ARISTOTLE'S POETICS

ARISTOTLE'S POETICS

Stephen Halliwell

The University of Chicago Press

STEPHEN HALLIWELL is professor of Greek at the University of St. Andrews, Scotland. He has translated and provided commentary on the *Poetics,* the comedies of Aristophanes, and Plato's *Republic.*

The University of Chicago Press, Chicago 60637

Gerald Duckworth & Co. Ltd, London W1V 5TA

Second impression 1998

First published in 1986 by Gerald Duckworth & Co. Ltd.

Printed in Great Britain

07 06 05 04 03 02 01 00 99 98   1 2 3 4 5

ISBN 0-226-31394-8 (paper)

Library of Congress Cataloging-in-publication Data

Halliwell, Stephen.
    Aristotle's Poetics / Stephen Halliwell.
        p.   cm.
    Includes bibliographical references (p.   ) and index.
    ISBN 0-226-31394-8 (acid-free paper)
    1. Aristotle. Poetics.   2. Poetics.   3. Aesthetics, Ancient.
    4. Tragedy.   I. Aristotle. Poetics. English.   II. Title.
    PN1040.A53H35   1998
    808.2—dc21   98-36373
                                                                  CIP

Contents

Introduction

Interpreters of the *Poetics* have long tended to regard the work more as a bundle of problems than as a unified argument - not altogether surprisingly, given the rather rough, and partly damaged, state in which the text survives. But this approach, which goes back to the scholarly habits of the sixteenth-century Italian commentators, takes an unduly limited view of our capacity to discern the armature of Ar.'s thinking about poetry. When the present book was first published in 1986, it was intended to offer a more sustained, integrated treatment of the *Poetics* than had often been previously attempted, and to do so, in part, by combining philosophical and literary perspectives on its ideas and arguments. Reactions to the book have suggested that this aim has been generally found successful and stimulating. If I were rewriting the book now, I would change much in the way of phrasing and detail, but would abandon none of my main interpretative contentions or emphases. This reprint gives me an opportunity, however, to say something about the development of my views over the past decade or so, and to supply some selective guidance to recent writing on the *Poetics* by others. In what follows, full bibliographical details of an item will be given only at the first occurrence; I include several references to reviews, to assist orientation.

Although, failing significant discovery of new evidence, some aspects of the *Poetics* will always remain elusive (the most obvious example is also the most controversial, the concept of *katharsis*: see below), I have tried to show that it is nonetheless feasible and rewarding to consider the treatise as preserving the framework of a philosophically mature, coherent view of drama and epic. Furthermore, I believe that careful study of the *Poetics*, especially when reinforced by relevant portions of Ar.'s other works - above all, the *Rhetoric* (on emotion), *Politics* (on musical education), and *Ethics* (on moral psychology) - can yield indications of the groundwork for a larger 'aesthetic' (covering the visual arts, music and dance, as well as poetry) whose foundations still deserve close attention, partly for its avoidance of the opposite extremes of moralism and formalism/aestheticism. Various general statements of my overall view of the work can be found in the introduction to my first translation, *The Poetics of Aristotle* (London & Chapel Hill 1987; translation alone extensively reprinted in A. Neill & A. Ridley (edd.) *The Philosophy of*

Art [New York 1995] 488-505); 'Aristotle's Poetics', in G. Kennedy (ed.) *Cambridge History of Literary Criticism*, vol. 1 (Cambridge 1989) 149-83; the introduction to my Loeb translation (which is independent of my 1987 version), in *Aristotle Poetics, Longinus on the Sublime, Demetrius on Style* [with D. Russell and D.C. Innes] (Cambridge, Mass. 1995); and, most briefly, 'Aristotle', in D.E. Cooper (ed.) *A Companion to Aesthetics* (Oxford 1992) 11-13.

The *Poetics'* combination of terseness with suggestive *aperçus* is one reason for its lasting, if frequently contentious, influence on criticism and aesthetics. My own interpretations have been increasingly shaped by a desire to read the *Poetics* in conjunction with an understanding of its *Nachleben* or reception: hence this book's final chapter, to which I have added in various respects in the introduction to *The Poetics of Aristotle*, 17-28 ('English' reactions to the treatise), and 'The *Poetics* and its Interpreters', in A.O. Rorty (ed.) *Essays on Aristotle's Poetics* (Princeton 1992) 409-24. (The conclusion of this last piece modifies what I now regard as the unduly narrow emphasis of the present book's final sentence.) I am continuing to work on the history of reactions to the treatise, and a project in progress, *The Aesthetics of Mimesis*, will bring together materials on both the Aristotelian and Platonic traditions in Western philosophies of literature and art, from antiquity up to the present. Some of my ideas in this area can be found in 'Aristotelian Mimesis Reevaluated', *Journal of the History of Philosophy* 28 (1990) 487-510, which tries to refine and extend considerations put forward in ch. 4 of this book by identifying in Ar. a 'dual focus' conception of representation that treats poems (and other works of art) both as objects in their own right and as images of possible realities (a conception far removed from the reductive accounts of Aristotelian 'imitation' that have had currency for far too long); and in 'Pleasure, Understanding and Emotion in Aristotle's *Poetics*', in Rorty (ed.) *Essays* 241-60, which tries to deepen some of the arguments of ch. 2 below by exploring the interdependence of various strands within Ar.'s thinking about poetry (and, once again, about other kinds of art too). Two other pieces which might be mentioned are 'Aristotle: Form and Unity', in M. Kelly (ed.) *The Encyclopedia of Aesthetics*, vol. 1 (New York 1999), which attempts to show how wrong it is to treat Ar. as a formalist; and 'Tragedy, Reason and Pity: a Reply to Jonathan Lear', in R. Heinaman (ed.) *Aristotle and Moral Realism* (London 1995) 85-95, in which I develop a case for supposing that Ar.'s view of pity is compatible with a strong tendency in Greek tragedy (and in Homer too) to conceive of pity as a force capable of expanding, even transforming, a person's sense of self and of his/her relationship to others.

I turn now to selective remarks on other scholarship since 1986. The peculiar character of the *Poetics* seems to invite repeated translation. For some reflections on the history of English versions see my article, 'Aristotle's Poetics', in O. Classe (ed.) *Encyclopedia of Literary Translation* (London 1998). Recent translations, apart from my own two renderings (above), include R. Janko, *Aristotle Poetics* (Indianapolis 1987), which helpfully incorporates materials pertinent to the lost second book (on comedy), but is marred by excessive literalism and some errors; and M. Heath, *Aristotle's Poetics* (Harmondsworth 1996). Although I cannot here survey translations in other languages, two Italian versions deserve a mention: D. Lanza, *Aristotele Poetica* (Milan 1987), with Greek text, large introduction and notes; and P. Donini, *Aristotele Opera 10**: Poetica* (Rome/Bari 1997), whose fine introduction and notes are especially strong on the work's relationship to Aristotelian thought in general.

The most substantial monograph devoted to the *Poetics* in the last decade is E. Belfiore, *Tragic Pleasures* (Princeton 1992), which deals in an often fresh and thought-provoking way with almost all the central themes of the treatise (including plot, *philia*, necessity, and the tragic emotions), but is marred, in my judgement, by a controversial and strained interpretation of *katharsis* as the removal of fearlessness and shamefulness: see my review in *CR* 43 (1993) 253-4. Also of note is V. Cessi, *Erkennen und Handeln in der Theorie des Tragischen bei Aristoteles* (Frankfurt 1987), a book which tries, if a bit too neatly, to connect tragic *hamartia* to Ar.'s moral psychology as a whole, and especially to his concept of *akrasia*. K. Eden, *Poetic and Legal Fiction in the Aristotelian Tradition* (Princeton 1986) appeared in the same year as my own book: its central aim, taken well beyond the *Poetics*, is to explore connections between theories of poetry and of forensic rhetoric. A very welcome sign of increasing interest in the *Poetics* on the part of Aristotelian specialists (who have traditionally been inclined to ignore it) is the wide-ranging collection, already cited, Rorty (ed.) *Essays,* which contains chapters on most of the major aspects and problems of Ar.'s theory of poetry (mimesis, plot, character, *hamartia, katharsis,* etc.) and is likely to remain a central reference-point in the secondary literature for some time. Important contributions to an integrated reading of the *Poetics* have been made by a leading Aristotelian, Martha Nussbaum: her *The Fragility of Goodness* (Cambridge 1986), esp. 378-94, places some of the *Poetics'* themes within a larger perspective on Greek poetry and ethics, a perspective whose focus is the nature of human vulnerability to misfortune (see my two reactions in *Ancient Philosophy* 8 [1988] 313-19, and 'Philosophy and Literature: Settling a Quarrel?', *Philosophical Investigations* 16 [1993] 1-17); and her 'Tragedy and Self-Sufficiency: Plato and Aristotle on Fear and Pity', *Oxford Studies in Ancient Philosophy* [*OSAP*] 10 (1992) 107-59 (shorter version in Rorty (ed.) *Essays* 261-90), develops a cogent argument regarding the interrelated elements of ethical judgement and emotion in Ar.'s model of the type of experience which tragedy offers its audience. Nussbaum's position, in both these publications, includes an attempt to integrate *katharsis* (to which I return below), as an ethically 'educative' dimension of the paradigmatic response to tragedy, into her analysis of the nature of pity and fear.

The following publications, which cover most of the spectrum of major issues arising out of the *Poetics,* represent a miscellany of worthwhile additions to the massive literature on the treatise (which is not to say, of course, that I necessarily agree with all their conclusions); space precludes more than sporadic comments: P.A. Cantor, 'Aristotle and the History of Tragedy', in D. Perkins (ed.) *Theoretical Issues in Literary History* (Cambridge Mass. 1991) 60-84, an interesting attempt, despite some unreliable details, to rehabilitate Ar.'s standing as literary historian (contrast pp. 92-6, 254-6 of this book, and Winkler's article, cited below); C. Carey, 'Philanthropy in Aristotle's *Poetics*', *Eranos* 86 (1988) 131-40, on the notion of *philanthrôpia* found in chs. 13 and 18; L. Edmunds, *Theoretical Space and Historical Place in Sophocles' Oedipus at Colonus* (Lanham 1996) ch. 1, on Ar.'s attitude to *opsis* (see my Appendix 3) *vis-à-vis* modern theories of theatre; G.F. Else, *Plato and Aristotle on Poetry* (Chapel Hill 1987), in part a résumé of the views of his big (1957) book (but see my review in *JHS* 109 [1989] 232-3); H. Flashar, 'Die *Poetik* des Aristoteles und die griechische Tragödie', in H. Flashar (ed.) *Tragödie: Idee und Transformation* (Stuttgart 1997) 50-64; D. Gallop, 'Animals in the *Poetics*', *OSAP* 8 (1990) 145-71, on Ar.'s 'organic' models and the quasi-philosophical pleasure of tragedy; S. Gastaldi, 'Lo *spoudaios* aristotelico tra etica e poetica', *Elenchos* 8 (1987) 63-104, on pre-Aristotelian as well as Ar.'s own use of the important term *spoudaios;* L. Golden, *Aristotle on Tragic and Comic Mimesis* (Atlanta Georgia 1992), which includes a restatement of his influential view of *katharsis* as intellectual 'clarification' (see pp. 354-5 below); E. Hall, 'Is there a Polis in Aristotle's *Poetics*', in M.S. Silk (ed.) *Tragedy and the Tragic* (Oxford 1997) 295-309, a critique of the allegedly non-political perspective of the *Poetics* (to be read in contrast with S. Salkever, 'Tragedy and the Education of the *Dêmos*: Aristotle's Response to Plato', in J. P. Euben (ed.) *Greek Tragedy and Political Theory* [Berkeley 1986] 274-303); M. Heath, *The Poetics of Greek Tragedy* (London 1987), esp. chs. 1-3 (with my review in *JHS* 109 [1989] 231); id., 'Aristotelian Comedy', *CQ* 39 (1989) 344-54; id., *Unity in Greek Poetics* (Oxford 1989) ch. 4 (with my review in *JHS* 111 [1991] 230-1); id., 'The Universality of Poetry in Aristotle's *Poetics*', *CQ* 41 (1991) 389-402; H.-J. Horn, 'Zum neunten Kapitel der aristotelischen *Poetik*', *Rheinisches Museum* 131 (1988) 113-36, on the sequence of thought in this important section; J.T. Kirby, 'Aristotle's *Poetics;* the Rhetorical Principle', *Arethusa* 24 (1991) 197-217; A. Köhnken, 'Terminologische Probleme in der *Poetik* des Aristoteles', *Hermes* 118 (1990) 129-49, on 'simple' plots and 'episodes'; A. López Eire, 'Aristoteles über die Sprache des Dramas', in B. Zimmermann (ed.) *Antike Dramentheorien und ihre Rezeption* [=*Drama* 1] (Stuttgart 1992) 74-84; S. Murnaghan, 'Sucking the Juice without Biting the Rind: Aristotle and Tragic Mimesis', *New Literary History* 26 (1995) 755-73; N. Richardson, 'Aristotle's Reading of Homer and its Background', in R.W. Lamberton & J. Keaney (edd.) *Homer's Ancient Readers* (Princeton 1992) 30-40; E. Schütrumpf, 'Traditional Elements in the Conception of *Hamartia* in Aristotle's *Poetics*', *HSCP* 92 (1989) 137-56, which stresses the influence of rhetorical/legal ideas on Ar.'s concept of tragic *hamartia;* G.M. Sifakis, 'Learning from Art and Pleasure from Art: an Interpretation of Aristotle *Poetics* 4 1448b8-19', in J.H. Betts *et al.* (edd.) *Studies in Honour of T.B.L. Webster,* vol. 1 (Bristol 1986) 211-22; M.S. Silk, 'The "Six Parts of Tragedy"

in Aristotle's *Poetics*', *PCPS* 40 (1994) 108-15; J.J. Winkler, 'The Some Two
Sources of Literature and its "History" in Aristotle, *Poetics* 4', in M. Griffith
& D.J. Mastronarde (edd.) *Cabinet of the Muses* (Atlanta 1990) 307-18. The
treatment of the *Poetics*, by the editor, in J. Barnes (ed.) *The Cambridge
Companion to Aristotle* (Cambridge 1995) 272-85 is regrettably little more
than a *jeu d'esprit*.

One topic requires separate attention, the perennially controversial *katharsis*, whose allure has been increased by the Freudian associations now
acquired by the term. My own position has become even more sceptical with
time, though I remain persuaded that a broadly ethical interpretation is most
plausible, and that the well-entrenched notion of purgation is hard to reconcile with the value attached to the emotions by Ar.'s moral psychology in
general: see my short article, 'Catharsis', in Cooper (ed.) *Companion* 61-3,
with further references, and cf. on Belfiore (1992), Golden (1992), and
Nussbaum (1986), (1992), all mentioned above. Various modern interpretations of *katharsis*, including the influential works by Bernays, Flashar and
Schadewaldt cited in ch. 6 (details in Bibliography), have been reprinted in
M. Luserke (ed.) *Die Aristotelische Katharsis: Dokumente ihrer Deutung im 19.
und 20. Jahrhundert* (Hildesheim 1991). A trenchant critique of several modern interpretations, including my own, is provided by J. Lear, *'Katharsis'*,
Phronesis 33 (1988) 297-326 (rpr. in Rorty (ed.) *Essays* 315-40), but Lear perhaps puts too much emphasis on the emotions of the ideally virtuous person, and his somewhat elusive view of *katharsis* as connected to a kind of
'consolation' raises problems of its own (cf. my 'Pleasure, Understanding etc.',
259 n. 47, and see my broader exchange with Lear in Heinaman (ed.)
Aristotle and Moral Realism 61-98). C. Segal, 'Catharsis, Audience and Closure
in Greek Tragedy', in Silk (ed.) *Tragedy* 149-72, relates the Aristotelian concept to scenes of shared emotion, including ritual laments, in surviving
tragedies. The important reference to *katharsis* in *Politics* 8 (see pp. 190 ff.
below) is reconsidered by R. Kraut, *Aristotle Politics Books VII and VIII*
(Oxford 1997) 208-12, who reaches the cautious conclusion that *katharsis*
may reduce the painfulness of certain emotions without eliminating the
emotions themselves. For the claim that references to Aristotelian *katharsis*
can be reconstructed in Philodemus's *On Poems* bk. 5, and that they support
an ethical construal of Ar.'s concept, see esp. R. Janko, 'Philodemus *On Poems*
and Aristotle's *On Poets*', *Cronache Ercolanesi* 21 (1991) 5-65 (at 59-63), and
Janko's essay in Rorty (ed.) *Essays* 341-58. The old view of *katharsis* as evac-
uative purgation is reasserted, with somewhat wilful disregard of recent
scholarship, in both T. Gould, *The Ancient Quarrel between Poetry and
Philosophy* (Princeton 1990) ch. 9 (see my review in *CP* 87 [1992] 263-9, at
267-8) and A. Nuttall, *Why Does Tragedy Give Pleasure?* (Oxford 1996) ch. 1
(see my review in *CR* 48 [1998] 205).

I have already mentioned the historical influence and reception of the
Poetics, a subject of which I try to give an overview in ch. 10 and which
remains of major significance for the history of criticism. The most original

work in this area during the last decade is undoubtedly T. Cave, *Recognitions* (Oxford 1988), which intricately and searchingly traces many ramifications of the idea of *anagnôrisis* in both literarature (from Homer to the modern novel) and literary criticism/theory, showing in the process how fertile the use of the *Poetics* can be in making connections betwen the literary forms of different periods. Some other recent items of note related to the *Nachleben* of the *Poetics*, and/or its comparative use in literary criticism, include: K. Barry, *Language Music and the Sign* (Cambridge 1987) 94-104, on Twining; D.L. Black, *Logic and Aristotle's Rhetoric and Poetics in Medieval Arabic Philosophy* (Leiden 1990); L. Deitz, ' "*Aristoteles imperator noster...*"? J.C. Scaliger and Aristotle on Poetic Theory', *International Journal of the Classical Tradition* 2 (1995) 54-67, on the unaristotelian cast of Scaliger's poetics (cf. p. 294 below); R. Dilcher, 'Furcht und Mitleid! Zu Lessings Ehrenrettung', *Antike und Abendland* 42 (1996) 85-102, vindicating Lessing against Schadewaldt (see also A. Kerkhecker, ' "Furcht und Mitleid" ', *Rheinisches Museum* 134 [1991] 288-310, with pp. 312-13 below); D. Javitch, 'Pioneer Genre Theory and the Opening of the Humanist Canon', *Common Knowledge* 3 (1994) 54-66, a piece which shows how the *Poetics* inspired 'modernist' theorists of genre in the 1540s; R. Kassel, 'Aristotle's *Poetics* in Germany', in his *Kleine Schriften* (Berlin 1991) 479-91; A.J. Minnis & A.B. Scott (edd.) *Medieval Literary Theory and Criticism c. 1100–c. 1375* (Oxford 1988, rev. edn. 1991) 277-313, on Hermannus' translation of Averroes (see p. 291 below); and, finally, Zimmermann (ed.) *Antike Dramentheorien,* which contains essays by R. Stillers on Italian humanist conceptions of drama prior to the 'rediscovery' of the *Poetics,* by A. Schmitt on Schiller's relationship to Ar., by B. Seidensticker on the concept of tragic *peripeteia* in Ar. and Peter Szondi, and by P. Thiercy on French reactions to the *Poetics* in the period of Corneille (cf., on this last subject, D. Clarke, *Pierre Corneille* [Cambridge 1992]). This may also be the place to cite R. Meijering, *Literary and Rhetorical Theories in Greek Scholia* (Groningen 1987), which is in large part a study of the persistence and modification of 'Aristotelian' concepts - which is not, though, to say of the *Poetics* as such - in the ancient critical tradition.

Finally, evidence from outside the *Poetics* for Ar.'s views on poetry has been documented, though mechanically, by D. Moraitou, *Die Äusserungen des Aristoteles über Dichter und Dichtung ausserhalb der Poetik* (Stuttgart 1994); see my review in *CR* 45 (1995) 438. Moraitou ignores the lost works, but the fragments of *On Poets* and *Homeric Problems* (see my Index) have been re-edited by O. Gigon, *Aristotelis Opera* III (Berlin 1987) 263-7, 526-39, and *On Poets* receives substantial discussion from R. Laurenti, *Aristotele: i frammenti dei dialoghi,* vol. 1 (Naples 1987) 211-300.

St Andrews   S.H.
May 1998

Abbreviations

1. Aristotelian works

An.Post.	*Posterior Analytics*
An.Pr.	*Prior Analytics*
Cael.	*De Caelo*
Cat.	*Categories*
De An.	*De Anima*
EE	*Eudemian Ethics*
EN	*Nicomachean Ethics*
GA	*De Generatione Animalium*
GC	*De Generatione et Corruptione*
HA	*De Historia Animalium*
Int.	*De Interpretatione*
MA	*De Motu Animalium*
Mem.	*De Memoria*
Met.	*Metaphysics*
Meteor.	*Meteorologica*
PA	*De Partibus Animalium*
Phys.	*Physics*
Poet.	*Poetics*
Pol.	*Politics*
Protr.	*Protrepticus*
Rhet.	*Rhetoric*
SE	*Sophistici Elenchi*
Top.	*Topics*

2. Pseudo-Aristotelian works (prefaced by ps.-Ar.)

Aud.	*De Audibilibus*
MM	*Magna Moralia*
Mund.	*De Mundo*
Probl.	*Problemata*

Rh.Alex. *Rhetorica ad Alexandrum*

3. Journals

CJ	*Classical Journal*
CL	*Comparative Literature*
CP	*Classical Philology*
CQ	*Classical Quarterly*
CR	*Classical Review*
CW	*Classical World*
G & R	*Greece and Rome*
GRBS	*Greek Roman and Byzantine Studies*
HSCP	*Harvard Studies in Classical Philology*
JAAC	*Journal of Aesthetics and Art Criticism*
JEGP	*Journal of English and Germanic Philology*
JHI	*Journal of the History of Ideas*
JHS	*Journal of Hellenic Studies*
JP	*Journal of Philology*
MH	*Museum Helveticum*
MLR	*Modern Language Review*
Mnem.	*Mnemosyne*
MP	*Modern Philology*
PCPS	*Proceedings of the Cambridge Philological Society*
Philol.	*Philologus*
SP	*Studies in Philology*
SR	*Studies in the Renaissance*
TAPA	*Transactions of the American Philological Association*

4. Ancient authors

Abbreviations of ancient authors and their works are standard. References to
fragments should be taken to standard editions, unless otherwise indicated. Note
that the fragments of Cratinus are cited from R. Kassel & C. Austin (edd.) *Poetae
Comici Graeci*, vol. 4 (Berlin and New York, 1983); the fragments of Cratinus are
cited from the edition of Kock (see Bibliography).

5. The text

The text of the *Poetics* followed for the purposes of both reference and translation is that of Kassel (see Bibliography), unless otherwise indicated. Note that references are abbreviated as follows: 1447a 8 becomes 47a 8, etc. In translating
words and phrases, I occasionally allow myself slight variation for the sake of clarity of exposition. Transliterated terms are usually explained in context, but brief
explanations can also be found in the Index.

I
The Setting of the *Poetics*

We would allow the champions of poetry – men who do not practise the art themselves, but are lovers of it – to offer a prose defence on its behalf, showing that poetry is a source not only of pleasure, but also of benefit to communities and to the life of man. And we shall listen graciously.

Plato, *Republic* 10, 607d

It may be no more than fanciful, and it is certainly chronologically difficult, to suppose that when near the end of his *Republic* Plato issued the challenge which forms the epigraph to this chapter, he had already encountered resistance to his view of poetry from the young Aristotle. There need be little doubt, however, that the roots of Aristotle's view of poetry do lie deeply embedded in the first period which he spent at Athens, when a member of Plato's Academy; and it is probable that already at this time, under the complex stimulus of Plato's arguments, he was developing some of the specific ideas which were to be formulated in his *Poetics*.[1] Whenever the *Poetics* as such took shape, it is my contention that Plato's invitation to the champions of poetry anticipates the riposte which his attack on the poetic core of traditional Greek culture was to receive from his own distinguished pupil. The *Poetics* can indeed be described as a defence of poetry which, like so much else in Aristotle's philosophy, presupposes the existence and the provocation of his teacher's system of thought. The Platonic challenge as such goes unmentioned, but the absence of Plato's name is undisturbing: Aristotle often argues against his predecessor without drawing explicit attention to the fact; and in his early dialogue, *On Poets*, which seems to have shared some of its ideas with the *Poetics* and which was written with circulation

---

[1] The extreme case for a connection between *Rep.* 10 and Aristotle's views is put by Else (1972), but it requires a dubiously late date for parts of Plato's work. On the chronology of the *Poetics* see my Appendix 1.

1

outside the philosophical school in mind, Aristotle probably did think it appropriate to name Plato.[2] It is, in any case, abundantly clear to anyone who reads the *Poetics* with a knowledge of Plato's treatment of poetry that Aristotle has Platonic material in his sights virtually throughout (see Appendix 2). Yet it is a widely held conception of the work that it addresses itself to only one part of the challenge issued in *Republic* 10, and that Aristotle's concern is only to show that there is a legitimate pleasure to be taken in poetry, but not that it has the moral or educational value which Plato seems to expect the true lover and defender of the art to claim for it. It will be a central argument of this book that such an understanding of the *Poetics* is inadequate, and that Aristotle does indeed set out to argue in his own way for poetry's intellectual and moral status, and hence for its potential place in the conception of the good life which is a common premise of all Plato's and Aristotle's thought.

I shall be returning to some particular aspects of the *Poetics'* relation to Plato later in this introductory chapter, and others will necessarily receive attention in various parts of the book. But there is no more pertinent way to approach an interpretation of the *Poetics* than by this general acknowledgement of the essential origin and context of the work, set against the inescapable background of Plato. This holds true, of course, for much of the whole system of Aristotelian thought, and the effort of setting the work in relation to Plato therefore can profitably be combined with the task of understanding how it fits into the general pattern of Aristotle's philosophy. That the *Poetics* is the work of a philosopher, not just in the trivial biographical sense, but by the nature of its ideas, its methods, and its underlying values, ought to be, but in fact is not, a platitude. A major reason for this is the division within modern scholarship between specialised study of Aristotelian philosophy, which regards the *Poetics* as marginal to the system (when it regards it at all), and study of the *Poetics* by literary scholars who often show

---

[2] If, as seems likely, the neo-platonist passages quoted by Bywater 94f. and Kassel 52 (= Lucas (1968) 52) refer to *On Poets*, there is a *prima facie* case for inferring both that the dialogue mentioned Plato and that at this stage Ar. already had a doctrine of poetic *katharsis*. Other evidence for the dialogue is assembled in frs. 70-77 Rose (the neo-platonist texts are in fr. 81). For speculative discussion and reconstruction see Rostagni (1955) 255-322; Brink (1963) 120-5 is more concise and cautious. Cf. also Appendix 1 §2(a).

On the importance of the *Poetics'* implicit engagement with Plato and with the ethics of poetry, one might adapt *Met.* 1078a 33-6: a work may have something to say on a subject without spelling it out by name.

little interest in the work's relation to its author's wider thought. The serious interpreter of the treatise will wish, so far as his competence allows, to resist this dichotomy.

It will be a recurring aim of this book to attempt to demonstrate to what extent and in which respects the interpretation of the *Poetics* needs to be set in the context of Aristotle's general philosophy. Although other parts of the corpus do not automatically unlock for us the meaning of the *Poetics*, they can provide invaluable help and clues in making sense of such matters as Aristotle's fundamental concept of art (ch. II below), his understanding of poetic structure and unity (ch. III), the nature of human action and character, and the relation between them (ch. V), the functioning and ethical importance of the emotions (ch. VI), and the connection between fortune and happiness in tragedy (ch. VII). There are, in addition, some cross-references between the *Poetics* and other works (the *Rhetoric* and *Politics*) to confirm the use of the former in a full course of Aristotelian instruction, but connections of the kind just listed are mostly signalled not explicitly but by the occurrence of terminology which Aristotle expects to be identified and comprehended within the framework of his own philosophy.[3]

Such a claim will seem paradoxical to some in view of the widespread conviction that, in reacting against Plato's view of art, Aristotle unequivocally divorced poetry from larger matters of morality, politics, and philosophical standards of truth. This conviction rests both on Aristotle's willingness to treat poetry in a separate treatise (thus acknowledging its status as an art) and on his resounding affirmation, in *Poetics* 25, that 'correctness in poetry is not the same as correctness in politics or in any other art' (60b 13-15, where 'politics' translates *politikê* and embraces moral philosophy). But a desire to draw as sharp a contrast as possible between Plato and Aristotle, and a reaction against the naive moralism of earlier, neo-classical interpreters, have too often led to the misrepresentation of Aristotle's position in this respect as some sort of aestheticism – as a declaration of the complete autonomy of poetic standards and principles. This is not something which Aristotle actually claims, nor

[3] Cross-references: *Poet.* 56a 35, *Pol.* 1341b 39f. (but cf. p. 31 and ch. VI n. 32), *Rhet.* 1372a 1f., 1404a 39, 1404b 7f., 28, 1405a 5f., 1419b 5f. Among the distinctive Aristotelian ideas and terminology in the *Poetics* are *prohairesis* (50b 9, 54a 18), various senses of 'nature' (48b 5, 49a 15 etc.), wholeness and unity (chs. 7-8), *eudaimonia* and *eutuchia* (see ch. VII pp. 202ff.), and 'universals' (esp. ch. 9). On the *Poetics* and the system cf. Stark 57.

something to which, given his philosophy as a whole, he could easily have subscribed. What Aristotle does assert, against Plato, is that poetry should not be subjected to simple and direct evaluation in terms of external criteria – moral, political or otherwise. Plato assessed art by the unqualified application of the canons of truth and goodness, so that art was wholly subsumed within the jurisdiction of his ethical and political philosophy (as well as his metaphysics). It is independence from such unmitigated moralism and didacticism which Aristotle's recognition of poetry's intrinsic qualities stands for.

This recognition is embodied in method and approach – in the attempt to define the nature of poetry and its genres, and to analyse the potential of the art. But to grant this degree of independence is not to claim or establish the exclusion of ethical and other values from poetry; the passage from *Poetics* 25 denies the *identity* of poetic and moral criteria, but it does not state that they are wholly unconnected. When, therefore, a modern scholar finds in this passage a suggestion of 'purely aesthetic values',[4] he projects onto Aristotle a fragmentation of experience which cuts right against the grain of the philosopher's thinking. Aristotle does not dictate to poetry as peremptorily as Plato had done, but he views poetry nonetheless within a unified and hierarchical conception of human life. If individual arts have particular aims, and bring their particular pleasures, they must still be placed within the purview of the philosophical perspective. 'The goal of politics and ethics (*politikê*) must embrace those of other branches of knowledge.'[5] This perspective is apparent in the *Poetics* at a number of points, but above all at the apex of the theory of tragedy, in chs. 13 and 14, where it is made explicit that the experience of tragedy depends intimately on a response to the moral features of the action of the play. Again a divergence from Plato can be discerned, for whom tragedy's sole function could be the protreptic assertion of moral truths: that is, the demonstration of the identity of virtue and happiness, and of their

---

[4] Lucas (1968) on 60b 14: for Lucas's use of 'aesthetic' cf. ch. II n.27. The case against aestheticism in Ar. is put by Bywater 325f. in one of his most judicious notes; see also Smithson's article, House 20f., Jones 52, and cf. n. 36 below and ch. VII n.37. Goldstein 568 and n.8 shows the perils of interpreting from translations: 'in itself', a standard translation of the third word of the treatise, does *not* mean 'divorced from all other considerations'; it means 'as a whole' or 'as a genus' (i.e. as well as by species).

[5] *EN* 1094b 6. The individual artist, of course, does not aim at some grand absolute, but at the particular goal of his art: *EN* 1097a 5-22, where the criticism of Plato's extreme moralism is unequivocal. Ps.-Ar. *MM* 1190a 31f. refers to the distinction between 'mimetic' and moral standards in art.

opposites. As I shall argue in more detail in later chapters, Aristotle, while avoiding such outright moralism, still expects tragedy (and mimetic art in general) to be conformable to a moral understanding of the world.

Two further points can be briefly made in objection to the tendency to find a type of aestheticism in the *Poetics*, and also, complementarily, as further emphasis on the need to locate the work in the context of the philosophy as a whole. Since one of the treatise's central concerns is with form and structure (the 'soul' of tragedy is its plot-structure, *muthos*), it is for some an immediate temptation to suppose that the *Poetics* 'deals with form at the expense of substance'.[6] But this brings with it a misconception, for it is no more the case with poetry than with other areas of Aristotle's thought that form can be so readily detached and divorced from substance. In particular, an examination of Aristotle's concepts of poetic unity and formal organisation reveals that our apprehension of them presupposes the cognitive experience of the material or substance (human action) contained within the poetic structure. One cannot, in Aristotle's theory, pass judgement on the formal aspects of a work of art without a grasp of the substance to which they give a form; one cannot discern poetic unity without comprehending the content of the mimetic representation. In the case of tragedy, this is borne out by the prescriptions offered in *Poetics* 13-14. These prescriptions cannot be said to deal with form at the expense of substance, since the plot-structure (*muthos*) with which they are concerned is not simply the abstract shape of the plot, but the totality of the represented action with all its causal connections and logic of development, as well as the integrated relation within it of action and character. That is also why the plot-structure of a play is compared in ch. 6 (50b 1-3) to a visual image – a *significant* form, to be perceived (like all Aristotelian forms) not as mere pattern but as the design of a particular entity.

If the *Poetics* does not present us with, in the strong sense, a formalist view of poetry, neither does it offer unqualified aesthetic hedonism. Here we encounter the dangers attendant on rigid application, in defiance of the closely-knit texture of Aristotelian thought, of the kind of dichotomy given classical expression by Horace's 'aut prodesse ... aut delectare' (*AP* 333) and perpetuated by

---

[6] Kaufmann 85. Cf. e.g. the claim of Rees (1981) 30 that what matters for Ar. 'is not the content of a poem ... but its structure.'

much later debate about the purpose of art. To set up an exclusive
distinction of this kind, and then to resolve the question in the case of
the *Poetics* by declaring that for Aristotle 'the purpose of poetry ... is to
give pleasure ...; he says so several times', is to indulge in
obscurantism, since this is to presuppose that pleasure is unitary and
self-explanatory.[7] For some it may be, but it was not for Aristotle,
who specifies in the *Poetics* both the generic pleasure to be derived
from mimesis, and the particular species of it which supervenes on the
experience of tragedy. Attention to the whole of the text, together
with consideration of Aristotle's general philosophy of pleasure, leads
to the realisation that in both cases pleasure is not to be taken as an
undefined and self-sufficient gratification, but rather as the result of
an underlying activity or experience. To understand the conception
of pleasure involved we need to understand the activity which it
completes. And thus an enquiry into the place of pleasure in the
Poetics takes one into the philosophical foundations of the treatise and
entails questions about the relation between cognition and emotion
in the experience of mimetic art.

These preliminary remarks are intended to signal some of the
leading themes and issues of this book, as well as to elaborate a little
on the importance of trying to read the *Poetics* with the assistance of
Aristotelian philosophy as a whole. In the final section of this chapter
I shall address the question of how much coherence it is legitimate to
expect from the treatise, in view of its condition. But before that, I
turn to the wider background to the *Poetics* furnished by earlier
Greek ideas on poetry.

*

In producing the *Poetics* Aristotle was not in a position to rely on an
established or sufficient set of expectations about what a work on
poetry should aim to achieve. Although earlier writers such as
Democritus and Glaucus of Rhegium had devoted individual works
to poetry and poets, and while many others had made contributions
to the subject, we are not aware of any close precedent for Aristotle's
treatise. Parts of the work may reflect existing types of criticism,
particularly the chapter on Homeric 'problems' (ch. 25); but the

---

[7] Gomme 49f. (and for his interpretation of *Poetics* 4 see ch. II n. 36 below).
Unqualified statements that for Ar. the end of poetry is pleasure are always likely to
mislead: cf. ch. II p. 81 and n. 46.

approach and organisation of the book cannot be extensively derived from the example of earlier writings. The treatise-form as such – the specialised or technical treatment of a particular topic – was a product of fifth-century intellectual life; one of its chief developments, continued by Aristotle himself, had been the application of method to rhetoric.[8] Here certainly was a partial model for a work on poetry, but despite some important points of contact between Aristotle's *Rhetoric* and *Poetics*, the latter cannot be explained simply by reference to the former. The *Poetics* is, however, at least parallel to the *Rhetoric* in its use of the distinctive analytical techniques of Aristotelian philosophy for the scrutiny of questions and issues which had roots far down in traditional Greek culture. In the case of poetry, as well as responding to an immediate Platonic challenge, Aristotle was able to look back beyond Plato to the larger horizon constituted by the poets' own conceptions of their art, and by the ideas on poetry which arose out of the great ferment of fifth-century thought. Although he is often unostentatious about rebutting or qualifying earlier views, Aristotle does at several points in the *Poetics* refer to previous works in a manner which is sufficient to confirm that he is conscious of engaging in an enterprise which others had broached.[9]

In the opening sentence of the *Poetics* – a sentence which gives an immediate impression of how Aristotle conceived of this enterprise – we find one of the aims of the work stated as being to examine 'how plots should be constructed, if the poetic composition is to be successful'. In Plato's *Protagoras* the sophist Protagoras asserts that the chief element in education or culture (*paideia*) is to be knowledgeable about language: that is, 'to be capable of understanding which of the things said by poets have been correctly

---

[8] There are references to technical treatises (*technai*) at e.g. *Rhet.* 1354a 12, 1399a 16, 1400a 4, Plato *Phdr.* 261b ff., 266d ff., 271c, *Soph.* 232d-e. Ar. is known to have made his own compilation of earlier rhetorical treatises. On the general subject of treatises see M. Fuhrmann, *Das systematische Lehrbuch* (Göttingen 1960) 122ff., and for a summary of the sophists' more technical work cf. Pfeiffer ch. II. Süss 91ff. and Rostagni (1955) 161ff. both seem to me to exaggerate the affinities between the *Poetics* and rhetorical theory.

[9] See Gudeman 9-28, though his argument is cavalier and faulty in detail: for a translation with small differences see 'The Sources of Aristotle's *Poetics*', in *Classical Studies in Honor of John C. Rolfe*, ed. G. D. Hadzsits (New York 1931, rpr. 1967) 75-100. Almost all the specific references in the *Poet.* to earlier theorists (in fact *all*, if we discount the uncertain case of Polyidos at 55a 6 and b 10) occur either in the linguistic chapters (19-22) or in the chapter on 'problems' (25) – perhaps an indication of the preponderance of technical criticism. But there remain general references to schools of thought: esp. 48a 28ff., 49a 28-30, 53a 13.

composed, and which not'.[10] Although Aristotle would not have
accepted the claim that education should be largely a skill in literary
judgement, and although Protagoras' own criticism, at least as
Plato goes on to portray it, has little in common with the *Poetics*,
there is a shared assumption between the sophist and the
philosopher.[11] Both proceed from the conviction that rational and
methodical understanding of poetic standards is important,
attainable, and teachable. While it had always been possible in
Greek culture to prefer one poet or poem to another, and to give some
reasons for doing so (witness poetic competitions, and poets'
criticisms of one another), the idea of a specialised, discursive theory
of poetic standards, or of communicable techniques of judgement,
was a new phenomenon in the fifth century, and in this general
respect Aristotle was heir to the sophists. The sophists mark the
beginning of an age in which theoretical and technical criteria are
superimposed on the more diffuse material of broad cultural attitudes
to poetry. It was the sophists who were responsible for instituting a
more systematic approach to many aspects of the subject: more
specifically technical ones such as grammar, metre and diction, but
also such larger matters as the place of morality and emotion in
poetry. Notwithstanding the traces of earlier Homeric exegesis and
criticism, the era of the sophists was the first great age of Greek
theoretical writings in these areas, as in many others, and the
treatises and handbooks which it produced were undoubtedly known
to the author of the *Poetics*.

A further preliminary point should be made in this connection.
The clause which I quoted above from the opening of the *Poetics*
begins with a prescriptive phrase: 'how plots should be constructed ...' If one has a precise, theoretical grasp of poetic principles
and standards, it may be tempting to suppose that one is equipped to
prescribe how poets ought to go about their work (especially in the
light of the belief that poetry is a technical craft). This supposition
certainly plays a part in the *Poetics*, and I shall examine the details of
it later in the chapter. Although it reflects some distinctively

---

[10] *Protag.* 338e 7ff. For the phrasing see the Platonic passages cited in Appendix 2
under 47a 9f. and 61a 4ff., together with Plato *Euthyd.* 277e and *Crat.* 384b on
Prodicus.
[11] Protagoras is criticised at *Poet.* 56b 13ff., but note that a more tolerant attitude
towards the relevance of such linguistic matters to 'rhetoric or poetry' is taken at *Int.*
17a 5f. For the kind of poetic self-contradiction which Protagoras is shown looking for
by Plato see *Poet.* 61a 31ff. (with Appendix 2 on this passage).

Aristotelian doctrine, I note it here also as a partial indication of sophistic influence. If we try to see beyond the strong moral attack launched against sophistry by Plato, it is possible to discern that the sophists based themselves, in theory if not always in practice, on the widespread assumption (fostered, for example, by the prevalence of craft apprenticeship) that knowledge of a subject could not be divorced from the capacity to teach it. Aristotle, at any rate, accepted such a premise: 'generally speaking, the proof of a man's knowledge or ignorance is his ability or inability to teach.'[12]

It was the sophistic age, then, which had first broached the possibility of the formal and systematic treatment of poetry as an art. But in order to place the *Poetics* more positively in relation to earlier Greek culture and thought, it is necessary to consider the range of views and ideas about poetry (and to some extent about the other arts) produced not only by the sophists but also by others, particularly the poets themselves. To do this with obligatory economy, I propose to sketch by way of introduction three major areas of contention which all have a bearing on the *Poetics*: the source and nature of poetic invention; the relation of poetry to nature and truth; and the purpose and function of poetry.

On the first of these subjects, Greek views seem from an early date to have contained two principal elements, given expression chiefly in the pronouncements of the poets themselves. The elements in question can be identified as the concepts of inspiration and craft. The first of these is archetypally embodied in prayers and references made by Homer and Hesiod to the Muses, and thereafter the literary tradition perpetuates inspiration in various ways as an emblem of the poet's privileged status and channels of potency.[13] Yet the idea of the poet's craft may well be just as old, and it can certainly be glimpsed in the Homeric portrayal of bards.[14] The developed Greek notion of poetic craft crystallised in the very noun 'poetry' (*poiêsis* = making), borrowed from the production of more

---

[12] *Met.* 981b 7-10; cf. *EN* 1180b 32-4, and e.g. Isoc. 15.205-6.

[13] For recent discussions see Russell ch. 5 and Murray's article.

[14] On poetic craft see Harriott ch. 5 and Murray 98f. Phemius' claim to be self-taught, *Od.* 22.347, implies by contrast the existence of a teachable poetic craft: cf. also the references to bardic skill or knowledge at *Od.* 1.384, 11.368, 17. 382-5, 518f. Craft and inspiration are nicely combined in the terms of Odysseus' praise of Demodocus at *Od.* 8.488, and for the combination see also *Od.* 22.347f., Solon fr. 13.51f. (West), Democritus fr. 21. On the use of craft terminology for poetry see M. Durante, in *Indogermanische Dichtersprache*, ed. R. Schmitt (Darmstadt 1968) 266ff.

tangible artefacts. It happens to be the case that this noun, as well as some cognates from the same verbal root, first appears in this sense in the fifth century;[15] but to infer from this that the concept itself was new in this period would be to confuse terminology with conceptualisation. Yet it is arguable that the development of terminology does reflect a shift in the balance of ideas about the nature of poetry. Although the claims of inspiration were not neglected (they received a forceful statement, it seems, from the materialist philosopher, Democritus), and although inspiration and craft could be combined into a compound view of the sources of poetic creation, it seems likely that the craft-conception of poetry did gain ground in the fifth century under the influence of the general increase in systematic theorising, particularly by the sophists. One of our main sources for literary ideas in this period, the contest of tragedians in Aristophanes' *Frogs*, shows clearly the pervasive implications of an understanding of the poet as a practical, purposive 'maker', in full rational control of his material, and standing on the same technical footing as other craftsmen.[16] Moreover, this contest reveals how such a conception of the poet is closely related to the new activities of technical theory and criticism: it is because the poet is regarded as a maker of artefacts, that it becomes possible to offer rational discussion and evaluation of what poets produce, analogously to the assessment of more obviously functional objects. The second half of *Frogs* is, in its presuppositions about dramatic poetry, a testament to the attitudes promoted by sophistic teaching and enquiry, and it is therefore not coincidental that it touches on issues of the kind which we later encounter in the *Poetics*.

Inspiration and craft may seem to form too drastic and simplified a dichotomy for the understanding of how poets produce their work, though I believe that in a condensed way they represent fundamental issues which have continued to underlie much later thinking about literature. At any rate, the two concepts conveniently prepare the way for one of the major differences between the theories of poetry advocated by Plato and Aristotle (see ch. III below).

As a heading for a range of not always clearly related ideas,

---

[15] *Poiētēs* first at Herod. 2.53, *poiēma* in Cratinus fr. 198 (with Kassel & Austin's *app.crit.*), *poiēsis* at Herod. 2.82. On this word-group see ch. II pp. 56ff.

[16] References to *technē* at *Frogs* 93, 762, 766, 770, 780, 786 etc., to *sophia* and cognates at 766, 776, 780, 872, 884, 895, 1108 etc. Cf. also the various references to testing, weighing and the like, esp. 1365ff.

suggestions and assumptions, 'the relation of poetry to nature and truth' is necessarily both grand and vague; yet it covers many of the crucial issues about poetry and the other arts raised by Greek thinkers: issues which are important both in themselves and for what Plato and Aristotle made of them. In this area, it is possible to identify a tendency towards polarisation behind much that was said on the status of poetry: the extremes are the views of poetry as literal truth and as outright falsehood. Both of these are to be found expressed within Greek poetry itself at an early date, though discussion of the dichotomy in theoretical terms may first have been stimulated by early philosophical criticisms of poetry in the later sixth century.[17] For the positive attitude to poetry as a medium of truth, the first reference point was perhaps the notion of epic poetry as a preserver of historical truth, a record and celebration of the glorious as well as the tragic heroic world of the distant past. The Homeric epics themselves make and imply such a claim, and it was taken seriously in societies where heroic song was not matched by other consistent means of access to the life of previous ages. The claim was subjected to increasingly sceptical scrutiny from historians and others in the classical period, but it was never completely undermined.

Yet if the possibility of poetic truth had rested wholly on epic's historical credentials, such a view would not have been so tenacious as to elicit some of Plato's most determined assaults on poetry in the fourth century. That poetry could continue to be regarded as a vehicle of truth did in fact depend on much broader assumptions, in particular on the supposition that poets could claim to portray, as no one else before the philosophers could plausibly do, the nature of the divine world and its control over the world of men. And if poets had religious truths to offer, they could also arrogate moral wisdom, for much Greek moral thinking and practice was shaped by the challenge of understanding the human predicament in relation to the gods' interests in, and power over, human affairs. More positively, since the material of a great deal of Greek poetry was derived from

[17] The *locus classicus* for poetry and falsehood is Hesiod *Theog.* 27f. See also Solon fr. 29 (West), said to be a proverb at Ar. *Met.* 983a 3f., Xenophanes frs. 1.22 and 11, Heraclitus frs. 56-7, Pindar *Ol.* 1.28f., *Nem.* 7.20-24, Thuc. 1.10.3, Plato esp. *Rep.* 377d (with Appendix 2 on 60b 33ff.). Homer too seems to recognise poetic falsehood: witness the tales of Odysseus, who is a sort of poet (*Od.* 11. 368, 17.518-21), and cf. 19. 203 (~ Hes. *Theog.* 27). But the idea of poetic truth is predominant in epic: see Macleod 4-6.

the sagas of a heroic world, the conviction grew, as we can again see
from Plato's antipathy to it, that poetry held up examples and models
of human excellence.

This view was naturally connected with the use of poetry for
educational purposes (see below), and it is important to keep in mind
this interrelation of theory and practice as the background to the
allegations of falsehood which began to be brought increasingly
against poetry in the early classical period, and which lead up to the
classic statement of the charge by Plato. Such criticisms are largely
moralistic and negative: that is to say, they express dissatisfaction
with the use of poetry to inculcate or sustain certain religious and
ethical beliefs, and their aim is not to contribute to the
understanding of poetry but only to demolish its pretensions. Their
effect, therefore, is not to illuminate the nature of poetry, but rather,
by accentuating the truth-falsehood polarity, to hinder a more subtle
appreciation of the distinctions between poetry and other types of
language and experience.[18]

What the more extreme criticisms of poetry as falsehood lacked, it
could be argued, was a positive conception of fiction:[19] of a relation
between poetry and its objects, to put the point minimally, which can
be described neither as a simple transcription of the truth, nor as the
invention of untruth masquerading as reality (Plato's polemical
imputation). The nature of the background against which Aristotle
attempted to solve the dialectic of poetic truth and falsehood is nicely
signalled by the philosopher's own wry phrase in *Poetics* 24 (60a 18f.),
that 'Homer has above all taught the rest how to speak falsehoods as
a poet ought'. It is significant that when in the later fifth century we
encounter some of the first serious attempts to define a concept of
fiction, a term such as 'deception' should play a prominent part in

[18] For the main philosophical criticisms of poetry before Plato see Xenophanes frs. 1,
11-12, 14-16, ?34, Heraclitus A22-3, frs. 40, 42, 56-7, 104.
[19] On the ancient development of a concept of fiction see Rösler's article. 'Fiction' is
used as an equivalent of mimesis as early as Twining 19f. and 25f. See also Gulley
167ff., but Potts goes too far in making 'fiction' a virtual title for the *Poetics* (and his
gloss on p. 7, 'the embodiment of a philosophy of life in stories', is inapt). For the
possibility of a Theophrastean emphasis on fiction, particularly in connection with
comedy, see Janko 49f.: are the titles *On the Pleasure of Falsehood* and *On Falsehood and
Truth* (Diog.Laert. 5.46, 48) relevant?
    Ar. cannot be said to have worked out a 'logic' of fiction. Passages such as *Cat.* 13b
15-19, *Int.* 17a 2-4 give no clear hint as to how Ar. would regard the logical status of
individual statements within the context of a *muthos*. Presumably, though, he
regarded the combined parts of a *muthos* as equivalent to general (*katholou*)
propositions.

them. A much cited fragment of the sophist Gorgias contends that
tragic poetry is a form of deception, in which 'the deceived is wiser
than the undeceived'.[20] Gorgias, it is true, was grossly addicted to
antitheses and to aphoristic compression, and this remark belongs to
such a context. This alone makes it difficult to know how much
serious thinking to discern behind the phrases, and tempting to
attribute the language of 'deception' to a sophistic penchant for
piquant paradox. But Gorgias was neither the only nor the first
person to use such language of poetry with approbation, and we
should perhaps attach more weight than is customarily done to the
linguistic difficulties that may have faced those who wished to
advance beyond the truth-falsehood dichotomy conceived on the
most literal level. That Gorgias did have some serious interest in
moving towards a refined understanding of the nature of poetry
receives a certain amount of support from other fragments of his
writings.

Apart from such relatively isolated glimpses of individual sophistic
theories, there is no doubt that general developments in attitudes
towards poetry centred around the language of *mimêsis* – a word, or
rather word-group, which is entitled to a chapter of this book to itself,
and whose increasing occurrence in the course of the fifth and fourth
centuries can be registered here as an index of a perhaps growing
recognition of the peculiar relation, neither simple truth nor blatant
falsehood, between poetry and its objects. But the language of
mimesis did not in itself provide an immediate solution to the
problems with which the notions of poetic truth and falsehood had, in
their own way, striven to cope. It was possible to interpret the concept
of mimesis so as to emphasise the potential for either falsehood or
truth, as the divergent arguments of Plato and Aristotle help to
show. For the philosophers, mimesis was drawn into, and made
central to, a debate which originally existed independently of it.
There is, in fact, an intricate set of difficulties involved in both the
Platonic and the Aristotelian applications of mimesis words to
poetry, and in trying to elucidate them I shall later have more to say

---

[20] Gorgias fr. 23, with Verdenius (1981) and Barnes (1982) 463-6. Cf. also ch. II
n. 24 and ch. VI n. 27 below. For the language of deception (disdainfully echoed by
Plato, esp. *Rep.* 598c and e, *Soph.* 234b) see also *Diss.Log.* 3.10, and cf. Dalfen 271ff.
'Deception' may be implicit in early passages such as Hes. *Theog.* 27f. (which is echoed
in *Diss.Log.* loc. cit.) and *Hom.Hymn Apollo* 162-4, and cf. the term *plasmata* ('fictions',
here pejoratively) in Xenophanes fr. 1. It is also tempting to take Empedocles fr. 23.9 to
intimate that deception is entailed in the visual mimesis of the preceding analogy.

about the philosophers' inheritance of the language of mimesis from earlier usage (ch. IV below). Mimesis can at any rate here be noted as a point of convergence for a number of strands in Greek thinking about poetry, as well as about the other arts, and it was therefore inevitably a point on which both Plato and Aristotle chose to focus much of their theorising about the subject.

The issues attendant on mimesis could not be disentangled from my final area of contention, the question of poetry's purpose or function, and of its effect on audience or readers. This association is illustrated by the assertion in an anonymous sophistic treatise, the *Dissoi Logoi*, that 'poets write in order to provide pleasure, not for the sake of truth'.[21] Here the author rejects the simple model of poetry as a medium of truth (and, in the same context, of moral values), and connects this negative view with a reliance on a purely hedonistic conception of the experience of poetry. We would naturally expect, in the Greek context, an advocate of the truth-value of poetry to be inclined towards favouring educational and didactic uses of it. Conversely, anyone who, like the writer of the *Dissoi Logoi* at this point, rejects poetic truth, is likely either to find no value in poetry at all, as seems to have been the case with some philosophical critics of literature (including, though only in his most polemical moods, Plato), or else to appeal to some notion of self-sufficient pleasure to justify the cultural status of poetry. This is, admittedly, a drastic and simplified way of looking at the matter, particularly since it assumes fixed and unproblematic senses for poetic truth and pleasure; such explicitly schematic use of the antitheses between truth and falsehood, instruction and pleasure, is in fact relatively unusual among Greek pronouncements on poetry before Plato, and it is a general virtue of the *Poetics* that it avoids facile and rigid assertions in these areas. There are, moreover, some pre-Aristotelian hints of more complex views than a simple alignment of truth and didacticism, or fiction and pleasure, would allow. In another passage of the *Dissoi Logoi* itself (the work is deliberately 'dialectical') we find an acknowledgement that the best tragedians and painters – and the conjunction is significant – are those who 'deceive the most by producing things which resemble the truth'.[22] This formulation,

[21] *Diss.Log.* 3.17. Cf. the similar antithesis at Thuc. 2.41.4 (Pericles' funeral speech).
[22] *Diss.Log.* 3.10. For the formulation see Homer *Od.* 19.203, Hes. *Theog.* 27, and later Plato *Rep.* 382d.

echoing early Greek poetic descriptions of verbal inventions, points towards a notion of the mimesis type – of a relation, that is, between poetry and its objects which at any rate is analogous to certain kinds of truth. If we combine this with the denial that poetry can serve as a vehicle of literal truth, we have at least a suggestion of a recognition that the dichotomy between truth and falsehood, and the corresponding antithesis between instruction and pleasure, could not fully cope with the problems and challenges involved in an understanding of the nature and purpose of poetry.

Yet the antitheses carried a potent appeal (as they still do), and despite the more refined standards of perception set by the *Poetics*, they were to become platitudes, and therefore impediments, in the framework of ancient thinking about art. Of their components, the didactic view of poetry is abundantly documented for the classical period partly because of Plato's repeated references and objections to it.[23] It need only be noted here as the dominant pre-Aristotelian attitude to the purpose of poetry, an attitude which both sustained and was sustained by the central educational use of poetic texts in at least Athenian culture. The principle of the pleasure of poetry was not, of course, a strict rival, since the two ideas could so easily be, and often were, combined. But the question of pleasure raised issues of its own, issues concerning the kind and quality of pleasure involved.[24] Two matters in particular can be picked out on this level as of prime importance to the Platonic and Aristotelian discussions of poetry. The first is the degree of compatibility between pleasure and other kinds of experience; the second centres on the type and implications of the special pleasure taken in the poetic portrayal of suffering and tragedy.

[23] The main Platonic references to the didactic view of poetry are: *Lysis* 213e-14a, *Phdr.* 245a, *Protag.* 325e 2ff., 338e 6ff., *Rep.* 598d ff., 606e, *Laws* 810e ff., 858d-e, 964c. A selection of other evidence: Xenophanes frs. 2.19 and 10, Heraclitus frs. 57, 104, Solon fr. 4.30 (West), Aristoph. *Frogs* 1008-10, 1026, 1030ff., Xen. *Mem.* 3.1.1-4, *Symp.* 4.6-7, Isoc. 1.51, 2.3, 13, 42-4, 3.2, 4.159, Lycurg. *Leoc.* 100, 103f., 106-9, *P.Oxy.* III no. 414 (= Lanata 214), Timocles fr. 6.7. As can be seen from this, Pohlenz 585-7 was right to retract his earlier claim, 441ff., that the didactic conception originated with the sophists, though this has been repeated by e.g. T. G. Rosenmeyer, in *The Legacy of Greece*, ed. M.I. Finley (Oxford 1981) 124. Germane to the didactic conception was the widespread practice of quoting poets as 'witnesses': see e.g. Plato *Rep.* 364c-d, Xen. *Mem.* 1.2.20f., Ar. *Met.* 995a 7f., *Rhet.* 1375b 28ff., with Dalfen 41ff. Note also that the sophists themselves can be considered as heirs to the didactic status of the poets (*sophistês* itself is used of poets at Pind. *I.* 5.28): cf. the implications of Plato *Protag.* 316d-e.

[24] On poetic pleasure see Harriott esp. 122ff.

Of the sparse evidence for pre-Platonic attitudes to these subjects, the traces of the sophist Gorgias' ideas about the emotional experience of poetry and the other arts deserve to be singled out. Echoing the poets' own early images of the power of their art, Gorgias used the language of magic and allurement in connection with the strong and moving gratifications of poetry, and we need here also to recall the notion of poetic 'deception' which I referred to earlier. Gorgias also described the soothing emotional effects of some poetry, and appears to have identified not a single poetic pleasure but a range of varying intensity.[25] In all this he can be seen to be putting in a theoretical form observations which had been given dramatic expression in the Homeric epics. A similar anticipation of the theorist by the poet can also be made out for Gorgias' apparent belief that the emotional experience provided by poetry could somehow mediate a kind of knowledge or understanding ('the deceived is wiser ...'), as well as for his sense of the specific paradox entailed in the enjoyment of tragic poetry. In both these respects Gorgias stands out, how adventitiously it is hard to know, from the scatter of pre-Platonic utterances on poetry, as a thinker who marks a transition from the insights of the poets themselves, above all Homer, to the two major fourth-century philosophers and their thoughts on the emotional force and pleasure of poetry.

As a supplement to this sketch of the central themes in Greek views of poetry before Plato and Aristotle, it may be worthwhile, for the larger perspective behind the *Poetics*, to provide a brief account of the categories of theory and criticism in which these themes were discussed or explored. At one extreme we have the committed judgements of philosophers who viewed poetry as a cultural phenomenon and addressed themselves to its moral and religious content, its influence on those educated by it, and its general status in relation to the sources of knowledge or wisdom valued and advocated by the philosophers themselves. It was to such a tradition of criticism, represented for us by Xenophanes and Heraclitus, that Plato looked back, and to which he himself in part belonged, when he adverted in the last book of the *Republic* to the 'long-standing quarrel between philosophy and poetry' (607b 5f.). Such criticism can hardly be called literary in any of the now usual senses. It raised some vital questions about the nature of poetry and the ways in

---

[25] Gorgias fr. 11.8-10 (cf. n.20 above). On the paradox of tragic pleasure see Hom. *Od.* 8.499-531 (with Macleod 7ff.), Plato *Ion* 535-6, *Rep.* 605-6, *Phileb.* 47-8.

which it was employed in Greek culture, but it did not stay for
answers, or, rather, it offered such brief and polemical answers that,
so far as we can see, it could not constitute anything more than the
negative and antagonistic position of a small minority of
intellectuals. Even Plato did not belong consistently in this camp; his
attitude to poetry was too complex and equivocal, as passages such as
the one from which I took the epigraph to this chapter indicate, where
the Platonic Socrates compares the love of poetry, ingrained from
childhood onwards, to the force of erotic passion. As for Aristotle, he
appears to have felt too detached from this tradition of philosophical
hostility to poetry to derive anything of explicit value from it; though
that is not to rule out altogether the possibility of its more subtle
influence on the *Poetics*.[26]

At the opposite extreme from the ideological objections to poetry
put forward by the philosophers was the type of linguistic criticism
whose development was largely a pioneering achievement of the
sophistic movement. Several of the sophists are known to have
engaged in discussion of linguistic usage, ranging (it seems) from
strict analysis of grammar, word-formation and similar matters, to
more evaluative and prescriptive ideas on the correct use of
language.[27] For all their historical importance, such subjects may
seem of little relevance to the evolution of Greek literary theory and
criticism, and indeed Aristotle himself says as much at one point in
the *Poetics* (56b 13-19). Yet the fact remains that linguistic questions
were not always properly separated from broader literary issues, and
this too can be seen in the *Poetics*, for it has left its mark on Aristotle's
own discussion of the style or language (*lexis*) of tragedy in chs. 20 to
22. Not only does this section of the treatise fail to focus at all clearly
on the language of tragedy as such, despite its formal place as part of
the analysis of this genre, but much of it is given over to a strictly
technical treatment of linguistic points. I shall attempt to draw out
some of the implications of these chapters in Appendix 4, but I
mention them here as an illustration of the way in which the
independent study of language, despite Aristotle's disclaimer, has

[26] For Ar.'s one explicit reference to this tradition see 60b 35ff. with p. 231 below;
he also alludes to part of Xenophanes' point (see his frs. 14-16) at *Pol.* 1252b 24-7.

[27] The slogan of the approach was *orthoepeia* ('correct speech'), a word associated
particularly but not exclusively with Protagoras. Pfeiffer 40 refers to 'Protagoras'
purely 'formal' *orthoepeia*', but I believe the term covered both technical matters (as at
Poet. 56b 13ff., *Rhet.* 1407b 6ff., Aristoph. *Clouds* 658ff.) and wider matters of sense and
style (as at Aristoph. *Frogs* 1180ff., Plato *Protag.* 338e ff., *Phdr.* 267c).

impinged on the work's approach to poetry.

Between the extremes of philosophical and linguistic criticism there lies a whole gamut of types of analysis and judgement of poetry. A certain amount of biographical study of poets was pursued, and Aristotle himself may have engaged in this in his early work, the dialogue *On Poets*; but the biography of poets was not practised extensively until after Aristotle's death, when it became a speciality of his own epigones in the Peripatetic school.[28] Somewhat akin to biography, however, was research into the data of literary history, particularly the evolution of genres. This was certainly a serious interest of Aristotle's in the later part of his career, and this line of enquiry, unlike the biography of individual poets, has probably left some traces in the *Poetics*, especially in the sketches of the history of tragedy and comedy in chs. 4 and 5. I shall argue later in this book, nonetheless, that Aristotle's concern for literary history is firmly subordinated in the *Poetics* to his *theoretical* understanding of genres; and the results might therefore be more aptly described as literary ideology than as history proper.[29]

Outside the types of work so far indicated, it becomes harder to classify neatly the kinds of literary issues which were raised and discussed by sophists and others.[30] But that a multiplicity of approaches and methods of criticism were available in the later fifth century is clear enough from the variety of material exploited by Aristophanes in the contest of tragedians in *Frogs*. Although this play confronts us in an acute form with the difficulties of interpretation that arise out of the comic poet's blend of satire and fantasy, we can still discern in it with a fair degree of probability a reflection of the areas of major interest in the contemporary analysis and judgement of poetry. In addition to fundamental themes such as the didactic function of the poet, on which I have already commented, and the reflection of contemporary preoccupations such as close verbal criticism (satirised in the weighing of words), we find in *Frogs* hints,

[28] Book 3 of *On Poets* seems to have dealt with biographical questions (frs. 75-6 Rose), but we should allow for the possibility that these were details that later readers were most interested in. For early interest in Homer's life see Pfeiffer 11, and for Peripatetic biography see A. Momigliano, *The Development of Greek Biography* (Cambridge Mass. 1971) 65-84.

[29] For a sketch of Ar.'s antiquarian researches see Pfeiffer 79ff., and cf. my Appendix 1 §2(c). On *Poetics* 4-5 see ch. III pp. 93ff. and ch. IX pp. 255ff., 269 below.

[30] One type of criticism which has no bearing on the *Poetics* is the allegorical, on which see N. J. Richardson, *PCPS* 21 (1975) 65-81. But there is a remnant of allegorical interpretation in *Homeric Problems* fr. 175 Rose (and cf. fr. 149?).

admittedly sometimes faint, of a number of topics which later find a place in the *Poetics*. I cannot examine these in detail here, but I list the most striking of them: an underlying sense of the poet's activity as a rational skill or art, and as therefore susceptible to systematic or technical scrutiny; an awareness of the structural properties of tragedy as a genre, including, for example, the importance of the opening of a play for the way in which a dramatist cuts into a block of mythical material; the significance of dramatic characterisation, and in particular the treatment of heroic figures in relation to the standards of the poet's own society; the role of choral lyric in tragedy, and its connection with general dramatic style; and finally a recognition of changing literary tradition, in which continuities and contrasts both play a part.[31]

The importance of *Frogs* as a document bearing on the history of Greek attitudes to literature lies not so much in these specific anticipations of the *Poetics*, interesting though they are, as in the fact that it provides us with our most vivid evidence on the subject before Plato. For the rest we have to be content, as this chapter has already intimated, with mere scraps and glimpses of sophistic thinking. While these are sufficient to show that the *Poetics* was written partly against the background of earlier theory and criticism of poetry, they leave an inadequate impression of the kind of intellectual energy and interest that must have gone into the thinking of Aristotle's predecessors in the subject. Although the *Frogs* cannot be trusted as an accurate historical record, it does at least comically reflect some of the passion and the liveliness of the fifth-century culture in which tragedy flourished and to which the *Poetics* later looked back. It also gives us indirectly a sense of the passions which poetry could arouse in the society that produced not Aristotle himself but the individual figure whose shadow falls across much of his treatise, Plato.

*

It has rightly become, despite an occasional denial, something of a commonplace that the *Poetics* is in large part concerned with issues

---

[31] Poetic skill: n. 16 above. Dramatic structure and prologues: *Frogs* 911ff., 946ff., 1119ff. Characterisation and heroes: 948ff., 1039-64. Choral lyric: 914-17 (with *Poet.* 49a 16-18), 1261-1363. Literary tradition: 910, 939ff., 1013ff., 1298-1300. Pohlenz's hypothesis (436-72) of a Gorgianic work as Aristophanes' source of ideas remains contentious. For some common terminology in *Frogs* and the *Poetics* see ch. III nn. 7 and 20.

which Plato had already raised and on which he had forcefully pronounced.[32] The preceding section of this chapter has offered an outline of some salient pre-Platonic attitudes to poetry and art, and there is no doubt that Aristotle was familiar with the various expressions of these attitudes in the works of poets themselves, in sophistic treatises and elsewhere. But Aristotle's own frame of reference was not simply cultural but philosophical, and within it the one central and unavoidable challenge, or set of challenges, was posed by Plato himself. Whether without the stimulus of this challenge Aristotle would anyway have been predisposed to direct his philosophical attention to poetry, is something now impossible to say; but it is clear that after some twenty years' exposure to Plato's insistent views on art, Aristotle could no more avoid his teacher's influence in this area than in any other prominent matter discussed by Plato. I have already referred to the indirect evidence that Aristotle may have explicitly countered some of Plato's strictures on poetry in his early dialogue *On Poets*. In the *Poetics* itself it is not difficult to discern the evidence for a constant, implicit engagement with the terms and the conclusions of the Platonic case against poetry. I have gathered a representative collection of verbal and other connections of detail between the *Poetics* and Plato in Appendix 2. Those connections supply much of the raw material for an understanding of the relation between the two philosophers, though we need to go deeper than details of comparison or contrast in order to grasp their chief ideas. Some of the more important questions will be taken up as appropriate in later chapters of the book: what I attempt here is a diagnosis of the main lines of relationship between Plato and the *Poetics*.

The first point which requires emphasis, particularly in view of the claims which are sometimes made to the contrary, is that this relationship is complex. To suppose that the *Poetics* was intended to offer a denial of Platonic doctrine on poetry at every stage would be to ignore the ample evidence in the treatise itself for a substantial Aristotelian indebtedness to Plato. It can be easily seen from the material collected in Appendix 2 that the *Poetics* contains many borrowings of terminology and ideas from Plato's references to

---

[32] For various assessments see Finsler, Solmsen 196-9, Gould (1964), and the balanced summary of Fuhrmann (1973) 72-90. The most vehement denial of Plato's relevance to the *Poetics* is that of Gudeman 21-8, but his scholarship does not match his animus.

poetry and art, though the borrowings may be juxtaposed with implicit disagreements or used in contexts which limit their force. The relation of the *Poetics* to Plato is a shifting one: it ranges from direct acceptance to flat contradiction of Platonic principles or arguments, through variously equivocal and qualified intermediate positions.

The central element in the relation between Plato and the *Poetics* is the concept of mimesis. This certainly did not derive purely from Plato, but he does seem to have made more use of it than any previous theorist. It is at any rate quite clear from a number of shared details that Aristotle's understanding of mimesis was specifically evolved, though not straightforwardly taken over, from Platonic arguments and suggestions. For Plato, mimesis was not only a commonly accepted view of the relation between art and its objects, but it was also a concept which allowed a serious philosophical insight into, and critique of, the status of art in relation to knowledge, truth and emotion. It is, in other words, the crucial idea in Plato's understanding of art, and the one to which he returns repeatedly. But this is not to say that Plato always approaches or discusses mimesis in quite the same terms; there are in his deployment of the language of mimesis, as also in the case both of earlier and of Aristotelian usage, significant variations. The immediate relevance of this is that there are passages on mimesis in Books 2-3 of the *Republic* and Book 2 of the *Laws* in which Plato accepts at least the limited validity of poetic mimesis, even though he may be critical of its results in existing poetry; and it is to these more positive treatments that some of the details in the *Poetics* (particularly in the theoretical framework of chs. 1 to 3) can be traced. The negative corollary of this is that Aristotle is largely unmoved by the major metaphysical assault launched against mimesis in Book 10 of the *Republic*, and occasionally touched on elsewhere too. To recognise the intricacy of the *Poetics*' response to Plato we need to avoid simplification of the Platonic view of art. Given his rejection of the idealist metaphysics on which the case against art in *Republic* 10 rests, Aristotle was not thereby obliged to turn away from Plato's whole notion of mimesis, for he was able to find elsewhere in his teacher's philosophy statements of a more fruitful and less dismissive interpretation of the concept. In particular, as ch. IV will attempt to show, it was under the influence of Platonic thinking that Aristotle elaborated both a general notion of mimesis as a fictional representation of the material of human life, and also a more technical sense of mimesis as the enactive or dramatic mode of poetry.

Mimesis, then, is not only a major connection between the Platonic and Aristotelian views of poetry and art, but also a pertinent instance of the subtle, revisionist position which Aristotle was capable of adopting towards his predecessor's arguments. The questions and issues which Plato had raised were too insistent to be simply evaded, and Plato's fervent exploration of them was too urgent for Aristotle to want to counter him on every point. Yet it would be absurd to deny that the two philosophers present widely divergent impressions in their attitudes to poetry and the other arts, and this divergence has much to do with the ways in which they employ the language of mimesis. The fundamental point to be made is that Plato strongly tends to judge mimesis by wholly external and objective standards of veracity. Mimesis is taken to be crudely parasitic on reality: the artist's aim, according to a passage of *Rep.* 10 which gives us the first occurrence of an idea with a long European legacy, is to produce the effect of a mirror held up to the world of the senses.[33] Plato, moreover, usually writes as though he regards the poet as directly responsible for, and assumes him to affirm, everything to be found in his works. Mimetic works are fake or pseudo-reality; they deceive, or are intended to deceive; their credentials are false, since they purport to be what in fact they are not. Despite maintaining the analogy between poetry and visual art, Aristotle reacts against this view of mimesis by releasing the artist from the obligation of transcribing or reproducing reality in any straightforward way, by charging mimesis with the power of embodying universals rather than particulars, and by treating the poet not as an affirmer (the poet is not truly a poet when he speaks in his own person: 60a 7f.) but as a skilful maker of dramatic fictions.

The repercussions of this contrast are pervasive, but they can be seen clearly in the divergent uses of the notion of *muthos* made by the two philosophers.[34] For both, a close relation exists between their understanding of the place of *muthos* in poetry and their conceptions of

---

[33] *Rep.* 596d-e; cf. the quotation from Alcidamas criticised at Ar. *Rhet.* 1406b 12f. For the wider use of the image see E.R. Curtius, *European Literature and the Latin Middle Ages*, Engl.transl. (London 1953) 336, E. Fraenkel, *Aeschylus: Agamemnon* (Oxford 1950) II 386.

[34] On this term see ch. II n.16.

mimesis. Plato and Aristotle also have in common a belief that *muthos* is the kernel or essence of poetry, but beyond that shared supposition their interpretations of the concept are opposed. Both, though Plato more than Aristotle, exploit existing connotations of the word, whose range of meaning encompasses the senses of speech, story, report, narrative, myth, fable and fiction. Plato is apt to treat poetic *muthos* simply but pejoratively: a *muthos* is a story or fable which embodies and asserts, without qualification, a set of propositions about the world; a *muthos* is equivalent to its paraphraseable content. *Muthoi* are the poetic products of mimesis, just as painted or other images are the products of visual mimesis, and Plato regards *muthoi* and images as closely analogous. His standard presupposition is that in both cases mimesis strives to reproduce objects as faithfully as possible, to mirror them: hence, the proper cognitive response to a story or poem, as to an image, is a direct judgement on its truthfulness; simple truth is in both cases the principal criterion of artistic success. There is no doubt that Plato knew better than this, as his own use of philosophical *muthoi* is sufficient to show. But the above is a fair statement of the polemical position which he widely adopts, and there is equally no doubt that he believed it to be an accurate account of the cultural status of much existing poetry. This being so, Plato's concern over the falsehood of poetic *muthos* focussed above all on moral values, to which I shall shortly return.

Although the term *muthos* remains central to Aristotle's theory of poetry, its sense has shifted markedly, and in a way which displays significant originality, from Plato's use of it. *Muthos* becomes in the *Poetics* a virtually technical term, yet the fact that Aristotle employs it from the outset without an initial definition may in part reflect the fact that he is elaborating a usage which retains some of the existing connotations of a story that is shaped in the telling, and of a fiction that may hold and entrance the attention regardless of its literal status in relation to reality. Other aspects of existing meaning are also relevant, not least the sense of traditional myth. But all this is certainly inadequate to explain the special force of the word in Aristotle's theory. In the *Poetics* (and the term is not used in this way even in Aristotle's other works, so far as I can see) *muthos* designates the formal product of the poet's art or craft: it denotes the plot-structure which is both the organised design and the significant substance or content of a poem. A poetic *muthos*, in Aristotle's most concise terms, is the mimetic representation of an action, and he devotes the core of his analysis of tragedy, in chs. 6 to 14, to a careful consideration of the properties of a tragic *muthos*: its unity and proportion, its principles of coherence and intelligibility, its special constituent elements (recognition and reversal), and the crucial shape of the ideal tragic action. *Muthos* in this new sense can be loosely rendered as 'plot', but only provided we understand by that not simply the contingent contents of a play or poem, but the formal organisation which is purposefully produced and fashioned to coherence by the poet. Because it is difficult to charge the trite term 'plot' with the necessary weight of meaning, I usually prefer 'plot-structure' as a translation. Aristotle's elaboration of this concept of a structured *muthos* turns the gaze more inwardly than the Platonic point of view had allowed onto the intrinsic properties of the poetic work of art. This is not, however, to say that the *Poetics* sets up poems as self-sufficient objects which can be intelligibly grasped in purely internal terms. Aristotle is not in this sense an outright formalist, nor could he have been, given his fundamental acceptance of mimesis. The shifts in Aristotelian thinking away from the Platonic position on mimesis and poetic *muthoi* do not commit him to arguing for the complete independence of art, only for the respectability of a status which is not wholly subjected to external standards of truthfulness.

For Plato, the issue of truthfulness was inextricable from that of morality, and the chief dereliction of existing poetry was the propagation of ethical falsehood by the failure to affirm and celebrate the identity of virtue and happiness. If mimesis could be justified at all, it would have to be capable of upholding this moral equation and its implications. Thus, in Book 2 of the *Laws*, where Plato explicitly takes mimetic 'correctness' in general to be a matter of accurate or truthful representation, the specific obligation laid on art is that it should portray moral goodness for our edification, or, perhaps less satisfactorily, the chastisement of evil.[35] I have already quoted in this chapter Aristotle's pronouncement that 'correctness in poetry is not the same as correctness in politics or in any other art' (60b 13-15), which serves as a response to both facets of Plato's compound requirement for art. But I have also cautioned against understanding Aristotle's point to be a statement of aestheticism. The fact that Aristotle does not set poetry explicitly in the larger perspective of

---

[35] *Laws* 654b ff. and 667-70. On 'correctness' (*orthotês*) in general see Pfeiffer 39f., 74f., and cf. Appendix 2 under 60b 13ff.

education and politics (as he does with music in *Politics* 7-8) does not mean that his treatment of it in the *Poetics* altogether lacks implications which could be articulated within such a perspective, nor that we can doubt that Aristotle intends his specialised theory of the poetic art to be conformable to the moral and political principles of his system of thought as a whole. A separate standard of poetic and mimetic 'correctness' is affirmed, but it is not one which is wholly autonomous.[36] Aristotelian mimesis still carries with it the presupposition that the artist aspires to produce plot-structures, or images, or forms of some other kind, which are consistent with reality, above all with that level of reality perceived through universals, which are also the concern of the philosopher (*Poetics* 9). Hence, also, Aristotle's belief, succinctly stated in *Poetics* 4, that the pleasure derived from mimesis is *au fond* a pleasure in cognitive recognition and learning. The passive, credulous audience of mimetic deception, as Plato saw it, is recredited with the positive capacity of comprehending the structured material of the poet's work.

In this way, through his refinement of the notion of mimesis, Aristotle moves towards (though scarcely with a wholly satisfying finality) a reformulation of the relation between mimetic works and reality; but that *some* such relation exists, or should exist, remains an unquestioned premise. It is one component of this premise, moreover, that art cannot be wholly divorced from ethical values, which are themselves for Aristotle, as for Plato, an aspect of reality. Aristotle's qualification of Platonic moralism is in accord with his redefinition of the nature of mimesis: if mimesis in general reflects reality by embodying universals, but without necessarily mirroring the world accurately in all respects, so its ethical content, while it may eschew simple didacticism, must in general be true to the good and evil in the world. Aristotle's assent to the premise can only be seen and assessed with any confidence in his theory of tragedy, where it gives rise to some difficult, perhaps irresolvable, tensions. In my examination of these in ch. VII I hope to confirm the existence, as well as to scrutinise some of the limitations, of the ethical dimension of the *Poetics*.

Most of the other significant differences between Plato's and

---

[36] Russell 32 goes too far in talking of 'conscious *isolation* ... from ethics' (my ital.) (his comments on p. 93 seem to me closer to the truth); similarly e.g. Hutton 18-20. For objections to such views see Grube (1965) 74f., and the articles by Eden and Smithson.

Aristotle's views of poetry can be regarded as either derivable from, or firmly tied to, the points already made. Plato's verdict on mimesis made it impossible for him consistently to attribute knowledge or skill to the poet and so to accept poetry's standing as an art (*technê*) in its own right. In so far as any value can be discerned by him in existing poetry, then, it is necessary to appeal to inspiration to explain it, though this explanation cannot always be taken at face-value. Aristotle, on the other hand, by his very willingness to devote a treatise to poetry, marks his acknowledgement that it is a rational, artistic activity with its own principles and dynamics; and it is a corollary of this that notions of inspiration are made redundant, and that the sources of artistic production are located within the intelligible sphere of knowledgeable craft (see chs. II-III below). Similarly, while Plato usually regards the pleasures afforded by art as false, irrational and pernicious, because grounded in the experience of wilful and immoral illusions, Aristotle adumbrates both a basic notion of aesthetic pleasure (pleasure taken in mimetic art) which relates it to the conscious, rational powers of the apprehending mind, and also a categorisation of this pleasure into particular types associated with individual poetic genres. And for both philosophers pleasure is connected with the emotions. For Plato this means that the immorality and irrationality of art indulge feelings which ought to be kept in check: in the case of tragedy, this is described tellingly as the watering of emotions which should be allowed to dry up (*Rep.* 606d). For Aristotle, by contrast, these emotions are based properly on a cognitive experience, and their arousal is intelligibly entailed in the poet's rational art. Thus tragedy, at its best, can offer an experience in which judgement and emotion are in harmony, as the complementary elements of a response to the pattern of action portrayed by the poet: and this is as it should be, given the general character of Aristotelian psychology (see ch. VI below). It should be mentioned as a revealing sidelight on these major disagreements between the philosophers that Plato, perhaps in part because of his Athenian origin, shows a more vivid sense of the public context in which much Greek poetry was encountered: primarily, this means, of the theatre, but also of the epic recital. This enables him to compare poetry to rhetoric and demagogy, because of the mass emotions which it can elicit and control.[37] But

---

[37] See e.g. *Gorg.* 501b-d, *Ion* 535b-e, *Rep.* 604e, *Laws* 817c. *Politics* 8 contains a few hints of a stronger sense of the public performance than we find in the *Poetics*: see esp. 1336b 20-23.

Aristotle goes far, though not all the way, towards separating even drama from the context of public performance (under the pressure, as ch. 26 indicates, of Plato's attitudes), and this accords well with his broader attempt to restore a cognitive significance and respectability to poetry in the face of Plato's criticisms.

These remarks on the relation between the *Poetics* and Plato cannot, of course, purport to be exhaustive. They have not been intended either to give a full account of Plato's approach to art, which has been studied elsewhere,[38] or to analyse in detail the many ways in which Aristotle adjusted his own thinking to that approach. My aim has been to pick out the main themes which underlie the connections and contrasts of detail that are catalogued in Appendix 2, and by so doing to alert the reader to questions of importance which will arise again in the later course of this book. Although I have been chiefly attending to matters of contrast, I reiterate what was said at the beginning of this section, that Aristotle's response to the Platonic critique of poetry should not be thought to be entirely adverse. There is a good deal of discreet continuity too. It may not be inappropriate to suggest, by way of conclusion, that we may recognise beneath the details of the *Poetics* a double movement in the direction of Aristotle's thought in relation to the stimulus of his teacher's views: first, a strong impulse away from the overt and uncompromising features of the Platonic case, especially the excessively rigid notion of mimesis, and the extreme moralism; but then, secondly, a more subtle and qualified inclination to reintegrate into his conception of the relative independence of poetry some understanding of the cognitive and moral values implicated in the invention and appreciation of mimetic art – values which Plato too would have liked to discern there.

*

Having so far urged the need to regard the *Poetics* seriously as part of Aristotle's philosophical *oeuvre*, and to place the work in relation to his predecessors, above all Plato, I turn now more narrowly to certain features of this small but immensely influential document itself. Even a casual reader of the *Poetics*, or perhaps especially a casual reader, will readily be struck by the rough state of the text. Quite

[38] The best survey of the Platonic material remains that of Vicaire, but see also Dalfen's book and the essays in the collection edited by Moravcsik and Temko.

apart from the likelihood that a whole section of the work (on comedy) has been lost, what remains is vitiated by unevenness of treatment, apparent inconsistencies, some unfulfilled promises (or lacunae), occasional disjointedness, and moments of obscurity which extend, even the most hardened Aristotelian will concede, to the point of the opaque. To determine in every instance how much of this can be attributed to the history and accidents of survival, and how much to internal or original Aristotelian factors, cannot be undertaken in a discursive work such as the present: it is principally the task of editors, some of whom have indeed derived creative delight from it.[39] Despite the variety of hypotheses that have been explored – that the text is a pupil's lecture-notes, or an epitome of a larger book, or heavily interpolated, or a work whose design has been badly confused in transmission – there probably exists a sound consensus that the *Poetics* is a document substantially produced by Aristotle himself, and that it provides us with a tolerably reliable impression of part of a course of philosophical instruction: that it is, in other words, an 'acroamatic' or (in the more usual terminology) an 'esoteric' treatise.[40] My aim here, however, is not to reopen this complex question in detail, but to examine the broader implications of the state of the text for the business of general interpretation. What I offer, therefore, is not an exegesis of the many individual points of difficulty in the text, but an introductory attempt to see how far they affect the basic conditions of understanding.

My contention is that the unpolished state of the *Poetics* need not impede us unduly from recognising in it the sharp lineaments of a developed theory of poetry (and, to a more limited extent, of mimetic art as a whole). For if the work is, as is commonly claimed, 'in parts little more than a series of jottings',[41] it is necessary to stress the countervailing fact that it purports in its own terms to be systematic

---

[39] For a summary of the attempts to explain (and rectify) the state of the text see Söffing 15-22. I note that Solmsen, whose 1935 article (applying the principles of Jaegerian *Entstehungsgeschichte*) pioneered the modern practice of discerning chronological strata in the *Poetics*, referred to the work as 'aus einem Guß' in *Gnomon* 5 (1929) 409 n.1. For a survey of inconsistencies etc. see Bywater xiii-xx. One hopes the nineteenth-century German view that the treatise is a series of compiler's extracts (cf. Gudeman 2f.) will not be revived.

[40] On the character of Ar.'s surviving works see Düring (1966) 32ff. (For the possibility of similar Platonic works note Ar. *Phys.* 209b 14f.) It must be frankly admitted, however, that we have little idea just how the esoteric works were used in the school: if we knew more, we would be able to read many works with fresh eyes.

[41] Lucas (1968) x.

and methodically organised. In order to try to see obscurities and shortcomings in the correct light, we must in the first place set them within the framework of the approach and aims which the work itself advances. On the scale of overall structure, there is certainly sufficient clarity of purpose, provided we allow for the tangential remarks, the *obiter dicta*, and the occasional loose ends which are characteristic of the corpus as a whole. The opening five chapters of the *Poetics* deal with general matters of mimetic categorisation, a psychological and cultural theory of the basis of mimetic activity, and an outline of the historical evolution of those genres of poetry with which the rest of the treatise will be concerned. These early chapters are concise and sometimes elliptical, but they embody a strong theoretical framework on which much that follows heavily depends. The start of ch. 6 signals the close of this introduction, and leads us to expect a discussion of tragedy, epic and comedy in turn. Of these sections we have only the first two. The completion of the section on tragedy is marked at the end of ch. 22, the beginning and end of that on epic at the start of ch. 23 and the end of ch. 26; what originally followed ch. 26 is a separate issue.[42] The way in which these limits of sections are indicated (as also at the end of chs. 3 and 25, on mimesis and 'problems') suggests that Aristotle supposes he has covered the given subjects sufficiently, as is indeed explicitly claimed for tragedy at the end of ch. 22.[43] With the exception of some anomalies to be discussed below, further subdivision can be discerned within the main sections of the analysis, yielding a reasonably coherent and progressive structure of argument. The following scheme gives a plain conspectus.[44]

Chs. 1-3 MIMESIS

ch. 1   The media of poetic mimesis: language, rhythm and music

ch. 2   The object of poetic mimesis: men in action, ethically differentiated according to genre

ch. 3   The modes of poetic mimesis: narrative, dramatic enactment, or an alternation of the two

---

[42] See Janko 63.

[43] 59a 16; cf. 54a 15, 54b 18.

[44] My diagram is intended only as a skeleton. Compare e.g. Söffing 26f. and the detailed headings in Hubbard's translation (tabulated in Janko 56).

Chs. 4-5 ORIGINS & HISTORY OF POETRY

ch. 4   Natural causes of poetry: mimetic instinct, and the pleasure of learning from mimetic objects

chs. 4-5   Literary history and teleology: Homer the pioneer of tragedy and comedy

Chs. 6-22 TRAGEDY

ch. 6   Definition; the six parts of tragedy, and their relative importance

chs. 7-14   Plot-structure (*muthos*)

  7-8   Coherence and unity

  9   Poetic universality (the distinction between poetry and history)

  9-10   Simple and complex plots

  11   Elements of the complex plot: reversal (*peripeteia*) and recognition (*anagnôrisis*)

  12   The quantitative units of tragedy

  13-14   The finest tragedy: *hamartia* and two approaches to the ideal

ch. 15   Characterisation (*êthos*)

ch. 16   Recognition: a typology

chs. 17-18   Miscellaneous precepts and observations

chs. 19-22   *Lexis*: the fundamentals of language and style

Chs. 23-26 EPIC

ch. 23   Unity of epic plot-structure: tragic principles applied to epic

ch. 24   Differences between epic and tragedy

ch. 25   Poetic 'problems' and their solutions: moral and fictional licence allowed to the poet

ch. 26   Comparison of epic and tragedy: the latter's superiority

Within the analyses of tragedy and epic there are many indications of an intention to sustain the methodical approach announced at the start of the treatise. The two simplest factors are, first, Aristotle's habit of frequently referring back to earlier points, and, secondly, his marking of the connective stages of his argument. These may of course be regarded as ordinary features of sequential discourse, but they cannot be taken for granted in a work that was never intended to be a self-sufficient text for readers, and they show that formally at

least the *Poetics* purports to consist of more than discrete or
ungathered notes, and strives for continuity of exposition. There are
in fact some twenty places where Aristotle refers back to an earlier
point; one or two of these references are uncertain, but only one is
seriously problematic.[45] This effect of cumulative coherence, and the
intermeshing of ideas, is strengthened by the design of the main
chapters on tragedy, where the progressive stages of the analysis are
unambiguously signed.

While these rudimentary details would pass without notice in a
treatise whose condition was not an issue, they are worth observing
in the *Poetics* as a rebuttal of the more extreme descriptions of the
work as a set of desultory *aperçus*. What, then, stands in the way of
our taking the *Poetics* to be a substantially finished work which has
perhaps suffered some damage in the course of its survival? It will be
as well to be explicit about the chief arguments which might be
adduced to support the claim that the treatise, even on its own terms,
is incomplete (I put aside, once more, the question of the lost book).
The first point is a piece of external evidence: the fact that a passage
in *Politics* Book 8 appears to promise a fuller discussion of the concept
of *katharsis* in the *Poetics*, while in our text the term *katharsis*, in this
special sense, occurs only once and quite without explanation. If we
discard, as I am inclined to do, the common but implausible
hypothesis that the promised discussion of *katharsis* was contained in
the lost section on comedy, it may be simplest to suppose that the
Politics passage is not a direct reference to our treatise, but to the
elaboration which Aristotle would give to the term *katharsis* in his
oral teaching on poetry;[46] there is much else besides on which we
might plausibly imagine that he expatiated more freely in this way.
But this one issue does not in any case go far towards establishing a
material deficiency in the surviving part of the *Poetics*, especially in
view of the likelihood that Aristotle had previously put forward a

---

[45] On the character of back-references cf. Else (1957) 615 and n.71. The most
problematic is 55b 32f.: see Lucas (1968) ad loc., and Allan (1972) for a special
explanation. The other main cases are: 48a 25 ~ 47a 16ff.; 49a 32 ~ 48a 17f., 48b 26;
49b 23: general; 50a 30 ~ tragic definition; 50b 13 ~ (?)49b 34; 50b 23 ~ definition; 52a
15 ~ ch. 7; 52a 23 ~ (?)51a 13f., (?)52a4; 52a 35 (corrupt) ~ (?)52a 4; 52b 10f. ~ preceding
section; 52b 15 ~ ch. 6 (cf. esp. 50a 13 with the text of Vahlen (1885)); 52b 30 ~ chs.
10-11; 53a 26 ~ 53a 13-15; 54a 9 ~ 53a 17ff.; 54a 18 ~ 50b 8ff.; 54b 19 ~ ch. 11; 56a 10f. ~
(?)49b 12ff., (?)55b 15ff.; 58a 33 ~ 57b 1ff.; 59a 30 ~ 51a 22ff.; 59b 7-10 ~ 55b 32ff.; 59b
18f. ~ 51a 3-15, 59a 31-3; 60a 3f. ~ 49a 24, 59b 31ff.; 60b 24f. ~ (e.g.) 50a 22f.; 62b 14 ~
esp. 53b 11f.

[46] See ch. VI p. 190 and n.32.

concept of poetic *katharsis* in an early work. The claim of incompleteness rests more firmly on internal factors, particularly the existence
of inconsistencies and contradictions. The salient difficulties in these
categories can be listed as follows:

1. 51b 33-52a 1 (on episodic plots) sits oddly in its present position: it
   would be arguably better placed at the end of ch. 10 (or perhaps of
   ch. 8). But there seems to be an associational link between the
   events of history, mentioned just before this, and the episodic plot,
   which might explain the presence of this material here.
2. Ch. 12 interrupts the sequence of argument (though hardly
   disfiguringly), as the reference back to chs. 10-11 as the beginning
   of ch. 13 indicates.[47]
3. Chs. 13 and 14 are notoriously held to be in contradiction, since
   they arrive at divergent conclusions about the best kind of tragic
   plot-structure.
4. After completing the section on plot-structure at the end of ch. 14,
   Aristotle moves on to characterisation only to revert to *muthos* as
   his subject for three sentences at 54a 37-54b 8.
5. Aristotle again reverts in ch. 16 to plot-structure, specifically to
   tragic recognition, which was discussed in ch. 11. The treatment
   of characterisation is therefore suspended once more, and this
   time it is not resumed (see next item).
6. Chs. 17 and 18 are miscellaneous in composition and content.
   They obscure the progress of analysis of the elements of tragedy,
   though ch. 19 opens as if the sequence of topics were still intact (cf.
   item 9 below).
7. Within ch. 18, at 55b 32ff., Aristotle produces a new scheme of
   four types of tragedy, and he relates this scheme to a previous list
   of four 'parts' of tragedy: even with a superabundance of
   ingenuity, and a tolerant latitude of interpretation, this reference-
   back is unintelligible for our text of the work (cf. n. 45 above).
8. Ch. 18, 56a 19-25 (an extremely vexed passage), appears to count
   as tragic those plots in which a wicked figure falls into misfortune
   (in contradiction of 53a 1-4).[48]

[47] On the status of ch. 12 see the opposing arguments of Taplin App. E and Janko
233-41.
[48] Allan (1971) 84-6 offers an elaborate but unconvincing treatment of the text.
Moles (1984b) 331f. argues against the existence of a contradiction, but an anomaly
remains; his suggestion that identification with wicked characters may after all be
possible can be firmly excluded: cf. e.g. *Rhet.* 1387a 12f., 1387b 11-13.

9. At the start of ch. 19 Aristotle says that of the six elements of tragedy only 'thought' (*dianoia*) and 'language' (*lexis*) remain to be treated. But there has in fact, in our text, been no formal discussion of two of the other elements, 'lyrics' (*melopoeia*) or theatrical 'spectacle' (*opsis*). The end of ch. 6 perhaps makes it clear why spectacle has not been separately dealt with: see Appendix 3. Lyrics have been touched on, with extreme brevity and deceptive simplicity, only at the end of ch. 18: see ch. VIII below.

10. Chs. 19 to 22 complete the section of the treatise on tragedy with an analysis of language, *lexis*. Unfortunately, the relevance of these chapters to tragedy will now escape most readers, since the focus is a wide one, and a majority of Aristotle's linguistic examples are picked from genres other than tragedy: see Appendix 4.

These problems and anomalies are not all of the same kind, and do not all warrant similar inferences. While I cannot tackle the intricate issues of detail attaching to the individual passages, I think it is worth summarising what seem to me to be the likeliest and most significant conclusions to be drawn from reflection on the above data.

In the first place, it is noticeable that the main chapters on plot (chs. 7-14), considered by Aristotle to be the 'soul' of tragedy, are relatively free of difficulties. The only substantial exception to this is the awkward relation between chs. 13 and 14 (item 3), and it is this which constitutes the major reason for believing that there is some important instability in the theory of tragedy. But it is pertinent that chs. 13-14 concern not the basic principles of plot construction, but the climax of the ideal tragedy; and I shall later argue that the issues involved here offered a sharp challenge to Aristotle's moral thinking about poetry. The uncertainty detectable at this point in the treatise may represent, I would suggest, not a contingent fact about the state of the text, but a deep dilemma in the theory of tragedy. The other oddities in the chapters on plot (items 1 and 2) are much more trivial; both could be due to textual displacement, or even (for 2) interpolation, in the course of the work's transmission. In any case, the most that they would establish is a slight degree of disorder in the text, and not any real obscurity or incompleteness in Aristotle's argument.

The majority of the difficulties I have tabulated are concentrated in chs. 15-18 of the *Poetics*, and I think that it is only here that we can fairly judge the treatise to be much less coherent than its own professions of design lead us to expect.[49] It is in these chapters that we are supposed to find the analysis of characterisation, choral lyrics, and theatrical spectacle. Even allowing for Aristotle's relative aversion to the latter, the fact remains that lyrics are hardly discussed at all, despite their central place in classical Greek tragedy, while the treatment of character, though more substantial, is twice interrupted by further observations on plot and is finally lost in the *mélange* of chs. 17-18. The extra material on plot is not in itself problematic; it is the postponed location of it, particularly the intrusion into ch. 16, which comes as a surprise, but for which various hypotheses can be devised. Whatever the explanation, the delay has little effect on the essential cohesion of the handling of plot. But what we *can* reasonably infer from the disjointed and inconsequential nature of chs. 15 to 18 is that Aristotle is either unwilling or unable to offer an analysis even of the element of most importance after plot, namely character, to match his study of plot-structure in scale or clarity. The impetus of his theory, which sustains itself cogently from ch. 6 to ch. 14, falls off when attention shifts from plot to subsidiary components of tragedy, and this is reflected in the double recurrence to plot in chs. 15 and 16 (items 4 and 5 above) as well as in the failure to integrate the miscellaneous material of chs. 17 and 18 into the scheme of argument founded on the six dramatic elements deduced in ch. 6. It is particularly telling that the intrusion of some remarks on plot into ch. 15 seems to be occasioned by the direct application to characterisation of one of the cardinal principles of plot-construction (necessity or probability, 54a 33ff.), so that we can see how the superficial desultoriness actually represents a circling back of Aristotle's thought on itself.

What should prevent us, then, from inferring that the inconcinnities of chs. 15 to 18 are simply the signs of the rough composition of the work as a whole is the combination of the clearly

---

[49] Bywater xiii and 250 (on 55b 32) notices the greater difficulties 'as the work advances': this is only a half-truth, since the chs. on epic are mostly free of difficulties; and Bywater's explanation (carelessness, in effect) is inadequate. Nor need we accept the argument of Solmsen 192-4 that most of the material on plot in chs. 15-18 must be later than chs. 7-14: cf. Hutton 38 n.52.

marked larger design, which is picked up again and followed with reasonable clarity from ch. 19 onwards, with the fact that it is precisely when moving on to aspects of tragedy which he holds to be of lesser importance that Aristotle's train of thought loses much of its cohesion and force. I would contend, in other words, that the condition of these chapters is to some degree a symptom of the priorities of the theory of tragedy on which the treatise is based. It is the corollary of the relative amplitude and integration of the chapters on plot-structure that the subordinate elements of tragedy should receive less space and much less incisive attention.

The hypothesis that the clustering of formal difficulties in chs. 15 to 18 of the *Poetics* may not be accidental, but rather be related to the intrinsic weighting of the theory of tragedy, would gain in plausibility if it were accepted that most of the central ideas of the treatise had been at least partially elaborated elsewhere. It is known that Aristotle had previously published, for general readers, at least one other work on poetry, the dialogue *On Poets*, and it is probably this to which he refers in the unfortunately opaque passage at the end of ch. 15 (54b 17f.). What is at any rate clear from this reference is that Aristotle considers he has dealt sufficiently in an already issued work with a point bearing (seemingly) on poetic characterisation. To this we must add that some of Aristotle's most emphatic pronouncements on mimesis, and on the criteria for the judgement of poetry, occur in ch. 25, the core of which almost certainly represents a summary of ideas elaborated at length in his *Homeric Problems*; it is therefore extremely probable that this work too predated the *Poetics*. When we supplement these points with the likelihood that the notion of tragic *katharsis* also goes back to an earlier stage of Aristotle's thinking on poetry (in fact to the *On Poets*), we have a *prima facie* case for supposing that he had some well-developed views towards a theory of poetry and tragedy before the *Poetics* was compiled, though this conclusion admittedly depends in part on one's dating of the *Poetics* itself (see Appendix 1). This case can, I think, be reinforced by drawing attention to Aristotle's tendency in the *Poetics* to employ terms and concepts before he has explained or defined them (though some allowance should be made for a factor which I earlier mentioned, the possibility of supplementary oral explanation). An obvious example of this is the central concept of mimesis, for which Aristotle presupposes both a general familiarity with the idea and a special awareness of Plato's treatment of it. But the following prominent instances should also be noted:[50]

ch. 6:   *katharsis* (49b 28), as earlier indicated, receives neither
         elucidation nor further mention, despite the fact that it
         merits a place in the definition of tragedy.

ch. 6:   reversal (*peripeteia*) and recognition (*anagnôrisis*) are first
         used here (50a 34f.), but not explained technically until chs.
         10-11.[51]

ch. 7:   the principle of probability or necessity (the order can be
         inverted) first occurs here (50b 27ff., 51a 12f.) but is best
         explained in ch. 9. These are, however, general logical
         categories used widely by Aristotle.

ch. 7:   it is at the end of this chapter (51a 13f.) that we find the first
         mention of a change of fortune in tragedy. It is striking that
         this essential idea does not appear as such in the definition of
         the genre, though it may there be implicit in the reference to
         pity and fear. Although the notion of a change of fortune is
         not itself obscure or technical, Aristotle's assumption that it
         may be shaped in either of two ways, towards favourable or
         adverse fortune, does require the elucidation of the
         alternative ideals of tragedy which he later sets up in chs. 13
         and 14.

ch. 9:   'simple' plots (51b 33) are defined only in the following
         chapter (52a 12ff.) but see item 1, p.32 above, on the section
         to which this first reference belongs.

ch. 15: the term *lusis*, 'dénouement', is first used here (54a 37), but
         not defined till ch. 18.

While individual explanations could be attempted for each of these
cases, as a group they tend to confirm the possibility that at least
certain parts of the theory of tragedy pre-existed the statement of it
which we have in our text of the *Poetics*. If we combine this
consideration with those I cited earlier, we can legitimately conclude

[50] Cf. Bywater xiv, but I would prefer not to resort to his explanation, which
hypothesises the pre-existing currency of these terms: for a fuller statement of his
argument see 'On Certain Technical Terms in Aristotle's *Poetics*', *Festschrift Theodor
Gomperz* (Vienna 1902) 164-72.

[51] One cannot safely follow Else (1957) 259 in using this anticipation as an
argument for his favourite obsession – the late addition of the sentence by Ar.: this
penchant of Else's is open to similar criticisms to those which he himself makes (40
n.153, 261 n.141) of De Montmollin.

that it is inappropriate to treat the work merely as a set of rough notes, or its contents as the materials of an inchoate theory of poetry. Despite some moments of disjointedness and obscurity, the main structure of argument is clearly delineated, and the evidence suggests that Aristotle regarded his theories as fully or sufficiently formed for his purposes. Where it appears to us otherwise, this may partly be due, I have tried to show, to the effect of the work's own priorities on the quality and balance of the various facets of the analysis. If this is so, the state of the *Poetics* can be taken to be adequate to justify the kind of critique which is undertaken in this book.

As a final preliminary to this critique, it is appropriate to make a few remarks on the type and level of theory which is embodied in the *Poetics*. In so far as a broad distinction can be made between descriptive and prescriptive criticism of literature, it should be beyond question that the treatise belongs somewhere in the second of these categories, though that is not to concede that Aristotle himself would have wholly accepted the distinction. It is not the primary purpose of the *Poetics* to examine or assess individual works of Greek poetry, but to establish a philosophical framework for the understanding of poetry in general, and to do so in a way which entails the statement and advocacy of criteria of poetic excellence. The treatise is in this sense both theoretical and prescriptive. But it has sometimes been believed that it is also prescriptive in a stronger and more pragmatic sense: that it sets out to instruct poets or would-be poets in the methods of composition itself.[52] I earlier noted the affinity between the *Poetics* and the various Greek *technai* or didactic manuals which were produced in a variety of fields, perhaps above all in rhetoric, but also in more practical crafts such as painting or sculpture. This affinity, which includes the association which I also mentioned between knowledge and teaching, helps to explain why Aristotle speaks with an assurance and directness which naturally have implications for the practice of poetry. This comparison might seem to imply that the *Poetics* too was intended to influence the activity of practitioners in the art, and so was directly analogous to a work such as the lost treatise, the *Kanon*, of the fifth-century sculptor Polycleitus: a treatise whose very title,

[52] E.g. Teichmüller vol.2, 404f., Bywater 206 and on 54b 9 (with a doubtful text), Collingwood 51, Post 247, Gomme 51, Else (1957) 535 and n.65, Söffing 154, Jones 21, 25.

meaning both a physical measuring rod and a standard or principle of proportion, appears to have nicely expressed the dual function of a workshop manual and the exposition of an aesthetic theory of form and proportion.[53]

The belief that the *Poetics* was meant to have practical value is ostensibly supported by the frequency of occurrence in it of didactic and prescriptive formulae. In more than two dozen places, beginning with the first sentence of the work, Aristotle employs phrases such as 'it is necessary', 'what one must aim at', and the like. But it is the scrutiny of these very passages which will provide the most immediate and compelling evidence that we need to appreciate the difference between theoretical and practical prescription, and that the *Poetics* is essentially an exercise in the former not the latter. The decisive factor is the abstract character of the principles and injunctions which the didactic phrasing is used to introduce. Consider the following representative selection: 'a plot-structure ... should be a mimesis of a single, entire action' (51a 30-32); 'the poet ought to be a maker of plot-structures rather than of verses' (51b 27f.); recognition and reversal 'ought to arise out of the very construction of the plot' (52a 18f.); 'the plot ought to be so constructed that even someone hearing the sequence of events would feel pity and fear' (53b 3-5); 'the chorus ought to be treated as one of the actors' (56a 25f.). In these and many other passages Aristotle's prescriptivism, while perhaps reminiscent of sophistic pedagogy, is aimed not at the practitioner but at the theoretical understanding of the philosophical student. If a young Athenian dramatist had taken the improbable decision of going to Aristotle for instruction in his work, he would have come away with material for reflection, but he would have had to develop his craft elsewhere. There is, in fact, no special status to be attached to those pronouncements in the *Poetics* which carry explicitly protreptic formulae; they simply confirm that the whole movement of Aristotle's thought is normative in the sense of being directed at a systematic and evaluative understanding of the

---

[53] On Polycleitus' *Kanon* see Pollitt 14-21, and for a play on the literal and metaphorical senses of the word cf. Aristoph. *Frogs* 799 and 956. Some other artistic treatises were: Agatharchus on scene-painting (Vitruvius VII Praef. 11: cf. Pollitt 234ff.), Ictinus on the Parthenon (Vitruv. ibid. 12), Democritus on painting (Diog.Laert. 9.48, Vitruv.ibid. 11).

nature of poetry and its genres.[54] But the *Poetics* lacks the detailed attention to practicality which one would expect to find in a true manual; the furthest that Aristotle goes towards this is in some of the miscellaneous advice of ch. 17, notably the least integrated part of the work, as we have already seen.[55] Moments in a pedagogic manner are easily incorporated into a theoretical treatise, the main impetus of which remains philosophical in Aristotle's own terms, for 'it is the task of the philosopher to be able to theorise about everything' (*Met.*1004a 34f.). Because poetry is by its very nature for the philosopher a productive activity, the explication of its principles cannot but present an instructive air, but the *Poetics* was nonetheless more distanced from its subject than many other *technai*; its context and its audience were within the philosophical school – a fact which I believe is discreetly echoed in the detached tone of voice to be heard in it from time to time.[56]

But the question of the work's theoretical status can also be approached from another angle, by asking what the relation was between the treatise and the existing corpus of Greek poetry. Some of my arguments in later chapters will depend on the assumption that it is necessary and valid to assess the doctrines of the *Poetics* against what we know of the literature which is its subject. But the possibility of judging the work in this way has often been impugned, most vehemently perhaps by Alfred Gudeman, who stressed that Aristotle knew some three hundred plays, as against our extant thirty-one, by the three great tragedians. Gudeman's point is part of a larger observation about the amount of Greek literature as a whole available to Aristotle but now lost to us.[57] This cautionary note certainly needs to be sounded, and its implications reckoned with.

---

[54] Both Pauw and Söffing tend to draw too strict and neat a distinction between descriptive and prescriptive elements (note Söffing's qualification on 37), and neither attends to how this dichotomy is undercut by Ar.'s teleological assumptions, on which see pp. 46ff. and 94ff. Cf. Fuhrmann (1973) 13.

[55] Solmsen 200 finds chs. 15 (second half) to 18 as a whole more empirical than the rest. Despite the fact that *technê* covers both theory and practice, the distinction is still open to Ar.: he draws it explicitly at *Met.* 981a 12ff. in a way which has implications for poetry and the *Poetics*.

[56] E.g. the third-person references to 'the poets' and the like, esp. 50a 25ff., 51b 12ff.

[57] Gudeman 11f., who does his case for Ar.'s 'thorough knowledge' of Greek poetry no good by observing (12 n.1) that 'talented pupils' may have gathered some of his evidence for him. Cooper (1923) 12 divertingly claims that Ar. could have read a thousand tragedies – as if he did nothing else.

But we also need to ask just what these implications are, rather than taking them for granted. It is certainly inadequate to presuppose, as Gudeman does, that Aristotle had necessarily availed himself fully of existing literature as a basis for his theories, since the *Poetics* omits altogether many major poets and whole tracts of Greek literature. We cannot, of course, infer that Aristotle was ignorant of what he omitted. Indeed, it is precisely because we can safely assume a broad knowledge of the authors and genres in question that it becomes worthwhile to ask why so little account was taken of them. I shall pursue this point in ch. IX.

But when we turn specifically to Aristotle's central subject, do we need to posit a multitude of tragedies as the relevant background to his theory of the genre, and should we feel inhibited in our evaluation of this theory by the paucity of the surviving material? If we examine the references to named plays in the *Poetics*, we discover that Aristotle mentions perhaps four works by Aeschylus, nine by Sophocles, and eight by Euripides.[58] Of these we have two of the Aeschylean tragedies, three of the Sophoclean, and five of the Euripidean – a total of ten out of some twenty. But when we scrutinise the distribution of references to these works, the sample becomes even more encouraging. By my reckoning, well over half of Aristotle's citations of named or identifiable tragedies involve plays which we still possess; this owes much to the fact that the two plays which are cited far more than any others, Sophocles' *Oedipus Tyrannus* and Euripides' *Iphigeneia in Tauris*, mentioned between them some ten times, have both survived.[59] Named plays are not the entire stock of tragic material on which Aristotle draws in his thinking about the genre, and for the fourth-century works in particular we remain largely in the dark. But the choice of illustrative cases in the *Poetics* is obviously significant, and our possession of a substantial portion of the texts to which Aristotle directly refers, above all the two plays

[58] There are some uncertainties of attribution and detail, but they do not affect my argument. The list in Gudeman llf. is defective; cf. Söffing 235 n. 98. It is worth noting that, in line with his fourth-century popularity, Euripides is the most frequently cited tragedian in the Aristotelian corpus as a whole: see Xanthakis-Karamanos 28-34.

[59] The *OT*: 52a 24-6, ?33, 53b 7, 31, 54b 7f., 55a 18, 60a 29f., 62b 2f. *IT*: 52b 6-8, 54a 7, 54b 31-5, 55a 18, 55b 3ff., 14f.

most prominent in his analysis, means that we can assess with some confidence the relation between the Aristotelian theory of tragedy and the practice of the major fifth-century dramatists.[60]

---

[60] Söffing 193-260 surveys the surviving plays rather mechanically in the light of what he takes to be Ar.'s five cardinal principles; his analysis suffers, particularly as regards Euripides, from a neglect of the implications of *Poetics* 14. Bremer (1969) chs. IV-VI considers surviving tragedy in relation to *hamartia*.

II

Aristotle's Aesthetics 1:
Art and its Pleasure

There is evidence to be found in the *Poetics*, and it receives some confirmation from material elsewhere in the corpus, that Aristotle's thoughts on poetry were not formed in isolation from comparative reflections on other related activities, especially the visual arts, music and dancing – activities which it is now automatic for us to describe collectively as 'art'. For Aristotle the most significant common factor shared by these activites, and their products, was mimesis, and it is directly in connection with mimesis that we encounter in the *Poetics* and occasionally in other works general pronouncements covering both poetry and one or more of the arts indicated above. Such pronouncements were not without precedent, and it is possible in particular to discern some influence on Aristotle of the analogy between poetry and painting frequently drawn and exploited by Plato. But Aristotle's use of the comparison was not merely conventional, and its repeated occurrence in the *Poetics* associates it with such vital matters as artistic form and unity, the relation between action and character in the portrayal of human life, and the nature of the pleasure to be derived from works of mimesis. It is for this reason that in the present and the following two chapters I shall be concerned with the broader foundations of the Aristotelian theory of poetry: that is, with concepts and principles which are presented in the treatise as the essential framework of an understanding of poetry, but whose scope it is clear that the philosopher regarded as encompassing the other activities too which I have mentioned.

In exploring the extent and the stability of these foundations, one must at once confront the question of whether Aristotle can legitimately be said to have possessed a unitary concept of art corresponding even approximately to the now prevalent use of this term. This basic issue elicited very different responses from the two most important English works on the *Poetics* written around the turn of the nineteenth century. The title of Butcher's influential study, *Aristotle's Theory of Poetry and Fine Art*, in itself boldly declares its author's position on the matter. Butcher was in fact contributing to a tradition already well established in Germany of attempts to reveal the existence of systematic aesthetic ideas in Aristotle, comparable to, and aligned with, his metaphysical, political and ethical systems. Butcher believed, with some minor qualifications, that 'the cardinal points of Aristotle's aesthetic theory can be seized with some certainty', and much of his book rather ambitiously undertakes to give substance to the claim. Bywater, however, in the preface to his edition of the *Poetics*, countered such views with the statement that 'the very idea of a Theory of Art is modern, and ... our present use of this term 'Art' does not go further back than the age of Winckelmann and Goethe'. Bywater conceded that there are ideas in Aristotle's work 'which we should regard as coming under Aesthetics', but he objected to the aspiration to supply a systematic elaboration of them, when Aristotle himself had never done so.[1]

While I do not accept that Aristotle's thought in this area is as fully structured or as accessibly close to our own as Butcher in his more confident flights tended to suppose, neither can I altogether share Bywater's negative approach. Not only is it virtually impossible in practice to dispense with 'art' and related terminology in discussing the *Poetics* and certain aspects of Aristotle's philosophy, but it also, and more positively, seems to me feasible and worthwhile to give to this term a faithfully Aristotelian significance which makes clear both where it coincided with, and where it diverged from, modern views of art. It will be the first task of this chapter to show that while Aristotle had a comprehensive concept (now lost) of *technê*, for which both 'craft' and 'art' in its older sense are rough but imperfect translations, he was also capable of demarcating within this larger notion a restricted group of activities for which the normal modern use of 'art' is the only simple equivalent, though 'mimetic art(s)' is perhaps a preferable description. In the later part of the

---

[1] See Butcher viii (though cf. 113f. for reservations) and Bywater vii. For judicious criticism of Bywater see H. Lloyd-Jones, *Blood for the Ghosts* (London 1982) 18 (where the quotation shows that Bywater to some extent confused conceptualisation with terminology: on this point cf. R. Wollheim, *Art and its Objects* 2nd edn. (Cambridge 1980) 103f.). Perhaps the most ambitious attempt to find an aesthetic system in Ar. is that of Teichmüller vol. 2; for a sketch of other nineteenth-century works see Svoboda 5-9, whose own book provides flat paraphrase of some of the relevant material.

chapter I shall go on to argue that it is also possible to identify an important Aristotelian theory of the pleasure properly entailed in the experience of these mimetic arts, but especially in poetry. I must emphasise at the outset that by referring to this and to other Aristotelian ideas as 'aesthetic' I do not mean to assume or appeal to any independent philosophy of art – least of all, any *aestheticist* philosophy. Except where otherwise indicated, 'aesthetic' is employed in a plain, unprejudicial sense, referring either to the properties or to the experience of those activities and works which Aristotle believed to be connected by the element of mimesis, and which most post-Enlightenment thinking takes, in its use of the term 'art', to be unified by expression or some other factor.[2] It must also be noted that since the first part of this chapter deals with the lineaments of the Aristotelian view of mimetic art, mimesis as such receives some attention here, but it is also reserved for the fuller treatment which it merits later in the book.

To elucidate Aristotle's conception of mimetic art, we must start with its foundation in the wider notion of *technê*. *Technê* had earlier become the standard Greek word both for a practical skill and for the systematic knowledge or experience which underlies it. The resulting range of application is extensive, covering at one end of the spectrum the activity of a carpenter, builder, smith, sculptor or similar manual craftsman, and at the other, at least from the fifth century onwards, the ability and practices of rhetoricians and sophists. It is therefore translatable in different contexts as 'craft', 'skill', 'technique', 'method', or 'art', and I mentioned in the introductory chapter the use of the term to denote a formal treatise or manual containing the exposition of the principles of an art. In the light of these linguistic facts, it is not surprising that in the classical period the word could be applied to the poet's ability, particularly if we take into account the close alignment between the range of meaning of *technê* and the usage of the term for productive activity, *poiêsis*, which had come to be employed specifically for poetry (p. 56 below). If *technê* and *poiêsis* had originally been restricted to skills directed to material results, they had at any rate developed so as to become capable of designating a much larger sphere of activity, and also so as to denote a

[2] On 'aesthetic' cf. also n. 27 below and p. 229 with n. 37. I limit the term in this way for the sake of historical, not philosophical, clarity: for a possible distinction between 'aesthetic' and 'artistic' see D. Best, *Philosophy* 57 (1982) 357-72 (revised as ch. 11 in his *Feeling and Reason in the Arts* (London 1985)).

characteristic type of disposition or procedure, or even a *theoretical* framework for procedure, as much as a particular kind of artefact. *Technê* implied method and consistency of practice; it represented a vital part of the ground of man's practical and inventive intelligence, as opposed to the forces of nature (including any uncontrollable elements in man's own nature). Hence the arguments which arose (so prominently in Plato) over whether certain activities could correctly be included in this category. Where poetry was concerned, *technê* could be set up, by Plato at least, as the antithesis of inspiration; but that is to anticipate a further issue which will receive consideration in my next chapter.

Aristotle accepts unequivocally that poetry, painting, sculpture, music and dancing are all forms of *technê*.[3] But the mere fact that the term can be readily translated as 'art' – a fact which depends historically on the persistence in English, as a secondary sense, of the original meaning of this word as derived from *ars*, the Latin equivalent of *technê* – evidently does not yield an Aristotelian concept of art in the desiderated sense, since *technê* as 'art' embraces a much larger range of activity than the mimetic arts alone. The contrast between the broad category of *technê* and the significance possessed by the standard modern use of 'art' is striking, and one element in this contrast is the fact that the distinction between art and craft which has come to seem essential to some modern aestheticians, and to be a common if not a universal assumption in general attitudes to art, had no existence for Aristotle.[4] The 'family resemblance' between the whole gamut of methodical skills and activities encompassed by *technê* was not weakened by the specific affinities which might be discerned between particular sets of *technai*. If mimesis is more in evidence, and more problematic, in the *Poetics* than *technê*, that is because the latter is actually more fundamental but also more easily assumed without explanation or explicit

---

[3] For *technê* in the *Poetics* see Kassel 75, *Index Graecus*. It is used of music and dance at 47a 21-8, and of the visual arts at 47a 20, as at *PA* 640a 32, 645a 12, *EN* 1141a 9-12, 1175a 24, *Pol.* 1281b 12-15. Outside Ar. *technê* is used of poetry especially by Aristophanes (see ch. I n.16); Plato sometimes but not always denies *technê* to poetry: see Appendix 2 under 47a 20f. For the visual arts compare e.g. Emped. fr. 23.2, Plato *Gorg.* 450c 9f., *Diss.Log.* 3.10, 17, and see A. Burford, *Craftsmen in Greek and Roman Society* (London 1972) 198-217.

[4] See e.g. Collingwood 15-41 (developing a Crocean aesthetic), whose statement of the concept of *technê* (esp. 18f.) is, however, not always reliable: for necessary reservations on this and other points see S. H. Rosen, *Phronesis* 4 (1959) 135-48. On *technê* in general cf. Pollitt 32-7.

definition. It is therefore all the more important for the modern reader of the treatise to be sure about what presuppositions are carried by Aristotle's adherence to the belief that poetry and the other mimetic arts mentioned were *technai*.

In the case of the visual arts, with their necessary component of material craftsmanship, it hardly needs to be stressed that Aristotle's acceptance of the concept of *technê* was in conformity with widely held attitudes. But for the musico-poetic arts too (whose *performing* practitioners – actors and instrumentalists – are not in question here, though they too had their *technai*: *Rhet.* 1404a 23f.) the connection, at least on the superficial level, is sufficiently clear: the notion (though not the name) of poetic *technê* was at least as old as Homeric epic, it was reflected in the later adaptation of the language of 'making' (*poiêsis*) to poetry, and it was reinforced by the strongly genre-based conventions of Greek poetry, in which the poet's task was often defined partly in terms of the requirements of a social, religious or other context. Aristotle's attunement to such attitudes was, moreover, implicitly close to that strand of sophistic thinking which had asserted the cultural importance of verbal skills, *technai*, particularly rhetoric. The whole ethos of the *Poetics* is to some degree a reflection of the sophistic development of the formalised theory and exposition of linguistic skills. And if, as I suggested in the last chapter, the *Poetics* is not a teaching manual as such, it at any rate presupposes the possibility of poetic teaching grounded in the principles and procedures of the *technê*: according to Aristotle, metaphor is the *only* thing in poetry which one cannot learn from someone else (59a 6f.).

To understand what the status of poetry as a *technê* entailed for Aristotle, however, it is necessary to go beyond popular Greek ideas or the sophistic importance of formal teaching of verbal skills. For Aristotle elaborated the concept of *technê* at a deeper level within his own philosophical thinking, and it is here that we must look for the assumptions which underlie his treatment of individual arts. In the *Ethics technê* is defined as 'a productive capacity involving true reasoning' (1140a 8-10, 20f.). This may not seem to carry us far beyond what has already been said about the scope of the term in ordinary Greek, but it does laconically indicate how *technê* fits into a fundamental Aristotelian mould of thought. *Technê* involves a true alignment of the axis of potential/realisation in human productive activity: it is concerned with bringing into being, by intelligible and knowledgeable means, objects whose existence depends on their maker (1140a 10-14). An immediate point to notice – it will recur – is the necessary entailment of objective, rational standards in all *technê*. A further implication of the definition is that Aristotle, more markedly than in general Greek usage, shifts the emphasis of the concept from activity as such to the potential or ability for a certain sort of activity. *Technê* is a capacity to act in accordance with reasoned procedures so as to produce designed results: the reasoned regularity and stability of the activity means that it is possible to abstract the theory of the practice from it, and it is in this theory, which constitutes a form of knowledge, that a primary locus of the *technê* can be situated: the philosopher is, indeed, sometimes prepared to treat *technê* and knowledge as virtually synonymous.[5]

One reason for attending carefully to Aristotle's refinement of this notion is to dispel any suspicion that the idea of a poetic or other mimetic *technê* necessarily brings with it crude associations of physical craft. It is essential to observe that this is not so for Aristotle, and had probably not been so for some time before him. But there are further, and more positive, aspects to Aristotle's understanding of *technê*. Although in Book 6 of the *Ethics* from which the earlier definition was taken *technê* is distinguished from nature ('art' cannot produce those things which come into being naturally, 1140a 14f.), Aristotle is often at pains to assimilate them. In several works we find him stating the principle that *technê* stands in a relation of mimesis to nature, a principle which is usually but perhaps misleadingly rendered as 'art imitates nature'. What the phrase affirms is that art follows procedures analogous to nature's, and that similar patterns and relations can be discerned in the workings of each; but it is vital to insist on the proviso that the claim does not apply exclusively to the mimetic arts themselves (whose own mimetic character is a separate matter) but to the sphere of *technê* as a whole. Aristotle's position is clarified by his observation that *technê* may sometimes complete the work of nature, or supply its deficiencies, and by a number of other

---

[5] *Technê* and knowledge (*epistêmê*) are carefully distinguished in *EN* 6.3-4, 1139b 14ff., but elsewhere they are often assimilated: e.g. *An.Pr.* 46a 22, *Met.* 981a1-b9, *EN* 1097a 4-8, *Rhet.* 1355b 32, 1362b 26, 1392a 25f. For the use of the two terms cf. Bonitz 759, s.v. *technê*. On the relation of the *Poetics* to Ar.'s wider concept of *technê* see Olson (1965) 175-86, and on the latter alone cf. K. Bartels, 'Der Begriff Techne bei Aristoteles', in *Synusia: Festgabe für Wolfgang Schadewaldt*, edd. H. Flashar and K. Gaiser (Pfullingen 1965) 275-86. For Ar.'s abstraction of theoretical *technê* from practice note esp. *Met.* 981a 30-b 6.

connections and comparisons made between the two forces.[6] From all the material bearing on this point it emerges that what *technê* and nature have in common is *teleology*: both, as Aristotle would say, control processes for bringing things into being, and both are guided, and in one sense determined, by the ends or purposes towards whose fulfilment they move.[7] It is presupposed in this theory that *technê* and nature both have a similar tendency to aim at the best, to effect the finest or most successful organisation of their material.

The most problematic feature of this philosophical thesis might well be thought to be what it predicates of nature, not its treatment of human *technê*, since the purposive procedures of the latter make at least a limited teleological definition of them readily intelligible. But even if we put on one side, as we here must, the general difficulties raised by Aristotle's natural teleology, the two spheres cannot be entirely disengaged, and there remains more to be said about the relation between nature and human productive activity. To the analogy posited between the two types of process as teleological, we need to add the conviction that, from one point of view at least, *technê* is itself a part of nature, and its ends are to be regarded as naturally given or determined. Because man is part of nature, and all *technê* involves his rational productive capacities, the teleology of 'art' is in some degree subordinate to and dependent on that of nature as a whole. The operation of this premise can be confirmed and exemplified specifically for poetry from the *Poetics* itself, and while I shall attempt a separate analysis of its implications for Aristotle's attitude to cultural tradition in my next chapter, it is apposite here to locate it in its broader context.

For my present purpose I emphasise only one passage, though there are others which are germane. In *Poetics* 4 Aristotle provides a brief account of the 'natural' causes of poetry, and in so doing advances a compound explanation of the reasons both for the production of poetry and for the pleasure taken in it. A preliminary point to be made

---

[6] 'Art imitates nature': *Phys.* 194a 21f., 199a 16f., *Meteor.* 381b 6; cf. *Protr.* B13, 14, 23 Düring (1961) (with his comments on p. 187), and ps.-Ar. *Mund.* 396b 12. Other analogies: *Phys.* 194a 21ff., 199a 8-20, b 1-4, 26-32, *PA* 639b 16ff., 640a 26ff., 645a 8, *GA* 730b 7, 743a 26, *Met.* 1032a 12ff., 1034a 33ff., *EN* 1099b 21-3, 1175a 23f., *Pol.* 1333a 22-4, 1337a 1-3, *Protr.*B47 Düring (1961). For the essentially shared teleology of mind and nature see *De An.* 415b 16f. On both Ar. and others see A. J. Close, 'Philosophical Theories of Art & Nature in Classical Antiquity', *JHI* 32 (1971) 163-84.

[7] See esp. *Phys.* 194a 27ff., *GA* 762a 16f., 767a 17, 775a 20-22, *Met.* 1032a 12-14, 1070a 6-8, *EN* 1140a 10-16, *Protr.* B11-15 Düring (1961).

about this passage is that, while it begins by reference to poetry, its perspective opens out, as sometimes happens elsewhere in the treatise, to include other mimetic arts, and we can therefore legitimately take Aristotle's arguments here to have a wider applicability to most forms of mimesis. The argument is, in fact, despite its characteristically plain and condensed presentation, an ambitious one, and it is crucial to the interpretation of more than one issue in Aristotle's aesthetic philosophy. Its significance for the present question lies not in the positing of natural human instincts for mimesis, but in the way in which Aristotle proceeds from this premise to sketch a theoretical view of the natural development or evolution of the major Greek literary genres. Nature enters into the sequence of thought at three stages, supplying a progressive series of reference-points: first (48b 5ff.) as the general provision of a human instinct and capacity for mimetic activity, encompassing musical and rhythmic instincts which are themselves mimetically charged (cf. n. 29 below); secondly (48b 22ff.) as the source of particular inclinations and talents shown by early poets, and hence as the motive force behind the first period of generic evolution (marked by the basic distinction between serious and base subjects); finally (49a 2-15), and most importantly, as the true process contained in the direction of cultural development, a process embodied in the gradual unfolding of the natural potential of specific poetic forms. On this last point Aristotle is most explicit in the case of tragedy (though we can fairly extrapolate for other genres), of which he says that 'it ceased to change, once it had acquired its own nature' (49a 15) – that is, its mature perfection, the fulfilment of its potential.

It is clearly implied in this last remark that the history of tragedy has to be comprehended ultimately in terms not of contingent human choices and tradition, but of natural teleology mediated through, or channelled into, acts of human discovery of what was there to be found. Aristotle's point need not be strictly deterministic, since he does not appear to believe that tragedy was bound to be invented and developed; but he does clearly affirm that once its development became a cultural possibility (once it had 'appeared' or 'been glimpsed', 49a 2) the end result was a naturally fixed goal. To return to the implications of this example for *technê* in general, we can now see that not only do human productive activities form an analogue to the generative and purposive patterns of nature, but their individual histories evolve in accordance with intrinsic seeds of natural potential. Although Aristotle seems nowhere to work the point out fully, it is corroborated by his belief that all *technai* have been repeatedly discovered and developed (and then lost) in the history of the world: this is because they are rooted in man's inescapable relation to nature.[8] Aristotle's concept of *technê*, it transpires, is a highly charged philosophical doctrine, and must therefore be differentiated both from ordinary non-philosophical Greek notions of skill, method and practical intelligence, and also from the standard modern understanding of craft. While the Aristotelian concept shares with these applicability to a wide range of activities in which rational, controlled procedures represent a structured relationship between means and ends, purposes and products, it goes beyond them in its theoretical entailments concerning the natural foundations of these activities.

Technê represents the first layer or level in Aristotle's concept of the mimetic arts; these arts count as arts, in the first place, precisely by virtue of belonging to the category of rational, productive procedures. It is important, however, to avoid the common distortion involved in reducing this doctrine to the belief that 'all arts are crafts', since the refined notion of *technê* includes, but is not simply equivalent to, craft. Nonetheless, we must not attempt to minimise the radical discrepancy between this aspect of Aristotle's thinking and the dominant modern view of art. It would be similarly wrong to try to reduce the discrepancy by placing weight on the passage in the *Metaphysics* where Aristotle distinguishes between arts of utilitarian value and those designed to give pleasure.[9] The distinction is, for one thing, broad, and not intended (in the case of the non-utilitarian, at any rate) to offer a careful delimitation of a particular set of activities; there is no reason to suppose that the arts of pleasure would be identical with, though they would evidently include, the mimetic arts. Nor is this passage of the *Metaphysics* designed to give a proper account of the types of pleasure derivable from *technê*, for this will reflect the nature of individual activities, and we shall see later in this chapter that the theory of aesthetic pleasure sketched in the *Poetics* cannot be understood simply as the antithesis of practical

---

[8] *Met.* 1074b 10-12, *Pol.* 1329b 25ff. It is clear in both these passages that the doctrine does not apply only to arts which cater for necessities.

[9] *Met.* 981b 17ff.; for the dichotomy cf. e.g. *Pol.* 1329b 27-9 and Isoc. 4.14. We must take account of the fact that non-utilitarian pleasures can be encompassed by Ar.'s concept of *diagôgê* – cultured leisure related to happiness: *Pol.* 1338a 1-34.

usefulness. Pleasure alone, therefore, will not make Aristotle's view of the mimetic *technai* conformable to modern attitudes. The primary reason for the remaining conceptual distance between the two is that Aristotle's acceptance of the framework of *technê* for the interpretation of poetry and related practices imports an inescapably objectivist element, as well as a naturalistic teleology, which is alien to the belief in creative imagination that has grown in strength since the Renaissance, and that has dominated Romantic and later aesthetic thinking. In Aristotle's system, the mimetic artist is devoted to the realisation of aims which are determined independently of him by the natural development of his art, and by the objective principles which emerge from this development.

I shall return to this contrast at the end of this section, but it is now necessary to move on to the second and the distinctive criterion of the mimetic arts, mimesis itself. Mimesis alone, it must be stressed, is insufficient to yield a definition of the mimetic arts, since there are mimetic activities (mundane forms of imitation) which are not *technai*. The combination of both *technê* and mimesis is therefore required to give us the core of Aristotle's concept of poetry, painting, music and the rest – the concept of *art*, in other words, in the fuller sense. For without prejudicing the question of where and how this concept is consonant with, or divergent from, later ones, there need be no serious doubt that the substantial coincidence between the activities counted as mimetic *technai* by Aristotle and those usually counted as art in modern European culture (the *Beaux Arts* of the Enlightenment) provides adequate justification for referring in this way to an Aristotelian concept of art or mimetic art. The centrality of mimesis to this concept calls for the extensive treatment which I give to it in ch. IV, where many details in the interpretation of the *Poetics'* understanding of mimesis are examined. Here a more synoptic view of the subject must be offered.

If *technê* is a definition or theory of the relation between the productive artist and his product, mimesis stands for, and purports to characterise, the axis between the product and reality. That mimesis can be written as an ordinary English noun (as it has been since at least the seventeenth century) is a testimony to the persistence of mimeticist thinking and terminology in the European tradition; and the fact that the language of mimesis and *imitatio* was for so long indispensable to neo-classicism (and that it still lurks, thinly disguised, around much that is said and thought about art) may suggest that its potential belies some of the more severe rejections which it has met with in recent times. But it need hardly be said that the influence of neo-classicism has also created a specious familiarity which is an obstacle in the way of attempts to recover the original Greek context and development of the idea. Indeed, the very familiarity of the whole question and problem of the relation between art and the world makes it difficult to realise the good reasons for the faltering movement of Greek thought towards a philosophical formulation of the issues involved, or towards a concept of the shared or analogous features of poetry, the visual arts and music (to go no further). As with *techné*, so with mimesis, it is important to appreciate the basis of Aristotle's thinking on the matter in already existing attitudes and assumptions, as well as the ways in which he builds on and reshapes this basis. In the case of mimesis Aristotle worked against the background both of Plato's persistent approaches to the idea, and also of the more widely held mimeticist views which Plato himself attests.[10] The notion of mimesis as a common or defining characteristic of a variety of cultural activities and products was not the discovery of a single thinker or period. It emerged untidily from a long development in the meaning and application of mimesis language, and may not have been wholly consciously articulated before Plato. But in the act of shaping a theory or doctrine of mimesis, Plato at the same time placed a considerable philosophical and often polemical burden on the concept, and as a result he did not pass on to Aristotle a freshly honed idea, but a whole set of suggestions, issues and challenges which were superimposed on the intricacies of existing non-philosophical uses of the word. Moreover, as I shall later show, Plato's own interests in mimesis were not as cut-and-dried, nor as entirely negative, as is often believed, and he demonstrated that the idea might have a contribution to make to a large area of philosophical enquiry.

Aristotle's pronouncements on mimesis, taken collectively, reflect the scope for uncertainty and instability produced by the earlier history of the word's applications. It is possible here to give some idea of the complexity of the problems raised by his view of mimesis, but also to bring some order into the relevant material, by trying to

[10] Esp. *Laws* 668b 9ff., where the speakers agree that everyone would accept that all products of *mousikē* (which here includes poetry, music and visual art) are 'mimesis and image-making'. Ar.'s acceptance of mimesis as a general view of art is seen most obviously at *Poet.* 47a 13-22 and *Rhet.* 1371b 4-8.

separate two salient dimensions of mimesis and two types of theoretical question associated with them. Starting from the minimal proposition that all Greek notions of mimetic art entail a necessary subject-object distinction, and that this must in some way structure a relationship between a mimetic art or work (in whatever medium) and an aspect or level of reality, it becomes possible to identify two main ways in which such a proposition might be elaborated. The first is to define what might be called a *formal* relationship between work and object, that is a relationship between the medium or mode of the mimetic representation and the relevant features of the represented object. Such a definition requires exemplification by particular arts, though the formal relationship established for one art may be, and often was, used as a model for the understanding of another, or even of mimetic art in general. The question of formal mimetic relationships points especially towards the importance in Greek thinking of an analogy between poetry and painting, an analogy which appears in the early classical period and is central to the interpretation of both Plato's and Aristotle's treatments of mimesis.[11] The formal aspect of visual mimesis is amenable to a straightforward formulation (however *simpliste* it might seem to some): colours and forms, as both philosophers would put it, correspond to, and so represent, the colours and forms of visible reality (and perhaps of more besides). There is no doubt that this formulation made it easier for the idea of poetic mimesis, and of mimetic art in general, to become acceptable. Plato can be demonstrably convicted of exploiting the elision in thought involved in taking visual as the paradigm for poetic mimesis, when he sets out to degrade artistic activity to the level of a shallow reproduction of the surfaces of the material world.[12] Despite the lack of a precise connection between poetic and visual mimesis, the analogy between painting and poetry was one which Aristotle was not prepared to surrender: it appears in the opening chapter of the *Poetics*, and repeatedly in later passages. It should be added that the visual model of mimesis was paralleled by, and in some contexts (such as acting and dancing) found in conjunction with, dramatic or enactive

[11] For various comparisons between poetry and visual art see: Simonides *apud* Plutarch 346f, Ion of Chios fr. 8, *Diss.Log.* 3.10, Plato e.g. *Rep.* 377e, 596ff. (cf. Appendix 2 under 47a 18ff.), Isoc. 9.73-5, Ar. *Poet.* 47a 18-20, 48a 5f., 48b 9-19, 50a 26-9, 39ff., 54b 9-11, 60b 8f., 17ff., 31f., 61b 12f., *Rhet.* 1371b 6f.

[12] On this flaw (or polemical tendentiousness) in *Rep.* 10 see Annas's article, and cf. more generally Keuls 33-47.

mimesis of human behaviour. In both cases the nature of mimesis can be intimated by noticing that it aspires, or might be held to aspire, to the condition of being indistinguishable from the original.[13] It is unclear how the same could be said of any conception of poetic mimesis, even if Plato was polemically ready to suggest this.

Aristotle was, however, undoubtedly aware of the specific issue of the formal relation between mimetic art and its objects. This is apparent in the passage from Book 8 of the *Politics* (1340a 28ff.) where he distinguishes between the true mimesis of human character which he states to be possible in music, and the weaker relationship – 'symbolic', rather than properly mimetic, representation – to be found in the portrayal of character in visual media. It is regrettably common for this passage to be erroneously paraphrased as claiming that music is, *tout court*, the most mimetic of the arts, but we must correct this by observing that Aristotle refers only to the mimesis of character. Understanding of the point is obscured by our ignorance of Greek music, but it appears to be the case that what is involved is a putatively precise correspondence between the expressive movement of music and the 'kinetic' dimension of active human character.[14] If this remains an alien instance, the *Poetics* itself, with its tendency towards the idea of dramatic enactment (which is not to be confused with performance as such) as the essence of poetic mimesis, is more easily comprehensible. What underlies this thrust in Aristotle's thinking is the concern for as close a formal match as possible between poetry and its human subject matter, and this leads to the stress on enactive mimesis in which the direct speech of agents gets us as near as language can come to the nature of significant action itself. Such a degree of correspondence is, however, not consistently adhered to as a necessary criterion of mimesis, and it is perhaps possible to see why. The more that certain types of formal equivalence are pressed, the weaker becomes the unifying factor in all the mimetic activities mentioned in the first chapter of the *Poetics*. Although interested in refining the concept of mimesis analytically by his differential scheme of media, objects, and modes, outlined in

[13] For this idea see e.g. *Hom.Hymn Apollo* 163f., Plato *Rep.* 598c, *Soph.* 234b (but note *Crat.* 432b-c for a logical qualification), and the famous story about Zeuxis and Parrhasius at Pliny *NH* 35.65. Note also the idea of visual works like *living* things, *à la* Daedalus: Pind. *Ol.* 7.52, Eurip. fr. 372, Plato *Phdr.* 275d. On artistic 'deception' cf. ch. I n.20.

[14] See ch. IV p. 125 and n.29.

the first three chapters of the treatise, Aristotle had nonetheless inherited, particularly from Plato, a general and loose concept of mimesis, and the preservation of such a concept depended on a willingness to accept a fundamental element of mimetic correspondence which cut across the divisions between the arts, and so made intelligible, for example, the kinship between poetry and painting.

The second dimension of mimesis, which is in theory independent of the first but in practice not always kept apart from it, concerns the cognitive status and value of the mimetic work and its content. However the formal relation, as I have called it, is construed for particular types of mimetic art (as direct equivalence, as a kind of symbolism, or as some more complex kind of representation), the question still remains to be asked about the truth-value of mimetic works. The question's importance can be seen in the context of Plato's discussions of mimesis, since if his polemics against art are characterised by a refusal to separate the cognitive aspect of mimesis from the formal (so that the supposed limitation of the latter to literal copying condemns its products to the realm of the derivative and spurious), Plato elsewhere intriguingly gestures towards a notion of philosophical mimesis which would allow its powers of signification to rise above its formal limitations (see ch. IV). Aristotle may have been influenced by this latter fact towards the development of his own doctrine that artistic mimesis is capable of representing universals or general truths, and need not be tied to the reproduction of particulars. It is far from clear, however, that Aristotle sees this capacity as belonging intrinsically to mimesis, for he continues to acknowledge cases of the mimetic representation of particulars, as well, of course, as non-mimetic ways, above all philosophy itself, in which universals can be communicated.[15] Because of this doubt, it might be legitimate to conclude that the chief refinement in Aristotle's view of mimesis pertains to its formal aspect, that is to the analysis of the various types of correspondence to reality which can

[15] *Poet*. 48b 15-19 clearly cites a visual instance of the mimesis of particulars (though the *implications* are wider: see pp. 73ff.) and 51b 14f. refers to the equivalent in iambic poetry: 48b 33f. shows, I believe, that *pace* Janko e.g. 61 iambus probably does count as poetry for Ar., though certainly of an inferior and negligible kind. The remarks in *Poetics* 9 show the strongly normative thrust of Ar.'s theory (cf. pp. 38f.): he is here attempting to define the nature of the best poetry (an important part of any *technê*: *Pol.* 1288b 10-21) and generalises from this position without quite trying to deny (as 51b 14f. intimates) that *some* poetry may deal with particulars. On iambus cf. ch. IX n. 36.

be achieved in different artistic media (visual, linguistic, musical, etc.); and, as a corollary of this, to regard the claims made in *Poetics* 9 for the quasi-philosophical potential of poetry as expressing a principle of the use of mimesis, rather than its necessary attribute. But as the *Poetics* stands, such a conclusion would be tidier than is warranted by the evidence, which suggests a coalescence, as in Plato, between considerations of the formal and the cognitive issues raised by mimetic art.

This preliminary approach to Aristotle's concept of mimesis should demonstrate the difficulty of reaching a clear-cut interpretation of it; but two broad inferences, which will receive further substantiation in ch. IV, can be drawn from the preceding argument: first, that Aristotle unquestioningly accepts the existence of a distinctive group of mimetic arts, and that by so doing he commits himself to a compendious criterion of mimesis as a form of correspondence in which some aspect of reality is reconstituted in a medium as close as possible in equivalence to the object; secondly, that he is prepared to attribute to some mimetic works a cognitive significance which goes beyond particulars to the embodiment of universals. The relationship between this notion of mimesis and the underlying idea of *technê* which I earlier examined can now be clarified by a brief look at a further area of terminology – the *poiêsis* word-group – which denotes poetry itself (and perhaps some other mimetic arts too) but is also closely related to *technê* as a whole. The root meaning of the *poiêsis* word-group is 'making' or 'producing', and for Aristotle all *technê* involves *poiêsis* of some kind: the former is the rationalised, systematic capacity for the latter. But the specific application of these same terms, *poiêsis* and its cognates, to poetry was a linguistic development well established by Aristotle's time. Extracted from their philosophical context, the remarks of Diotima in Plato's *Symposium* furnish a reliable description of the phenomenon: 'You know,' she says to Socrates, 'that making (*poiêsis*) takes many forms. It is making which is responsible for any case in which something comes into being from non-being, so that the activities of all crafts and arts (*technai*) are types of *poiêsis*, and the craftsmen are all makers (*poiêtai*) ... Nevertheless ... some have different names, and a determinate part of the whole area of *poiêsis*, the part concerned with music and verse, is called by the name that belongs to the whole. For it is only this part that is called *poiêsis* (making/'poetry') and its practitioners *poiêtai* (makers/'poets')' (205b8-c9).

Since Aristotle himself used *poiêsis* terminology both for the definition of *technê* in general and to describe a particular type of mimetic *technê* (poetry), it is reasonable to suppose that the latter took some of its colouring from the former. In this respect we can both compare and contrast Aristotle's position with ordinary usage, since twice in the *Poetics* he adverts to the normal conception of the poet as a maker (*poiêtês*) of verses (47b 13-16, 51b 27-9). Against this Aristotle opposes his own conception of the poet as a maker of plot-structures (*muthoi*), that is unified mimetic representations of human action. An immediate point to note is that this new definition of poetic art clearly presupposes, similarly to the case of *technê* (p.47 above), that the language of *poiêsis* has lost any unnecessary material connotations: what the poet 'makes' or produces is not a tangible object, but a mimetic construct in language (and other media) to be apprehended by the mind. It is profitable to draw a further contrast here with the passage in Plato's *Phaedo* (61b) in which Socrates describes the content of poetic composition as *muthoi*, the term adapted to his theory by Aristotle: but what Socrates has in mind is setting Aesop's fables (*muthoi*) to verse, so that the making (*poiêsis*) which is the 'poetry' would precisely be the making of verses.[16] In ch.

---

[16] It is true that Socrates thinks of setting already existing fables as a *pis aller*, since he cannot invent his own. This still does not bridge the gap between Plato's and Ar.'s positions.

The original sense of *muthos* was anything said or told: an utterance, speech, story, report, etc. It later acquires the idea of something intrinsically false: a myth, fable, fiction, etc. Cf. LSJ s.v. II 1-4. References to *muthoi* in poetry before Plato (e.g. Hom. *Od.* 11.368, Pind. *Ol.* 1.29, *Nem.* 7.23) simply reflect the ordinary meanings of the term. Plato, exploiting the connotations of falsehood (as well as associations with idle tales and the like), treats *muthologia* (story-telling) as the essence of poetry: e.g. *Phaedo* 61b 4f., e2, 70b 6, *Rep.* 377d ff., 380c 2, 392d 2, 394b 9f., *Laws* 941b-c.

Outside the *Poetics*, Ar.'s use of *muthos* and cognates almost invariably carries implications of falsehood, though not always as disparagingly as at *Met.* 995a 4f., 'fictional (*muthôdê*) and childish'. He applies the words chiefly to: myth and legend (*Phys.* 218b 24, *Cael.* 284a 18ff., *HA* 580a 17, *MA* 699a 27ff., *Met.* 982b 18f., *EN* 1100a 8, *Pol.* 1257b 16, 1269b 28, 1284a 22, 1341b 3), poetic theology (*Met.* 1000a 18, 1074a 38ff., 1091b 9), fable (*Meteor.* 356b 11-17, *HA* 578b 25, 579b 4, 609b 10, 617a 5, *PA* 641a 21). Although there are some general references to poetic *muthologia* (e.g. *EE* 1230a 3), I cannot find the *Poetics'* special sense of *muthos* anywhere else in the corpus. What this means is that Ar. has taken a term with the senses of story-fable-legend-myth, and without erasing these altogether (they can be seen within the *Poetics* itself at 51b 24, 53a 18, 37, 53b 22) he has given the word a new critical edge and significance. We must observe in particular the subtle movement away from the associations of *traditional* myths: a poetic *muthos* need not be traditional (51b 23ff.), and it may even borrow from history (ibid. 30-2). But whatever the source of material, it must be made afresh – i.e. shaped into a coherent design – by the

9 of the *Poetics*, on the other hand, Aristotle argues that, whether or not the poet's raw material is pre-existent (traditional myths being an equivalent to Socrates' Aesopic fables), his task as a poet-maker (*poiêtês*) is still to design and organise his plot-structure in such a way as to give its content the universal intelligibility of which Aristotle believes poetry to be capable.

The elements of *poiêsis* in the Aristotelian concepts of *technê* and poetry are mutually reinforcing. In neither case does the maker necessarily produce a tangible artefact, though in some *technai* he will do so. But whatever his media, the maker aims, by the application of rational method, to bring something into being, and in the case of the mimetic arts this is, if successful, a unified construction which must be comprehended as embodying a representation of a possible reality.[17] Although the *Poetics* elaborates this doctrine in relation to poetry, there is no doubt that Aristotle presupposes a comparable attitude to arts such as music and painting. Thus we can be confident that he would have said that the painter, for example, is not a maker of shapes and colours: these are his media, but they are used to produce, to bring into being by rational art, an image of possible human reality, and an image capable of being understood, at its best, in universal rather than particular terms. Consideration of either the specific *poiêsis* of poetry or the generic *poiêsis* of all mimetic art therefore brings us back round to the question which was earlier raised about the cognitive value of mimesis in Aristotle's aesthetic thinking. The 'making' which is the procedure of the poet's or the painter's art is the imparting of design and order to his material, and this design will carry a mimetic correspondence to a conception of reality. But the Aristotelian emphasis on coherence and unity, as we find it applied to the concrete doctrine of poetic plot-structure, gives the poet a very different responsibility for his artistic product from the one assigned to him by Plato, in whose eyes the artist must be accountable for his raw material, not just for what he makes of it. Aristotelian *poiêsis* is a positive, potent force, whose implications of productive control and purpose should dispel any lingering

---

maker-poet, and the true *muthos* is the result, not the original material, of this act (esp. 51b 27-9). See also ch. I pp. 22f.

[17] Ar.'s underlying notion of *technê* puts the stress on the maker-product axis, but this should not be formulated as a focus on the art rather than its products, as it is by Else (1957) 6, 9, 12, 237, 279f. etc. To take just one detail, note how 'thought' (*dianoia*) is defined at 50b 4-12 as *both* a poetic capacity *and* a property of poems.

associations of the derivative or passive from the understanding of mimesis. *Poiêsis* and mimesis are tightly interwoven strands of the thinking which lies behind the *Poetics*; and if *poiêsis* cannot solve all the problems of mimesis for us, it does at any rate help to bond together the elements of *technê* and mimesis in the Aristotelian concept of mimetic art which it is my aim to delineate.

The argument up to this point has deliberately tolerated the linguistic intricacy and cumbersomeness which are entailed in any attempt to stay close to Aristotle's own language, and so to avoid superficial assimilation of his ideas to later views of art. There is also, however, the lesser danger that the peculiar features of Aristotle's thought will be allowed to exaggerate the alien ethos of his concept of mimetic art, and to impede recognition of the affinities it may have with later attitudes. It will consequently serve a purpose to draw some provisional conclusions about Aristotle's understanding of the mimetic *technai*, and to try to relate it to some of the more characteristic modern beliefs on the subject. The basis for such a comparison, as earlier indicated, is the fact that the range of activities circumscribed by mimetic *technê* agrees approximately with the standard modern categorisation of the arts. The historical link between the two lies in the transmission of ancient notions of mimesis and imitation to the Renaissance, and the elaboration of these notions in the period of neo-classicism into the foundation for a system of fine arts whose central principle was the 'imitation of nature'.[18] But we saw earlier (p. 47) that the origin of this principle in Aristotle is very far removed from its later use as an aesthetic slogan, since in contrast to the vagueness of the latter the Aristotelian formula stands for a philosophy of all rational productive activity, both mimetic and non-mimetic. If neo-classical imitation of nature is manipulable to various effects (including, for instance, a strong idealism) the original analogy between *technê* and nature not only has broader scope but commits its holder to a specific teleology of mimetic art.

This teleology differs less from the orthodox neo-classical aesthetic, however, than it does from the attitudes to art which have

[18] On the emergence of this system see Kristeller, but in pressing the lack of an ancient version of eighteenth-century aesthetics too hard (166-74) he gives an inadequate account of the place of mimesis in Ar.'s theory (171f., with some *naïveté* regarding Plato too). The general comparison of ancient and modern views of art by W. Tatarkiewicz, *JHI* 24 (1963) 231-40, is also marred by a neglect of mimesis and a misunderstanding of Ar.'s concept of it (233).

grown up since the eighteenth century and to some extent in reaction against neo-classicism. Typical theorists of the sixteenth and seventeenth centuries might have understood Aristotle's insistence on an objective concept of art, structured by the rational relation between the artist and his work, much better than could the Romantic or his modern epigone. The shift represented by the rise of Romanticism can be located, for present purposes, in the new aesthetic centrality of the idea of creative imagination, an idea for which the eighteenth century discovered that Longinus was a much more sympathetic classical source than Aristotle or Horace. The contrast with Aristotle can be illuminated by observing that the origins of this concept of imagination are to be traced in the ascription to the artist of free, creative powers analogous to those of a God who can bring a world into being *ex nihilo*.[19] For Aristotle, on the other hand, the model for *technê*, which embraces all mimetic art, is a nature whose generative workings are regulated by the teleological realisation of form in matter. Creative imagination is inimical to tradition and sees the spring of art within the exceptional capacities of special individuals. Hence the importance in modern aesthetic attitudes of various notions of *expression*, usually centring around the idea of that which is brought forth from the mind of the artist and given new or unique form. While Aristotle can of course acknowledge the unusual abilities of certain individuals, above all Homer, and the importance of their contribution to the development of an art, this development itself is not only the essential framework within which particular achievements must be placed, but the unfolding of a *natural* potential: it constitutes a large-scale dimension of teleology to arch over the small-scale teleology of individual mimetic works. Aristotle's artist may be gifted, but his gifts are not unique or *sui generis*; they are at the objective service of his art, to be harnessed to the realisation of aims which have a potential existence that is independent of the individual (and which, as we saw, have been realised before and will be realised again). And if mimetic art can be said at all, in Aristotle's scheme of things, to be expressive, it is certainly not expressive of the artist himself. For not only is Aristotle's concept of art objectivist, but its accent falls on the universal significance to which mimesis can attain: mimesis makes art outward-facing, and locates its subject in general human reality,

[19] See ch. III n.1.

not in the privileged inner experiences of the artist.

A caution must be entered here. My characterisation of one of the dominant strands in modern attitudes to art is not meant to imply that free, creative imagination is a universally accepted principle, or that aesthetic objectivism has altogether disappeared. The contrast I have drawn is a deliberately schematic one, designed to put Aristotle's views in perspective. The danger of simplification, both of Aristotle's and of later positions, becomes acute when we reach the question of the purpose or function of art. Without raising this question, and seeking an answer to it in the *Poetics* and in Aristotle's other references to mimetic art, it is difficult to feel that the concept I have so far analysed is a fully rounded one. But we here encounter a striking paradox which may serve as an appropriate introduction to the next stage of my argument. In the two broadest phases which can be demarcated in European theory and criticism of art since the Renaissance, those of neo-classicism and the Romantic reaction (with all its modern off-shoots) against neo-classicism, it is remarkable that Aristotle has been enlisted within both as a supporter of the prevailing view of the function of art. Under neo-classicism, the *Poetics* was used as a pillar of the dominant moralism, according to which art could be justified in terms of its capacity to be ethically edifying and improving. In the reaction against such views, the last two centuries have seen a growing, though hardly uniform, adherence to the belief that art's ultimate legitimation lies in some sort of self-sufficient pleasure or gratification. Such a belief does not require Aristotelian sanction, but it is nonetheless discernible that it has influenced the common reading of the *Poetics* and has led to an orthodoxy in which Aristotle's view of art is held to be essentially formalist and aestheticist: that is, one which attributes an autotelic status to poetry and the other arts, which grounds the experience of them in pleasure, which identifies the properties of works of art as purely internal attributes of form, and which entails a strong divorce between art, on the one hand, and morality, religion and politics, on the other. Thus the *Poetics*, despite the major differences from modern views of art which I have tried to locate in it, is brought into line with the aesthetic consensus which has evolved since the Enlightenment, and in which art has been freed from what is often considered to be the taint of a direct concern with, or effect on, the ideas and values belonging to the realms indicated above.

Alert to the possibility that it may be wrong to hope to adjudicate between these two antithetical views of the *Poetics*, the didactic and the formalist, in the terms in which their proponents themselves formulate the dichotomy, I want now to undertake a scrutiny of Aristotle's references to the pleasure or pleasures of mimetic art, in the expectation that it will bring to light a vital area of the treatise's philosophical foundations.

*

That art is pleasurable, and in its own peculiar ways, is a datum of experience which the Greeks did not need to wait for theorists or philosophers to call to their attention. The seductive pleasures even of works of art which portray exceptional suffering are attested from the beginnings of Greek poetry, and not only attested but illuminated in a number of Homeric scenes with a dramatic insight which is irreducible to prosaic paraphrase.[20] But from the philosophical point of view, there remained much scope, and much need, for the investigation of the subject. Aristotle had more than one good reason to be interested in discriminating between the types of pleasure which might enter into the experience of poetry and the other arts, not least because the need to take pleasure in the right things was a pervasive principle of his educational and ethical thought. Aristotle's own philosophical psychology posited a rich and complex range of pleasures, related to particular types of activity and the human faculties employed in them. He conceives of pleasure primarily as a level or aspect of experience which supervenes on and completes (like the 'bloom' of those in their physical prime) any activity in which man's abilities are put successfully to their natural use. Pleasure marks the fulfilment of a natural potential, and to understand how and why pleasure arises in individual cases, we must comprehend the special character of the given activities.[21] In view of the cohesiveness which we have seen his attitude to the mimetic *technai* to possess, we

[20] In particular *Il*. 3.125ff. (Helen's embroidery), 9.186ff. (Achilles' song), *Od.* 1.325ff. and 8.499ff. (Phemius' and Demodocus' songs of the Trojan War). For sensitive comment on such material see Macleod 6-12.

[21] Ar.'s most extensive discussions of pleasure are in *EN* Book 7, chs. 11-14, 1152b 1ff., Book 10, chs. 1-5, 1172a 16ff., and (less subtly) *Rhet*. Book 1, ch. 11, 1369b 33ff. For a recent and full discussion see J.C.B. Gosling & C.C.W. Taylor, *The Greeks on Pleasure* (Oxford 1982) chs. 11, 14-15. On the relation of pleasure to virtue cf. ch. VI n. 39.

would reasonably expect a conception of aesthetic pleasure to be an integral element of Aristotle's thinking about mimesis.

A further factor to prompt reflection on the subject was the variety of references to pleasure in Plato's discussions of art. In the *Laws* and elsewhere Plato claimed that the ordinary man's expectation of art was that it should provide pleasure, and he alleged contemptuously that pleasure was the sole popular standard of artistic merit.[22] The Athenian at first rejects such a mentality as 'blasphemous', and later observes that the decadence of recent Greek poetry has followed from an indiscriminate belief in the audience's pleasure as the aim of art and the criterion of success. Yet Plato's spokesman himself comes round to arguing that a certain, very different kind of pleasure *is* to be desired in art: the pleasure of the educated and morally upright man. This correct and laudable species of pleasure will be the result simply of the artistic presentation of moral truth – the dramatic portrayal, for example, of virtuous men. Elsewhere, in the difficult *Philebus* (51), Plato argues that the apparent pleasures of art are actually false and synthetic, and he contrasts with the specious pleasure taken in an artistic form the true pleasure which may be derived from contemplation of intrinsically, that is geometrically, beautiful shapes, and perfect pure colours. Without venturing any further, then, into the shifting significances of Plato's treatments of this subject, we already have glimpses in these two passages alone of four different kinds of pleasure arguably relevant to art: the ordinary man's uncultured pleasure, which will involve the gratification of the lower part of the soul; the good man's moral pleasure in the celebration of virtue; pleasure from the sensual forms used in mimetic works; and the pleasure of contemplating pure shapes, colours and musical tones.

In the *Poetics* too we encounter a wide range of references to pleasure. Before attempting to provide a synthesising interpretation of these, it will be as well to offer a preliminary tabulation of the types or occasions of pleasure mentioned in the treatise, roughly in the order in which they occur.

(a) Ch. 4, 48b 8ff.: *natural* pleasure taken in mimetic works (*mimêmata*), even when these represent objects, such as corpses, which

---

[22] See the whole of *Laws* 655c-660e, and later 667b ff., 700e, 802c-d; cf. *Hipp.Maj.* 297e-8a, *Gorg.* 501d-2d, *Rep.* 607a.

are inherently unpleasant.[23] The cause of this pleasure is that the experience entails a process of understanding and learning. I shall contend below that we have also to put in this category the pleasure which, according to ch. 24, 60a 17, derives from 'the wonderful', which is itself closely related, as ch. 9, 52a 1-11 indicates, to the arousal of pity and fear by tragic poetry.

(b) Ch. 4, 48b 17-19: pleasure due to the execution, surface or some other such aspect of a work of mimetic art; this pleasure is *independent* of the work's mimetic status.

(c) Ch. 6, 49b 25-31: 'pleasurably garnished' language is given in the definition of tragedy, and then explained as 'language with rhythm and melody' – that is, the sensual elaborations (both verbal and musical) of the lyric sections of tragic drama (called 'the greatest of the garnishings' or embellishments at 50b 16), and probably also the rhythmical dimension of the ordinary spoken parts of a play. Similarly, in ch. 26, 62a 16f., *mousikê*, which here means something close though not identical to the 'pleasurably garnished' language of ch. 6, is cited as a source of vivid pleasures which give tragedy an advantage over epic. This is evidently not meant to deny pleasurable embellishments altogether to the epic poet's art: the pleasure of epic style may be at least part of what is meant in the reference to Homer at 60b 2.

(d) Ch. 6, 50b 16f.: although denying that theatrical spectacle is strictly part of the dramatist's art, Aristotle does describe it as 'stirring' or 'seductive'. The word he uses is *psuchagôgikon*,[24] and its cognate verb is found earlier in ch. 6, 50a 33, applied to the effect of tragic reversal and recognition. This helps to establish that Aristotle is prepared to attribute a strong emotive potential to spectacle, though it is less well defined, and obviously much less valuable for him, than

---

[23] Note the implicit relevance of this example to tragedy and the paradox of tragic pleasure; similarly in the parallel passage at *Rhet.* 1371b 4-10, and compare the pleasurable memory of things not pleasant at the time, *Rhet.* 1370b 1-7.

[24] *Psuchagôgein* (and cognates), originally meaning 'to conjure souls', became used in various ways of the captivating power of language, particularly poetry and rhetoric, and also of the visual arts (*contra* Pollitt 101 n.34): see esp. Aristoph. *Birds* 1555 (a pun?), Xen. *Mem.* 3.10.6, Plato *Phdr.* 261a, 271c, Isoc. 2.49, 9.10, Timocles fr. 6.6 (echoing Ar. himself? cf. Appendix 5 §2), and LSJ with Suppl. s.v. for later passages (to which add Marc.Aur. *Med.* 3.2 and 11.6). This metaphorical development was probably influenced by Gorgias's theory of the magical and bewitching powers of language, *Helen* (fr. 11) 10-14, which itself is a development of the archetypal Homeric idea of poetry as enchantment: on this and related points see ch. VI pp. 188ff. and nn. 26-8.

the potential of the complex plot-structure. Such emotional effects carry implicit pleasure with them. The point is confirmed in ch. 14, 53b 8-11, where the use of spectacle to produce the specious effect of 'the portentous' is frowned on as supplying a pleasure alien to the true tragic experience of pity and fear, for which see (g) below.

(e) Ch. 6, 50a 39- 50b 3: reference is here made to the contrasting types of pleasure afforded by the (hypothetical) painting which consists of random patches of colour, and the colourless outline sketch or drawing. The latter is said to be analogous to the plot-structure of tragedy.

(f) Ch. 9, 51b 23, 26: Aristotle here touches in passing on the pleasure of tragedy, in making the point that it is unaffected by whether the material of a play is conventional or invented. For another general reference to pleasure see 62b 1, in connection with the superiority of tragic concentration over epic diffuseness.

(g) Finally, there are four important references in the *Poetics* to the particular pleasure of tragedy (to which there are corresponding comic (53a 36) and epic (59a 21, 62b 13f.) pleasures): ch. 6, 50a 33-5; ch. 13, 53a 35f.; ch. 14, 53b 10-14; ch. 26, 62b 13f. The third of these passages, which stipulates 'the pleasure arising from pity and fear through mimesis', is the fullest, and indicates that the proper pleasure of tragedy is linked directly with the experience of its distinctive emotions, pity and fear (hence the justification for the inclusion of the first passage in the list), while resting on the basis of the generic pleasure of poetic mimesis ((a) above). The notion of pleasures proper or peculiar to individual activities appears prominently in Aristotle's mature views on the subject in *EN* Book 10.[25]

I think it is possible to advance beyond this preliminary catalogue, and to integrate most of this material into a coherent pattern, by deducing three main levels or types of aesthetic pleasure – that is, to reiterate, pleasure derivable from the mimetic arts. It would certainly be fanciful to try to forge a completely systematic theory out of this collection of passages: Aristotle draws analogies with the visual arts, but even so it is not always easy to see just how his

---

[25] *EN* 1175a 22ff.: the phrase 'peculiar pleasure' (*oikeia hēdonē*) occurs at 1175a 31, b 14, 21, 27 etc. It was also used by Plato, but to denote pure, 'true' pleasures: *Phileb.* 51d, 63e, *Rep.* 586e, 587b. The attempt of Else (1938) to connect Plato and Ar. on this point is misguided, and involves him in the claim (194) that the proper or peculiar pleasure of the *Poetics* is not specific to individual genres: this will not stand up to scrutiny.

principles could be elaborated for mimetic art in general. But the following scheme of analysis is economical, positive, and based squarely on the evidence cited above, with supplementary guidance from other relevant passages in the corpus. I shall attempt to define and analyse the three types of aesthetic pleasure in ascending order of both importance and delicateness of interpretation.

In the lowest position in the scheme comes the inessential, and potentially inappropriate, enjoyment of theatrical spectacle, *opsis*, by which Aristotle probably means chiefly the visual presentation of the actors (see Appendix 3). In this first case, there are no grounds for extrapolating from poetry to other arts; *opsis* is not even a feature of all poetry (epic lacks it: 59b 10, 60a 14), but only of dramatic poetry in performance. Furthermore, in his animadversions on spectacle Aristotle does not have in mind the general visual aspect of performance, but the specific exploitation of it for emotional effect. Thus, properly used, *opsis* can contribute to the tragic effect of pity and fear (53b 1f.), and I suggested earlier that this must also be part of Aristotle's point at the end of ch. 6, when he describes the potency of spectacle with a term already applied to the elements of the complex plot-structure. It is also in this latter passage, however, that spectacle is relegated to the status of an accessory art. This severely limits Aristotle's attention to it within the theory of tragedy, but the brief acknowledgements of its capability should not be wholly forgotten. We can probably infer that the correct use of *opsis* would be regarded simply as visual reinforcement of the intrinsic dramatic effect, and the pleasure accruing from the former should therefore be categorised as a secondary manifestation of the true and proper pleasure of tragedy, to which I shall be returning. In any case, Aristotle's concern at the start of *Poetics* 14 seems to be more with the *incorrect* use of spectacle to produce a purely sensational pleasure that would distract from, or impede, the appropriate tragic emotions and their concomitant pleasure. The 'portentous' is dismissed as a spurious substitute for these emotions,[26] and whatever else one may think about Aristotle's sharp divorce between dramatic poetry and its performance, his attitude at least confirms his philosophical interest

[26] The basis of the portentous, as *GA* 770b 8ff. helps us to see, would be unnatural phenomena (grotesque horrors), which means that they would flout necessity or probability: hence their spuriousness, in contrast to the intelligibility of events which cause pity and fear. For the possibility of a reference to Aeschylus at 53b 9 see ch. III n.20.

in discriminating between types of pleasure, and in evaluating their relative worth.

The devaluation of *opsis* is also a reflection of Aristotle's aim of shifting the locus of the poet's art from the realm of the sensual to that of the cognitive. But a more subtle and significant indication of this aim is provided by the distinction drawn in *Poetics* 4 between the natural pleasure derivable from mimetic works, and the sensual pleasure which may be taken in them independently of their mimetic status. It is the latter which is the second of the three main levels of aesthetic pleasure to be analysed.[27] Outside the *Poetics* there are other passages in which Aristotle differentiates between sensual and intellectual pleasures, and it is evidently in the former category that we must place the pleasure noted in item (b) in my earlier list: a pleasure which can be given by works of art entirely in respect of their sensible properties, and without any specifically cognitive or emotional element. Into this category we must also bring item (c) and the first of the types referred to in item (e). The objects of this species of pleasure are the forms, textures, patterns and sounds of art, apprehended in and for themselves and not as the medium of mimetic significance. This is the disjunction which Aristotle makes explicitly at 48b 17-19, by immediate reference to a visual example, but as part of a larger argument whose scope covers also the whole of poetic mimesis. Although condensed, this passage is sufficient to establish that sensual pleasure cannot, in Aristotle's terms, properly account for the experience of any mimetic art, though it is recognised as having a legitimate, secondary part to play. That such pleasure seems to be most readily identifiable in the case of the visual arts is suggested by the fact that in two of the three relevant passages of the *Poetics* cited above Aristotle makes his point by reference to painting (items (b) and (e)). If we ask what the applicability of the concept is to the non-visual arts, Aristotle's answer is embodied in what he has to say about the rhythmic and musical enhancements of language ((c) above): it is the most directly sensible aspects of the language of poetry, its rhythmical and melodic 'garnishings', as the philosopher regards them, which supply the closest equivalent to the sensual

---

[27] The use of 'aesthetic' by Lucas (1968) on 48b 13 and 17 to refer *only* to this type is question-begging, and is rightly criticised as such by M. Hubbard, *CR* 20 (1970) 177. On the distinction between purely sensual and cognitive pleasure, parallel to *Poet.* 48b 10-19, see *PA* 645a 7-15, and cf. e.g. *EN* 1175a 26f., 1176a 2f. This distinction is related to that between the sensible and the knowable, e.g. *De An.* 431b 21ff.

forms and colours of visual art.[28] But the inference is not easily to be
elaborated, since Aristotle's view of the mimetic nature of music
reduces the scope for the derivation of a purely sensual pleasure from
it, and the evidence of both the *Poetics* and the *Rhetoric* implies that
this qualification holds good even for rhythm independently of
melody.[29]

It is at any rate clear that any sensual pleasure afforded by poetry
cannot in Aristotle's theory be of more than secondary significance,
and it is worthwhile to note that this inference has a bearing on his
attitude to *performance*, since the availability of pleasure from the
rhythmic and melodic aspects of poetry clearly depends on this. In
the case of the rhythms of spoken verse, this condition would be
satisfied by the standard practice of reading aloud (alluded to
perhaps, for different purposes, at 53b 3-7),[30] but for sections of lyric
poetry presumably no alternative to musically accompanied
performance would be sufficient. Various lines of thought therefore
converge to produce a devaluation of lyric in the *Poetics*: the
conception of its distinctive features as an embellishment or
'garnishing' of tragedy (and consequently inessential); the
separation of poetry proper from performance and its attendant arts;
and the relegation of the sensual pleasure of poetry to the level of the

[28] For the translation 'garnishings' see ch. VIII n.3. The comparison of
characterisation to colour at 50a 39ff. ((e) in the text), which effectively reiterates the
emphasis of 48b 15-19, does not, of course, imply that character is sensually
apprehended, only that it needs the formal framework of plot-structure to have its
proper significance.

[29] For general references to musical pleasure see *EN* 1173b 30f., 1175a 13f., 34f.,
EE 1230b 27f., *Pol.* 1339b 20f., 1340b 16f. The mimetic nature of music is indicated at
Poet. 47a 14-16, 23-6, *Pol.* 1340a 28ff. (and cf. 1340a 13f. with Susemihl's emendation:
see Anderson 126, 186-8). The question arises how far Ar. allowed a sensual pleasure
to musical tones *independently* of their mimetic significance, as Plato does at *Phileb.* 51d.
Poet. 47a 15 implies that some music is not mimetic, but the adverb 'most vividly' at
62a 17 implies a mimetic force (cf. the same word at 55a 24). The general impression
left by *Politics* 8 is of music as a naturally mimetic art. The point affects rhythm too, for
which some degree of intrinsically mimetic or expressive value is posited at *Poet.*
21ff., 59b 31ff., 60a 4, *Pol.* 1340a 19ff., b 8ff., 1341b 19-27, *Rhet.* 1408b 21-9a 23:
compare e.g. Plato *Laws* 669c, 798d (but note 669e on the difficulty of understanding
rhythm and music *without words*). Isocrates 9.10-11 appears to treat the pleasure of
rhythm as autonomous. Finally, *Pol.* 1341a 14f. distinguishes between the 'common'
and evidently sensual pleasure of music and rhythm (available even to some animals)
and the sensibility to enjoy 'beautiful melodies and rhythms', which probably entails a
mimetic significance.

[30] Ar. also refers to *epic* recitation at 59b 30. Note that Plato describes poetry as the
form of mimesis which operates through our *hearing* at *Rep.* 603b 6f. On the Greek
practice of reading aloud see B. Knox, *GRBS* 9 (1968) 421-35.

subordinate. That this devaluation does indeed result in a failure on Aristotle's part to do justice to the lyric dimension of Greek tragedy is something I shall argue in greater detail in ch. VIII.

But it is not only the particular connection of sensual pleasure with performance and with lyric poetry which explains its status in the *Poetics*, for we have seen that the passage in ch. 4 where Aristotle distinguishes between a cognitive and a sensual pleasure from works of art refers directly to a visual example, and suggests that the principle ought to be applicable to mimetic art in general. If so, the reason must be sought in a larger aspect of Aristotle's philosophy. At the opening of the *Metaphysics* Aristotle makes the famous pronouncement that 'all men by nature desire knowledge', and he goes on to relate this postulate to the observation that we value the senses, regardless of utility, for the pleasure they afford us. This pleasure, however, particularly that of sight, is not merely sensual; its cause is the cognitive content of our perceptions, the contribution which they make to the acquisition of knowledge to which our very nature predisposes us. Hence the supreme value of sight, for 'this is the sense which allows us to apprehend the most, and which reveals the most discriminations'.[31] This passage in fact generalises the principle which is enunciated specifically for the experience of mimetic art in *Poetics* 4, and it indicates the broader foundation on which Aristotle bases his claim that the true pleasure of this experience entails a process of understanding and learning. The negative corollary of this is that the purely sensual enjoyment of form, colour, texture, rhythm and so on, does not involve the full use of the senses' natural cognitive capacity.

It is, then, to the elucidation of the third and highest level of aesthetic pleasure posited by the *Poetics* that I must now turn. Two items from my original list are left for consideration: the natural pleasure of learning and understanding through mimesis (a), and the proper pleasure of tragedy (g), 'the pleasure arising from pity and fear through mimesis' (taking the passages in (f) to represent indefinite allusions to the latter). What I wish to argue is that these two items in fact present aspects of the same phenomenon, or, more precisely, that they are related as genus to species, so that the pleasure proper to tragedy is one example, and perhaps for Aristotle the supreme instance, of the generic concept of pleasure from mimetic works

[31] *Met.* 980a 21-7. On the general love of knowledge cf. *Protr.* B17, 72-7, 97-102 Düring (1961).

sketched in *Poetics* 4. But to establish the cogency of this position, which has not been widely adopted in interpretation of the treatise, will require some close reasoning, and in the first place a scrutiny of the crucial passage in ch. 4.[32]

It is a paradoxical part of the difficulty of dealing with *Poetics* 4 that its train of thought is ostensibly so plain and unremarkable. It is possible to carry away from a reading of it, seduced by its very simplicity, and undisturbed by consideration of how Aristotle's reasoning here must be integrated with what he offers later in the book, the impression of nothing more than the concise formulation of rudimentary and preliminary points. Nor is this impression entirely erroneous; but it is essential to dissociate the straightforwardness of the argument from the question of how far-reaching the implications of it can be seen to be.[33] The theme of the first half of the chapter is the original causes of poetry, though the progression of thought, with its general references to mimesis and its visual examples, leaves little room to doubt that the enquiry applies to all mimetic art. Aristotle suggests, with typical ingenuousness, two 'natural' causes for poetry. It is possible, I believe, to discern that these are really facets of a single explanation. The first cause or reason is the instinct in human beings from childhood onwards to engage in mimesis, for which we here need to have in mind at least the two ideas of 'imitation' and 'enactment' (static or active representation). Moreover, even early mimesis involves learning, though Aristotle makes the point so briefly that it is impossible to determine how wide a range of behaviour he means his audience to understand.[34] At any rate, we

[32] Ross 280 calls ch. 4's explanation of the mimesis-instinct 'too intellectualistic' and misses its significance. Lord (1982) 90f. talks of a 'purely intellectual' understanding of mimesis, and Else (1957) 128-30 finds the 'emphasis on the intellect' a sign of a marginal addition (cf. ch. I n. 51 above). These judgements all seem to me to misconstrue the implications of the passage. The essential import is that the basic cognitive pleasure takes particular forms, such as that from tragedy, in which it is engaged with emotion and other factors. For a recent philosophical attempt to use *Poetics* 4 as a starting-point for an aesthetic thesis see A. Savile, *The Test of Time* (Oxford 1982) ch. 5, esp. 86f., 95f.

[33] It is specifically the simplicity of the passage which has led scholars such as Twining 186-91, Butcher 201f., Rostagni (1945) LXIV, and Lord (1982) 90-2 into underestimating its importance: against Rostagni and Lord it is particularly pertinent to observe that the educative effect of poetry on the passions (for which they rightly argue: cf. ch. VI n. 40) cannot be divorced from the cognitive experience of the mimetic structure of a poem (see esp. 53b 12 for an indication of this).

[34] The obvious parallel is *Pol.* 1336a 32-4, where children's games are said to be imitations or enactments of adult activities and to 'prepare the way for their later occupations'. See Plato *Rep.* 395d 1f., and cf. ps.-Ar. *Probl.* 956a 14.

can say that alongside man as a political creature and a rational creature, we may juxtapose, in Aristotle's perspective, man as the most mimetic of creatures. Mimesis is rooted in human nature, and is implicated in distinctively human patterns of action. We recognise readily that within the naturalistic terms of Aristotelian philosophy mimesis is thus vindicated in the face of the intrinsically suspect and shallow status to which Platonic metaphysics had often condemned it, and that the mimetic *technai* now have a doubly natural grounding and sanction: first, as I earlier demonstrated, in the teleological character of *technê*, productive art, in general; secondly, in the human propensity towards mimesis. The mimetic arts consummate this propensity by developing it into various types of rational art.

Aristotle's second cause of poetry also concerns mimesis,[35] but adjusts the point of view to that of the recipient or spectator, rather than that of the agent or artist. To the universal instinct for engaging in mimesis Aristotle now adds the equally natural pleasure which is taken in the mimetic activities or works of others, and from his elaboration of the point we gather that these two factors coalesce as elements of a single phenomenon. For the underlying explanation of the pleasure taken in the apprehension of mimetic objects (which need not be *physical* objects) is the primary human pleasure in learning: learning and understanding therefore appear as the basis of both the active and the receptive interest in mimesis (48b 12f. refers back to 5-8). Moreover, the cognition involved in mimesis is equally a source of pleasure in both cases, since Aristotle's claim that there is a natural human instinct for mimesis entails, given his philosophy of pleasure, that men take a natural pleasure in exercising it as well as in appreciating its products. The two causes of poetry, then, and of mimesis in general, turn out to be aspects of a single psychological and cultural hypothesis, and one which contains the nucleus of a highly serious concept of aesthetic pleasure.

One reason for a common refusal to take that last step in my argument seems to be a sense, to which I have already referred, that ch. 4 of the *Poetics* represents a preliminary or marginal part of the treatise, and can offer no insight into the centre of Aristotle's idea of

---

[35] There has been much disagreement on this point (and the issue is old: cf. Weinberg 462). I take *mimeisthai* at 48b 20 to refer to *both* causes, and the instinct for melody and rhythm to be an additional but *closely related* factor (a point usually overlooked) in view of Ar.'s understanding of these things as naturally mimetic (n.29 above).

poetry or art. It is, of course, the case that this passage is initially
offered by way of accounting for the *origins* or causes of poetry: it
furnishes what might be regarded as the psychological and
anthropological premises from which Aristotle can advance to the
sketch of poetic evolution which follows in the rest of the chapter. But
to infer from this that Aristotle's causes of poetry have only a
hypothetical or historical reference, and have no bearing on the
developed forms of art, would simply be to overlook the fact that
these causes are presented as putatively permanent, because natural,
data about human engagement in mimetic activities. Origins
correspond to fulfilment: in Aristotle's beginning is his end. The
argument is, in fact, not properly historical at all, but philosophical –
committed, that is, to the explication of underlying and universal
causes. It should be remarked, moreover, that Aristotle's verbs are
all in the present tense in this passage: 'mimetic activity is natural to
men from childhood onwards ... man is the most mimetic of
creatures ... we enjoy looking at pictures ...', and so on. Aristotle's
conclusion that 'if one has not seen the object of a picture before, it
will not produce pleasure *qua* work of mimesis, but by virtue of its
execution etc.'[36] therefore unequivocally states a principle about the
status and comprehension of mimetic works in general, though its
implications remain to be drawn out. While external confirmation of
this is hardly needed, it happens to be available in the fact that
Aristotle makes the same point in very similar language in Book 1 of
the *Rhetoric*, where he affirms, without reference to anything but
existing forms of mimetic art, that the aesthetic pleasure derived from
them contains a process of recognition and understanding implicit in
the appreciation.[37]

[36] That this latter, purely sensual pleasure could be for Ar. 'the true pleasure', as
Gomme 64f. suggests, makes nonsense of the treatise and flatly contradicts the
reference to mimesis in the definition of tragic pleasure at 53b 11-13. *Pol.* 1340a 25-8
provides an important parallel: there the form (*morphē*) is an attribute of the human
subject of the image (cf. *Poet.* 54b 10), and the pleasure derived from it is cognitive (the
recognition of physical strength, athletic beauty, etc.) and dependent on mimesis; the
reference to 'another reason' is parallel to *Poet.* 48b 18f. The difficult passage, *Mem.*
450b 21ff., is also germane: for the interpretation see R. Sorabji, *Aristotle on Memory*
(London 1972) 84. It confirms that the proper appreciation of visual mimesis involves
treating a work as an image of a possible reality (for an image, *eikōn*, is precisely the
product of mimesis: *Top.* 140a 14f.). It might be possible to discern allusions to
cognitive and non-cognitive pleasure in visual art at, respectively, *EE* 1230b 31-4, *EN*
1118a 3f.
[37] *Rhet.* 1371b 4ff.: the relevance of the passage is correctly indicated by Hubbard
134 (though the word 'just' does not belong in the translation), in line with her brief

That Aristotle should regard the basis of aesthetic pleasure to be an experience for which he finds the language of 'learning', 'comprehending' and 'reasoning' apt, is a conclusion of major import for his philosophical view of art, and particularly of poetry.[38] Yet the clarity of this position belies the problems which confront a deeper interpretation of it. Perhaps the most immediate of these problems arises from the fact that in explaining the natural human roots of poetry, Aristotle chooses, as he also does in the passage from the *Rhetoric* mentioned above, an illustration from visual art, and one, moreover, of arguably disappointing simplicity. The example of a picture, or other visual work, which portrays an identifiable (though not necessarily a real) figure, and to which the mind of the beholder may respond with the reasoning, 'this is so-and-so', might well be thought to shed little enough light on the type of cognition involved in the experience of paintings, and none at all on the understanding of poetry. Given the ambitious scope of the context – an explanation of the psychological causes of poetry, and implicitly of all mimesis – we must assume both that Aristotle gives a visual instance of something which can take non-visual forms, and also that he is deliberately citing a simple case of an experience which must have more complex varieties (in the apprehension of both visual and non-visual art).[39] In one respect the simplicity of the illustration does serve well to mark the tenor of the passage as a whole, for Aristotle is sketching a view of a large range of human activity but contending that there is a fundamental unity in the experiences which underlie it; the fact that the passage contains references to both the playing of

but exemplary explanation of the theory of aesthetic pleasure on pp. 86f. Cf. also Tracy's article, Redfield 52-66, and Goldschmidt (1982) 212-17. Closely related passages are those on metaphor (*Poet.* 59a 7f., *Rhet.* 1410b 10-26), on 'wit', including types of metaphor (*Rhet.* 1412a 17-b 23), and on other kinds of comparison (*Rhet.* 1394a 5). It is regrettable that an emphasis on the importance of *Poetics* 4's explanation of aesthetic pleasure has been confused with the issue of *katharsis* in Golden (1962) and later articles: see Appendix 5 §5(a).

[38] *Manthanein* leads to knowledge: e.g. *De An.* 417b 12f., *Rhet.* 1362a 30f., 1363b 31f. For *sullogizesthai* cf. *Poet.* 55a 7, 10f., 61b 2, *Rhet.* 1371b 9. Although this latter term should not everywhere be pressed in its technical logical sense (cf. Appendix 1 p. 326), the language of *Poet.* 48b 16 allows for a process in which new understanding may be reached (cf. e.g. Plato *Euthyd.* 277e-8a). See n. 42 below.

[39] The point is reinforced by the reference to non-philosophers at 48b 13f.: the following example is intentionally rudimentary, with the implication that more sophisticated forms are possible. Cf. the parallel drawn between the study of art (dramatic performances) and philosophical study at *Protr.* B44 Düring (1961).

children and the philosopher's pleasure in knowledge, is significant of the potential scope of the argument. The implicit comparison between the pleasure of mimetic art and the pleasure of philosophical knowledge recurs more pointedly in the *Parts of Animals* (645a 7-15), where we also find the example of unattractive animals – animals which, because *ex hypothesi* repellent, cannot be a source, whether in art or in life, of *sensual* pleasure. Although this passage is explicit on the reason for philosophical pleasure (the understanding of causes), it leaves that of art less than clear; but given its analogy between art and nature (a theme explored earlier in this chapter) it may not be unreasonable to infer a kind of cognition of causes in the pleasure derived from mimetic works too.

The outline of a cognitive theory of aesthetic pleasure in *Poetics* 4 accords with Aristotle's mature view that pleasure involves the natural exercise of human faculties. In the experience of mimetic works any element of purely sensual pleasure must be subordinate to the processes of recognition and learning which constitute the proper response to mimesis. Without cognitive recognition, the status of the mimetic work – the representation of a possible reality which it embodies – cannot be grasped and therefore cannot be enjoyed, though the senses may take separate pleasure in certain material aspects of the work (48b 17-19). But the use of a rudimentary visual example at *Poetics* 48b 15-17 (a general mannerism, incidentally, of Aristotle's philosophical method) seems at first sight to impede further illumination of this fundamental layer in the thought of the treatise. In order to make headway with the interpretation of Aristotle's concept of aesthetic pleasure, we need therefore to explore the possibility of implicit connections between what is said in the first part of ch. 4 and some of the work's other doctrines. Two lines of enquiry can be initially distinguished. The first is to examine the relation between the general cognitive pleasure of ch. 4 and the 'proper pleasure' of tragedy referred to elsewhere in the work. After this, it will be necessary to consider more closely the idea of comprehension or learning which Aristotle ascribes to the enjoyment and appreciation of mimesis.

An attempt to combine *Poetics* 4 with later parts of the treatise is encouraged, among other things, by the passage from Book 1 of the *Rhetoric* which I mentioned earlier. Aristotle there associates understanding with 'wonder', both of which he says are usually pleasurable: understanding, because, in short, it fulfils man's nature, and wonder, because it involves a desire to learn. Elsewhere we find Aristotle repeating what Plato had said before him, that wonder is the source or origin of philosophy itself, because it represents man's primary thirst for knowledge.[40] We have here a pointer to one possible link between parts of the *Poetics*, for there are a number of passages in the treatise where Aristotle touches on the poet's use of 'the wonderful'. The most revealing of these occurs near the end of ch. 9, where it is proposed that pity and fear are best aroused in tragedy by events which happen 'unexpectedly but on account of one another', and that such events will produce wonder more than would chance happenings. It emerges here that there is a kinship, in tragedy, between pity and fear and 'the wonderful': the same kinds of tragic events (in the ideally complex drama, at any rate) should elicit both. Furthermore, the effect of wonder to which Aristotle here refers is explicitly related to the intelligible causation of the events of tragedy (notwithstanding the immediate impact of surprise), and that this is so is corroborated by the following remark that even chance events arouse more wonder when they appear to happen for a purpose – that is, *appear* to be part of an intelligible sequence.[41] If, then, we put this passage together with the one from *Rhetoric* 1, wonder becomes a link between the tragic emotions, on one side, and our understanding of the structure of a dramatic action, on the other. Wonder itself does not seem to be simply identifiable either with the particular emotions elicited by tragedy, or with the process of understanding: yet it has both an emotional and a cognitive significance, in that it is felt alongside – as part of the same experience as – pity and fear, and offers a challenge to the mind which, ideally, stimulates and leads on to comprehension or knowledge. Aristotle's comments on wonder in the *Poetics* and *Rhetoric* help a little to strengthen the case for trying to see the general thesis of *Poetics* 4 and the detailed analysis of tragedy later in the

[40] *Rhet.* 1371a-b, cf. 1404b 12, *Met.* 982b 12ff., 983a 12ff., Plato *Theaet.* 155d. Ar.'s 'wonder' all too easily became *admiratio*, hence admiration, for neo-classical readers of the *Poetics*: cf. ch. X n.21. Ar.'s and Plato's views on wonder deserve closer study. For a sensitive general essay on the subject see R. Hepburn, *Wonder and Other Essays* (Edinburgh 1984) 131-54.

[41] It is true that at 60a 11ff. 'the wonderful' is related to the irrational, which is undesirable in poetry. Although there may be something of a tension here, it is reasonable to infer that there are degrees of wonder, which lies on the boundary of the explicable and the inexplicable, and so can slip into the latter (and hence become the irrational) or, properly used, may stimulate and challenge understanding, as at 52a 4ff. Cf. Else (1957) 624f., and ch. VII n. 16.

treatise as interrelated and mutually illuminating.

In the juxtaposition of the tragic emotions with wonder in ch. 9 of the *Poetics* we have an indication that the peculiar pleasure of tragedy, which Aristotle defines in ch. 14 as 'the pleasure arising from pity and fear through mimesis', should be regarded as one species of the generic aesthetic pleasure whose elements are sketched in ch. 4. Such a claim gives some illustration of the need to seek out associations which our text of the treatise omits to make explicit, and which Aristotle may either have taken for granted or else have drawn out orally in his philosophical teaching. The cogency of such claims depends on the possibility of discerning multiple signs of underlying relations between superficially discrete ideas or doctrines, and this can, I believe, be plausibly achieved for my argument that the peculiar pleasure of tragedy represents in one specific form, adapted to the particular characteristics of the genre, Aristotle's essential or primary concept of aesthetic pleasure, in which cognition and emotion are integrated. In *Poetics* 6 Aristotle picks out the components of the complex plot as the most potent of the resources of tragedy, a remark which can only be understood in terms of the distinctive tragic emotions of his own definition. This observation is borne out by the later concentration on the complex plot in the prescriptions for the ideal tragedy. Recognition and reversal are the focus of the finest tragic plot-structure, and so the focus of the emotions aroused by it. In the passage from ch. 9 to which I have already drawn attention it can reasonably be inferred that Aristotle has these aspects of the complex plot, perhaps particularly reversal, in mind: for he says that pity and fear will be best produced by events which happen 'unexpectedly but on account of one another', and this can be taken virtually as a definition of reversal (*peripeteia*). It is, therefore, telling that in *Rhetoric* 1 Aristotle singles out precisely sudden and unforeseeable reversals of fortune (*peripeteiai*) as a source of wonder (1371b 10): they both surprise us and arouse our minds to look for an underlying explanation of the ostensibly inexplicable. Once again we see a convergence of ideas, the sign of a nexus of associations between the complex plot, the tragic emotions, and wonder, with the latter's implications for learning. To this we must add the crucial fact, which can only be stated here but will be discussed in detail in ch. VI, that Aristotle's conception of the emotions, pity and fear, itself rests on a cognitive basis: properly educated, at any rate, these emotions are not arbitrary or irrationally impulsive, but are aligned with the recognition and understanding of certain types and patterns of suffering or misfortune.

The provisional conclusion can therefore be drawn that the peculiar pleasure of tragedy is not a wholly autonomous phenomenon, a self-sufficient category of experience. It is, in the first place, a species of the genus of aesthetic pleasure, the pleasure taken in mimesis, which Aristotle defines in ch. 4 as entailing a necessary process of recognition, learning or understanding. The particular tragic species of aesthetic pleasure involves distinctive emotions, but these emotions are themselves only fully intelligible and justifiable in terms of the cognitive apprehension of certain kinds of human actions and their consequences. The proper tragic pleasure not only shows the relevance of Aristotle's general comments on aesthetic pleasure, by providing an instance of their embodiment in the theory of an individual genre, but also gives some idea of the ways in which we can expect the elementary model of ch. 4 – the identification of a subject in visual art – to be complicated and made more sophisticated by internal factors of a genre. Most obviously, the example used in ch. 4 posits a case of simple recognition without an emotional dimension, whereas Aristotle's whole theory of tragedy assumes an interplay and integration of the intellect and the emotions. Furthermore, the illustration in *Poetics* 4 involves particulars ('the man in the picture is so-and-so') while Aristotle's theory of poetry assigns to the art the potential to deal with universals: the cognitive experience of such art needs correspondingly to be framed in far richer terms than those used in ch. 4's outline of Aristotle's position.[42]

If my argument so far has attempted to orient us in the direction in which the interpretation of Aristotelian aesthetic pleasure ought to lie, it also could be said to force us back to consider the notions of learning, understanding and reasoning of which both *Poetics* 4 and the passage from *Rhetoric* 1 speak in connection with mimesis. Since it is doubtful whether a scrutiny of Aristotle's terms will in itself allow

[42] In the full understanding of universals in poetry it is not easy to know what would correspond to the pre-existing knowledge of *Poet.* 48b 17. Certainly not factual acquaintance with myths: see 51b 21-6. Perhaps knowledge (which for Ar. is not true knowledge) of particulars, from which we are led to a grasp of the universals embodied in the poetry: cf. *Top.* 108b 10-12 for the movement from particulars to universals through 'likenesses'. For the movement from existing to new knowledge in a different context see *An.Post.* 71a 1ff.

us to make much progress on this point, for their range of meaning is too broad, we need to look for other clues to the elucidation of the type of cognitive experience which he takes to be implicit in the proper appreciation of mimetic works. One such clue may be furnished by a further detail which the passages from the *Poetics* and *Rhetoric* have in common. In the latter, Aristotle describes wisdom, which is virtually synonymous with philosophy, as 'the knowledge of many wonders', thus reinforcing his observations in the *Metaphysics* on the status of wonder as the motive of philosophising.[43] Philosophy is also mentioned in *Poetics* 4, where it is said that 'learning is highly pleasurable not only to philosophers but likewise, if to a lesser degree, to all other men'. While this reference to philosophy sharpens the paradoxical simplicity of the instance of cognition which Aristotle goes on to give, it should not be lightly underestimated; I cited earlier the passage from the *Parts of Animals* where the experiences of philosophy and of mimesis are also connected. It ought to be stressed that *any* direct comparison between philosophy and the mimetic arts, however seemingly casual and qualified, could hardly fail to strike someone familiar with the Platonic background as bold; and the comparison was not one which most philosophers would have easily accepted.[44] That Aristotle should have drawn it in several of his works is evidently significant. It intimates that the cognition involved in the appreciation of mimesis is not wholly different in kind, though it may be in degree, from philosophical thought, and the *Parts of Animals* passage suggests that the understanding of causes can play a part in both. We have, therefore, corroboration for the interpretation of *Poetics* 4 as of fundamental importance for the assessment of Aristotle's view of art and the experience of art, and we also have a prompting to draw into the enquiry the other passage in the *Poetics* where philosophy is mentioned.

'Poetry is more philosophical and more serious than history' (51b 5f.). If we look to this famous sentence from ch. 9 for further light on Aristotle's idea of the comprehension implicit in the experience of mimesis, we can notice at once that ch. 9 as a whole offers a more refined notion of intellectual activity than the one suggested by ch. 4's example from the visual arts. Part of the dissatisfyingly *simpliste*

---

[43] *Met.* 982b 12ff., *Rhet.* 1371b 27f.

[44] It does not seem to have been accepted, for instance, by Ar.'s successor, Theophrastus: see fr. 65, translated in Russell 203f. On Plato's comparisons between poetry and philosophy see Appendix 2 under 51a 5f.

impression given by that earlier illustration lies in its apparent equation of understanding with factual knowledge, so that it remains uninstructive just what the value is of being able to recognise that a picture of, say, Achilles in his tent is just that. Part of the importance of *Poetics* 9 is that it helps to rectify this impression, by providing a more elaborate account of the kind of cognition which poetic mimesis calls for, as well as a more detailed placing of poetry in relation to other intellectual activities. *Poetics* 9 represents a broadening out into general poetic principles of the particular prescriptions given in the preceding chapters (6-8) for the structure and unity of tragic plot. Unity of plot, as I shall argue in ch. III, is not for Aristotle a purely formal matter, for the essential reason that plot itself, *muthos*, is not an exclusively formal concept, but a concept of significant (because mimetic) form. The criterion of unity on which so much emphasis is laid is that of 'necessity or probability', which is a principle of the logical and causal relations between actions or events. For poetry to conform to this criterion is for it to produce plots – mimetic structures of human action – which embody generalised patterns of universals, as opposed to the random particulars of history. Such universals are meant to be intelligible precisely as such: that is, the mind which contemplates poetic mimesis can perceive it and understand it as the dramatic communication of universals. This notion of poetic significance is so far from the impression given by *Poetics* 4 that, if we were to take the latter's example of visual mimesis at face-value, and infer from it a poetic equivalent, the result would be closer to ch. 9's view of *history*, with its alleged restriction to the particular, than to its claims for a quasi-philosophical art of poetry.[45] But this is an argument not for ignoring the general implications of ch. 4, but for adjusting our interpretation of it, and particularly of the status of its illustration from visual mimesis, in the light of what is to be learnt about poetic mimesis later in the treatise.

Thus *Poetics* 9 serves to carry Aristotle's view of the cognitive experience of mimesis beyond the limitations of the earlier formulation. As a further reason for treating ch. 4 as a simple

[45] Else (1957) 131f. can hardly be right to see a reference to universals in the visual example of ch. 4, but this is tied up with his belief (128) that the point concerns scientific models and diagrams, a belief refuted by *Poet.* 48b 17-19 and the parallel passage, *Rhet.* 1371b 4ff. (On Ar.'s independent use of diagrams cf. ch. VII p. 218 and n. 23.)

statement of a principle capable of much more complex elaboration
for particular arts and genres, we can now add the overall tendency
of Aristotle's handling of mimesis, which I shall be returning to in
ch. IV. Given that Aristotle repudiates the need for mimetic works to
involve a one-to-one correspondence with reality, the simplicity of the
visual example in ch. 4 is best regarded as a deliberately minimal
and uncontroversial process of cognition, but one which would
clearly be insufficient where the nature of the mimetic work is richer.
Once this qualification on the argument of ch. 4 is accepted, it
follows that further enlightenment on Aristotle's concept of aesthetic
pleasure can only be pursued within the context of the study of his
treatment of individual genres. I have already argued that the proper
pleasure of tragedy is to be taken as a species of the generic type
indicated in *Poetics* 4; the pleasure provided by the genre matches the
distinctive emotional experience of it, and this emotional experience
is itself integrated with the understanding of the structure and
causation of human action dramatised in the tragic plot. It therefore
becomes impossible to specify more closely the nature of the proper
pleasure of tragedy other than by investigating the *Poetics*' theory of
tragedy as a whole, and by attempting to ascertain whether the
treatise allows us to identify a particular area of universals in the
apprehension of which the particular cognitive-cum-aesthetic
pleasure of tragedy resides. This investigation will be undertaken in
later chapters of this book.

The interpretation of aesthetic pleasure in the *Poetics* is, then, not
readily to be brought to a definitive conclusion. The brevity of
Aristotle's explicit remarks on the subject stands in the way of a
complete exposition of his views. But it must also be said that if the
line of argument I have followed is correct, then it is not altogether
surprising or objectionable that Aristotle should have failed to supply
a full statement of his concept of aesthetic pleasure, since the hints
that we are given gesture in the direction of a theory which does not
separate off aesthetic experience as discrete and self-contained, but
relates it both to natural human instincts and to the 'higher'
intellectual activity of philosophy. While we may regret that Aristotle
did not examine these relations in more detail, he says enough to
establish the fundamentally cognitive character of the experience of
mimesis, and so to imply the kind of framework within which the rest
of his discussion of poetry must be placed. And if we associate, as I
have contended, the particular pleasure of tragedy with this

underlying notion of aesthetic pleasure, then we are now in a position to see why it is so misleading, as I suggested in my introductory chapter, to attribute to Aristotle, without the necessary qualifications, the belief that the aim of poetry is pleasure:[46] misleading, principally because such a formulation of his position is likely to import an idea of aestheticism, in which the autonomy of works of art is linked with the autonomous character of our enjoyment of them. The central role of pleasure in Aristotle's aesthetics needs to be understood, as I have tried to show, in close conjunction both with the broad indications given in the treatise of the essentially cognitive experience of mimetic works, and with the particular content of the theory of tragedy. Seen in this way, aesthetic pleasure complements the analysis of the Aristotelian concept of art which I offered earlier in the chapter, for the pleasure of those who experience mimetic works is a response to the intelligible structure imposed on his material by the artist's rational capacity. And these two things, the maker's art and the recipient's pleasure, are a reflection of the natural status of mimesis and of the framework within which its individual types evolve: successful mimesis is of significance in Aristotle's eyes, and can be vindicated against Platonic condemnation, because it fulfils man's natural potential to understand reality by reconstituting it in some of the materials over which he has rational control.

---

[46] E.g. Twining 399-401, Butcher ch. 4, Gudeman 99, Allan (1970) 155, Schadewaldt 225, 228f. Cf. ch. I p.6. For the comparison between poetry and philosophy there is an analogue in the affinities allowed at *Rhet.* 1356a 20-7 between rhetoric and dialectic (and *politikē*), and at *Rhet.* 1359b 8-12, *An.Post.* 71a 9-11 between rhetoric and logic, ethics, and dialectic.

III

Aristotle's Aesthetics 2: Craft, Nature and Unity in Art

In the previous chapter I examined perhaps the two most fundamental dimensions of Aristotle's treatment of poetry and the other arts: the concept of art itself (representing the mimetic *technai* as a cohesive group), and the concept of aesthetic pleasure (grounded in the cognitive experience of mimetic structures). Aristotle's thinking can in both cases be seen ultimately to centre on the notion of mimesis, which will receive an independent analysis in ch. IV. In the present chapter I offer some observations on a further group of important questions concerning the conceptual and evaluative categories which constitute Aristotle's understanding of art, but especially poetry: first, the character of the individual artist's capacity to produce or invent his works; secondly, the relation between nature and tradition in the evolution of genres; and finally, the principles of unity in works of art.

No area in the theory and criticism of art is given more to *a priori* arguments and unsubstantiated assertions than that of the sources and processes of artistic invention – or 'creativity', to employ a term which itself has roots in a particular movement of thought on the subject.[1] I noted in the introductory chapter that ancient Greek view of the resources which the artist draws on to produce his work

---

[1] 'Creativity' is strictly inappropriate as a historical concept in the Greek context. Ar. himself holds the view that everything which comes into being must do so out of something pre-existent: e.g. *Met.* 1032a 14, b 30-2, 1033b 11. Moreover, the artist must know in advance the form of that which he intends to produce: see esp. *Met.* 1032b 6ff. On the incompatibility between general Greek ideas of cosmic rationality and the notion of creation *ex nihilo* see A. Dihle, *The Concept of the Will in Classical Antiquity* (Berkeley 1981) 1-5, 71f. For the extension of the idea of creativity from the divine to the human in the Renaissance and later see Lieberg 159-73, P.0. Kristeller, ' "Creativity" and "Tradition" ', *JHI* 44 (1983) 105-13, and R. Williams, *The Long Revolution* (Harmondsworth 1965) 19-24. Wehrli (1957) examines the ancient roots of a more naturalistic concept of 'das Schöpferische'.

moved from an early date around the poles of the dichotomy between 'craft' (or knowledge and skill) and inspiration. But to this fact we have to add the relative lack of emphasis within classical (and neo-classical) attitudes to art as a whole, in contrast to the modern consensus fostered by Romanticism, on the personal or special qualities of the artist himself.[2] That in this respect Aristotle is largely typical of the tradition has already emerged from the construction of his concept of art around the ideas of *technê*, mimesis and *poiêsis*. These ideas characterise either the objective relation between the artist and the artistic product (*technê*, *poiêsis*), or that between the work of art and reality (mimesis). If the understanding of art is framed entirely in terms of these relations, then it would seem that Aristotle's thought leaves nothing of importance to be predicated of the individual artist as such. In order to seek confirmation or qualification of this inference, it is worthwhile to ask whether attention to particular passages of the *Poetics* allows us to detect any operative assumptions about the source of artistic production in the poet or painter himself.

The issue is one which elicited so unequivocal a response from Plato as to provide us with an important test and point of comparison for Aristotle's views. Plato seems to have followed the fifth-century philosopher Democritus in attributing the force of artistic invention to an inspiration which he was inclined to represent as madness. The case is presented in its most sustained form in the *Ion*, where its corollary, the poet's lack of a systematic or rational skill, a *technê*, is given full weight.[3] While the idea of inspiration had been propounded by poets themselves in order to arrogate a religiously privileged and inimitable status, Plato manages to twist it round so as to lend to it the largely unrespectable appearance of a force which is opposed to true knowledge – the very value which inspiration was supposed to vouchsafe. In the *Ion* the conclusion that poets must be inspired is arrived at ironically as a *pis aller*, for once it is putatively established that poets have no knowledge or expertise which can be intelligibly accounted for or relied upon, there is apparently nothing left to assign to them but an exotic motivation which can be safely – because in the context of the dialogue meaninglessly – clothed in the traditional

---

[2] At Aristoph. *Thesm.* 149-70 there may be a comic allusion to a contemporary view which takes account of the individual nature (*phusis*) of the poet himself, but it is equally a possibility that the idea is a humorous invention.

[3] On poets' lack of knowledge and skill see also *Apol.* 22b-c, *Meno* 99c-d.

language of divine afflatus. By pursuing this polemical line of argument Plato can, in his own terms at least, undermine the status of poets as teachers and educators, and he can reduce the pleasure afforded by art to an irrational type, of low or dubious value. But there remain two potential tensions within the Platonic position as a whole. The first arises from the fact that Plato does at times attempt to rescue the language of inspiration for his own philosophical purposes, as part of his paradoxical enterprise – paradoxical, given the strength of his dismissal of poetic culture – of defining a new philosophical substitute for poetry and its truth-claims: a new *mousikê*, to use a term which itself bears traces of the notion of inspiration.[4] Plato therefore cannot allow more than a specious or limited form of inspiration to poets. But there is also a tension between *any* idea of inspiration and the common Platonic emphasis on mimesis as an activity of mechanical image-making, carried out, in the reductive terms of *Republic* 10, by a kind of inferior craftsman.

While these anomalies within Plato's critique of art are in part due to the fluctuations in his own attitudes, they can also be taken as a reflection of the inherent inadequacy of the inspiration-craft dichotomy for the interpretation of the artist's sources and procedures. Yet, in however stereotyped a form, the two concepts could at least be said to acknowledge the observable gulf which exists between the explicable and inexplicable elements in the production of poetry and art, and it is an immediate question about any theory of art which treats either one of these poles as sufficient in itself, whether it can expect to cope convincingly with the range of relevant phenomena and achievements. There is, it must be said, a *prima facie* case for raising just this question in connection with the *Poetics*. If Plato's treatment of the subject involves inconsistencies (or eristic variations), Aristotle's apparently offers a rigorous but one-sided adherence to a single principle. The *Poetics* creates an unmistakable impression, from the first sentence onwards, of a craft-based view of poetry and art. Again and again Aristotle flatly contradicts both the *Ion* and other germane Platonic passages by asserting and assuming that poetry is a complete *technê*, a rational productive activity whose methods can be both defined and justified.

---

[4] On Platonic *mousikê* see Vicaire 265-7, Dalfen 287-304. For desirable forms of madness in Plato see esp. *Phdr.* 243e ff. (poetry is mentioned at 245a, where the inadequacy of *technê* is noted). On the whole subject cf. E.N. Tigerstedt, *Plato's Idea of Poetical Inspiration* (Helsinki 1969), and see Appendix 2 below, under 55a 32-4.

One relevant negative factor is the likelihood that the concept of inspiration, in its essential religious sense, was not one to which Aristotle could have given serious credence.[5] But if inspiration was discarded, the ostensible consistency and coherence of the craft model of artistic production was nonetheless open to obvious objections: principally, the difficulty of accounting for some of the exceptional achievements of existing Greek poetry, especially the unique status of Homeric epic; but also the challenge of the poets' own claims about the nature of their art. In order to see to what extent Aristotle anticipated the force of such objections, I propose to examine in turn those passages in the *Poetics* where he explicitly touches on the relationship between the artist and his work.

Near the start of the book we are told that some visual artists work by rational skill (*technê*), others by experience or habit (47a 19f.). The contrast is illuminated by, for example, the opening of the *Rhetoric*, where Aristotle observes that all men engage to some extent in the component activities of rhetoric, its primary argumentative aims. But some do so randomly, others by experience: the task of an art (here meaning theory embodied in a treatise) is to explain and systematise the necessary skills (1354a 4ff.). We can therefore deduce a tripartite structure of categories which it will be appropriate to bear in mind: ordinary indiscriminate activity, which will achieve its aims, if at all, only by chance; regularised experience or habit, which develops consistencies of procedure that nevertheless fall short of art; and *technê* itself, in which a self-conscious and rational understanding of the subject establishes secure techniques for success in it. We find, then, in ch. 1 of the *Poetics* a preliminary acknowledgement of the coexistence, at least in the visual arts, of the latter two categories of ability (the first being, of course, here beneath consideration).[6]

[5] *Rhet.* 1408b 19 (poetry is inspired, *entheon*) is sometimes cited as if it suggested otherwise, but the context, where orators too are described as 'inspired', intimates that Ar. is talking metaphorically (perhaps with some irony too) in concession to traditional attitudes: see Hubbard 146 n.3, Russell 78f. Compare the language of 'possession' in a metaphorical sense at e.g. *EN* 1179b 9, in contrast to Plato *Ion* 536c, *Phdr.* 245a. The point is purely psychological, not religious, in the references to *enthousiasmos* as an effect of poetry at *Pol.* 1340a 11, 1341b 34, 1342a 7: cf. ch. VI pp. 190ff. At *EE* 1225a 28-30, it should be noted, Ar.'s discussion of prophetic inspiration emphasises the *involuntary*: this would be inconsistent with *technê*. (Plato's apparent combination of *technê* and inspiration in poetry at *Laws* 719c and in prophecy at *Phdr.* 244c (and cf. Aesch. *Eum.* 17, Soph. *OT* 562) hardly represents a positive doctrine.)

[6] At *Met.* 981a 14-24 Ar. concedes that theory without practice may be inferior to experience alone; experience matters in art because it is possible to have universal knowledge but still make mistakes over particulars: cf. *An.Pr.* 67a 27f., *Pol.* 1269a 11f.,

A further factor seems to be introduced in ch. 4 (48b 22-4, 49a 2-14), where, in sketching the historical development of poetry, Aristotle mentions the 'nature' of individual poets and describes their improvisatory activities as having 'begotten' particular genres.[7] He posits a correspondence between poets and the nature of the works which they produce, or of the genres to whose discovery and development they contribute. I commented in the previous chapter on the general relation in Aristotelian philosophy between human *technê* and the processes of nature, and in the next section I shall draw out some of the implications of this relation for his interpretation of cultural history and tradition; but what calls for immediate attention here is the limitation on the reference to the 'nature' of individual poets, which might at first sight suggest an important qualification on the dominance of *technê* within the *Poetics*.

In the first place, there is no indication of true individualism entering into the early stages of poetry's growth: the 'nature' of each poet is conceived of as a typical characteristic, inclining him, in particular, either to a serious or to a humorous style of performance; it is a heightened form of the universal and natural propensity of humans to mimesis (48b 5ff.). The cultural model which Aristotle here hints at is therefore relatively *im*personal, hypothesising no more than the existence of individuals with a greater than normal aptitude for mimetic experiment. This aspect of the passage is clarified by the fact that the operation of the individual's nature is seen within the larger framework provided by the 'nature' of the genres whose discovery and evolution are in question. Artist and art-form are parts of a compound natural pattern and process, and the relation between them is not a matter of purely contingent historical circumstance. And it is precisely because the phenomenon involves the realisation of a somehow already existing natural potential, that the process will ultimately lead to the stage of *technê*: paradoxically, therefore, Aristotle's acknowledgement of a natural factor in the invention and advancement of poetic genres serves not to reduce the validity of the

---

Rhet. 1393a 17f. On the importance of experience and practice in art see also *EN* 1103a 32-4 and *Protr.* B48 Düring (1961); and for the Aristotelian scheme of sense-perception/memory/experience/art or science see *An.Post.* 100a 3ff., *Met.* 980a 27ff.

 [7] For *phusis* as natural ability cf. Plato *Phdr.* 269d, *Laws* 700d 4, Aristoph. *Thesm.* 167, *Frogs* 810. There is no question in Ar. of *phusis* in the sense of 'inspiration', for which see Plato *Apol.* 22c 1, *Laws* 682a 2, and Democritus fr. 21.

concept of *technê*, but only to reinforce its natural origins and foundations. Even if this passage of the *Poetics* were less elliptical than it is, and even if our ignorance of the early forms of Greek poetry were less grave than it is, it would be inapt to challenge Aristotle on the basis of historical data alone, for what he offers, in embryo, is a set of theory-laden suppositions about the relations between the individual poet, the genre, and the dynamics of cultural change.

These suppositions can be studied further in the passage of ch. 8 (51a 24) where Homer's grasp of the principle of poetic unity is attributed uncertainly to either *technê* or his natural endowment (*phusis*).[8] It seems most appropriate to relate this reference to Homer's 'nature' to the more general use of the term in ch. 4 just considered, and to treat it not as an acceptance of the possibility of a purely personal source of poetic achievement, unintelligible without the supposition of unique individuality, but simply as a specific application of the idea of an affinity between the artist and the natural requirements of his art. There are, in other words, despite Aristotle's recognition of Homer's greatness, no Romantic overtones of 'natural genius' here, for the connotations of free and inimitable creativity attaching to such a concept are alien to Aristotle's underlying cultural teleology. On contextual grounds alone we can discern the limitations of Aristotle's point: the very pairing of *technê* and 'nature' bespeaks a *technê*-oriented point of view; it is simply not a conjunction which would be utilised in this way by anyone who believed in the essentially inspirational or strongly creative character of poetry, since it inescapably implies that *technê could* achieve the same results, whether or not it did so in this case. Moreover, the feature of Homeric epic which Aristotle here commends is not an unrepeatable achievement, but a grasp of the fundamental principle of poetic unity and organisation on which the *Poetics* places maximum emphasis. There is, therefore, no compromise on the treatise's central assumptions: the apparent concession is made primarily for obvious historical reasons, in that a *technê* of poetry needs to be regarded as the outcome and fruition of a period of actual experiment and experience, and could not be projected back with complete plausibility onto the early period of epic.

There is also a historical dimension in the next pair of passages to

[8] With this antithesis compare Sophocles' alleged remark on Aeschylus, *apud* Athen. 428f. At *Met.* 1025b 22f. Ar. mentions intelligence (*nous*) or 'some faculty' alongside *technê* as possible sources of productive activity (*poiêsis*).

be cited. In ch. 13 (53a 17-22) Aristotle claims that tragic poets
originally picked their mythical subjects arbitrarily, but that the best
tragedies now concentrate on the sufferings of just a select group of
families. The point is reformulated and expanded at 54a 10-12: it was
originally not by rational choice and art but by chance that poets
discovered how to achieve the right effect in their tragedies.[9] These
passages deserve a brief mention as illustrating, negatively at least,
Aristotle's attitude to poetic invention. Aristotle appeals to current
practice to confirm his prescriptive theory of the ideal tragedy: the
theory, that is, is not directly based on practice, but can receive
secondary ratification from it; for the theory purports to analyse the
essence of the genre and its inherent potential, which emerges not
simply from scrutiny of existing practice but from rational reflection
on its 'nature'. The implication of this is that when practising
tragedians are successful, their success is a matter of the
materialisation of generic potential, not of their own original insight
or inventiveness. We can trace here, therefore, the tripartite scheme
which I cited earlier: the original choices of tragic material represent
ordinary random activity, whose occasional success would be due
only to chance; out of this emerges the gradual regularisation of
experience, which may indeed be the level at which some tragedians
still work; and, finally, the discoveries of the genre's natural potential
which experiment has brought to light can now be rationalised into
the art of which the *Poetics* is the theoretical embodiment. The
underlying teleology, operating through the stages of cultural
evolution, is not difficult to discern: the primary sources of poetic art
are located, once again, beyond the individual, and even, in a sense,
as I shall argue in the next section, beyond strictly human tradition.

Some might argue, however, that what has been so far said needs
to be qualified in the light of ch. 17, 55a 32-4 – a vexed passage, since
the insertion of one word, as advocated by some scholars, virtually
inverts its sense.[10] Despite some difficulty over the wording of the

---

[9] Cf. *Met*. 1034a 9f., *EN* 1140a 17-20 on the relation between art and chance.

[10] See the long note of Lucas (1968) on 55a 32-4 for a good discussion. Note that
ekstatikos (55a 34) is not easy to reconcile with Ar.'s general conception of poetry: in
addition to the passages cited by Bywater on 55a 34 see esp. *EE* 1229a 25-27 on
uncontrollable passion (including that of wild boars!). For Ar.'s general attitude to
inspiration cf. n. 5 above.

Ar.'s idea of composition at 55a 22ff. may have been readily intelligible in a society
where recitation and dictation were familiar; it is wholly and anachronistically
misconstrued by Else (1957) 489f. Compare the comically exaggerated behaviour of
Agathon in Aristoph. *Thesm*. 101ff. (cited on p.114).

preceding passage, it is clear enough that Aristotle is discussing the convincing presentation of emotion by the poet, and is arguing for a psychological link between the poet's technique of composition and the achievement of this aim. His suggestions bring the poet into line both with the actor and with the rhetorician, and the injunction that the poet should visualise his dramatic events as vividly as possible (as if he were present: a traditional formulation), even to the point of acting them out with gestures, loses its superficial peculiarity once we take account of the tradition of the poet-producer in the Athenian theatre (and also recall the standard practice of reciting poetry aloud). The rhetorician would similarly need to imagine and anticipate how a piece of oratory, with its full vocal and visual delivery matching the language, could effectively communicate emotion. As the text stands, Aristotle concludes his suggestions by saying: 'therefore poetry is the task of a naturally gifted person or manic one; for the first is inventive, the second ecstatic.' If this is allowed to stand, then we must take him to be identifying two types or degrees of nature suitable for the poet. If, however, we insert a word to convert 'or' into 'rather than', then we actually produce a rejection of inspiration, in favour of a flexible quality of mind, a type of imagination,[11] of a kind which can be controlled and, so the tenor of the passage as a whole intimates, deliberately cultivated. It is in fact this latter point which deserves to be emphasised, whether or not we are prepared to alter the text. In other words, even if we accept that Aristotle here makes a concessive gesture towards the traditional notion of inspiration, this is outweighed not only by the fact that he does so nowhere else in the *Poetics*, but also by the clear implication of the full context in the first part of ch. 17 that the imaginative requirements of poetic writing, though they may be assisted by certain natural talents, can be accommodated and practised within the framework of a *technê*-based concept of the subject. Even if these considerations do not compel us to emend the text, they do, I maintain, show that nothing in this section of the *Poetics* disturbs the balance of Aristotle's general argument.

Continuity of interpretation is possible between ch. 17 and Aristotle's description of metaphor in ch. 22 (59a 6f.) as 'the only thing one cannot acquire from someone else, and a sign of natural ability': first, because the occurrence of the term for natural ability –

---

[11] For the reference to imagination at 55a 23 see ch. VI n.17.

euphuïa, the noun cognate with the adjective used of the talented poetic nature in ch. 17 – helps to confirm that Aristotle's main alternative to a capacity founded purely on *technê* is not inspiration, but a disposition less remote from ordinary mental experience;[12] and secondly because the recognition of metaphor as exceptional unquestionably implies that most elements or resources of poetic production *are* firmly within the ambit of a rational and teachable art. The point is reinforced by the parallel passage in the *Rhetoric* (1405a 3ff.), where alongside the acknowledgement of the special status of metaphor we also find some analytic treatment of its types and properties, designed to indicate that even metaphor must be controlled by general canons of appropriateness (here rhetorical, but there are equivalents for poetry). The natural endowment which enables a poet to excel at metaphor is therefore productive of results which, although unteachable, can be judged from the secure standpoint of the art; and this is confirmed by the definition of the endowment not as a mysterious instinct but as 'the capacity to see resemblances' (59a 8).

Aristotle's brief remarks on metaphor have the paradoxical force of conceding the limits of *technê* only in such a way as to strengthen the underlying sense of its dominance within the *Poetics'* conception of poetry, as of the mimetic arts in general. We have here, then, as in the other passages considered above, testimony to what could anyway be taken to be an implication of the treatise-form itself, namely the belief that poetry is a rationally intelligible and teachable art, because it rests, like all Aristotelian arts, on determinate and discoverable principles which are rooted in man's nature and in his relation to the rest of the natural world. If Aristotle can be said to enter the traditional debate about the sources of poetic activity, he does so with a supreme assurance which allows him hardly even to mention the opposing point of view: we may infer that it is his intention not so much to contradict the possibility of inspiration as to

[12] *Euphuïa* corresponds to *phusis* as used elsewhere in the *Poetics*. *Euphuïa* and practice are contrasted at *Rhet.* 1410b 7f., analogously to *Poet.* 51a 24. The language used for the uniqueness of metaphor recurs in a moral context (where, however, the sentiment is not Ar.'s own) at *EN* 1114b 9-12.

It is perhaps surprising that Ar. nowhere in the *Poetics* employs *sophos* terminology for poets or artists (for its currency cf. ch. I n.16), despite its close connection with *technê*, as e.g. at *EN* 1141a 9-12 (of the visual arts). He may have been deterred by his use of *sophia* as a synonym for the highest philosophy, though *sophos* does occur, applied to poets, in *Protr.* B43 Düring (1961), = fr. 58 Rose.

demonstrate that an understanding of poetry need not take any account of it. Given the use made by Plato of the idea of inspiration, there can be no doubt that Aristotle's virtual silence on this score is meant to be eloquent.

It is important to emphasise that the various references in the *Poetics* to the natural aptitudes and abilities of poets justify little or no qualification on the conclusion just stated. The main reason for this is that, as I explained in the previous chapter, the notions of nature and art are ultimately complementary within Aristotelian philosophy. The ends of art, and its basis in human behaviour, are given by nature: by man's tendency, in the case of mimesis, to try to understand the world by producing representations of it and taking pleasure in the experience of these. If, therefore, certain poets (or other artists) can be said to depend on their natural endowments, rather than on a systematic craft, that offers no challenge to the notion of the craft as such, but only a comment on a contingent factor such as the stage of development reached by a particular genre at a particular time, or the circumstances in which a given individual happens to produce poetry. For if someone is able to rely on nature in this way, that is only because there is an underlying alignment between human potential for mimetic invention and the natural cultural movement towards the realisation of generic goals, that is of forms of poetry which have a precise scope for the mimesis of certain aspects of life. Nature is the starting point from which, by processes of experiment and discovery, progress may be made towards the mature genres of art in which the perfected techniques of a productive craft will be discernible to the analytical eye of the theorist, and become codifiable into rational canons for the continuation of the art. And when this mature stage of the elaborated art is reached, the fulfilment is one which, to complete the conceptual circle, Aristotle holds to be a manifestation of a natural goal accomplished (49a 14f.).

But if this is a just statement of the Aristotelian position, we are now equipped to observe a curious feature of it. The traditional dichotomy between craft and inspiration can be formulated as a distinction between a view of the artist as the master of productive or inventive skills, and a view of him as one who has access to a force which derives from outside and works through him. The tenor of the *Poetics'* advocacy of a strongly craft-based conception of poetry is such as to confirm the sense of art as a procedure in which the maker rationally controls and shapes his material. Yet, if my elucidation of

the relation between *technê* and nature in Aristotle's philosophy is
right, then it seems that from this larger perspective the artist may
once again come to be seen as a medium through which the
operations of natural and greater forces are channelled. Inspiration,
it could be argued, has been 'naturalised' within the Aristotelian
view of art. To discover whether this judgement can be sustained, it
is necessary now to open the argument up from the narrower
question of the individual artist's resources, to the broader issues of
Aristotle's treatment of poetic history and tradition.

*

I tried to show in the previous chapter how, in the interpretation of
Aristotle's concepts of art and of aesthetic pleasure, it is important to
refer to the naturalistic framework of his whole philosophy. The
conclusions reached there may be complemented, and given more
concrete application, by a consideration of the hints which the *Poetics*
contains on the historical status of poetic genres within the theory. A
number of passages in the *Poetics* reveal an Aristotelian belief in the
natural essence of genres and their attributes. The following are
among the most important:[13]

Ch. 4, 49a 14f.: 'and after undergoing many changes, tragedy ceased
  to change, once it had acquired its own nature.'[14]
Ch. 4, 49a 23f.: 'when dialogue came into being, nature itself
  discovered the metre which suited it.'
Ch. 7, 51a 9f.: 'the limit [of dramatic size] which corresponds with
  the very nature of the material ...'
Ch. 24, 60a 4f.: 'nature itself teaches [poets] to choose the metre
  which suits an epic structure.'

'Nature' in the first of these passages is a matter of the whole generic
potential of tragedy. In the second and fourth quotations, 'nature
itself' refers to particular elements of the genres and to what Aristotle

---

[13] Others are: 49b 24, the definition of tragedy's 'being' or 'essence' (*ousia*), which
is the same as its 'nature' and 'goal' (*phusis* and *telos*: cf. e.g. *Met.* 1015a 11ff.); the *phusis*
terms at 50b 28f.; and the analogies with living creatures at 50b 34-51a 4, 59a 20. Cf.
Pfeiffer 68f., who underestimates, however, the degree to which teleology is to be
understood literally in this context.

[14] For some Aristotelian parallels to the pattern of tragedy's development see Else
(1957) 153.

takes to be the given natural attributes of individual rhythms:[15] in both these cases too, in fact, 'the very nature of the genre' would be an equally apposite translation. In the third passage, where Aristotle has just before appealed to natural standards of beauty (illustrated by the forms of living creatures, 50b 34ff.), there appears to be a compound concern with objective standards or criteria of unity and beauty, as these apply to the plot-structure of tragedy. It is particularly striking that in three of these cases, either 'nature' or the genre itself is the subject of a clause. The formulation is indicative of the belief that the significance of the history of poetry resides not in the contingent acts or inventions of individuals, but in processes of a teleological kind in which the fundamental determinants are truly natural. These passages, then, collectively create a presumption that Aristotle's application of the language of 'nature' to the history of poetic genres is neither a mere metaphor, nor simply the codification of the contingent path made for itself by cumulative poetic tradition. That this presumption is merited can best be confirmed by a closer look at the first of the passages listed, for it is here that the context is fullest and gives us the clearest view of the character of the argument and its underlying assumptions.

It is hardly accidental that what history there is in the sketch of Greek poetry's development in *Poetics* 4 and 5 is obscure and questionable in a number of respects; and to remark that Aristotle perhaps here fails to match even his own rudimentary and limiting definition of history in ch. 9 of the treatise is not to indulge in irony at his expense, but to suggest a point of importance about these two chapters. Whether indeed Aristotle can by his own standards be deemed to be even attempting to write any history here is at least doubtful: for if, as ch. 9 claims, history deals only with particulars, it cannot be the appropriate mode for Aristotle's argument in a passage where he is manifestly concerned to trace the pattern of natural poetic growth *beneath* the particulars. Thus the accent of the argument falls, for example, on the way in which Homer prefigures both tragedy and comedy, and on the supposed way in which, once these latter genres have been discovered, they supersede epic and are turned to by poets whose 'natures' are correlated with the poetic types which they are instrumental in advancing. If some of the precise historical details get garbled (or lost) in the course of the

[15] On rhythm see ch. II n.29.

argument, that is of less importance to Aristotle than the discernment of the larger pattern.[16]

When, therefore, tragedy is described as moving through various stages of growth and change before it attains its 'nature', Aristotle's claim ought to be confronted at face-value. It should not be assumed that, because he sometimes draws a basic distinction between the principles of nature and art, he cannot also see the latter in the larger perspective of his view of nature. This is precisely what he does in the case of poetry. While individual poems are directly the products of individual makers, it is still open to Aristotle to regard the evolution of a genre, as he does in *Poetics* 4, as a matter of naturalistic teleology. If the course of tragedy's history depended primarily on the choices or the originality of individuals, and the cumulative tradition arising out of them, then a conclusion concerning the genre's 'nature' could be no more than the most tenuous metaphor, and Aristotle could not afford to be as brief and elliptical as he is over the data of innovations.[17] It is because he considers these to be stages in the growth towards a perfect form, and not as independently valid moments of cultural history, that the emphasis of his account is placed on the supposed direction of progress within the development of the genre. And it is necessary to perceive that even the achievement of the *telos* is not strictly located in historical terms: to say, as is commonly done, that ch. 4 implicitly attributes perfection in tragedy to Sophocles, is to obscure the abstract and *a priori* quality of this section. Aristotle had no need to identify perfection with a particular playwright: the nature of the full-grown genre is precisely the subject of the subsequent chapters of the treatise, and one might well suppose that the ultimate vindication for Aristotle of his claims about tragedy's evolution is the possibility of the *Poetics* itself.[18]

[16] On Ar.'s reconstruction of literary history cf. Dale 176f. n.2. Lord (1974) does not accept that Ar.'s approach in this chapter is theoretical, but the contorted argument which he uses to show that Ar.'s case is lucid and coherent helps to confirm the very opposite. Cf. also ch. IX nn.6 and 25 below.

[17] The vagueness is particularly striking if we suppose Ar. to have been carrying out his documentary research on tragedy (cf. Appendix 1 p. 328), and if we compare the remains of his *On Poets*: frs. 71, ?72, 75 (Rose) touch on matters of chronology. Moreover, the whole early history of Greek poetry, including questions of chronology and influence, had received attention before Ar.: see esp. the frs. of Glaucus of Rhegium (Lanata 270-7), regrettably ignored by Pfeiffer.

[18] Attempts to locate the roots of Ar.'s theory in a particular playwright are unnecessary and inconclusive: e.g. Söffing 217-26 (Sophocles' *OT* – a common view), Kannicht *Poetica* 8 (1976) 327f. n.5 (Euripides), Fuhrmann (1973) 12 (Sophocles *and* Euripides), and, least convincingly of all, the articles of Webster and Kitto

The sketch of poetry's development, then, in ch. 4 (and, to a lesser extent, ch. 5 too), is in Aristotle's own terms largely *ahistorical*. Its chief purpose is to discern a natural pattern of progress towards a natural *telos*: that is, an end or fulfilment which is intrinsic and determined, not simply the result of choices, processes and acts which might have turned out otherwise. It is worth reminding ourselves at this point of Aristotle's view (p. 50 above) that all arts (*technai*) have been repeatedly discovered and evolved in the history of the world. What Aristotle therefore rules out is a purely cultural and man-made tradition, and one whose essential course can only be anlaysed *post eventum* as a matter of historical detail.[19] It is on the basis of such an alternative explanation of the development of tragedy and other genres that Aristotle's naturalistic assumptions can be questioned – and, indeed, *ought* to be questioned by anyone who sees the implications of his scheme for, among other things, Aeschylean tragedy.[20] Nor is there any danger of conceptual anachronism in such a challenge, since the issue between a naturalistic or teleological and a contingent historical understanding of cultural development can be traced back to the roots of a distinction which had been a central discovery of fifth-century Greek thought: that between nature (*phusis*), on the one hand, and tradition, cultural continuity, and man-made convention (*nomos*), on the other. Aristotle was of course familiar with this antithesis, but the firmness of his allegiance to *phusis* as the ultimate explanatory principle, in

---

(fourth-century tragedy). But Radt (1971), esp. 201-5, goes too far in concluding that Ar.'s ideal is wholly 'unhistorical'.

[19] For a sketch of a flexible notion of tradition see Quinton 97-101.

[20] Aeschylus is the most scantily treated of the major tragedians in the *Poetics*. 49a 15-18 implies an important historical role for him, but seems to place him before the attainment of the canonical *phusis* (*pace* Brown 3-5) and also gives a hint of the problematic status of the chorus in Ar.'s theory of poetry (see ch. VIII below). 56a 17 gives a brief, complimentary mention, 58b 19-24 an unfavourable one. 60a 32 is also unfavourable, but may not refer to Aeschylus's *Mysians*. 55a 4-6 cites the *Choephori* in a garbled fashion for the second-best type of tragic recognition. The considerable scope of Aeschylean lyrics, with their concomitant dramatic techniques, is probably the main reason for Ar.'s relative lack of interest in the playwright; but the theory does not seem accommodating to trilogies either: cf. Vahlen (1911) 254 and note, Söffing 195-204. Aeschylus, it should be noted, is by far the least often cited of the great trio in the corpus as a whole: the only references outside the *Poetics* appear to be at *HA* 633a 19ff., *EN* 1111a 10, and *Rhet.* 1388a 8. For the possibility that *Poet.* 53b 9 alludes to Aeschylus (though I take the primary reference to be to fourth-century *producers*) see not only 56a 2f. and the usual citation from the *Vita Aeschyli* (e.g. Lucas (1968) ad loc.) but also Aristoph. *Frogs* 834. Cf. Taplin 44-6.

poetry as elsewhere, is uncompromising.[21] And it is in this light that
the acknowledgements of individual contributions to generic
development in *Poetics* 4 and 5 must be seen: the recognition of the
importance of Homer or Sophocles is outweighed by the fact that
tragedy can in the final resort be made the proper subject of its own
evolution.[22]

I suggest, then, that the considerations adduced in this section
complement those put forward in the previous chapter on the relation
between nature and art in Aristotelian philosophy. The result of this
is to provide corroboration both that Aristotle's notion of poetic *technê*
has implications which do not conform to ordinary Greek (or
modern) ideas of craft, and also that the elucidation of this
Aristotelian notion carries us not into a deeper sense of the artist's
own creative resources, but into the wider, impersonal perspective of
cultural teleology. Hence, behind the *Poetics'* recurring references to
the aim, function and potential of tragedy, there is a strongly *a priori*
and prescriptive set of presuppositions, which derive from the
theorist's own perception of the natural history of poetry and of the
intrinsic perfection of which tragedy is capable, rather than from the
strict observation of established practice or the major existing
achievements in the genre. Aristotle's assurance is such as to tell us
in advance what standards any further achievements in the genre
would satisfy; and if it appears ironic that, as a result of the
irreversible decline into which we can now see that Greek tragedy
had slipped, this assurance was never to receive historical
vindication, it may be doubted whether Aristotle would have
regarded that as in any way invalidating his philosophy of poetry.

*

I turn, finally in this chapter, to another of the central tenets of that
philosophy. The concept of unity, in one version or another, is one of
the most pervasive and arguably indispensable criteria in the
understanding of art. Yet its fundamental status makes it
exceptionally difficult to come to terms with on the level of articulate

[21] For the antithesis see e.g. *Int.*16a 26-8 (linguistic forms), *EN* 1134b 18ff.
(justice), *Pol.* 1253b 21f. (slavery), 1257b 11 (money).

[22] In other fields Ar. sometimes acknowledges the importance of individuals in
historical development: see esp. *Met.* 993a 30-b 19. On the particular importance of the
starting-point (*archê*) in the arts (n.b. for Homer's status in Ar.'s scheme) see *SE* 183b
17ff., *EN* 1098a 21-6.

theory, for not only do presuppositions concerning it lie so deeply embedded in discourse about art as to be hard to bring clearly to the surface, but unity is by its very nature a notion which tends to coalesce with, or transform itself into, other categories employed in the evaluation of works of art. It is certainly to Aristotle's credit in the *Poetics* that he offers some firm and unambiguous indications of the canon of unity which he brings to bear on poetry, and while the tendency for unity to merge into other concepts is sometimes in evidence here too (so that, for example, it cannot effectively be separated from the *Poetics'* standard of beauty),[23] Aristotle's efforts at definition do give us some solid grounds on which to base an assessment of the vital function of unity within his theory of poetry. It will also be seen that, although the concept of unity is elaborated in specific application to poetic genres, Aristotle holds it to be basic to the experience of all mimetic art.

The notion of poetic unity is insinuated at the very start of the treatise in connection with that of *muthos*, 'plot' or 'plot-structure'. Aristotle refers in his opening sentence to the construction of plots in such a way as to imply that this is an essential part of all poetic composition, and the verbal idea of 'construction' involved here might itself be aptly glossed as 'to make a unity of'. We consequently find that the noun cognate with this verb is used by Aristotle in one of his periphrases for plot – namely, 'the structure of events' (*sustasis tôn pragmatôn*). It becomes evident in the course of the work that a poetic plot-structure can indeed only be properly so called when it is unified in the requisite ways. Aristotle builds the requirement of unity into his definition of tragedy as 'the mimesis of an action ... which is complete and of ample scale'. These elements in his definition he proceeds to expand and clarify in chs. 7 and 8, where he produces the formula of 'beginning, middle and end', as well as the analogy between the beauty and unity of poetic structures and the same properties in living creatures. *À propos* of this last point, it needs to be firmly stated that Aristotle's principles of order and beauty are

---

[23] Ar.'s notion of beauty rests primarily on criteria of form, order and proportion: esp. *Met.* 1078a 36ff. Ar., unlike Plato, separates beauty from ethical goodness: ibid. 31ff. For artistic proportion (*summetria*) see *Pol.* 1284b 8-10, and cf. Pollitt 14-22, 160-2 on the general concept. But *summetria* is insufficient for beauty: magnitude, too, is required (*Poet.* 50b 25f., *EN* 1123b 7f.). The claim of Else (1938) 187 that beauty is the 'master-concept' of the *Poetics* is part of an over-zealous attempt to connect Ar. with the doctrines of Plato's *Philebus*. For appropriate caution see Butcher 161f., and cf. Svoboda ch. 2.

not 'biological', as often claimed; they are universal standards, applying, as he affirms, to 'everything which consists of parts', and the case of living creatures is just one instance and illustration of them.[24] Neither the beginning-middle-end schema nor the comparison of a poetic structure with a living form is peculiarly Aristotelian; both occur in Plato, most strikingly in the remarks made on unity in the *Phaedrus*.[25] But what does deserve to be regarded as characteristically Aristotelian is the further underpin-ning given to the concept of unity or integration by its exposition, in chs. 7 and 8, as an interlocking set of factors and criteria.[26] Since this compound concept of unity – whose constituents are wholeness, order, singleness, and appropriate scale – concerns the representation of human action, the perception of poetic unity, as will be confirmed, rests inescapably on the cognitive understanding of the action portrayed. Aristotle's interpretation of unity is emphatically not aestheticist.

This is true even of the dimension of appropriate scale or size, which may at first sight strike a modern reader, in view of the analogy with living creatures, as a purely formal matter of beauty. But what this analogy signifies for Aristotle is not the mere sense-experience of an animal's shape and proportions, but the understanding (by teleological criteria) of the interrelated functions of its parts; scale cannot, from this point of view, be divorced from purpose.[27] Correspondingly, the appropriate scale for a tragedy is

[24] The scale and unity of a poetic *muthos* can, from the point of view of the analogy between art and nature, be seen as the imposition of standards of the kind which in nature are intrinsic (e.g. *De An.* 416a 16f.). The essential thinking is teleological (see *De An.* 412b 8f., and cf. n.27 below) not 'biological'. This last term is often applied to Ar.'s view of tragedy or to his methodology without sufficient reason: e.g. Atkins vol. l, 77, Henn 2 ('the plot is the skeleton of the animal' - but the plot is the *soul* (50a 38)!), Rees (1981) 28ff. (mistaking *logical* concepts and method which are used in the biological works for being themselves biological). Aristotelian biology is itself subsumed within the framework of larger philosophical ideas of form, function and purpose.

[25] See Appendix 2, under ch. 7's references. Cf. also Gorgias fr.11.5, and see Brink (1971) 77ff.

[26] The point is made tersely by Hubbard 100 n.4. Teichmüller vol. l 68f. (cf. vol. 2 436-40) argues for a strict separation of wholeness and unity (or 'singleness'), but the former is defined by Ar. so as to presuppose the latter (even if the reverse need not always hold). Cf. *Met.* 1023b 26ff.

[27] Perhaps the passage which best confirms this is *Pol.* 1326a 34ff., where the interrelations between excellence (beauty), scale and function are spelt out; cf. also *PA* 645a 23-6 for the teleological aspect of beauty. Given Ar.'s way of looking at nature, it is inconceivable that the perception of order (*taxis: Poet.* 50b 37) could be divorced from

defined, as are all the other aspects of unity, by reference to the cardinal principle of 'necessity or probability', which represents the internal and intelligible cohesion of the action dramatised in the poetry. It is, therefore, in the scrutiny of the notion of necessity and probability that we must look for a fuller understanding of Aristotelian unity. The correctness of this procedure is corroborated by the way in which the observations of *Poetics* 7 and 8 lead up to the central philosophical generalisations of ch. 9, where we encounter the heaviest density of reference to necessity and probability in the treatise. Although I shall retain the phrase necessity and/or probability for convenience of description, it is obviously important that it should be taken unprejudicially in its Aristotelian sense, and that any irrelevant associations of the English terms should be disregarded.[28] Aristotle cites the pair of ideas again and again in the main chapters of the treatise, either singly or, more often, in combination. Little is offered, however, by way of direct explanation of necessity and probability, though ch. 9 in particular gives some important clues. It is clear that we are dealing here with terminology with which Aristotle presupposed some familiarity, and for whose interpretation it is therefore useful to draw on assistance from his wider philosophy.

The more problematic of the two concepts is undoubtedly necessity, since the language of necessity is employed by Aristotle outside the *Poetics* in a wide variety of contexts and applications, the fine details of which are beyond the scope of my argument.[29] On the broadest level, necessity can be considered as a category of cause or explanation; together with nature, chance and human agency, necessity belongs to the scheme of four major types of cause at *EN* 1112a 32f. Within the framework of this scheme necessity reappears in more specific forms. It is evidently most pertinent to its place in the

---

the understanding of the function or purpose of the structure and its parts; compare the relation between form and intelligibility in the periodic style defined at *Rhet.* 1409a 35ff. It is instructive to observe how Lucas (1968) on 50b 37, while grasping the essential point about the teleological view of beauty, struggles with it because of his own concern with 'aesthetic satisfaction': cf. ch. II n.27.

[28] 'Probable' and 'probability' have been used in this context since at least the time of neo-classicists such as Dryden and Rymer, and it is difficult to think of a less imperfect translation for the purpose. The main qualification to attach to the term is the exclusion of statistically based ideas, *pace* House 60, whose discussion of necessity and probability (58-62) is otherwise illuminating.

[29] For a short survey see Sorabji 222-4.

Poetics to ask what part necessity plays in the sphere of human action,
since the poetic plot-structure, for whose coherence and unity
Aristotle invokes necessity as a principle, is precisely a structure of
actions. One of the clearest statements of the role of necessity in
human action can be found in the first Book of the *Rhetoric*, where it
is said that of those actions which men themselves do not cause
necessity is one of the two chief explanations, the other being chance
(1368b 32ff.). But necessity in this context can be subdivided into
nature and compulsion, and when in this same passage Aristotle
draws up his final list of the seven causes or explanations of human
action, it is these two particular forces, rather than necessity as such,
which he includes. Where action at least is concerned, therefore,
necessity encroaches on the territory of nature, and is clearly
distinguished only from chance and from the various internal motive
forces of human agency (desire, reason, etc.).

Elsewhere in the *Rhetoric*, however, Aristotle makes the
observation that little or nothing in the area of human action can be
attributed to necessity (1357a 22ff.). He does so in connection with
the subject of rhetorical arguments (enthymemes) and the kind of
premises which can be used in them; and he moves from the point
that most human actions could be other than they are, to the
conclusion that rhetorical 'syllogisms' (which consist of propositions
about action) will generally have the force only of probability, not of
necessity. This passage helps to illustrate what can be argued on
more substantial grounds, that Aristotle's notions of causal and
logical necessity are not altogether separable, and there is no good
reason why we should have to make a choice between the two in
attempting to relate the necessity of the *Poetics* to parts of the larger
philosphical system.[30] In the case of unity of dramatic plot-structure,
causal necessity might be thought to be more immediately relevant,
since it is evident in most of the treatise's references to the principle
that what is at stake is the causal sequence of the human actions
which constitute the material of the plot: 'it makes a great difference
whether things happen because of, or only after, what precedes
them.'[31] But the *perception* of dramatic sequence and structure is
comparable to the understanding of a logical or quasi-logical
argument; the audience's sense of intelligible structure is a matching

[30] Cf. Sorabji 223. There is insufficient reason to follow Else (1957) 295 n. 30, 297,
and 303 n.7, in taking *sumbainein* at 51a 13 and b 9 to mean 'follow logically'.
[31] 52a 20f.: cf. e.g. *An.Post.* 73b 10ff., *Rhet.* 1401b 31.

response to the causality within the plot.

It is for this reason, among others, that there is for Aristotle an affinity or analogy between poetry and rhetoric. One indication of the awareness of this is precisely the common occurrence of the conjoined concepts of necessity and probability in his treatments of the two subjects. Just as the orator constructs arguments with a view to what his audience will understand and be prepared to believe, so the playwright must order the material of his plot-structure in such a way as to convince his audience of its intelligibility as a sequence of human actions. In both cases there is, in the strict sense, a subjective and an objective side to the matter. For the orator, the subjective resides in what his hearers can reasonably be expected to believe; the objective consists in the claims which his arguments make to represent the truth, the facts of the case. For the playwright, the subjective element is of the same kind; but the objective inheres in the action which he portrays by mimesis.[32] Before returning to the question of how necessity can fit into this, I turn now directly to probability (*eikos*).

Aristotle defines *eikos*, again in the *Rhetoric*, as 'that which happens for the most part' (1357a 34): a concept for which I have accepted the translation 'probability', but which could be rendered, depending on the precise setting, as likelihood, plausibility, or generality. *Eikos* represents, therefore, a degree of regularity or consistency which falls short of the invariable or the necessary. This is probability in its objective aspect noted above, and is equally applicable to the propositions of the orator's argument and to the actions which a dramatic plot-structure comprises: and it is on this plane that Aristotle can juxtapose general considerations of probability with the known facts of reality, as he does at *Rhet.* 1400a 7. But probability also has a subjective dimension, and it is in this respect that it can be described as a central principle – perhaps *the* central principle – of rhetoric, the foundation of the rhetorical function of persuasion. Subjectively, probability is to be seen in terms of what people suppose and are prepared to believe – their common assumptions and prejudices. From this point of view, rhetorical *eikos* can be conceived

---

[32] For the subjective-objective dichotomy note *Rhet.* 1402b 15: arguments from probability concern things 'which either *are* or are *thought to be* usual'. A similar ambivalence can be discerned in Plato's *Phaedrus*, where *eikos* is defined as 'the plausible' (*pithanon*: 272d-e) and hence as 'what most people think likely' (273a), yet it can also be said that *eikos* involves a likeness to the truth (273d).

and analysed not so much by reference to objective regularities as to the mentality of an audience, the set of attitudes, suppositions and expectations which most of them share and to which, if he is to be persuasive, the orator's arguments must conform and appeal.[33]

But the subjective and objective aspects of probability are, of course, potentially complementary, and the subjective may be thought to mirror or reflect the objective (though some, hardly Aristotle, would invert the relationship). The difference between them depends on one's point of reference: if the focus is on an audience, and on the task of persuading or convincing them, then it is the subjective sense of probability which is more appropriate; if on the inherent relations between the components of an argument or an equivalent structure of thought, then the objective sense is predominant. It can now be additionally noted that probability is parallel to necessity in virtue of the fact that it has a status which bears both on logic and on causality. On the one hand, *eikos* can be used to categorise the conclusion of an argument as plausible but not certain. On the other, it may describe a causal regularity which is less than that of necessity. In both these senses however, it is unquestionable that Aristotle regards probability as much more characteristic of matters of human action than necessity.

This latter point raises a question about the necessity-and-probability principle of the *Poetics*, to which we can now return with the wider evidence for these two concepts in mind. If necessity scarcely enters into the sphere of human action, and therefore into the construction of dramatic plots which represent such action, why does Aristotle repeatedly mention both necessity and probability, rather than simply the latter, as the requisite canons of poetic unity? If an answer to this question is possible, it will need to emerge from an attempt to piece together the implications of all the relevant passages of the treatise, beginning with the least elliptical of them in ch. 9. Here Aristotle invokes necessity and probability as the defining feature of the proper subject-matter of poetry. Poetry deals, he says, not with things that are known to have happened, but with 'the kinds of events which might happen and which are possible according to

---

[33] Note the connection between *eikos* and plausibility (*pithanon*) at 61b 11-15, *Rhet.* 1400a 8f. See also *An.Pr.* 70a 2ff., where *eikos* is defined as an agreed premise, i.e. 'what people know to be, or not to be, the case for the most part'; similarly ps.-Ar. *Rh.Alex.* 1428a 26-29a 20. Note that *Poet.* 56b 2-7 indicates a connection, or analogy, between rhetorical *eikos* and the implicit *eikos* of the dramatic plot.

probability or necessity'. It is this which, as he goes on to state, makes the poet's material 'more philosophical' than the historian's, for the poet is concerned with general propositions or universals, by which Aristotle means 'the sorts of things which certain sorts of people will say or do, according to probability or necessity'.[34] These formulations have a deceptive simplicity about them, and as much as anything in the work they signal Aristotle's concern with abstract theorising rather than practical protreptic. This is not to question that on one level Aristotle shows in this passage a grasp of the need for a dramatic structure to conform to what I have called subjective probability: that is, to convince an audience of the plausibility of the plot. But that is not his emphasis, either here or elsewhere in the *Poetics*. If it were, it would be difficult, for one thing, to explain the telling reference to the nature of philosophy. The implicit connection with rhetoric, carried by the notion of *eikos*, is insufficient to account for Aristotle's concern in ch. 9, which is more with the status of poetic content itself (the causal sequence of the action) than with its direct relation to the mentality of the audience.[35]

Ch. 9 is, in other words, directed more towards the objective presentation than the subjective reception of the general propositions which the poet's dramatisation of human action embodies – more towards their intrinsic validity, in terms of necessity or probability, than their capacity to convince an audience (whose credence will anyway, it is assumed, follow from successful plot-construction). This accords not only with Aristotle's general reluctance to appeal to the mentality of audiences as a standard of poetic practice (though he is occasionally prepared to do so in a negative fashion), but also with the fact that the work's other references to necessity and probability show little inclination to emphasise the quasi-rhetorical element of persuasiveness, but firmly imply that what is at issue is the inherent credibility and intelligibility of the poetic plot-structure. If ch. 9 concentrates on the status of poetic meaning in comparison to the

[34] 51b 8f.: cf. the similar formulation at *De An.* 434a 17f. On universals see n.38 below.

[35] One important divergence between rhetorical and poetic *eikos* is that in the former various types of manipulation are both possible and pragmatically necessary (given an opponent, audience resistance, and other factors): see e.g. *Rhet.* 1395b lff. on appeals to vulgar prejudice. Such things have a slighter place in poetry: *Poet.* 60a 18f. perhaps suggests a mild instance. Ar.'s theory as a whole presupposes a constancy of relation between the play and the audience's perception of it. It was Renaissance theorists who turned the probability of the treatise into pure *vraisemblance*: see ch. X p. 298.

criteria of philosophy and history, most of the other relevant passages
in the *Poetics* place the accent on the causal connections between the
components of a dramatic sequence of events. In ch. 7 necessity and
probability are cited in connection with the turning-point of a
tragedy, the critical transformation of fortune (*metabasis*). In ch. 8
the lack of suitable coherence between certain events in Odysseus's
life is described as not matching the requirements of sequential
necessity or probability, and it is the same standard which is
appealed to in ch. 9 to characterise the deficiency of the episodic plot.
The point is put positively again in ch. 10, where the crucial
transition which defines the complex plot is yet another opportunity
for necessity and probability to be applied, and Aristotle makes the
remark which I quoted earlier, that 'it makes a great difference
whether things happen because of, or only after, what precedes them.'
Not only do we here find the causal dimension of the principle
explicitly mentioned, but we also learn that necessity and probability
are to be expected even of the vital turning-points of fortune which for
Aristotle lie at the heart of tragedy. The same is true of the passage
from ch. 7 cited above, and the idea is later reinforced by further
references to the causal principle in immediate connection with the
components of the complex plot – reversal and recognition. Since it is
also into the mechanism of the complex plot that Aristotle introduces
hamartia in *Poetics* 13, the nature of necessity and probability raises
substantive issues in the interpretation of the core of the theory of
tragedy, with which ch. VII of this book will try to deal. The
essential point to be observed here is that the complex plot central to
Aristotle's theory does not represent a qualification of the principle of
necessity or probability, but gives this a deliberately paradoxical
embodiment – 'paradoxically but on account of one another' being
an approximate translation of the phrase used at 52a 4, effectively for
the key stages of the complex plot.[36] The arousal of pity and fear in
their most intense form hangs on a pattern of action which does not
follow a linear progression (the schema of the 'simple' plot), but
which incorporates a tragic twist of fortune. Yet even this pattern, in
Aristotle's theory, must leave intact the underlying necessity or
probability of the plot-structure. It is emblematic of the philosopher's
whole view of the genre that intelligibility must be preserved even at
the heart of tragic instability.

[36] On this passage, and *peripeteia* generally, see ch. VII p. 212f. and nn.15-16.

But it is not the theory of tragedy as such with which the present argument is concerned, and it is now time to take stock of what has been said about necessity and probability, in order to draw together the strands of Aristotle's conception of poetic unity. We have seen that the framework within which this conception is elaborated is that of poetic plot-structure (*muthos*), which the *Poetics* from its first sentence onwards normatively assumes as a feature of all poetry. Since the *muthos* is a structure of human actions, or, more strictly, of the mimesis of human actions, the notion of unity which is applied to it turns out to be related to categories which are employed by Aristotle elsewhere in the understanding of the causality of action, and in the interpretation (in rhetoric, philosophy, and ordinary rational discourse) of propositions and arguments concerning human action. Adapted to poetic theory, these categories, necessity and probability, bear both on the intrinsic causality of the action, and on the 'logic' which the construction of the plot requires us to apprehend in it. From this it emerges that the one negative judgement which can be made with assurance on Aristotle's concept of poetic unity is that it is not a purely formal criterion, for it is grounded in the representation and understanding of human action: one cannot judge poetic form or unity without reckoning with the principles (that is, the causes and motivations) of human action itself.[37] Aristotle's underlying preoccupation, in other words, is with intelligibility, not with formality in itself or for its own sake. We have here, therefore, a conclusion parallel to that which I reached in the previous chapter on the concept of aesthetic pleasure. In both cases it has transpired that the experience of poetry is inescapably cognitive, and that the ordering of the work of art, together with the proper pleasure to be derived from it, is, for Aristotle, inseparable from the universals which ideally furnish its content.[38] Moreover, it is as clear for unity as it was for aesthetic pleasure, that Aristotle is elaborating in detailed application to poetry a principle which he would hold as valid for all mimetic art: 51a 30.

It is, I believe, the strength of Aristotle's stress on the causal

[37] Russell 91 calls Ar.'s criterion of unity 'wholly aesthetic', but he refers to 62b 1ff., which concerns concentration rather than basic unity, while the main treatment of unity in chs. 7-8 indicates that it is a function of intelligibility in the plot-structure. Will 159-62 is similarly mistaken in seeing the justification for necessity and probability as narrowly 'aesthetic'.

[38] For universals see esp. *Met.* 1038b 1-39a 23, *Rhet.* 1394a 21ff., 1356b 30ff. Universals are the true object of knowledge: *De An.* 417b 22f., *Met.* 982a 21ff.

intelligibility of the tragic plot-structure (as a paradigm for other types of poetic *muthos*) which explains the fact, to which I earlier drew attention, that the *Poetics* repeatedly mentions necessity alongside probability, even though, on Aristotle's own admission elsewhere, necessity plays little part in the sphere of human action outside the limited factors of compulsion and unavoidable facts of nature (neither of which would have much scope in the types of plot recommended in the treatise). We need not suppose that Aristotle imagined the causal sequence of a play could often have the degree of cohesion which a necessary relation between events would entail. But necessity stands for an extreme or ideal of unity which Aristotle clearly finds it theoretically important to emphasise. It has, that is, the significance of overstating the requirement of unity of action. Probability (*eikos*) is sufficient, but since in a sense *eikos* aspires to the condition of necessity, necessity itself can be held up as the perfect accomplishment of an integrated plot-structure: it represents a degree of causal and logical cohesion which, even if human action can rarely if ever achieve this, would constitute a perfect embodiment of dramatic meaning.[39] If necessity does stand in the *Poetics* as an ideal though scarcely attainable standard, this is congruent with Aristotle's remarks in ch. 9, where the distinction between poetry and history, and the comparison between poetry and philosophy, seems to imply that poetry heightens as well as generalising reality. It is precisely, as ch. 8 makes clear, the lack of patterns of coherence in the events of much ordinary life (or even in the life of a single hero) which makes them inadequate material for the demands of a poetic plot-structure. Poetry should in some sense rise above mundane life (though not with a necessarily optimistic import) and elevate human action to a higher level of intelligibility, so that it acquires something which even the philosopher might recognise as significant. If, then, Aristotelian poetic unity has the anti-formalist virtue of relating to the mimetic content, the constituent actions, of the poem, it equally represents a movement away from the realistic portrayal of ordinary life towards the universalised status of philosophical propositions of general (or probable) validity.

---

[39] An analogy to the relation between probability and necessity in the *Poetics* is Ar.'s observation at *Rhet.* 1370a 6-9 that 'habit resembles nature, since frequent occurrence is akin to invariability'. On the assimilation of probability ('that which happens for the most part') to necessity cf.De Ste Croix 47-50. But the two should not be casually interchangeable: see *Top.* 112b 1ff. The fact that Ar. considers tragedy to

One final implication of Aristotle's concept of unity deserves to be drawn out, and that is what it precludes. The *Poetics* is unequivocal on this point, but since most of the relevant passages occur in the later chapters of the work, in the analysis of epic, there is some risk that their relevance to the central theory of poetry will be underestimated. On a number of occasions Aristotle comments directly on the need, except in certain qualified circumstances, to eliminate from a poetic plot any trace of the unintelligible or 'irrational'.[40] This is precisely the negative corollary of the positive requirement of unity of plot. That Aristotle should have enjoined the exclusion of the irrational from a tragic, epic or other poetic construction, appears at first sight unobjectionable, but reflection on the point in relation to existing Greek poetry may prompt the view that it is in some degree contentious. On the level on which Aristotle is simply concerned, as to some extent he certainly is, with the avoidance of anomalies in human action, his principle is perfectly understandable. But insofar as it can be taken to entail that all the action of poetry should be both fully intelligible and intelligible in wholly human terms, it raises the issue of how far such a demand is compatible with some of the major presuppositions of traditional Greek religion, as we find this dramatised in poetry. One facet of this issue touches on the status of chance both in traditional religious thinking and in Aristotle's philosophy. Both the positive principles of unity and the warnings against the irrational which we find in the *Poetics* clearly exclude the play of chance in the sense understood by Aristotle himself: indeed, one Aristotelian definition of chance – that which happens neither always nor for the most part – is simply the reverse of necessity and probability.[41] But the main Greek term for chance, *tuchê*, carries a much more indeterminate sense and value within the unsystematic outlook of traditional religion and myth, and in particular it shades into belief in divine causation. If Aristotle's notion of unity rules out the possibility of this and other religious ideas of the irrational, then this clearly has serious implications for the relation between the *Poetics* and existing Greek epic and tragic poetry. Whether such a conflict does exist between

---

be capable of greater unity than epic does not justify the attempt of Friedrich (1983) 51 to refer necessity to the former, probability to the latter.

[40] 54b 6-8, 60a 11-14, 28-32, 60a 34-b 2, 61b 14f., 19-24.

[41] *Phys.* 196b 10ff., *Rhet.* 1369a 32-5.

the theory and earlier poetic practice is a question to which I shall return in ch. VII, but I have mentioned the possibility of it here in order to end this section with a further pointer to the strongly cognitive and rationalist tenor of the concept of poetic unity adumbrated in the treatise, and indeed of Aristotle's aesthetic thinking as a whole.

IV
Mimesis

There has been more than one occasion in the earlier chapters of this book to notice the centrality of mimesis to Aristotle's understanding not only of poetry but also of the visual and musical arts. For Aristotle, as for Plato before him and subsequently for most other classical and neo-classical thinkers, mimesis was the key to the primary question of the relation between works of art and the world (characteristically referred to as 'nature' in the later tradition); and since this question has dominated all other considerations about art in this long classically-oriented era of thought, the historical value of attempting to reconstruct the views on mimesis of the first two major figures in the tradition calls for no justification. That on this subject perhaps more than any other Aristotle's ideas require to be related to the Platonic background, is a proposition which I stressed in the introductory chapter; both the significance and the complexity of this relation will become apparent in greater detail in the course of the present enquiry. How far back beyond Plato it is worth extending the enquiry, it is harder to say. Some account must certainly be taken of the evidence for earlier conceptions of mimesis, since it is clear that to some extent Plato presupposes existing uses of the language of mimesis. But I am neither able, given the inevitable restrictions of scope, nor inclined, given the nature of the material, to offer a systematic analysis of the vestiges of pre-Platonic thinking about mimesis. There is, in my view, both too much variety of usage and too much obscurity about individual details to allow any linear scheme for the semantic development of the mimesis word-group to be successfully traced. I shall therefore be trying in the first part of this chapter to do little more than illustrate the chief uses of mimesis terminology in the earlier period, before proceeding to closer scrutiny of Plato's and Aristotle's discussions of the subject.

Speculation about the original sense of mimesis and its cognates is not particularly profitable, and I begin by mentioning this issue only in order to note the danger, which the endeavour of reaching back to tell the story *ab ovo* easily brings with it, of unnecessarily limiting the interpretation of mimesis language in surviving texts. This can be demonstrated from the work of those who have argued both that the original sense of mimesis was choreographic or dramatic enactment (for which there may well be something to be speculatively said) and that the application of the word to the reproduction of appearances first occurs in Plato.[1] As a counter-example to this latter claim one could cite, for instance, Herodotus 2.78, where the historian reports the Egyptian custom of carrying round at banquets a miniature wooden effigy of a corpse as a *memento mori*, which he describes as 'extremely realistic (*memimêmenon*) in both painting and carving'.[2] The verb *mimeisthai* here refers, and surely can only refer, to the reproduction or copying of appearance. Yet it has been suggested that 'we do not find before Plato ... the use of the term *mimêsis* or its cognates for purely static simulation of appearance', and in order to come to terms with the Herodotean passage (which, as we shall see, is not unique) this same writer falls back on the tendentious claim that 'the artist had conveyed the notion of a dead man'. Indeed he had, one presumes, but only by virtue of having simulated the appearance of one; and it is purely to the matter of appearance, not to some 'underlying notion of enactment', that Herodotus applies the language of mimesis in this passage.[3]

This example illustrates the possibility of over-interpreting pre-Platonic occurrences of mimesis terminology in order to make them conceptually richer than their contexts warrant, and in order to make a case for a more determinate evolution of the usage of the word-group than the evidence really permits us to discern. It is important to stress that excessive interpretation of this kind is particularly inappropriate where authors are concerned who, like Herodotus, evince no interest in, or concern for, theoretical nicety in

[1] See the books of Koller and Keuls, and cf. Nehamas 56ff. Although he accepts the original sense of dramatic enactment, Else (1958) differs from these scholars in acknowledging that the range of meaning for mimesis words broadened out before Plato. Else is followed by Pollitt 37ff.

[2] Cf. the similar phrase applied to the models of embalmed corpses at Herod. 2.86.2.

[3] The quoted phrases are from Keuls 20 and 11. The nature of Keuls' thesis leads her into confusion over the meaning and implications of enactment: on 11 'the notion of enactment' is peculiarly glossed as 'one object takes the place of another or symbolises a notion'.

the use of mimesis words. The simple and unprejudicial procedure which I propose to follow in preparing the way for consideration of the Platonic and Aristotelian material, is to start from the demonstrable datum that by the classical period (whatever had earlier been the case) the language of mimesis was employed to denote what can collectively be described as a number of types of *correspondence*, to use a term whose looseness serves aptly to avoid presuppositions about what, if anything, these various relations of correspondence have in common. It is indeed the fact that the range of phenomena to which mimesis terms could be applied was wide and far from homogeneous that provides us with a basic interpretative difficulty in dealing both with general usage and with the philosophers' theories. The first task in confronting this problem must therefore be to undertake a preliminary categorisation of the pre-Platonic material. It should be noted that the following categorisation does not purport to be either complete or definitive, if only because in the very nature of the subject certain passages could be cited or understood under more than one heading; so that, for instance, at least some cases of impersonation might be thought also to fall under the description of general behavioural imitation. My scheme should nonetheless give a sufficiently clear idea of the main lines of usage, and of those applications of mimesis terminology which are most pertinent to the philosophical treatments of the topic.[4] I distribute the material in the following categories (whose order is not significant): visual representation; behavioural imitation; impersonation; vocal imitation; metaphysical mimesis.

In addition to the passage cited above, Herodotus furnishes us with a number of clear instances of the use of mimesis language to refer to visual copying or resemblance. Thus the carved columns around the tomb of Amasis are said by him to look like palm trees: mimesis here is again inescapably a matter of perceived visual correspondence and not of 'enactment', since columns cannot enact anything.[5] In another passage of his *History* (3.37) Herodotus says that he will make clear to anyone who has not seen it what the appearance of the statue of Hephaestus at Memphis is, by describing it as the 'image (*mimêsis*) of a pygmy': all that is being predicated of

---

[4] For alternative schemes see Else (1958), esp. 79, and Keuls 14-22; and for a survey (though a tendentious one) of most of the relevant passages see Sörbom 28-36, 41ff.

[5] Herod. 2.169.5: 'enactment' is falsely diagnosed by Keuls 21, with 11, 19.

the statue is, once more, a certain set of visual features. Where a
mimesis term is used of a gold disk placed between the horns of a
wooden cow to represent the sun, it is arguable that an element of
symbolism is involved, but the notion of resemblance remains
central.[6] Herodotus is not the only classical author to supply
evidence for this sense of mimesis. At Euripides *Helen* 74 Teucer,
seeing Helen but thinking her only Helen's double, exclaims: 'what
an image (*mimēma*) of Helen you are!' Of course, Helen is more than
a static image, but the dramatic context, together with the language
of the preceding lines, establishes that Teucer is making a point only
about the woman's appearance.[7]

   The examples just given provide cases of what in an earlier chapter
I called *formal* mimesis (pp. 53f.): that is, they entail or presuppose a
direct correspondence between the mimetic subject and its model, a
use of visual means to represent a visual object. This need not mean,
however, that the two things be identical in all respects, so that while
the woman whom Teucer sees could not be visually distinguished
from Helen (since she *is* Helen), the corpse carried around at
Egyptian banquets differs from a real corpse at least in scale. The
category of visual mimesis is wider than the visual arts, but evidently
includes them: a medical text, for instance, states that sculptors
produce 'a mimesis of the body'.[8] But it is most obviously with the
visual arts, as opposed to ordinary visual phenomena, that a further
and important issue arises, and one which is interestingly raised in a
passage of Xenophon's *Memorabilia* (3.10.1-3). Xenophon reports a
conversation between Socrates and the painter Parrhasius, whom
Socrates asks, after obtaining consent to the proposition that painting
involves the reproduction of visual appearances, whether it is possible
for the art also to show the characters of men's souls in its images.
The difficulty of translating the mimesis language of this passage lies
precisely in the fact that Socrates is shown attempting to stretch its
sense and its scope. Parrhasius at first rejects Socrates' suggestion,
on the grounds that mimesis can deal only with things which have
physical and therefore visual attributes; but Socrates manages to

   [6] Herod. 2.132.1; cf. Aristoph. *Thesm.* 17 for a related case.
   [7] Note in particular the language of lines 72f., and cf. 875. Eurip. *Bacch.* 980 is a case
where it is impossible to distinguish between appearance and impersonation: by being
dressed 'in imitation of a woman', Pentheus both looks like one and is acting the part
of one.
   [8] [Hippoc.] *De victu* 1.21. Another instance is Aeschylus fr.17.7 Mette (on which
Keuls 20 is again tendentious).

bring him round to accept that the painter can imitate facial looks
which are themselves revealing of character and emotion: the latter
are therefore brought within the range of visual mimesis. But do we
still have *formal* mimesis in such a case? The question in fact admits
of two answers: if the painter's object is taken to be, say, a certain
look on the face, then what he does could be said to be formally
parallel to his portrayal of any other kind of appearance; but if his
object is understood to be the emotion or character itself, then we
have moved beyond strictly formal mimesis, to which visual
correspondence is essential, into a wider sphere of mimetic
significance. This ambiguity, and the problems which it raises, points
towards the theorising of Plato and Aristotle.

My second category, behavioural imitation, is abundantly
illustrated in surviving texts and calls for little comment. It should
be noted, however, that the frequency of the usage may have tended
to lend a general colouring of enactment to the mimesis word-group.
I simply list a number of typical cases: Thucydides 2.37.1 ('we
provide others with a model rather than imitating them'); Euripides
Electra 1037 (a wife tends to follow the example (*mimeisthai*) of an
unfaithful husband by committing adultery); Xenophon *Mem.* 1.2.3
(Socrates' followers hoped that by imitating or emulating him they
would become like him); Aristophanes *Eccl.* 278 (by their gait and
manner the disguised women are to copy or ape the behaviour of
countrymen).[9]

Impersonation, my next category, can from one point of view be
seen as the extreme case of behavioural imitation, though in most
contexts it can be distinguished from the latter in terms of intention
and effect. The conceptual distinction does not always, however,
make it easy to decide on the precise force of mimesis language in
passages where either ordinary imitation or impersonation would be
in place. A perhaps doubtful instance is to be found at Lysias 6.51,
where Andocides is described as putting on a priestly outfit in order
to parody religious mystery rites: the use of costume, and the very
idea of parodying a ritual, both perhaps tilt the balance in favour of
interpreting the verb *mimeisthai* here to denote impersonation (of a
role, not an individual) – that is, acting out the part of a priest *in full*.

There remains no doubt, at any rate, that the language of mimesis
was used of impersonation in the classical period. A straightforward

[9] Further examples: Herod. 2.104.4, 4.166.1, Thuc. 1.95.3, 7.67.2, Democritus frs.
39 and 79, Aristoph. *Clouds* 559, *Wasps* 1019, *Eccl.* 545, Xen. *Mem.* 1.6.3.

instance occurs in Aristophanes *Frogs* 109, where Dionysus uses the term *mimêsis* of his own action in dressing up as Heracles in order to pass himself off as his brother in the Underworld. Yet it may be no coincidence that the passage belongs to a dramatic text, and that Dionysus himself is closely associated with drama, for the most striking example of mimetic impersonation that we have in this period directly concerns the fictional enactments of drama. In Aristophanes *Thesmophoriazusae* the tragic playwright Agathon is presented as costuming himself in the apparel of his own characters in order to stimulate his poetic imagination. He justifies his behaviour with a piece of literary and aesthetic theory, including the claim that the poet must use mimesis to supply what he cannot find in his own nature (*Thesm.* 156). There is more than one strand in the humour of this passage. For one thing, Agathon is in part being assimilated to the theatrical actor; he is, with a degree of comic exaggeration, doing part of the actor's work in the process of composition (precisely what Aristotle enjoins at *Poet.* 55a 22-30). But there can be no serious question that Aristophanes is also picking up and parodying fragments of contemporary dramatic theory, the key element in which is the idea of mimesis. Mimesis on the level of direct impersonation therefore shades here into the mimesis which is part of the dramatic poet's art *per se*. The passage provides oblique and distorted, but nonetheless intriguing, evidence for two distinct but related conceptions of mimesis, which could be concisely described as the actor's and the playwright's arts. Aristophanes' parody involves, and deliberately confuses, both an ordinary usage of mimesis terms (for impersonation) and a newly developing application of the language of mimesis to the fictional status of dramatic poetry: both are relevant to the philosophers' later interests in mimesis.[10]

Under my fourth heading, vocal imitation, belongs the earliest occurrence of a mimesis term in surviving Greek.[11] In the *Homeric Hymn to Apollo* 162-4 a chorus of Delian maidens is said to be able to

[10] Other uses of mimesis language for impersonation or dramatic enactment: Aristoph. *Thesm.* 850, *Plut.* 291, 306, 312 (virtually 'act a mime'), Eurip. *HF* 1298 (?), *Rhesus* 256.

[11] Cf. (without direct reference to mimesis) Hom. *Od.* 4.279, Helen's mimicry of the Greek wives' voices. Various other sound effects can be called mimetic: e.g. Pind. *P.* 12.21 and fr. 94b.15 (with Else (1958) 77) and Aristoph. *Birds* 266, all for imitative uses of the 'flute'; Plato *Rep.* 397a, 423c, and ps.-Ar. *Aud.* 800a 25-9, for vocal imitation of non-human sounds.

copy or reproduce the voices of all men, and what seems to be meant, puzzling though the passage to a degree remains, is some kind of vocal mimicry. More easily intelligible is Aeschylus *Choephori* 564, where Orestes and Pylades plan to imitate a Phocian accent as part of their ruse to gain admittance to the palace. These passages help to indicate how vocal mimesis sometimes coalesces with a more general kind of imitation or even impersonation, and one would expect vocal mimesis to have been acknowledged as a specific component in the art of the actor.[12]

With the possible exception of the mimesis of character in visual art, mentioned earlier, all the material I have cited in the previous four categories entails formal mimesis: in each case, there is a directly perceived match between the medium of the mimetic object or act (whether appearance, behaviour or sounds) and the relevant aspect of the corresponding phenomenon. My final category, metaphysical mimesis, is by definition not of this kind. We are told, on Aristotle's testimony, that certain Pythagoreans conceived of the relation between the sensible world of men and objects, and the hidden, ultimate, metaphysical world of numbers, as one of mimesis.[13] Mimesis here is a concept of correspondence, though certainly not of an obvious or transparent kind, between the visible and the invisible. Aristotle actually compares this Pythagorean conception to Plato's doctrine of Forms (and the relation to them of material reality).[14] Whether or not the same point was made or emphasised by Pythagorean thinkers, there is no doubt that Plato was to interpret the relation in question as one between inferior and superior, the false and the true. It is perhaps appropriate also to include in this category a fragment of thought from a fourth-century

---

[12] *Poet.* 47a 20, referring to those who engage in mimesis 'through the voice', may include actors (it certainly does not refer to poetry as such, *contra* Ross 276, who ignores its status as an analogy): cf. *Rhet.* 1404a 21f., where the voice is called the 'most mimetic' of our parts, and the source of the arts of the rhapsode and actor. For the actuality, though not the term, of histrionic vocal mimesis cf. Aristoph. *Thesm.* 267f.

[13] *Met.* 987b 11ff., and note the phrase 'participation and resemblance' at *EE* 1217b 9f. in reference to the Platonic Form of the Good. There may, however, be a polemical note in Ar.'s comparison: on the difference between Pythagorean and Platonic mimesis see W. Burkert, *Lore & Science in Ancient Pythagoreanism*, Engl. transl. (Cambridge Mass. 1972) 43-5.

[14] Nehamas 60 and 77 n.71 denies that particulars can stand in a relation of mimesis to Forms, but he ignores the Aristotelian testimony and fails to consider all the relevant Platonic passages. In addition to those cited in the text cf. *Phdr.* 250a-b, where earthly beauty is said to involve images and likenesses of eternal beauty.

medical text, where it is stated that men are incapable of comprehending how the arts and crafts (*technai*) which the gods have given them actually 'imitate' the divine world itself: men use these arts without recognising what it is of which they are producing a mimesis.[15]

This concise sketch of the range of mimesis terminology before Plato should at least have served to demonstrate variety of usage, but it may also have given some preliminary indication of potential difficulties in developing such a flexible word-group for the purposes of strict theory. It is certainly necessary to keep this flexibility in mind when approaching Plato's views of mimesis, and important to be alert to the different ends for which Plato exploits the vocabulary of mimesis. There is a strong tendency in discussions of this subject to concentrate on a small number of Platonic passages and on a restricted conception of mimesis, but in what follows I shall be attempting to open up a larger perspective, if only in outline.

To do so, my analysis naturally starts with the most comprehensive type of mimesis to be found in Plato, which we have already seen that Aristotle refers to in the *Metaphysics* in his comparison between Platonic and Pythagorean philosophy. Aristotle specifically suggests that the difference between the two doctrines is only one of terminology: Pythagorean mimesis becomes Platonic *methexis* ('participation'). Leaving aside the historical claim, we can qualify this by observing that Plato is on occasion prepared to appropriate the language of mimesis for his own philosophical speculations. In Book 7 of the *Laws* the Athenian hypothesises how the organisers of the new ideal polis will reply to the tragedians who request access to their city. They will say: 'we too are poets of tragedy, the finest and best tragedy. Our whole state is a mimesis of the finest and best life, which we say is in reality the truest tragedy.' (817b) Mimesis is here applied to the *politeia*, the constitution and state itself; but, since this state exists only in the minds of the dialogue's interlocutors, this mimesis must in a sense be embodied only in Plato's book itself – a fact which gives piquancy to the mention of tragic poetry. The philosophical quest merges with the

---

[15] [Hippoc.] *De victu* 1.11: on the date of this text cf. Else (1958) 82f. The passage is superficially reminiscent of Ar.'s own principle that 'art imitates nature' (p. 47 above): the latter should not however be thought of as a metaphysical use of mimesis terminology, only a metaphorical one (which is not to deny that the doctrine as such has a metaphysical dimension).

imagined life of the new city, and both are contained within the dramatic mimesis of the Platonic presentation of them. That Plato should be ready to go this far in borrowing the notion of mimetic activity which he elsewhere condemns is highly significant. It entails a recognition of a seriousness of conflict between tragedy and philosophy which goes far beyond their dramatic forms, and extends to the objects of their mimesis, their rival views of the life of man and its relation to the divine.[16] Even so, on the basis of this passage alone it might seem unnecessary to claim anything more than that Plato is willing to talk analogically of the mimesis of his own philosophy. It need not be implied that he is conceding the existence of a mimetic correspondence of some sort between this world, or the philosophical endeavour, and a grander metaphysical reality.

That Plato could, however, posit a mimetic correspondence between the material and the metaphysical is demonstrated elsewhere, above all in the *Timaeus*. In his account of the creation of the world by the Demiurge, Timaeus explicitly describes the visible world as being as like as possible to the eternal 'in the mimesis of unchanging nature': the world is a *mimêma* of a model, and all the transient shapes and properties which come into being in the stuff of the world are themselves '*mimêmata* of eternal objects'.[17] Thus we have here that direct relationship of mimesis between the temporal and the eternal which Aristotle attests in the *Metaphysics*. What remains deeply problematic, of course, is just how this mimesis is to be characterised or interpreted: in particular, whether it is to be thought of as quasi-symbolic mimesis, in which a correspondence exists despite fundamental differences between the nature of subject and object. Metaphysical opacity aside, it is certainly necessary to understand mimesis in a special symbolic or expressive sense in the claim that 'time is a mimesis of eternity' and a moving image of it, for Plato regards eternity as strictly outside time.[18] Yet the reference here to an 'image' shows how Plato draws on more than one of the existing associations of mimesis, and in the course of the dialogue there are others to be encountered. The activity of the Creator, the divine 'poet', is reinforced by the lesser divinities who both imitate him in their own activities (as to some extent men too

---

[16] Cf. Halliwell 50-8.

[17] *Tim.* 39d-e, 48e, 50c.

[18] *Tim.* 37d-38a: cf. R. Sorabji, *Time, Creation and the Continuum* (London 1983) 108ff.

can do) and engage in mimesis themselves by their fashioning of the human body after the model of the spherical universe.[19]

Two general remarks can be made about this strand of the *Timaeus*. In the first place, the dialogue leaves the impression that mimesis is a key to the structure of the world and of reality, which is to be comprehended in terms of correspondences and interrelations between mimetic subjects and objects. It seems at least arguable that everything can be taken to be in some way a copy or expression or representation of a higher model or paradigm – everything, that is, until one reaches the supreme 'poet' himself. This latter qualification leads to the second point, which is that the posited structure implies a hierarchical, and to some extent a purposive, conception of mimesis. Mimesis is both the means by which the eternal produces and fashions the world, and correspondingly the means by which the human mind can ascend or aspire in its search for knowledge: mimesis carries an active philosophical and theological significance.

Such an idea will appear incredible to anyone who thinks of Platonic mimesis only in the terms of *Republic* 10 and other related passages. But the enormous discrepancy between the two things can to a considerable extent be explained by reference to the notion of a mimetic *hierarchy* which I have pointed out in the *Timaeus*. This notion also enables us to see how the philosophical and poetic types of mimesis in *Laws* 7, mentioned earlier, can be placed within the larger Platonic perspective. At the start of the *Timaeus* Socrates compares himself, in the inadequacy of his portrayal of an ideal state (that is, the *Republic*), to 'the tribe of imitators' (19d-e). This phrase not only alludes to the activities of poets and other artists, but it also carries the specific irony that the Socratic *Republic* is being judged wanting by the very standards which within that work were so astringently applied to art. Yet this, as we have seen, is at the beginning of a dialogue which proceeds to project relations of mimesis onto the entire universe. Although Socrates suggests that his companions Timaeus and Critias are superior philosophers, and can make up for his own deficiencies, the reservation about *human* mimesis can be seen to concern also the account of the world which Timaeus goes on to give. Timaeus himself claims no more than an approximate likeness for his account, since his model (the model of his 'image') is

[19] The divine poet: *Tim.* 28c. Imitation of the Demiurge by lesser divinities: 42e, 69c. Human imitation of the divine: 88d (cf. *Phdr.* 252c-d, 253b, *Laws* 713e). Body and universe: 44d.

only the visible world (28a-29d). The philosopher too, then, is engaged in mimesis, but it is inferior mimesis by the standards of the divine mimesis which, at the risk of conceptual circularity, the dialogue hypothesises and pictures. That mimesis has at this stage of his thinking become central to Plato's understanding of all human discourse, philosophy included, is confirmed by the subsequent dialogue, the *Critias*, in which Critias argues that 'everything we say is mimesis and image-making'.[20] But unless these late dialogues are to be read as wholly ironic and self-destructive texts, Plato wishes the notion of higher kinds of mimesis to be seriously and sympathetically considered.

It is now possible to begin to locate Plato's view of specifically artistic mimesis within a larger framework of the kind adumbrated in the *Timaeus* and perhaps alluded to in the passage from *Laws* 7. That the aspect of Platonic thought to which I have drawn attention is not purely a late development can be seen in the *Republic*'s image of the philosopher-artist engaged in the mimesis of eternal truths, and even perhaps within *Republic* 10 itself, where the mimetic activities of painting and poetry are juxtaposed with the at least quasi-mimetic relation between the material world and eternal Forms.[21] The comparison is given all too solid expression in the passage on the triad of beds: eternal, material and mimetic. A related chain or ladder of being can be traced in the *Sophist*, where, although Forms as such are not mentioned, a major division is made, within the complex diaeretic analysis, between divine inventiveness and human inventiveness, and one of the two main sub-divisions of the latter is classed as mimetic. But we find in the *Sophist* that the vocabulary of mimesis as such has reacquired a wholly derogatory force, being attached, among other things, to the deceits of sophists: Plato here exploits as emotively as anywhere the distinction between reality and image, which he aligns with that between truth and falsehood; and it is to the latter that mimesis seems wholly to belong.

Here, then, we have a reaffirmation of what is usually, though too simply, thought of as the characteristic Platonic mistrust of the image and the mimesis which produces it, yet in a work which

---

[20] *Crit.* 107b-d. Cf. the 'image' of reason needed to avoid the blinding experience of looking into the sun of reason itself, at *Laws* 897d-e.
[21] See *Rep.* 500c-501b for philosophical mimesis on the analogy of painting (the Forms are the models (e 3, compare 472d) to which the 'artist' refers in his attempt to capture them mimetically), and *Rep.* 596a ff. for the hierarchy of Forms-matter-mimesis.

propounds a hierarchical view of things for whose expression Plato is elsewhere prepared to employ the language of mimesis, as we have seen, to very different effect. What calls therefore for primary recognition is that there exists a complex and significant ambiguity in the collective evidence for Plato's attitude towards mimesis. If it is generally the case that underlying Plato's references to mimesis there is 'a contrast between the work of imitation and something else which is, in comparison, real',[22] we can nonetheless identify a radical divergence between his attempts to arrogate the language of mimesis for philosophy's relation to metaphysical truth, and his condemnations of the specious and meretricious status of works of artistic mimesis. In the former case there is what might be called an elevating function for mimesis: within the hierarchy of things, mimesis directs the mind upwards towards higher reality, in a way which anticipates the spirit of later neo-platonic views of art. With existing art, however, the reverse holds: poet and painter are castigated for pulling their audiences down below even the level of material reality, which is itself ephemeral, to that of the merely counterfeit. It is noticeable that for the purposes of his adverse case against art Plato is particularly fond of the notion of mimesis as mere copying of appearances: the mimetic artist *par excellence* is an image-maker. Where, however, he borrows the model of mimesis for the philosophical enterprise, image-making is less conspicuously implied in the concept – understandably so, since this strand of Platonic thought tends, as we have seen, towards a much freer and more expressive idea of mimesis, if only because it concerns a subject-object relation in which the object may not be independently accessible to the human mind. Yet even here there is some talk of images: a fact which indicates, I suggest, that the imagistic sense of mimesis was well established by Plato's time and represented one prominent aspect of general usage of the term.

As a postlude and supplement to this outline of an interpretation of Platonic mimesis, it may be worthwhile to draw up a list of the main

---

[22] McKeon 152, whose whole demonstration of the pervasiveness of the language of images in Plato, though somewhat different from my analysis, is highly interesting. Cf. also Golden, *CP* 64 (1969) 148-51 (independently of the conclusion on *katharsis*).

uses of mimeticist terminology in the dialogues (not all of which have been mentioned above).[23]

(a) Linguistic: language reflects the essence of things.
(b) Philosophical: the philosopher's thought aspires to provide a copy of truth – the mimesis of an eternal model.
(c) Cosmic: the material world may in various ways stand in a mimetic relation to eternal models.
(d) Visual: the painter's mimesis pictures the appearances of things.
(e) Mimicry: the voice and the body can be used to reproduce certain properties of the animal and natural world.
(f) Behavioural: ordinary imitation or emulation.
(g) Impersonatory: the (non-artistic) acting out of a role (but see (h) below).
(h) Poetic: apart from unspecified references to poetic mimesis, Plato usually treats poetry either as an art of verbal image-making, comparable to the painter's, or (in some of its forms) as a special case of (g) above, i.e. dramatic impersonation.
(i) Musical: musical modes and structures can give expression to certain human actions and experiences. (It is sometimes impossible to disentangle music from poetry in Plato's references to *mousikê*.)
(j) Choreographic: dancers can act out representations of human life.

*

In view of the recurrent emphasis placed by Plato on the mimetic character of art, it is hardly surprising that the concept should have

---

[23] Linguistic: *Crat.* 423b ff. (cf. Ar. *Int.* 16a 3ff., *Rhet.* 1404a 21ff.). Philosophical and cosmic: see text. Visual: esp. *Rep.* 596ff., *Crat.*430b ff., *Soph.* 233d-6c, 265-8, *Laws* 667-70 (see also under poetic (b) below). Mimicry: e.g. *Rep.* 397a-b, *Crat.* 422e ff. Behavioural: e.g. *Phdr.* 252d, 264e, *Protag.* 326a, *Phaedo* 105b (and cf. the special case of shadow boxing *vel sim.* at *Laws* 830b, e, 865b). Impersonatory: *Soph.* 267a, *Laws* 836e. Poetic: (a) general – e.g. *Phdr.*248e, *Rep.* 595b, 597e, *Tim.* 19d-e, *Laws* 668b-c, 719c; (b) associated with visual art – e.g. *Rep.* 596c ff., *Crat.* 423d, *Polit.* 288c, 306d, *Laws* 669a; (c) dramatic – *Rep.* 392d ff., *Laws* 798d ff. Musical: *Rep.* 399a-c, 400a, *Laws* 655d ff., 798d ff. Choreographic: see Appendix 2 under 47a 26-8.

The attempt of Verdenius (1949) to synthesise all Plato's mimesis terminology into a single theory leads him to the curious conclusion that for Plato 'art ... strives to transcend the material world' (18).

occupied a place at the centre of Aristotle's thinking on the subject. There is also some likelihood that the variety of both general and Platonic usage of the mimesis word-group will have had its influence on Aristotle. To take one instance, we have some evidence that in an early work, the *Protrepticus*, he closely followed the Platonic distinction between philosophical and artistic mimesis.[24] But by the time of the *Poetics* direct dependence on his predecessor is much less prominent, and we have for the most part to deal with an unspoken and oblique relationship whose strands are not easy to disentangle. There is, furthermore, a particular Aristotelian factor which makes for complications. If Plato's attitudes to mimesis are problematic because of their fluctuations, Aristotle's cause interpretative difficulties for the rather different reason that relatively little is explicitly said about the meaning of mimesis, and much appears to be left tacit. If Plato is sometimes dogmatically forthcoming on the nature of mimesis, and openly grades it against his scheme of philosophical values, Aristotle's *Poetics* leaves us with little more than suggestive *aperçus* and laconic observations to piece together his conception of poetic and related types of mimesis. Yet the effort of reconstruction is undoubtedly essential to an understanding of the treatise, since the vocabulary of mimesis, first used without definition or comment in the work's second sentence, is pervasive and fundamental.

A first step towards elucidation of Aristotle's position, if we approach it from Plato, is to recognise that his focus is narrower than Plato's, and more firmly held. There is no clear trace in the *Poetics* of a concern with the possibility of philosophical mimesis, and hardly an allusion to any other mimetic activities than those of poetry, music, dancing, the visual arts and some related *technai*. It is precisely as the defining characteristic of all these, as the common element in them which distinguishes them from history, philosophy and many other human enterprises, that mimesis matters to Aristotle. The first divergence from Plato on this topic is therefore a determination to compartmentalise poetic and related mimesis consistently in a category of its own, and to speak of it in its own 'technical' terms, rather than from a grand metaphysical perspective. But to see this much is only a prerequisite for seeing further: in itself the restriction

---

[24] *Protr.* B48, 49, (44) Düring (1961), with Düring's comments on p. 220. The sense of this philosophical mimesis seems in context to depend for part of its force on the ordinary senses of copying and behavioural imitation.

of the conception of mimesis to a particular group of arts still calls for justification and explication. For although the language of mimesis had already been applied to most if not all of the arts referred to in the *Poetics*, and while Plato suggests (*Laws* 668b 9ff.) that mimesis was a commonly accepted notion of art in general, there is no evidence that a stable, agreed sense of mimesis had been defined which would account for the common element which is predicated of the various activities cited in the opening chapter of the treatise. In Plato's case this negative fact is reflected perhaps above all in the anomalies which arise in *Republic* 10's attempt to treat poetic mimesis without qualification in the terms of mimetic *image-making*, especially after, and in contrast to, the work's earlier discussion of poetry, in which the notion of mimesis as enactment was predominant. But a more awkward impediment to a unitary conception of artistic mimesis was the simple fact that in ordinary usage, as has been demonstrated, this single set of terms covered a number of distinguishable types of subject-object relationship. Aristotle's theorising, for all its technical concentration, could hardly be altogether immune to this linguistic fact.

It is necessary now, against this background, to consider the ways in which Aristotle turns mimesis into the defining characteristic of a particular group of arts, but with special reference to poetry. We need to look primarily at the occurrences in the *Poetics* of the two main types of mimesis already identified in art by both Plato and existing classical usage: first that of image-making (in which poetry is compared to or grouped with the visual arts); and, secondly, that of impersonation or enactment, whether in the strongest sense (exemplified by dramatic performance) or simply as the poetic mode of direct speech. Since Aristotle himself identifies drama by reference to this mode, and not to performance as such, I shall use the terms 'enactive', 'impersonatory' and 'dramatic' in what follows without implying any necessary element of *physical* mimesis of the kind which they would usually suggest.[25]

Aristotle frequently follows Plato in equating poetry at the level of mimesis with the visual arts, particularly painting. In the opening

[25] Else (1957) 93-8 states that Aristotelian mimesis 'has nothing to do with impersonation', but he has predictable difficulty with the quasi-Platonic formulation of mimesis precisely as a kind of impersonation (whether or not *we* would call it that) at 48a 21f. Twining 25f. correctly identifies Ar.'s two chief senses of mimesis as 'fiction' and 'personation': the whole of his First Dissertation (reprinted in Olson (1965) 42-75) remains enlightened and enlightening.

chapter of the *Poetics* the visual arts as a group provide a direct
analogy to the mimetic status of the musico-poetic *technai*, and a close
parallel can be seen between this observation and a passage from
Republic Book 2.[26] There are a further seven contexts in the *Poetics*
where a comparison is drawn between poetry and visual art, and in
most of these mimesis is an issue.[27] Although more than one earlier
writer had noted some connection or similarity between these groups
of arts (most memorably Simonides, with his description of poetry as
'talking painting'), the frequency with which we meet the analogy in
Aristotle's short treatise may well reflect Platonic influence.
Certainly, some of the relevant passages of the *Poetics* involve an
arguably naive shift from poetic to visual mimesis, in a manner
which we also encounter at times in Plato, and which compounds
rather than solving aesthetic problems. Perhaps the most striking of
these is in ch. 4, where the natural and psychological aspects of poetic
mimesis are illustrated with an example from painting. But in my
discussion of this passage earlier in the book I suggested that
Aristotle's example, though deceptively simple, does not altogether
obscure or invalidate the seriousness of his argument about poetry at
this point (see pp. 73ff.). The reason for this is that the reference to
visual art, if not ideally suited to Aristotle's purpose, nonetheless
clearly stands as an analogy and not as a reductive conception of
poetry. This point can be generalised to cover the other passages in
question, thus allowing us to discriminate between Aristotle's use of
visual analogy and Plato's occasional attempts to erase all the
significant distinctions between the two arts. The *Poetics* suggests
that poetic and visual mimesis can be usefully compared, but it is not
committed to the belief that the model of image-making is wholly
adequate to explain the work of the poet.

   Aristotle places a further qualification on the Platonic exploitation
of the concept of visual mimesis. In *Poetics* 25 we find the following
pronouncement: 'since the poet, like the painter or any other
image-maker, is a mimetic artist (*mimêtês*), it follows that he must
produce (at any one time) a mimesis of one of three things: reality

---

[26] See Appendix 2 under 47a 18f. Ar.'s main coupling of poetic with visual mimesis
outside the *Poetics* is at *Rhet.* 1371b 6-8. For a neutral reference to poetic mimesis see
EN 1113a 8, '... the ancient constitutions which Homer portrayed' (where *mimeisthai* is
equivalent to *poiein*).

[27] 48a 5f., 48b 10-19, 50a 26-9, 50a 39-b 3, 54b 9-11, 60b 8f., 61b 12f. Cf. also the
metaphor from painting at 55a 34-b 2. Mimesis is used of the visual arts alone at *Pol.*
1336b 16. Cf. ch. II n.11.

past or present; things as they are said or seem to be; or things as they ought to be' (60b 8-11).[28] It will be necessary to return to this passage later, but for the moment it should be recorded that it not only frees poetry from the literalistic model of a transcription of material reality, to which Plato had tended to restrict it, but similarly liberates the visual arts themselves from the narrowness of this conception. Aristotle is edging towards a redefinition of mimesis as well as of the language of the 'image' so often associated with it: the object of the artist's mimesis not only need not be actual, but may in some sense be ideal. In this last implication anyone familiar with the Platonic inheritance must recognise a strong thrust away from the debasing, trivialising quality which Plato had polemically ascribed to artistic mimesis.

These points and others will have to be integrated into a synoptic view of the *Poetics* after we have examined the part played in the argument of the treatise by the notion of mimesis as enactment. It is worth remarking that outside the *Poetics* we encounter an important case of enactive mimesis in Book 8 of the *Politics*, where Aristotle distinguishes between the indications or signs (*sêmeia*: perhaps 'symbols') of character seen in visual art, and the mimetic representations of character possible in the musico-dramatic arts.[29] This passage is especially telling in that it demonstrates a possible tension between the imagistic and enactive senses of mimesis, for by emphasising the immediacy of the latter's mode of representation Aristotle is drawn into limiting or qualifying the power of static images, and even, in a way which we shall see is significant for a passage in the *Poetics*, into denying the full status of mimesis to the image where the representation of character is concerned. Within the *Poetics* itself mimesis as enactment can be readily found. One simple

[28] Ar. regards all images as the product of mimesis at *Top.* 140a 14f.

[29] *Pol.* 1340a 28ff. (where the distinction may be in part between *natural* likenesses and *conventional* signs or symbols: cf. *Int.* 16a 3-8, 26-8). Ar. is here talking about mimesis of moral character (*êthos*), and to understand why enactment, including music, is necessary for this, we should take account of the 'kinetic' nature of character referred to at *EN* 1128a 10-12: cf. ps.-Ar. *Probl.* 919b 26ff., 920a 3ff. But it should be noted as a reflection of Ar.'s neglect of *melopoeia* in the *Poetics* (see ch. VIII below) that the only reference to the mimetic potential of music is in the opening chapter, 47a 14-16, 23-6.

For other behavioural and enactive senses of mimesis in Ar. see *HA* 597b 24, *EN* 1115b 32, 1124b 2, 1150b 4, *Rhet.* 1404a 35f., *Protr.* B44 Düring (1961) = fr. 58 Rose, and cf. ps.-Ar. *Probl.* 917a 8, 918b 15-17, 28f.

index of it is the application of mimesis terminology to actors,[30] though it should not be supposed that what Aristotle means by dramatic mimesis is simply or primarily theatrical performance. But more revealing than this is the passage in ch. 24 where Aristotle states that the poet is not a mimetic artist (a *mimêtês*) when he speaks in his own person. The phrase 'speak in his own person' may at first sight mislead, since it might wrongly be taken to mean first-person utterance of the kind we identify directly with the poet himself, or at least with his persona. But Aristotle does not immediately have in mind such things as the passionate utterances of the love-poet or the moralising of the elegist (though these would be covered, *a fortiori*), for in ch. 24 he is discussing epic poetry, and he observes that epic poets other than Homer 'very rarely engage in mimesis'. This somewhat startling remark can refer only to the prevalence outside Homeric epic of the ordinary narrative mode, narrative without direct speech. For the epic poet to rely on narrative is for him to fall below the standards for the genre set by Homer, and Aristotle specifically regards these standards as dramatic.[31]

What we have, therefore, in *Poetics* 24 is not only a case of enactive mimesis, the mimetic mode of drama, but a momentary identification of this as the *only* true poetic mimesis, even in epic. Earlier in the treatise, in ch. 3, Aristotle had used the same phrase, 'to speak in his own person', of the narrative mode of epic, but he had there categorised this as a mode *within* his analytical scheme of poetic mimesis. Interpreters of the *Poetics* commonly regard this passage as carrying more weight than the later; it is not easy to see why this should be so. The inconsistency should be understood not as a casual insouciance on Aristotle's part, but as an acute reflection of his attempt to incorporate more than one notion of mimesis into his poetic theory. The wider notion, which depends for much of its force on the analogy with visual image-making, and the narrower, enactive sense, are both found in Plato's *Republic*, where no

[30] This is certainly the case at 47a 28 (dancers), 49b 31, 62a 10f., and 61b 31 (flute-players' miming), perhaps also at 48a 1 and 48b 25 (poet-actors? note the pertinent reference to improvisations at 48b 23f.). Cf. also *Protr.* B44 Düring (1961) = fr. 58 Rose, and ps.-Ar. *Probl.* 918b 28 (the actor is a *mimêtês*).

[31] 60a 7ff.: note the dramatic metaphor, 'brings onto the stage' (*eisagei*), used of Homer at 60a 10, and found also at *Rhet.* 1415a 32, 1417b 7 and 1418a 34 (coupled in the latter with the verb 'to turn into episodes', on which cf. ch. IX n. 10). The attempt of W. Ridgeway, *CQ* 6 (1912) 235-41 to eliminate the inconsistency in Ar.'s attitude to the mimetic status of narrative cannot be accepted: it would require us to suppose that Cyclic poets spent most of their time invoking Muses (the point is obscured on 238f.).

reconciliation between them is attempted. Of the two, the sense of enactment is the clearer: not only can it be seen as a special species of behavioural imitation, but it can be categorically defined by reference to dramatic poetry and related modes. It is the broader concept of image-making mimesis which, once applied beyond the limits of the strictly visual, becomes ill-defined and question-begging: it denotes a general mode of representation and a relation of correspondence between a work and its object, but without carrying the necessary criteria by which it could be judged that poetry but not, say, history is mimetic.

In order to enquire further into the uneasy juxtaposition of the two given ideas of mimesis, and to try to discern more precisely the orientation of Aristotle's position on the matter, I propose now to look closely at the first four chapters of the *Poetics*, in which Aristotle addresses himself more immediately than elsewhere to questions about the nature of poetic mimesis. The thrust of my analysis is intended to show that the anomaly between chs. 3 and 24 to which I have drawn attention is only the most obvious symptom of an underlying tension in Aristotle's treatment of mimesis.

An uncertainty can be detected almost from the opening sentences of the work, for it soon becomes apparent that the announcement of a concern with 'the art of poetry in general, and the potential of each of its types ...' translates itself into attention to a particular group of genres. I shall be considering in ch. IX the fuller implications of Aristotle's neglect of certain areas of Greek poetry, but for present purposes it is sufficient to notice that the genres he does refer to (first at 47a 13f., then at 47b 25-7) are all either fully dramatic or, in the case of epic, partially so (and essentially so, Aristotle will later suggest, in the Homeric paradigm). In addition, the prose genres which Aristotle seems prepared to bring within his definition of poetry are themselves dramatic: mime and Socratic dialogue (47b 10f.). The mention of these genres must be explained by reference to mimesis, since Aristotle specifies mimesis as the true differentia of poetry. It is by this criterion that the status of poet is denied to Empedocles.[32] Now as Aristotle has not defined mimesis, we have to infer the sense in which he is using it from the line of his argument:

---

[32] Also by the criterion of subject-matter, as 47b 16 and 19 indicate. But mimesis is more fundamental: history and ethical philosophy, for example, which have human action as subject-matter, are still not varieties of mimesis for Ar. (though historians' speeches at least ought to count as it).

and it is clear enough that by the standard of general poetic 'image-making', as propounded by Plato and elsewhere in the *Poetics* by Aristotle himself, Empedocles would have to be classed as, among other things, a poet. There is here, then, together with the observable concentration on dramatic genres of poetry, a *prima facie* case for suspecting that Aristotle's guiding notion of mimesis is implicitly that of enactment: poetry proper (which may include some works in prose) does not describe, narrate or offer argument, but dramatises and embodies human speech and action.[33]

Such a suspicion receives some confirmation at the start of ch. 2, where mimesis, now firmly embedded in the unfolding theory, is elaborated into what it will remain for most of the treatise, the mimesis of 'men in action'. Yet this formula, although apparently reinforcing the movement towards a predominantly dramatic conception of mimesis, need not in itself tie poetry down to a purely enactive or impersonatory mode, as Aristotle confirms by proceeding directly, in ch. 3, to stipulate enactment and narrative as the *two* principal modes of mimesis (the third mode being a mixture of the two). The structure of the analysis offered in ch. 3 is virtually taken over from a passage in *Republic* Book 3, though there is a slight adjustment in the details of terminology.[34] But whereas Plato's restriction of the term mimesis in *Rep.* 3 to the dramatic mode of poetry has no effect on the concept of poetry as such, the question of what is included in Aristotelian mimesis is necessarily bound up with the definition of the poetic art. The tension within Aristotle's position, as this emerges from ch. 3 and later passages of the *Poetics*, is highlighted by the equivocal treatment of epic. We find, in fact, that epic is located in Aristotle's theory in three different ways:

i. In ch. 3 Homer is cited as an example of the mixed mode of poetic mimesis, which combines narrative and enactment. It is

[33] The reference to dancing at 47a 27f., within the analysis of poetic media, helps further to give an enactive force to the initial concept of poetic mimesis. On Ar.'s view of dance see Appendix 3 n.8.

[34] See *Rep.* 392-6. Plato divides the genus *diêgêsis* into (a) simple *diêgêsis* (which is also '*apangelia* of the poet himself', 394c 2f.), (b) '*diêgêsis* through mimesis', 393c 9, (c) '*diêgêsis* through both', 392d 6. But Plato also uses the verb *apangellein* of (b) at 396c 7f. Ar.'s terminology therefore differs from Plato's first by using mimesis for the genus rather than one of the species, and secondly by restricting both *diêgêsis* and *apangelia* to species (a) above, i.e. narrative. But Ar. notably retains the formulation of narrative as the poet speaking 'himself' (48a 22, 60a 7 cf. *Rep.* 393a 6f., 394c 2f.), and the underlying tripartition is shared. Cf. Bywater 118f.

likely, though not stated, that other epic poets belong to the narrative mode.

ii.   In chs. 23 and 24 (59a 17, 59b 33 and 36f.) epic is designated, without qualification, as the narrative art of poetic mimesis.

iii. In ch. 24 (60a 7-11), as earlier noted, Homer is praised for his dramatic technique, and epic poets who 'speak in their own person' (the narrative mode of ch. 3) are said thereby not to engage in mimesis.

If the commendation of Homeric epic's dramatic technique and quality, which is stressed in other passages as well, were purely a judgement of poetic merit, and represented a contingent observation on the supreme achievement in the genre, it would call for no special comment. But what is problematic is that Aristotle's acknowledgement of the Homeric paradigm complicates his notion of the *nature* of the genre, and consequently his notion of poetic mimesis as a whole. An evaluation of the finest standards within the genre partly becomes converted into a redefinition of the mimetic character of the genre as such. Not only is Homer to be regarded as a great dramatist, but epic at its best (which is for Aristotle its true nature) is seen to be a form of drama and thus to be consistent with a conception of poetic mimesis as a primarily dramatic or enactive art. (This presentation of Homer incidentally helps to accentuate the dispensability of theatrical performance to Aristotle's view of dramatic mimesis.) Yet it remains the case that there is operative in the treatise as a whole a looser sense of mimesis which will allow for the inclusion of epic as either essentially a narrative genre, or a genre of mixed modes, both narrative and dramatic.

Moving on now to *Poetics* 4, we find here again signs of more than one idea of mimesis. The enactive sense must be uppermost in Aristotle's reference to the natural mimetic propensities of the human species (man as a mimetic creature), and this carries over into his sketch of early poetry further on in the chapter, where the crucial premise is that men improvised performances in accordance with their natural talents for either serious or humorous mimesis (48b 22-4). Set against this, however, is the unequivocal example, or analogy, of the mimetic *image*, which Aristotle employs in explication of the claim that men naturally take pleasure in contemplating and understanding mimetic works. The stress here falls on mimesis as accurate reproduction of an individual model, and Aristotle goes further than anywhere else in implying a one-to-one correspondence between the mimetic work and its model, so that the appreciation of the former is said to depend on prior experience of the latter. Although I have already argued that we need not, and indeed, given a passage such as 60b 8-11 (p. 124 above), *cannot* take this analogy to be meant as a sufficient account of poetic mimesis, it nonetheless draws poetry towards the visual arts, but without indicating how such a notion of mimesis is to be reconciled with the enactive sense which we find lying alongside it in ch. 4.

   This uneasy relationship between the two views of poetic mimesis which we have seen that Aristotle takes over with qualifications from Plato, resides in the fact that they are not strictly comparable. As applied to poetry, mimesis as image-making and mimesis as enactment are incompatible at a fundamental level, because they categorise poetry from the logically distinct points of view to which I drew attention in an earlier chapter (pp. 53 ff.). In its original context, mimesis as image-making represents the *formal*, iconic correspondence between works of visual art (or impersonatory acts) and their visual models. Dramatic or enactive mimesis also arguably entails a formal match or equivalence, in either of two ways: first, in its fullest form, which Aristotle does not require, in complete performance (which of course also has a dimension of visual mimesis), where action directly represents action; but, alternatively, as a category of poetic mode distinguished from narrative, namely as the direct *verbal* representation of human action. Imagistic mimesis, however, once used as an analogy for poetry, loses its formal definition, and instead purports to describe the general status of poetry (or any other relevant art) in relation to the world. Thus, it is this concept of mimesis, in a crudely reductive form, which Plato employs in *Republic* 10 to condemn the poet's as well as the painter's work as emptily and derivatively imitative: the artist works to produce a copy of the surface of material reality, and the supposedly counterfeit nature of this visual activity is predicated by direct transference of poetry also. But the notion of dramatic mimesis, by contrast, is best understood as referring to one possible *mode* of poetry, not as in itself implying anything general about poetry's relation to reality. A poetic mode is precisely what enactment is for Aristotle in ch. 3 of the *Poetics*, but I have tried to show that this idea infects his larger concept of mimesis, which correspondingly tends towards *identification* with dramatic poetry. But the chief significance of enactive mimesis is that it provides an account of the manner in which poetry deals with its material, whatever cognitive status that material as such is supposed to have: dramatic enactment, whether in performance or just in the verbal presentation of human action, can be distinguished, as Aristotle in places seems to imply, from description, narration, analysis, argument, and other forms of discourse. Through the enactive mode the poet exhibits his drama of human action without himself appearing or participating in the content of his poetry: hence Aristotle talks of Homer 'bringing on' his characters (60a 10), like a playwright or dramatic producer; and it is the negative counterpart of this that, as we have seen, narrative can be designated by the phrase 'to speak in his own person'.

On the basis of this distinction between mimesis as a general formula (however unsophisticated) for the relation between art and the world, and mimesis as a mode of poetic representation, it is now possible to see a duality in the *Poetics'* use of the language of mimesis, even if the movement of Aristotle's argument tends in places to obscure this. To pursue the further elucidation of the role of mimesis in the treatise, it is therefore desirable to keep the two aspects of it properly apart. I have already pointed out that, as a poetic mode, the enactive sense of mimesis is not to be confused with dramatic *performance* as such. Performance, the actor's art, certainly has its own claims to mimetic status (it may be covered by the category of vocal mimesis at 47a 20), and we should not rule out the possibility that this fact exercised a latent influence on Aristotle's thinking. But even if we allow for the recitation-performance of epic, which was of course usual, this is inadequate to explain Aristotle's theoretical conception, for poetry is analysed as a mimetic art independently of *any* possibility of performance. The enactive mode of mimesis represents the intrinsic manner in which the poet presents his material, and, where this mode alone is employed, it stands for the complete effacement of the poet's own 'first-person' from the content of his work. Although this fact lends itself naturally to translation into performance, it is strictly speaking an inherent feature of the poetic structure, apprehensible as such even without the assistance of actors. It is worth adding that the same cannot be said of either dancing or music (score-reading not being a Greek experience), the two other arts whose enactive character Aristotle acknowledges.

Aristotle's emphasis on enactive mimesis, reflecting as it does the dominance of drama within his theory of poetry, allows him to intimate something of importance for his understanding of the poet's function: Aristotle's poet is not expected to assert or argue (though he must know how to make his characters do so, 56a 34ff.); his task is to display organised structures of action through direct verbal representation; and any attitude which the poet may be assumed to have towards his material must be wholly implicit, embodied in his shaping and structuring of the events of his dramatic work.[35] But this dimension of the prescriptive theory of the *Poetics* now needs to be supplemented by closer examination of that aspect of the treatise which addresses itself to poetry's correspondence to its objects, the relation, that is, between poetry and reality. It was over this relation that the heavy shadow of Platonic disapproval had fallen, carrying with it the associations of falseness and deceit which Plato felt deserved to be attached to the image-making concept of mimesis. Aristotle, we have seen, was sometimes content to take over this concept, yet manifestly without Plato's critical intentions. How, then, does he reinterpret the subject-object relation entailed by mimesis so as to restore respectability and value to it?

Once again, in attempting to find an answer to this question, we face the difficulty of Aristotle's inexplicitness and laconicism, but one of the more promising leads to be found in the *Poetics* is the principle enunciated at the start of ch. 25, that the object of both the poet's and the painter's mimesis can be 'reality past or present, things as they are said or seem to be, or things as they ought to be' (60b 10f.). It would be possible to limit the force of this passage on the grounds that Aristotle's immediate concern is with the solutions to poetic 'problems', and that his approach is consequently defensive.[36] While this is a valid qualification, it does not entirely detract from the implications of this section for the status of mimesis. Together with the statement, which follows closely on the above quotation, that 'correctness in poetry is not the same as correctness in politics or in any other art', the ascription to poetry of the freedom to depict things other than present or past actuality contains a vital expression of Aristotle's response to the Platonic strictures on artistic mimesis. Perhaps the most useful way of formulating the answer to Plato's

---

[35] In this connection it should be remarked that 'thought' (*dianoia*) is only one element – a rhetorical element – within poetry, and does not represent the poet's own thought.

[36] Witness, for example, 61b 14f., where even the central principle of probability is compromised.

charge is to say that Aristotle is arguing for the independence of art from straightforward subjection to standards and criteria of truth-telling and virtue (Plato's expectations of it) and that, against the Platonic castigation of mimesis as falsehood, he is adumbrating a concept of *fiction* which allows the poet's stance towards reality to be more oblique.

As in ch. 4, Aristotle goes on at this point (60b 16 ff.) to elaborate an important argument in terms of a seemingly simple analogy from the visual arts. The details of the text are partially corrupt, but the distinction which Aristotle draws between an essential and an accidental artistic error remains intelligible enough. He illustrates the point with the example of the painting of an animal, and says that a zoological mistake in such a picture is less important than 'if the painter's depiction was unmimetic' (60b 32).[37] Whatever the standard of mimetic success that Aristotle here posits, it is certain that it cannot be the Platonic canon of mere faithfulness to appearances, for on this assumption it would make no sense to distinguish a zoological error in the painting from some other kind of mimetic failure. Instead, Aristotle appeals to the 'aim' or 'purpose' (*telos*) of the particular art to provide a criterion of effective mimesis. That Aristotle still seems to expect general conformity to optical accuracy in the visual arts is both a reflection of the aspirations of contemporary painting and sculpture, and also tellingly parallel to the requirement – confirmed at 61b 19f. – that the poet will not stray from basic ethical and rational standards except where it is necessary to do so.[38]

It can legitimately be argued, however, that Aristotle's reliance on a visual analogy for the explication of a poetic principle is a weakness, and that he follows Plato in comparing the two arts at the very point

[37] The adverb *amimêtôs* should not be translated 'with less realism' (Janko 126, who also misconstrues the syntax). As the full context indicates, Ar.'s point is not a simple one, but needs to be translated into the terms of particular arts and genres; it covers the full range of factors referred to in ch. 25, rather than any single criterion of mimetic effectiveness.

[38] There are therefore good grounds for caution against over-interpretation of Aristotelian mimesis. To say that mimesis 'is what ... we call "creative imagination" ...' (Potts 10) is simply to shirk the problems of understanding. G. Hagberg, *Philosophy* 59 (1984) 365-71, in correctly arguing against too literalistic an interpretation of Aristotelian mimesis, overstretches his case to reach the conclusion that it involves 'fidelity to the abstract connections between things and the movements of the spirit' (367). I believe the common view that Ar. takes mimesis necessarily to involve universals is also misleading, though understandable: *Poet.* 48b 15ff. shows that mimesis of particulars, while inferior, is still possible. Cf. ch. II n.15.

at which he is in fact abandoning Plato's reason for exploiting the comparison: namely, the desire to convict art of being slavishly parasitic on actuality perceivable by the senses. Aristotle can be partially defended against this criticism on the grounds that part of the force of his analogy is to suggest that his rejection of a literalistic canon of mimesis applies equally to poetry *and* to the visual arts. But while this is true, it does not alter the fact that the references to painting in ch. 25 concern specific points of visual accuracy, rather than, say, the painter's relation to mythic subject-matter; and the result of this is to leave the analogy less illuminating than it might have been (as with the visual example in *Poetics* 4) about Aristotle's primary interest, poetry.

A further drawback with ch. 25 derives from the fragmented way in which Aristotle attempts to give some substance to his general principles. This is understandably due to the focus on 'problems' and their solutions. Individual instances are cited, and a brief indication is given in each case of how they might be tackled. But this atomistic approach – which Aristotle could afford, since he had written a separate and fuller work, *Homeric Problems* – allows only glimpses of insight into fundamentals. One positive hint, however, is given, where it is stated that an error such as an impossibility within a work of art can be justified if it contributes to the aim, the *telos*, of the work. What counts as a serious fault, in other words, is to be determined not by immediate reference to the standards of other activities, as Plato had insisted, but in terms of the particular purposes of the mimesis. Aristotle gestures here towards standards which are grounded in the nature of individual genres, since he nowhere gives any reason to suppose that all poetry, let alone all art, pursues precisely the same *telos*. In particular, he alludes at 60b 25 back to the intense emotional impact which his theory of tragedy had earlier explicated. At this point, therefore, the issue of mimesis shades into the interpretation of specific kinds of poetry and their generic characteristics. To pursue the understanding of tragic or epic mimesis any further, Aristotle implies, would be to enter into the analysis which he has already offered of the type of emotional and cognitive experience, and the pleasure arising from it, which these genres distinctively aim to produce.

We have seen so far that, had Aristotle formulated his view of mimesis in an integrated statement, two necessary components of it would have been, first, an emphasis on the enactive mode which he regards as a defining feature of poetry, in contrast to discursive, analytical and even narrative uses of language; and secondly, an acceptance of poetry's fictional freedom to imagine human action of more than one kind, or to derive its models of action from sources other than common reality. But to these two we must now add a further point, and one which, to some extent unlike the pronouncements of ch. 25, not only signals Aristotle's repudiation of the Platonic case against poetic mimesis, but allows us to form a more positive conception of his own alternative. The critical evidence for this alternative is to be found in *Poetics* 9, in the distinction made there between poetry and history, and in the claims also made for the generalising status of the poet's treatment of his material. This passage confirms some of the implications which I have already drawn from *Poetics* 25: it establishes that the poet is not to be tied to transcribing reality in any straightforward manner, and indeed reinforces the idea of poetic fiction by its argument that even if the poet were to take his material from history, he would still have to fashion and structure it in accordance with the requirements of his art. On the nature of these positive requirements I have already commented in dealing with Aristotle's notion of poetic unity. I have argued that the principle of generality or typicality which *Poetics* 9 sketches means that the events of a dramatic poem should exhibit a higher level of intelligibility, particularly *causal* intelligibility, than is usually to be found in life. The plot of a dramatic poem, which is its essential structure of action, is not to be understood as simply corresponding to reality past or present (though certain elements in it may do so), but as representing a heightened and notional pattern of possibility, and as therefore more accessible to rational apprehension than are the events of ordinary experience. On the argument of *Poetics* 9, it is not immediately to life that the poet must turn for his material, but to an imagined world (including that of inherited myth) in which the underlying designs of causality, so often obscured in the world as we encounter it, will be made manifest.[39]

[39] The term 'ideal' should be applied to the status of this material only with caution: Butcher 150-62 constantly imports optimistic implications which are inappropriate for Ar.'s main interest, tragedy; similarly with the term 'Wunschwelt' (Koller 117, followed by Söffing 46). The phrase things/characters 'as they ought to be' at 60b 11 and 34 does not refer *directly* to moral goodness, but to the status of general conceptions: Lucas (1968) on 60b 11 is confused on this, but the point was seen by Lessing, *Hamburgische Dramaturgie* no.94 (with the final footnote). This does not, of course, rule out the possibility of an element of idealisation, particularly in

Such ideas remain abstract, as they are in Aristotle's outline of them. But some concluding remarks can be usefully made on them. In the first place, *Poetics* 9 makes clear how far Aristotle has moved beyond the reductive view of mimesis propagated in such Platonic texts as *Republic* 10. Mimesis does not even aim to give access to common reality, to the surfaces of life: its function is not at all merely reproductive. Aristotle has, in other words, suggested a much more cognitively rich status for mimesis than Plato ever conceded to art. This is marked above all by ch. 9's comparison between poetry and philosophy, which can be read as a riposte to the Platonic sense that the two are opponents in an irreconcilable rivalry (*Rep.* 607b). But the paradox of this Aristotelian position is that, after starting out from a restricted attention to artistic mimesis, and excluding the more ambitious Platonic attempts to elaborate a grander concept of philosophical mimesis, Aristotle has come round to regarding poetry from an angle which endows it with at least something of the force which Plato had speculatively attributed to philosophical mimesis in his late work: the capacity to enlarge understanding and to direct the mind from particulars to objects of higher significance. If it would be misleading to exaggerate these implications of Aristotle's theory, or their affinities to aspects of Plato's thinking, it is equally indefensible to overlook the connection altogether.

Aristotle's willingness in *Poetics* 9 to define the object of poetic mimesis in terms of generalised human action underlines the need to keep a comprehensive view of poetry's mimetic relation to the world separate and distinct from a theory of the mimetic mode or modes of poetry (and the other arts). Aristotle's concern with the enactive or dramatic status of poetry could be argued to draw poetry paradoxically towards the concrete and the particular, since enactment can only in itself be of particulars. Yet *Poetics* 9 shows that the engagement of poetic mimesis ought, for Aristotle, to be with universals, in contrast to the particulars which form the subject of history. There is in fact no contradiction here, only a superficial uncertainty which is due to Aristotle's refusal to disentangle the

---

characterisation (cf. *Rhet.* 1404b 13f.?). See 54b 8-11, where the reference to painting is not surprising: for the visual arts cf. *Pol.* 1281b 10-15, Xen. *Mem.* 3.10.1, Plato *Rep.* 472d (with Appendix 2 under 54b 10f.), and note what is said of the statues of the gods at *Pol.* 1254b 35. For the influence of these and other ancient passages in the history of concepts of artistic idealisation see E. Panofsky, *Idea: A Concept in Art History*, Engl. transl. (Icon edn., New York 1968).

various strands of his concept of mimesis. The *Poetics* contains, side by side and sometimes overlapping, attempts to refine the understanding of two different aspects of poetic mimesis: in short, its true mode (enactment) and its true meaning (the portrayal of universals). Aristotle's philosophical interest in the latter should not impede us from recognising that he also feels some compulsion to emphasise the former, for unlike Plato, who saw art's approximations to reality as a matter of beguiling simulacra, Aristotle certainly attached value to mimetic directness and vividness as qualities of the *modes* which mimesis might use to embody its material. This vividness is not, however, an end in itself, but a means to the successful communication of mimetic significance; for vividness concerns concrete details – actions and characters – which are taken, in their unified presentation, to be capable of signifying universals. The immediacy of the mode of poetic enactment is not required for the sake of a deceptive simulation of life, but in order to be the vehicle of a structure of meaning which Aristotle believes can nourish the understanding and move the emotions with ethical force. In this way, Aristotle's interpretation of mimesis perhaps restores to the poet at least something of the possibility of the knowledge and wisdom which Greek tradition had always claimed for him, but which Plato had been impelled to deny.

V

Action and Character

Tragedy is a mimesis not of people but of actions and life ... It is not the function of the agents' actions to allow the portrayal of their characters; it is, rather, for the sake of their actions that character is included ... Moreover, a tragedy without action would be an impossibility, but one without characterisation would be feasible ... And so, the plot-structure is the first principle and, as it were, the soul of tragedy, while character is the element of second importance. (*Poetics* 50a 16-39)

Having considered in the previous three chapters the essential framework of Aristotle's understanding of the mimetic arts in general, and poetry in particular, I proceed in the next four chapters to analyse and assess the major tenets of his theory of tragic drama. I begin in the present chapter with a pair of topics, action and character (and the relation between them), which might be regarded as pertinent to the wider sphere of poetry as a whole, since the two concepts in question are introduced at the start of ch. 2 as necessary aspects of all poetic mimesis (48a 1f.). But the principal treatments of the issue which occur later in the work belong to the discussion of tragedy, and it is chiefly in connection with this genre that Aristotle's position must be interpreted. Although some of what follows will have a bearing on other kinds of poetry, especially epic, it is therefore to the further scrutiny of the theory of tragedy that the argument will lead naturally on.

If the categories of action and character have come to seem unavoidable or indispensable to many readers and critics of drama, it is a historical fact that their fundamental place in the theory of drama was first established and explored in the *Poetics*. Yet such an observation carries the risk of importing a preconception into the reading of the treatise, since the very familiarity of notions of action and character may beguile us into supposing that what Aristotle has to say on the subject ought to be readily intelligible in our own terms. In fact, in this as in many other respects the heritage and apparent influence of the *Poetics* has often been a matter more of superficial and merely terminological alignment than of serious continuity of thought, and Aristotle's judgements on the nature and relative importance of action and character have frequently been misconstrued even by those propagating supposedly Aristotelian doctrine.[1] Although modern scholarship has made some significant contributions to the elucidation of the priorities which Aristotle unequivocally states in *Poetics* 6, the main obstacle in the way of a correct appreciation of this aspect of the treatise lies at a deeper level than that of academic exegesis. Modern readers of the *Poetics* are likely to continue to experience dissatisfaction and unease over Aristotle's pronouncements on action and character, and particularly his firm subordination of the latter to the former, on account of the wide discrepancy between the view of drama which this subordination represents and the dominant post-Romantic belief in the centrality of psychological characterisation both to drama and to other forms of literature (above all, the novel).

Such dissatisfaction is a reminder of the need to take nothing for granted in approaching this side of the *Poetics*, but to be open to the possibility of a radical difference between Aristotle's and the typical modern idea of the relative status of action and character in drama. In order to reach an understanding of what may separate these two points of view, we must turn first to the concept of action in the *Poetics*. But before attempting to explicate the most important, and the most problematic, features of this concept, it will be useful to prepare the ground by indicating the various, if closely related, areas of meaning which the terminology of action covers in the work. The value of starting from these apparently dry data of usage lies in the fact, widely traceable in the corpus as a whole, that Aristotle starts from and works with the given scope of ordinary Greek terms and ideas, but seeks to refine them into more sophisticated notions for

---

[1] This can be seen in, for example, attempts such as that of E.E. Stoll, 'Plot & Character: on the Stagirite's Behalf', *MLR* 39 (1944) 209-14, to find modern testimony in line with Ar.'s: the consequence is too often a misleading assimilation of disparate ideas, and a failure to reckon with Ar.'s specific concept of character. The latter is equally true of many who contradict Ar.: e.g. E.M. Forster, *Aspects of the Novel* (Harmondsworth 1962) 91, who, after telling us that Ar. is wrong on this matter (but without any attention to what he might have meant), goes on to concede, somewhat illogically, that his remarks hold true for drama. Lucas (1957) 137ff. similarly gives no indication of what is distinctive about Ar.'s concepts.

theoretical and critical use. On this basis, we can find in the treatise three salient categories of lexical usage which will illuminate facets of Aristotle's concept of dramatic action.

(1) Aristotle frequently uses the plain verb 'to act' (*prattein*) of the human subjects of drama: he has a certain penchant for the participial form according to which these subjects are denoted as 'the agents'.[2] Correspondingly, the noun *praxis*, 'action', is sometimes applied in a general sense to the involvement of the agents in the plot.[3] This lowest and broadest level of usage may look unremarkable, but its repetitive emphasis does in fact lend a colouring to Aristotle's view of poetry, and it gives recurring support to the principle, quoted at the head of this chapter, that tragedy is 'a mimesis not of people but of actions and life'. The notion of action is capable of bearing a very wide significance in Aristotelian philosophy, as a comprehensive description of the purposive behaviour of mature living beings: 'if action is taken away from the living person ... what remains except contemplation?'[4] Aristotle's stress on action and rational agency accords with the meaning of the word *drama* itself (cf. 48a 27-9), but it would also, and more tellingly, intimate an essential point for the philosopher's audience: it implies that the fabric of tragedy, or indeed of all poetry, is the representation of human purpose striving for realisation, and therefore falls within the purview of 'practical' or ethical philosophy – a point to which I shall later return.

(2) The plural noun *pragmata*, cognate with *praxis* but sometimes possessing a more concrete force than it, is employed in the *Poetics* for the individual constituents or elements of a play, though without quite the directness of reference to agency which *praxis* usually

---

[2] 'Agents' (*prattontes*): e.g. 48a 1, 23, 27, 49b 37, 50a 6 (and *drôntes* in the same sense at 48a 28f. and 49b 26, in the definition of tragedy). The verb *prattein* is arguably sometimes used of the *actors* of a play: 49b 31 (*contra* Else (1957) 233f.: cf. Appendix 3 n.4) and 59a 15, and possibly also at 50a 21 and 48a 23 (the latter very unlikely). But Lucas (1968) on 49b 37 and Else (1957) 239 are wrong to find a reference here to actors, since moral characterisation would be absurdly predicated of the latter. Jones 59 argues too loosely for a general merging of the two senses of the verb.

[3] E.g. 48b 25, 50a 16f., 22, 51b 29, 54a 18. *Pragmata* in this same sense at 50a 22, but for the normal sense see n.5 below.

[4] *EN* 1178b 20f. Ar.'s concept of action does not apply to children or animals: *EN* 1139a 20, *EE* 1222b 19f., 1224a 28-30. For a full philosophical treatment of the subject (but one which ignores the *Poetics*) see D. Charles, *Aristotle's Philosophy of Action* (London 1984).

carries. *Pragmata* is thus best translated as 'events' rather than
'actions'. Its most prominent occurrence is as part of the phrase 'the
structure [or composition] of events', which is a definition of plot.[5]
Both the verb *prattein* and the noun *praxis* are occasionally found in
related senses.[6] The importance of this range of usage is that it
somewhat counterbalances the positive emphasis on purposive action
already noted, and helps to prompt a central question which will
shortly be raised about the vocabulary of action in the *Poetics*.

(3) Superimposed onto the normal uses cited above, the *Poetics*
contains an original development of the word *praxis* to mean the
organised totality of a play's structure of events, its complete
dramatic framework.[7] *Praxis* in this sense is larger than, and
embraces, all the terminology of action so far considered. This new
piece of poetic and dramatic vocabulary also represents a new
concept, since it is not simply a compendious way of referring to
everything within a play, but imports the specific implications of
Aristotle's formal ideas about the nature of a plot-structure. *Praxis*
might, indeed, be thought to be a synonym of plot-structure (*muthos*),
which is itself a term elaborated beyond its ordinary meaning and
refined by Aristotle to the status of a technical term. Strictly
speaking, however, synonymity cannot be claimed, since *muthos* is
defined (as is tragedy itself) as the mimesis or enactment of the (or
a) *praxis*.[8] Analytically, in other words, the 'action' (*praxis*) is the

[5] E.g. 50a 4f., 15, 32f., 36f., 50b 22, 51a 32f. Other occurrences of *pragmata*: e.g. 51b
22, 53b 5 (where the phrasing indicates that the word is less active than *praxis*), 13f.,
54b 6f. *Pragma* at 51a 10 might conceivably be synonymous with Ar.'s new sense of
praxis, but the context makes certainty impossible.

[6] For *praxis* used in a similar way to *pragma* see 52b 1 and 11. Likewise with various
forms of *prattein*: 52a 22, 29, 55a 25, 59b 24.

[7] This usage is not properly recorded by LSJ s.v. *praxis* II, where 54a 18 (n.3 above)
is wrongly connected with 59a 19 and 51b 33: these last two passages do not mean
'action in drama, opp. *logos*'.

[8] E.g. 50a 3f., 50b 3, 51a 31f. Other occurrences of the new sense of *praxis*: 49b 24,
50b 24, 51a 19, 28, 59a 19, 22. Note that some cases of *praxis* (e.g. 49b 36, 50b 3) could
in themselves be translated either simply as 'action' or in the developed sense of a
unitary structure of action: this highlights the way (best seen in the whole sentence,
49b 36ff.) in which Ar.'s refined usage grows out of the existing meaning. 'Action' in
English is capable of approximating to the distinctive Aristotelian sense of *praxis*
precisely because of the *Poetics*' influence: the OED s.v. Action I 4 cites Addison's
papers on *Paradise Lost* for the earliest examples. But the dramatic sense of 'action' in
English rarely if ever carries the full implications of structure and unity which Ar.
lends to the Greek term. (The Latin *actio* seems never to have been used for a unitary
dramatic plot: OLD s.v., 2b, gives a Ciceronian usage equivalent to *praxeis* or *pragmata*
in the *Poetics*.)

structure of a play's events viewed as a dimension of the events themselves; it is the pattern discernible in the 'actions and life' which the poet dramatises. As such, it can be described as the object or content of the plot-structure (*muthos*), which can in turn be understood to be the design or significant organisation of the work of art. By the finest logic, it is the *muthos* which the poet makes and shapes (he is a maker of *muthoi*, 51b 27 f.), but since for Aristotle the events of which a dramatic action (*praxis*) consists need not exist except as the imagined material of the playwright's plot-structure, the distinction between *praxis* and *muthos* is of little or no practical weight. Hence the occurrence of passages such as ch. 9, 51b 33f., 'of simple plot-structures (*muthoi*) and actions (*praxeis*) the episodic kind are worst'; ch. 10, 52a 12-14, 'plot-structures may be simple or complex, for such are the types of actions of which the plots are enactments'; and ch. 11, 52a 36-8, 'the type of recognition which is essential to the plot-structure and the action has been stated ...' The complementarity of plot and action is a function of Aristotle's concept of poetic unity: on the principle that a unified mimesis (the plot-structure) must be a mimesis of a unified object (the action), as this is propounded at the end of ch. 8 of the treatise, the formal properties of plot and action are necessarily correlative. Consequently, in the model of the Aristotelian complex tragedy, recognition and reversal can be conceived of interchangeably as elements in the *praxis* or in the *muthos*.[9] The English terms 'plot' and 'action', in fact, both become serviceable for either of the Greek terms in question, and I use them (though with a continuing preference for 'plot-structure' over 'plot') without any attempt to preserve a nice distinction.

In the above three categories of terminology, all connected with the root sense of 'action', we have moved from a general account of drama in terms of the agents who are its human subjects, through the conception of events which form the component materials of the plot-structure, to the overarching framework of the 'action' which represents the essential design – and therefore the intelligible substance – of the work of art. Each of the first two of these elements, which constitute the same dramatic fabric seen from slightly different angles, must be referred for their ultimate significance to

[9] Cf. e.g. 52a 14-18, 22f. (= *praxis*), 52a 18f., 52b 9f. (= *muthos*). On *muthos* and *praxis* see Vahlen (1914) 236-9.

the third, the action which is virtually synonymous with the plot-structure. For the action of a play is not simply the sum of the component actions or events; it is a coherent and meaningful order, a pattern which supervenes on the arrangement of this material and arises out of the combination of purposive individual actions. Aristotle makes the point succinctly, but in a way which delicately emphasises his development of a new poetic concept, at the start of ch. 8: 'one man may perform many actions (*praxeis*), but these need not produce a unified action (*praxis*)' (51a 18f.). While there is a deliberate air of the paradoxical about this formulation, there is certainly no intention to sever the notion of the overall action from the normal sense of *praxis*. A combination or succession of discrete actions does not result in a single unified 'action', the fabric of an ordered drama; but it remains clear from the general thrust of Aristotle's theory that the term *praxis* has been chosen for the structure of a play's content in order to corroborate the underlying insistence in the *Poetics* on drama's concern with human agency.

But if the new concept of a unitary dramatic action rests on the firm basis of a broader interest in the actions of individuals, it also rises far above that basis, and in so doing it suggests a question about the precise relation within Aristotle's theory between actions and the single action of the plot – that is, between actions and poetic structure. Both the degree of continuity between Aristotle's two senses of 'action', and also the problematic aspect of the relation, are initially indicated by the sentence early in the analysis of tragedy, in ch. 6, which begins: 'since tragedy is a mimesis of (an) action, and (the) action is engaged in by certain agents ...' (49b 36f.).[10] What is striking here is that although 'action' is used to refer to the structure of a play's content (later in the same sentence the *muthos* is defined as 'the mimesis of the action', 50a 3f.), yet Aristotle talks as though the figures of a tragedy are its agents or subjects: the action, the 'structure of events', is performed by them. In itself this might seem to imply that the framework of dramatic action is merely the outcome of individual acts, but the subsequent analysis of plot shows that this cannot be so. Later in ch. 6 Aristotle again makes a strong

[10] This is one of the two main passages (the other is 48a 1-2) which necessitate some qualification on the thesis of Belfiore that *praxis* in the *Poetics* never means an ethically characterised action. Belfiore makes the distinction between action and character a little too rigid: 50b 9-10 (which should be kept: n.20 below) intimates that *some* actions may have an intrinsically ethical quality, and one may doubt whether Ar. could regard a killing as a *mere* event (Belfiore 110).

connection between the agency of the stage-figures and the design of
the plot, when he says that a tragedy is 'a mimesis of (an) action, and
principally on account of this a mimesis of the agents' (50b 3f.).
While the subordination of character to action is here clearly
reaffirmed (following 50a 16-22), no elucidation is given of the
relation between the individual actions of agents and the totality of
the plot-structure. Such elucidation must be gathered, if at all, from
the doctrine of unity which I examined in ch. III, for unity is the
principal property of the *muthos* and of the action which it embodies.
Unity arises out of the causal and consequential relations between
the actions or events of a tragedy, and it is the connective sequence of
these events which constitutes the intelligible structure that Aristotle
terms both the action and the plot-structure.

The use of the word 'events' in that last sentence, as a kind of
mediation between the level of individual actions and the
superstructure of the plot, reflects the *Poetics'* own procedure. In the
language of the treatise, actions are also perceived as events, which are
then composed by the plot into the coherent 'structure of events' – into,
that is, a *single* action. This is, of course, to schematise the train of
thought beyond Aristotle's own exposition of it, but to do so is
nonetheless fairly to clarify the orientation of the theory. The
mediating function of 'events', *pragmata*, is due to the fact that in Greek
(as in English) this term both embraces the possibilities of human
agency, but also allows for a more complex interplay of factors than the
stress on personal agents can cover: it occupies the theoretical space
which would otherwise exist between the 'many actions' of these
agents and the single action in which the dramatic structure should
bind them. But Aristotle's fluctuation between 'actions' and 'events'
in his discussion of tragic poetry does not solve, but only heightens, the
difficulty of seeing how his extreme concern with purposive agency is
to be reconciled with the requirements of the cohesive design of the
plot-structure. And if this difficulty appears abstract or theoretical, it is
vital to realise that it is in fact of great significance for the conception of
tragedy, for it should lead us to ask how Aristotle imagines that
distinctively tragic material can be created or handled within a
scheme that is primarily determined, so the treatise insists, by the
intentions of individual agents. Or, to formulate this question in its
most concrete and pointed form: how is the emphasis on action
expected to be consistent with the inescapable factor of tragic *suffering*,
as posited by the defining criterion of pity and fear?

What is at issue here can be appreciated more fully in the light of a comment on the weighting of the work's argument as a whole. Most of Aristotle's references to the characters of drama as 'the agents', as well as to their separate actions, occur in the earlier sections of the *Poetics*: either in the discussion of the objects and modes of mimesis in chs. 2 and 3, or in the long and crucial ch. 6. Correspondingly, the few explicit mentions of passive experiences in poetry and drama are mostly to be found later in the treatise. There is no direct reference to the poetic representation of suffering or passive experience in the first seven chapters, though there are some oblique allusions to it.[11] It is only in ch. 8 that Aristotle's analysis of plot-structure, whose components have so far been denoted either positively as actions or more neutrally as events, clearly betrays the possibility of a passive dimension of experience in drama. Even here the possibility is principally acknowledged in the two negative remarks (with the same verb in both) that 'many random things can *happen* to a man which do not form a unity' (51a 17f.), and that Homer 'in composing the *Odyssey* did not tell of everything that *befell* Odysseus' (51a 24f.). The implications of the phrasing in these two cases may seem to be limited, and they are further qualified by the fact that one of the illustrations used to support the second of them concerns a positive and deliberate action on Odysseus's part. Further on in the *Poetics* the only explicit references to passive experience are the brief definition of *pathos*, 'physical suffering', in ch. 11 (a definition which significantly includes the term 'action', *praxis*);[12] the instances of reversal cited in ch. 11, 52a 24-9; the merest glances at *pathos* in ch. 14; and a pair of phrases in chs. 13 and 14 describing the terrible sufferings involved in the histories of those families who make the best tragic subjects.[13] It is not surprising that it is in the section of the work dealing with the constituents of the complex plot that we meet an unavoidable recognition of the passivity entailed in certain tragic myths, but it ought to be observed how little Aristotle makes

[11] 47a 28 (dancers portray *pathê*, but the word may mean 'emotions' here); 49a 35, where the description of the comic mask implies a contrast with tragic *pathos*, physical suffering (cf. 52b llf.); 49b 27, pity and fear in the definition of tragedy.

[12] On *pathos* see Rees (1972a), and cf. ch. VII n.30 below. For a similar sense of *pathos* see e.g. *Met.* 1022b 20f., *Rhet.* 1382b 30.

[13] 53a 21f., 54a 12f. One might add the implications of 51b 11: the subject of history is (e.g.) 'what Alcibiades did or suffered' (a wry echo of Hom. *Od.* 8. 490? and an allusion to Thucydides, according to De Ste Croix).

of the point even here.[14] It is of major significance that Aristotle does not relax his concentration on purposive agency when defining the pattern of his tragic ideal.

Although the attention paid to action in the earlier parts of the *Poetics* to some extent reflects Aristotle's interest in the dramatic *mode* of mimesis (as I tried to bring out in my previous chapter), it is also a sign of the larger agent-centred view of drama which the treatise consistently offers. To explore the specific relevance of this view to the understanding of tragedy would carry us into a study of the core of Aristotle's theory of the genre, and to consideration of the question whether Aristotle sufficiently allows for the scope, and the causes, of tragic suffering, as this is known in the surviving plays. Part of the answer to this question will be attempted later in ch. VII, but I must here briefly anticipate some of the argument which I shall there advance. Scrutiny of the theory of tragedy outlined in the *Poetics* warrants us, I believe, in concluding that Aristotle is concerned to exclude from the structure of a plot all those sources of causation which are external to the actions of the human figures themselves. These sources encompass, most importantly, the full range of traditional religious explanations for events in the world. The figures of tragedy are primarily characterised as 'the agents' because it is this description which best fits the agent-centred perspective within which dramatic poetry is seen in the treatise: it is the agents themelves who are the prime causative force in the action of the play; it is they who direct, or, through the failures of action for which *hamartia* stands, *misdirect*, the development of events which gives the plot its structure and unity. For the possibility of distinctive tragic patterns of action to occur, some place needs to be reserved in Aristotle's theory for suffering, as well as, more broadly, for a combination of actions or events which cannot be directly attributed to the main agents. But, as I have suggested, the whole dimension of passive experience is minimised, since Aristotle's view of tragedy is focussed not on the actuality of suffering, but on the lines of causation within the sphere of human agency which lead towards it.

[14] On action as against passive experience in Ar.'s theory see Else (1957) 306f. For the distinction within tragedy itself note Soph. *OC* 266f. It helps to set Ar.'s stress on action in relief to observe the common view that suffering (in a wider sense than Ar.'s *pathos*) is the essence of tragedy: e.g. Herod. 5.67.5 (Sicyonian tragedy), Plato *Rep.* 380a, 605c-d, 606b, Menander *Aspis* 329f. Cf. also the Byzantine treatise in Browning 68 §2: tragedy portrays 'sufferings more than actions', though it is odd of Browning 73 to comment that this is 'implicit in Aristotle's *Poetics*'.

Hence, in ch. 14 of the treatise we find this tendency brought to fulfilment in the prescription for an ideal tragic plot-type in which irreversible suffering is averted: such an ideal permits the full demonstration of the conditions in which agency can unwittingly advance towards 'the incurable' (53b 35), yet it makes this movenent in the plot-structure compatible with prevention of the ultimate suffering.

Ch. 14 reinforces the point in a further respect. Aristotle here considers four possible plot-types derived from permutations of two factors: the knowledge or ignorance of the agent, and the fact that a tragic deed is or is not carried through. The general pertinence to my argument of these two factors is not hard to discern, for both are firmly agent-centred and concern the nature of certain courses of action. One negative entailment of this is that the main figure of a tragedy which conforms to Aristotelian requirements cannot be a passive *victim*. Accordingly, to take first a clear-cut instance, when Aristotle rejects a play such as Euripides' *Medea*, he does so because of the plot's implications for the agent not for the victims. In a subtler case such as that of the admired *Iphigeneia in Tauris*, it may be relevant to Aristotle's judgement of the play that it is hardly possible to distinguish a victim from an agent; both Iphigeneia and Orestes can be regarded as agents (as well as, in a sense, victims) since, up to the point of recognition, both are implicated by their actions, though beyond their knowledge or intentions, in the chain of events which leads towards tragic suffering. The force of the *Poetics'* theory must be seen in relation to the fact, which Aristotle himself clearly perceives, that many of the prominent tragic myths revolve around family relationships. One might have expected this to mean that the plays dealing with these myths would give as great a role to victims as to agents. Aristotle's conception of tragedy, however, frames the matter sharply in terms of the erring tragic agent, and in doing so it arguably reflects the character of at least the majority of the Greek tragedies known to us. As representative instances of works in which a tragedy between members of the same family is nonetheless dramatised largely as the tragedy of a single individual, one might cite Aeschylus's *Seven Against Thebes* (though without its context in a trilogy), Sophocles' *Oedipus Tyrannus*, and Euripides' *Bacchae*. Although various qualifications may need to be put to this claim, there remains a strong congruence between the *Poetics* and the tendency of the tragedians to build their treatments of tragic myths around a preeminent and *active* figure, usually of heroic status: and Aristotle signals his recognition of this most clearly in ch. 13 by defining his conception of the ideal complex plot around the assumption of a central tragic agent.

If this agreement between theory and practice owes something to the traditional attributes of Greek heroism, with its stress on individual status and the assertive, often egoistic values of action, it is equally true that the the world in which such heroes belonged was one in which powers other than those of human agency were a major source of suffering and tragedy. It is this latter fact for which Aristotle's theory of the genre does not make full provision, and it is in this respect that theory and practice are no longer in harmony. Although there will be more to say on this subject in a later chapter, it is my present contention that a direct connection can be observed between the *Poetics'* insistence on the primacy of human agency and the work's neglect of the religious element in Greek tragedy. If this is right, the claim must be extended to take account of Aristotle's notion of a coherent dramatic *praxis*, and for two reasons: first, because this new notion is influenced, as I earlier argued, by the basic concern with agency; secondly, because the unity which is the prime attribute of the *praxis* has to be understood in terms of the intrinsic causation of human action. Unity of action, which is also unity of plot-structure, is regulated by necessity and probability, whose operation is much less easy to interpret with reference to passive experience than to the scope of purposive action. The intelligibility of tragedy, for Aristotle, resides in the fact that the configurations of events of which dramatic plots are made up lie entirely within the field of human intention and agency, and the potential error, ignorance or failure in which they can be implicated.

Success or failure in action is very much to the point within the Aristotelian view of tragic poetry, but it is largely so because this view presupposes the terms of the philosopher's general understanding of human behaviour. When, at 50a 2f., Aristotle states that 'it is in their actions that all men experience success or failure', the context reveals that he is linking his theory of poetry expressly with his wider ethical thought; and his talk of success or failure functions as a gesture towards ideas with which he would expect his audience to have some familiarity. Aristotle's theory requires poetry to portray men in pursuit of the goals of action, and in the case of tragedy (and epic) these goals are taken to bear on the supreme moral aim of 'happiness' (*eudaimonia*).[15] Happiness, within the philosopher's system, represents the ultimate standard of success in action, the virtuous perfection of human agency, and it provides a model against which the serious actions and events which provide material for tragedy must be measured. But Aristotle's conception of happiness also illustrates in its extreme form his basic presupposition that human excellence and success call for *active* embodiments, rather than being regarded as achieved or static conditions. And this presupposition brings us to the point at which it is necessary to expand the analysis of action in the *Poetics* so as to bring the question of character into the frame of reference.

The nature of the relation between Aristotelian character and action can be given a preliminary definition by the complementary propositions that the true locus and realisation of character is in action, and that action in its strong sense of purposive behaviour cannot be fully understood without the explanatory quality of character. But these propositions are likely only to produce an immediate paradox in the eyes of the modern reader of the *Poetics*, who there finds action and character analytically separated, together with a statement of the possibility of tragedies which dispense with character altogether. We clearly cannot claim for Aristotle complete inseparability of character and action of the kind implied by Henry James's questions in 'The Art of Fiction': 'What is character but the determination of incident? What is incident but the illustration of character?'[16] Yet James seems to imply a view of character of precisely the kind which my two propositions above formulate. Starting from ostensibly similar postulates, Aristotle and James are led to rather different conclusions. Thus James rejects the categorisation of novels into those of action and those of character, whereas Aristotle not only seems open to such a categorisation for tragedy in his general remarks in ch. 6 (50a 23ff.), but actually puts forward a scheme of tragic plot-types at 55b 32-56a 2 which incorporates the character-action dichotomy. This seems difficult to reconcile with the close link between action and character which I have attributed to Aristotle, and it also recalls the discrepancy which I emphasised near the start of this chapter between Aristotelian and

---

[15] For a discussion of in just what way, see ch. VII pp. 202ff. On happiness and action see e.g. *Phys.* 197b 5, *Met.* 1078a 31f., *EN* 1169b 28ff., 1173a 14f., *Pol.* 1325b 14-16.

[16] *Henry James: Selected Literary Criticism*, ed. M. Shapira (Harmondsworth 1968) 88.

modern attitudes to character and its function in literature. It may
be profitable to approach the first of these problems by way of some
further observations on the second.

A significant element in the divergence between Aristotelian and
modern ideas of character lies in the contrast of the relative
narrowness and determinacy of the former with the fluidity and
uncertainty of the latter.[17] One of the implications of the quotation
from Henry James in the preceding paragraph is that character may
pervade, or inhere in, everything that human beings do. This has the
effect of turning character into something which it would be difficult
to define or circumscribe, and it suggests a strong connection of
character with action only by going far towards dissolving the
distinction between them. But to this we must add another
dominant feature of modern notions of character, namely the
psychological. The suggestion that character may be bound up with
all our actions, from the trivial to the portentous, does not contradict
the prevalent belief in a firm, internal locus for the individual
character. Psychological inwardness is a major assumption in
modern convictions about character, and this in turn leads to typical
emphases on the uniqueness of the individual personality and on the
potential complexities of access to the character of others. If
character is thought of in strongly psychological terms, then the
possibility readily arises that it may remain concealed in the inner
life of the mind, or be only partially and perhaps deceptively revealed
to the outer world; but, equally, that it may be glimpsed or intimated
in various unintended or unconscious ways. Such ideas and
possibilities, which find their quintessential literary embodiment in
the novel (whose conventions allow privileged access to the minds of
characters), are by their very intricacy and indefiniteness the
antithesis of the theory of dramatic character presented in the *Poetics*.
Aristotle defines *êthos* (which is both 'character', an attribute of
persons, and 'characterisation', a property of the work of art) twice in
the course of the treatise, first in ch. 6 and later at the start of ch. 15,
both times in very similar language. The first of these passages reads:
'character (characterisation) is that which shows the nature of

[17] Grube (1958) xxi states the very opposite, but where does Ar. treat *êthos* as a
man's 'whole personality'? For the contrast between Ar.'s and modern notions of
character see Jones, esp. 32-8. The idea of 'access' to that which is essentially inward
is common to much modern thinking on the subject: see e.g. E.M. Forster loc.cit. (n.1
above) (' ... the secret life ... to which ... the novelist has access'), and Gould (1978)
43 ('what they say and do gives us access to the kind of people they are ... ').

deliberate moral choice ... consequently there is no character in those speeches in which there is nothing at all that the speaker chooses or rejects' (50b 8-10). The word which Aristotle uses here for choice, *prohairesis*, is not a casual ingredient in anything that people do or say, but a carefully delimited matter of conscious desire and intention, based on dispositions which are those of virtue and vice. The *Poetics'* definition of character, in other words, precisely echoes Aristotle's moral philosophy, and he could expect his original audience to appreciate the relevant ethical background to this part of the theory of tragedy.[18] It is a background very different from that from which modern readers are likely to come to the treatise.

The basis of character for Aristotle is constituted by developed dispositions to act virtuously or otherwise. These dispositions are both acquired and realised in action; they cannot come into existence or continue to exist for long independently of practical activity. In contrast to much modern thinking, the Aristotelian distinction between character and action is not a matter of internal as against external aspects of behaviour;[19] rather, character represents the ethical qualities of actions: it is that, as Aristotle puts it in the *Poetics*, in virtue of which 'we say that the actions are of a certain sort' (49b 38f.). Character is most clearly realised in the deliberate framing of ethical intentions which Aristotle calls *prohairesis*, and it is this which, as we saw, he puts at the centre of his definition of character or characterisation in tragedy. Out of this definition, inspected against the setting of the philosopher's ethics, two essentials must be grasped before we proceed to consider the further implications of character in the *Poetics*. The first, already indicated, is that character (*êthos*, or commonly the plural *êthê*) is a specific moral factor in relation to action, not a vague or pervasive notion equivalent to modern ideas of personality or individuality – least of all to individuality, since *êthos* is a matter of generic qualities (virtues and vices). The second point, which follows on from the first, is that dramatic characterisation, to correspond to Aristotle's concept, must involve the *manifestation* of moral choice in word or

[18] For the general sense of *êthos* in Ar. see Schütrumpf ch. I; on the relation between character and action in the *Poetics* cf. Vahlen (1911) 236-52, Lord (1969), and Rees (1975).

[19] Still less should Aristotelian action be thought of as encompassing 'everything that expresses the mental life', or as 'an inward process, a psychical energy working outwards', to cite one of the more deleterious instances of Butcher's Hegelianising tendencies (123f., 334ff.).

action (50b 8, 54a 18); if this is lacking, then characterisation cannot properly be predicated of the play.[20] Together these points show that there is continuity between the *êthos* of the *Poetics* and the *Ethics*, and that the interpretation of poetic *êthos* takes account of the limitations imposed by practical circumstances on the judgement of character in others. For, while Aristotle holds the connection between action and character to be direct and fundamental, he does not pretend that it is in all cases transparent to the beholder (if indeed there is a beholder at all). Because of a range of contingent factors, we may not always be able to make a secure judgement on the function of character in individual actions. It is this which explains Aristotle's attitude to character in drama: if character is to play a part in tragedy, as it is ideally required to do, there must be no uncertainty or ambiguity about it; we must be able to identify it as a specific dimension of the action, embodied in clear evidence for the ethical dispositions of the agents.[21]

The demarcation of dramatic character as the manifestation of deliberate moral choice or intention provides the conditions which enable Aristotle to make a clean conceptual distinction between action and character, and also to arrive at judgements on the relation between, and the relative importance of, these two salient aspects of dramatic poetry. To elucidate further his view of this relation, it is advisable to examine in turn the passages of the treatise where it is touched on, beginning with ch. 2. An apparent anomaly is at once encountered here, given the remarks which Aristotle later makes about the possibility of characterless tragedies. At the start of ch. 2 (as again later at 49b 37f.) Aristotle seemingly states that since poetry is a mimesis of 'agents' or 'men in action', the moral characterisation of the agents necessarily follows. In fact, there need be no contradiction between this passage and the later one in ch. 6,

[20] 50b 9f., which should be retained, *pace* Kassel's text, in some form (cf. Vahlen (1885) 125f.), indicates the difference between implicit and explicit *prohairesis*: it is the latter which Ar. mostly has in mind by *êthos* in the *Poetics*, though 54a 18 alludes to the intrinsic moral quality (whether good or bad) which some actions might possess.

[21] Although deeds may be signs of character (e.g. *EE* 1228a 5-7, *Rhet.* 1367b 27), and while in practice we tend to infer character from action (e.g. *EE* 1219b 11), the two are sometimes separable: cf. *EN* 1111b 5f., *EE* 1228a 2-4, *Rhet.* 1374c 14. To be sure of inferring character from action, we may need more information than individual deeds sometimes allow (*Rhet.* 1367b 22ff.), since character depends on habituation and consistency of disposition. Ideally, of course, character and action go closely together: e.g. *EN* 1127a 27f., 1178a 34ff. But to make the firmest moral judgements we must be able to be sure of *prohairesis*: *EN* 1105a 28ff., 1144a 13ff.

since in the first case we are offered a generalised contention about the nature of poetry, whereas in his later observations on the variable scope of characterisation in tragedy Aristotle is making and pressing a more specific point about the dramatic balance of action and character. What is said in ch. 6 should therefore check us from supposing that ch. 2 advances the strict thesis that there is no dramatic action which does not entail character. What this passage does assert is that the agents of poetry are in general morally characterised, since character is the natural concomitant of most human action of any significance; and Aristotle can probably also be taken to be enjoining the inclusion of character in poetry, in order to lend full ethical intelligibility to the portrayal of action. But the possibility remains that individual instances of action, or even whole plays of a certain sort, will dispense with explicit characterisation, and it is this possibility to which Aristotle will later draw attention.

The generality of what *Poetics* 2 states on the subject of character is indicated both by the broad and unqualified use of moral categories ('good or bad ... vice or virtue ... better or worse than present humanity ...') and also by the fact that at this stage in his argunent Aristotle is still concerned with the whole genus of poetry, and with the essential differences between its species. Most of this short chapter is taken up with what, in embryo, is the first formulation of a principle which was later to become a standard component in the definition of the dramatic genres of tragedy and comedy, until these were undermined by the development of 'bourgeois' tragedy and of tragicomedy. Later doctrine, however, placed stress on the worldly and social status of the characters with which each genre typically deals, so that tragedy and comedy become distinguishable by reference to the opposite extremes of the scale of social standing. There are those who would discern in the *Poetics* a more precise anticipation of such views by arguing that Aristotle's ethical terminology carries overtones of social status or other types of preeminence, and by appealing to the general Greek use of such terminology in which it is certainly often difficult to divorce ethical judgements from wider social and related considerations. Moreover, the heroic figures represented in epic and tragic poetry are exceptional in a number of respects, from personal qualities such as courage to external matters of honour and power, and the poets' images of them do not customarily stress the separability of these various attributes. These two arguments make it tempting to align Aristotle's references to tragedy's 'better' characters with the values of heroism and with popular Greek ethics; but they are, in fact, inadequate to establish this sense as more than a secondary factor in Aristotle's thinking, and they are outweighed by other points. Paramount among these is Aristotle's own unequivocal definition of character in terms of moral choice and intention (*prohairesis*). This fact is buttressed by the clear ethical force given to the terminology applied to character in the *Poetics*, particularly in ch. 15, where the reference to women and slaves in connection with goodness indicates that status, though material, is not primarily in question. But even more significant is the separation emphatically drawn in *Poetics* 13 between the ethical virtue of the tragic agent (which should not be extreme) and his status, fortune and circumstances, which *should* be extraordinary (53a 7-12). I shall return at the end of this chapter to the implications of this for Aristotle's estimation of heroic values in tragedy, but it is sufficient here to note that the separation reinforces the *Poetics'* delineation of dramatic character by reference to clear-cut (Aristotelian) criteria of ethical virtue.[22]

Most of Aristotle's important pronouncements on character, and its relation to action, occur in ch. 6 of the *Poetics*, where he approaches the subject three times. On the first occasion, at 49b 36ff., he begins by echoing the opening of ch. 2 and the idea that characterisation ought to play a part in the dramatic portrayal of human action; but the postulate is now extended by the addition of 'thought' (*dianoia*): the figures of tragedy should be 'of a certain sort in respect both of character and of thought, for it is through these that we say that the actions too are of a certain sort'. Although later in this same sentence Aristotle defines character alone as 'that in respect of which we say that the agents are of a certain sort', it appears from the former remark that a close association may exist between character and thought. 'Thought' is defined both in the present passage and again in ch. 19 in such a way as virtually to identify it with rhetorical

---

[22] The arguments for a wider than moral reference in Ar.'s terminology is put by e.g. Butcher 231-8, Else (1957) 73-8, Jones 56f., and cf. Twining 68 n.7 and 183f. (with 214-16 for the corollary on comedy). On the other side see e.g. Grube (1958) xxi-ii, House 82f., Schütrumpf 55-9, Held 166ff. The matter can hardly be settled on the terminology alone (on Ar.'s use of *spoudaios* see Teichmüller vol. 2, 172-8). I rest my case ultimately on the unambiguous separation of ethical from status-defined attributes in *Poetics* 13, without wishing to deny that Ar. does not sustain the separation cleanly throughout.

The broad sweep of the argument in *Poetics* 2 can be brought out by comparison with *Cat.* 12a 13-20.

argument: it is the province of verbal demonstration, refutation, and kindred matters. But thought can evidently impinge on characterisation too. This is illustrated ouside the *Poetics* in a passage such as *EN* 1112a 15f., where it is stated that the moral choice (*prohairesis*) which is the basis of character is accompanied by 'reasoning and thought'.[23] Within the *Poetics* the connection is reaffirmed further on in ch. 6, at 50b 4-12: here a definition of character, including a reference to the expression of character in speech, is enclosed between two explications of the significance of dramatic thought. We can also append the mention of 'ethical speeches which are well composed in language and thought', in Aristotle's hypothetical case of a tragedy which concentrates on characterisation but is deficient in action (50a 29-31).

A number of observations can be made on these passages and their implications. In the first place, they provide evidence for characterisation through speech and argument. What this entails, given Aristotle's definition of character in terms of conscious moral choice, is hardly obscure. For speech to function in such a way as to characterise the speaker, it must involve the assertion or revelation of determinate ethical desires and intentions, and in a discernible relation to action. We can be confident that Aristotle would have recognised a strong element of ethical characterisation in some of Oedipus' speeches in Sophocles' *Oedipus Tyrannus*: the King's declaration of his attitude to his city's well-being, for example; or his account to Jocasta of his attempt to escape from the predictions given to him by Apollo's oracle; or his explanation to the chorus of his reasons for blinding rather than killing himself. Despite Freudian interest in the play, such characterisation, communicated through rhetorically powerful exposition, does not correspond to the psychological notion of personality held by most modern readers of literature, according to which character is something that can be constantly and implicitly intimated, often unconsciously on the person's own part, through utterances of every kind. Certainly, whatever we may make of Sophocles' play, Aristotle's notion is much narrower and stricter than this, and has little to do with Oedipus' inner consciousness. Because of the importance of *prohairesis* to character, there is not much scope in the *Poetics*' theory for the unconscious revelation of character on a speaker's part. Character,

[23] Cf. also *EN* 1138b 35f., 1139a 33f., *Pol.* 1281b 7, 1323b 3. But the 'thought' of the *Poetics* is more rhetorical than in any of these cases.

on this view, is not fluid and does not pervade all speech; it is embodied in definite moral dispositions, which can be estimated by reference to equally clear-cut criteria and standards of virtue. The explicitness of the type of characterisation which Aristotle has in mind is illustrated by the last quotation in my previous paragraph: when he wishes to frame the hypothesis of a play which takes characterisation to an extreme, it is a series of 'ethical set-speeches' (50a 29) which he imagines, and the nature of surviving Greek tragedy, with its heavy dependence on the formal speech, allows us to envisage the kind of material which he means.

It is the premise that, when communicated through language, characterisation will take the form of declarations of decisions, intentions or motives, which leads to the association I have noted in the *Poetics* between character and thought, an association which, in view of the rhetorical sense of 'thought', would be much less cogent if character were something that might be obliquely indicated through any kind of speech. As it is, the explicitness of verbal characterisation sits well alongside the techniques of argument and exposition which rhetorical thought requires. In proposing an affinity between these two elements of tragedy, Aristotle reflects the influence of the existing and well-established practice of the genre, in which modes of rhetorical speech are prominent in shaping the utterances of the leading figures. Yet Aristotle only associates thought and character; he does not identify them.[24] The reason for this lies in the fact that thought belongs, on Aristotle's definition, to the realm of language and reasoning, while character must stand in a discernible relation to action. The scope of rhetorical thought, moreover, is very wide, and can encompass facts and issues which do not directly bear on the speaker's own behaviour. The same cannot be said of character, whose basis is constituted by moral dispositions: and moral dispositions are dispositions to act in certain ways.

We are brought back round, therefore, to the fundamental relationship between dramatic action and character. Aristotle's

---

[24] Note the distinction between older and more recent tragedy at 50b 6-8, which implies that the former used rhetorical thought with a stronger moral emphasis (*politikôs*), while the tragedies of the present employ rhetoric more for its own sake. On character and thought see Vahlen (1911) 252-68 and Dale 139-55, though there is something of a tension between the latter's recognition of Ar.'s fidelity to tragic practice (esp. 145-7) and her attempt to judge him by a distinctively modern notion of character (e.g. 143, 'the whole compound of personality in action').

disapproval of concentration on the latter to the detriment of the former is unequivocal, but it is now possible to see a little more clearly what underlies it. When in ch. 6 Aristotle contrasts a play dominated by 'ethical set-speeches' (or 'speeches of character': the alternatives are only apparent) with one deficient in characterisation but possessing a structure of action, he is not offering a mere preference for one kind of drama over another, or propounding an arbitrary aesthetic principle. His judgement is grounded in his understanding of the concepts of action and character themselves, and in the assumption that poetic mimesis will reflect accurately the main lineaments of human life. The play which elevates characterisation above action displaces the element of primary significance by that of secondary, in that it deprives the ethical character which it presents of that framework of action without which character cannot find its full realisation or meaning. The reason for Aristotle's evaluation of the relative importance of dramatic action and character, in other words, is his wider philosophical evaluation of the relative importance of action and character in life. The moral dispositions revealed in the speeches of the type of play hypothesised at 50a 29-31 would lack a true object, and would necessarily be, for Aristotle, sterile and incomplete. His hypothetical case both elucidates, and is elucidated by, the sententious remark a little earlier in ch. 6, that 'tragedy is a mimesis not of people but of actions and life' (50a 16f.). What Aristotle means by the negative part of this proposition is that drama should not take as its aim the static portrayal of human character divorced from the active processes of life. 'Actions and life' is practically a tautology within the Aristotelian vocabulary, as is suggested by the sentence from the *Ethics* which I quoted near the start of this chapter: 'if action is taken away from the living person ... what remains except contemplation?' The fundamental premise of much of what is said in *Poetics* 6 turns out to be nothing more, and nothing less, than that tragedy should deal with the essential fabric of life, as this is conceived by the philosopher. It is from this premise alone that Aristotle is able to deduce the primacy of action.

But the primacy of action does not imply the insignificance of character, and it remains to scrutinise further the scope and weight of the latter in the *Poetics*' conception of drama. We must therefore move on to examine ch. 15 of the treatise, where we find the formal discussion of characterisation in the sequential analysis of the six 'parts' of tragedy.[25] Few will want to deny that after the detail and forcefulness of the treatment of plot-structure, ch. 15 is disappointingly thin and slight: nor need we shirk the inference that this contrast in scale and care of analysis is a symptom of Aristotle's priorities, as I suggested in my opening chapter. Since the argument is presented at this point with schematic brevity, it will be worthwhile to consider in turn the four requirements set out here for characterisation.

The first and the most important principle of characterisation is goodness or excellence. Aristotle elaborates this, boldly and simply, with the statement that the moral choices revealed in speech and action should be virtuous ones. While the implications of this for the nature of characterisation as such call for no further comment, two points can be made about the ethical standard invoked. The first is that Aristotle's principle must be read in the light of the claims earlier made about tragedy's typical object, 'men better than present humanity', in *Poetics* 2. His concern, in other words, is partly with what might be called generic tone or ethos, with the gravity and ethical seriousness of tragedy's characteristic material. While this concern owes something to the heroic conceptions contained in tragic myth, it is not entirely reducible to them, as we see both from the general ethical colouring of Aristotle's language for the characters of tragedy, and also from the reference which is made in the present passage to the goodness of women and slaves. It is particularly clear from surviving plays that tragedy's portrayal of the latter involves a deliberate elevation and moral refinement, and this must be taken to be part of Aristotle's point. There is also no reason to deny a degree of Platonic influence here in the requirement that tragedy should conform to basic moral standards, though Aristotle qualifies Plato's moralism in two ways: first, by allowing some elements of evil to be incorporated where necessary for the purpose of the work (see below, and cf. 61a 4ff.); secondly, by refusing to demand of tragedy a simple affirmation of the identity of virtue and happiness. For Aristotle does not accept this identity outright, and over and above the generic attribute of seriousness, goodness of tragic character is required precisely (and unplatonically) because at the crux of the ideal plots defined in the *Poetics* lies the idea of

---

[25] Jones 38 n.1 thinks that ch. 15 does not maintain the earlier sense of *éthos* – a peculiar view, since at the start of the chapter (54a 17f.) Ar. reiterates the earlier definition (from 50b 8ff.).

undeserved suffering, whether actual or threatened: and it is on this premise that other features of the theory, such as the distinctive combination of tragic emotions, depend. On this account, the requirement of goodness applies with special force to the central figures of tragedy, but we will see below that it has to be tempered by consideration of other factors.

Aristotle's second principle of characterisation, appropriateness, needs scarcely any explication. It derives from the belief in a strong link between moral character and the objective conditions of life, including age, sex, social origins and status. This belief is more fully attested in Aristotle's *Rhetoric*, and was a prevalent attitude in the ancient world.[26] Although the principle is illustrated negatively, by reference to the inappropriateness of attributing certain values to women, it has positive implications for the figures of tragedy, especially those of heroic stature, and Aristotle subsequently confirms this by the illustration of dithyrambic portrayal of an unheroic Odysseus. Appropriateness should therefore be interpreted closely in conjunction with the requirement of goodness in the agents of tragedy. But it should not be supposed that the canons of appropriateness, and the assumptions behind them, compromise the ethical basis of Aristotle's conception of character: material and social factors help to define the conditions within which virtues and vices can be acquired and exercised, but this does not interfere with the possibility within Aristotle's system of a distinction between the ethical and the non-ethical.

The third of the requirements for character, 'likeness', is the most difficult to interpret, since Aristotle does not elaborate the point, and if we take 'like' in the same sense as it is given in *Poetics* 2, where it does not apply to tragedy, we appear to commit him to a contradiction. Such a contradiction can, I think, be avoided if we keep two points in mind when considering all four passages in the treatise where 'likeness' is mentioned in connection with characterisation: first, as Aristotle observes at *Rhet.* 1387b 26-8, likeness can exist, or be perceived, in relation to a variety of attributes; secondly, as I have already mentioned and will later reiterate, the agents of tragedy are viewed in the *Poetics* in terms of both ethical character (*êthos*) and external status. While this latter

---

[26] Cf. *Rhet.* 1388b 31ff. and 1408a 27ff., and see Brink (1971) 190ff. Similarly, appropriateness will cover what might be termed the 'accessories' of character, for which cf. *Rhet.* 1417a 22-4.

distinction has a crucial function in the definition of the ideal tragedy (53a 7-12), it is not, however, of immediate importance in *Poetics* 2, where Aristotle is concerned with broad differences between genres and artists, and for this purpose produces the convenient tripartite scheme of characterisation, better than – worse than – the same (like). Likeness here, then, represents a middle way, below the general elevation typical of tragedy; but such a wide focus does not rule out the possibility of more precise perceptions (as the later remark about the characters of Sophocles and Euripides, 60b 33f., helps to remind us). When we reach ch. 13, where likeness is posited as a condition of tragic fear (53a 4-6), Aristotle is applying a more refined and specifically ethical criterion: the likeness which the audience must be able to recognise in the tragic agents is a basic moral affinity, keeping the characters within the range of our experience and sympathy. This affinity does not entail moral mediocrity, as 53a 16 indicates and as the requirement of goodness in ch. 15 later confirms; but it does impose a kind of ethical upper limit, while in terms of status, by contrast, the tragic characters can be allowed a more striking preeminence. Not only, therefore, does likeness have a more exact reference here than in ch. 2, but Aristotle's earlier synoptic view of tragedy's characters as 'better than present humanity', in which no differentiation was made between ethics and status, has now given way to a more analytical appreciation of the separate factors involved.

The principle of likeness in *Poetics* 15 is best taken as a reaffirmation of the point made in ch. 13 – that the characters should not stand at an ethical extreme, but should be such that an audience can experience a sympathetic moral affinity with them.[27] If there is felt to be something of a tension between this requirement and the primary requirement of goodness, or still more with the idea of tragic characters as better than present humanity, that must in part be explained by the nature of tragedy itself, in which Aristotle is right to discern both an essential elevation and yet also the need for an intense sympathy with the agents' sufferings. We must be able, like the Theban elders, to recognise in Oedipus the qualities and

[27] The alternative (held by e.g. Bywater and Lucas (1968) ad loc., and Schütrumpf 127-9) is to suppose that likeness at 54a 24 means faithfulness to the mythical prototype. But in addition to the difficulty of interpreting such a requirement, is it conceivable that Ar. would have made fidelity to poetic tradition a canon? Cf. 51b 23f. and see Radt (1971) 201 n.1.

grandeur which raise him above other men, but also his true humanity.[28] That Aristotle was aware of the necessity of allowing for both these factors, and that he believed some reconciliation or balance of them was feasible, seems to me to be clinched by the reference to likeness towards the end of *Poetics* 15. 'Since tragedy is a mimesis of men better than ourselves,' he says, reiterating the premise of ch. 2, 'one ought to emulate good portrait-painters' who manage both to preserve a likeness and to improve on the beauty of their subjects (54b 8-11).[29] The poetic analogue to physical beauty here, as the continuation of the argument shows, is moral character: tragic figures such as Achilles should be portrayed with the particular ethical failings which keep them within the range of the audience's understanding and sympathy, but should also be characterised with a favourable enhancement. If there is a lingering uncertainty or instability in Aristotle's position (and the visual comparison is, not for the only time, less cogent than it might be), we ought to attribute this, I suggest, to the fact that he has not sufficiently elaborated the relation between his own criteria, which permit a separation of the ethical from the non-ethical, and the traditional values embodied in heroic and tragic myth. I shall return to this point at the end of the chapter.

The fourth and final requirement of character, consistency, refers straightforwardly to the relation between different elements in the characterisation of a figure in the course of a play. The understanding or expectations created by the characterisation of one scene should not be undermined, except for deliberate effect, by that of subsequent ones. This rudimentary principle allows Aristotle to introduce a reminder of his cardinal criterion of 'necessity or probability', which he here indeed cites three times within a single sentence (54a 34-6). The emphasis of this reminder, which includes a reference back to the analysis of plot-structure, confirms the contention of ch. 6 of the treatise that character is neither the primary component of tragedy, nor a component of independent interest, but should be integrated into the framework of a play's structure of action and conform to the design of this structure.

[28] See Soph. *OT* 1186-1222, where the chorus's pity is all the deeper for their sense of Oedipus' previous stature.

[29] Compare *Pol.* 1281b 10-15, where the relations between *spoudaioi* and ordinary men (note the relevance to tragedy), between beautiful and plain men, and between paintings and reality, are all aligned.

Character, that is, is a subordinate aspect of the play, but one which must contribute to the unity, and therefore the significance, of the action. The mention of consistency of characterisation enables Aristotle to affirm his priorities once more.

The four requirements set out in *Poetics* 15 can be seen, then, as bearing respectively on the general moral tone and level of tragedy (goodness), the particular types of figure involved in it (appropriateness), the possibility of a powerful emotional response to the sufferings and experiences of these figures (likeness), and the incorporation of character into the structural design and unity of the play (consistency). For the purposes of my argument as a whole, it is the last of these points which is most telling. The conformity of character to necessity or probability means not only that characterisation must be self-consistent, but also that it has a function within the causal or logical sequence of the plot-structure. Characterisation is, in the best drama, a necessary qualitative and explanatory factor within the scheme of the action: it is through character and thought, as Aristotle puts in in ch. 6, 'that we say that the actions too are of a certain sort' (49b 38-50a 1). Much the same idea is communicated by ch. 9's formulation of the universals which are the substance of poetry, for these are 'the sorts of things which certain sorts of people will say or do according to probability or necessity' (51b 8f.). Here, in phrases of typical Aristotelian spareness, character and action are combined and integrated in a unitary conception. For in the best poetry (as in Homer: 60a 11) there can be no doubt that Aristotle does expect action and character to be interlocked in a way which reflects the full ethical nature of human life. It is precisely and only this premise which explains the inclusion of an ethical term in the very definition of tragedy – 'the mimesis of a morally good action', by which Aristotle means an action involving morally good characters striving to realise their goodness.[30]

If this position remains somewhat abstract and generalised, that is because of the style and purpose of the treatise. But it may nonetheless be worth attempting to press the further question of how far, and in what ways, the *Poetics*' explication of the nature of tragic

---

[30] Argument over the meaning of *spoudaias* in the definition is part of a larger dispute over this and related terminology in the *Poetics*, on which see n. 22 above. Other details which indicate that Ar. does expect characterisation in poetry are the passages cited in n.10 above, and the phrases describing comedy, tragedy and epic as representations of certain sorts of *people* at 49a 32f., 49b 10 (commonly overlooked references).

plot allows for the explanatory and enriching function of characterisation. The answer I shall briefly contend for contains a mixture of positive and negative comments on the theory of tragedy. On the positive side, it is principally to Aristotle's account of the distinctive emotional experience of tragedy, and its translation in *Poetics* 13 and 14 into patterns of dramatic action, that we must look for some indication of the possible contribution of characterisation. Each of the emotions of pity and fear carries with it conditions for the content of the tragic plot, and these conditions also have implications for character, that is for the ethical dispositions and motivations of the agents. 'Pity is felt for the undeserving sufferer of misfortune, fear for the sufferer who is like ourselves' (53a 4f.). On the 'likeness' of the tragic figure or figures I have already said something. It is as evident in the case of innocence, the precondition of pity, as it is in that of likeness, that the action of a play cannot fully measure up to Aristotle's theory without the assistance of moral characterisation to demonstrate that the agents and their actions are such as to elicit and merit our emotions. In this context, we should recollect that while in *Poetics* 6 Aristotle notes the possibility of dispensing with tragic characterisation, he does not recommend it, any more than, to adapt his own analogy, he would have been inclined to advise the avoidance of colour in painting.

But to reflect on the necessity of characterisation to establish the innocence of a tragic figure and the possibility of sympathy with him, is to realise how limited is the scope for this element within Aristotle's vision of the genre. The potential of character is restricted not only by the principle that it must have a direct ethical bearing on the sequence of actions of which the plot-structure consists, but also by the fact that the two specific prerequisites entailed by the emotions of pity and fear are both effectively *negative*. For a playwright to reveal the innocence of an agent need call for no subtlety or complexity of dramatic technique: to meet the conditions laid down in the *Poetics*, it ought chiefly to involve the display of an area of ignorance relevant to the agent's motives or intentions. The second requirement, that of 'likeness', is admittedly less determinate, and there is perhaps a hint towards the end of ch. 15 of ways in which a poet may choose to incorporate some finer ethical details into his treatment of a character in order to allow an audience to recognise his essential humanity. But the hint is only a slight one, and the treatise elsewhere invites us to construe likeness too as a largely negative aim for the dramatist, namely the avoidance of extreme virtue. These negative implications of the theory can be supplemented by noting that the two components of the complex tragedy, reversal and recognition, are features of the action of the play, and offer only minimal opportunities for characterisation in Aristotle's sense, as the illustrations of them in chs. 11 and 16 make evident. Reversal and recognition must be grounded in the ignorance of the agents, and in the instability of their control over the outcome of their own actions. Ignorance may play a part in characterisation, most obviously in the dramatisation of moral innocence. But not all ignorance is pertinent to character, and even where it is, the reversal and recognition which rest on it remain significant primarily on the level of action itself: the value and potential tragic charge which they carry is located in their contribution to a pattern of action, the pattern of a *metabasis* or transformation of fortune, of the kind which may to a great degree be independent of the exact ethical qualities of the agent.

The main tenets of the theory of tragedy, therefore – the stress on unity of action, on pity and fear, and on the nature of the complex plot – confirm that characterisation should be integrally involved in the composition of the ideal tragedy, but also show the limits on Aristotle's expectations of it. If these limitations seem striking, however, that is in part, as I earlier suggested, because of the presuppositions likely to be made by the modern reader of the *Poetics*. Where psychological conceptions of character tend to posit a complex background of inner mental life, and a consciousness which may or may not be congruous with action, and while they correspondingly support a strongly individualist notion of persons, Aristotle's understanding of character is essentially ethical, rests on a belief in a necessarily close relation between character and action, and interprets the behaviour of persons less in terms of individuality than by reference to a set of objective and common standards: it is, quite fundamentally, in virtue and vice that the characters of men differ (48a 2-4). In both these respects, and in the firm subordination of character to action in drama, a strong case can be made for arguing that Aristotle's precepts come closer to the practice of the Greek tragedians than modern psychological categories, or a critical frame-of-mind suited to the reading of novels, will easily enable us to do.[31] In particular, it can be said that the

---

[31] See Jones's book, Gould (1978), and cf. H. Lloyd-Jones, *Classical Survivals* (London 1982) 111-15. The attempt of House 79f. to argue that Ar. aims to 'guarantee

traditional myths used and reshaped in epic and tragic poetry allow relatively little scope for a strong sense of individuality. The figures at the centre of these myths are exceptional in various respects, but the power and interest of their stories resides above all in the typical implications which they carry for the place of men in the world. This is, indeed, intimately tied up with the distinctive nature of tragedy, which aspires to strip the human condition down to some of its bare essentials. The emphasis of the *Poetics* on the fundamental patterns of tragic action – on the great transformations of fortune which mark its myths – can be seen to be congruous with this central strand in the poetic tradition. But that is not to suggest that Aristotle's theory can in all respects be regarded as codifying this tradition. One especially problematic aspect of the relation between them, the questionable extent to which Aristotle allows for the interplay between human and divine which is so basic to epic and tragedy's material, was mentioned earlier in the chapter. I shall return to this issue in ch. VII below, but it is right to draw attention to it again here since it might well be felt that Aristotle's construction of dramatic characterisation around the notion of deliberate human choice (*prohairesis*) fails to take sufficient account of the impingement of divine influence on the sources of human action in tragedy.[32]

Alongside this question about Aristotle's treatment of the religious aspect of tragedy, some qualification must also be placed on the *Poetics*' handling of the heroic stature of the major figures of tragic myth.[33] From the general evidence of Aristotle's work two preliminary propositions can be advanced. The first is that he does not appear to have discerned a basic ethical shift between the values embodied in the material used by Homer and the tragedians, and those of his own society or his own thought. On the other hand, there are undoubted traces of a recognition of the exceptional status of heroes, as, for example, in the application of the term 'heroic'

---

the individuality of character' is wishful thinking: *Poetics* 17 yields nothing of the sort (cf. House's uneasiness on the point, 86-91).

[32] Cf. Vernant 13 on the relation between *êthos* and *daimôn*, with Winnington-Ingram 173-8 on the latter in the *Oedipus Tyrannus*.

[33] Jones 11ff. is right to criticise the grafting of Romantic ideas of the tragic hero onto the *Poetics*, but two qualifications remain basic: first, that Greek tragedy does mostly deal with major individuals who belong to what can properly be called a heroic tradition of myth (I note that Jones 57 accepts 'heroic worth' in the Greek context, and cf. the comments on 60); secondly, that *Poetics* 13 *does* essentially posit a central figure in the ideal tragedy (cf. ch. VII n.21).

(together with a Homeric exemplum) to the 'superhuman' virtue mentioned at the start of Book 7 of the *Ethics*.[34] A similar recognition might be thought to lie behind the *Poetics'* description of the characters of tragedy as 'better than present humanity' (48a 17f.) and other related passages. But some reservations are in place.

For one thing, Aristotle tempers this description, as we have seen, by his stress on 'likeness' as the condition for sympathy with the tragic agents. This need not cut entirely against the grain of heroism, since the latter does not entail remoteness from, only superiority over, ordinary human nature; but it may still be suspected that Aristotle's concern with the possibility of tragic fear inhibits the scope for heroic excellence within his ideal tragedy. However, we must also reckon with the fact that some of the prominent features of heroic status (noble breeding, physical and military prowess, power and wealth, honour) do not properly fall within the scope of Aristotelian virtue, but belong to the realm of 'external goods'. These are certainly allowed for in the *Poetics*, particularly at 53a 10-12, but under the description of good fortune (*eutuchia*), not of moral character. By bringing to bear the categories and criteria of his own philosophy, within which the virtues proper are held apart from 'external goods' such as status with more consistency than in traditional Greek attitudes, Aristotle seeks to disentangle a finer ethical from a looser non-ethical strand in heroic myth, and to cater for the former by his principles of characterisation (but without positing exceptional virtue on the part of the agents), and for the heroic factor by the element of great prosperity or good

---

[34] *EN* 1145a 18ff. (on this difficult passage see W.F.R. Hardie, *Aristotle's Ethical Theory* 2nd edn. (Oxford 1980) 401-4). *Pol.* 1285b 4f. and 21 imply *some* notion of a heroic age (as perhaps at *Poet.* 48a 17f.), *Pol.* 1332b 17-20 suggests that 'heroes' are preeminent firstly in *physical* terms, and *An.Post.* 97b 17ff. associates certain heroes with one type of *megalopsuchia*. The passage from *EN* and the second from *Pol.* show traces of the religious sense of *hērōs*, but the predominant reference is to the warriors of epic-tragic tradition (on the two senses see M.L. West, *Hesiod: Works & Days* (Oxford 1978) 370-3). For the special qualities of these heroes compare e.g. Aristoph. *Frogs* 1058-61, Plato *Rep.* 391d.

Poet. 54b 11-15 indicates that heroes can be judged by ordinary moral criteria: cf. e.g. *EN* 1116a 21-9 (not a heroic extreme, but patriotic bravery), and compare Plato *Hippias Minor*. Ar.'s own ethical system differs from heroic values principally in giving slighter importance to honour (*timē*): see esp. *EN* 1107b 21ff., but cf. 1095b 22ff. (happiness cannot be equated with *timē*) and 1123b 17ff. (*timē* is the greatest of *external* goods, but it must come from the right sources). Adkins (1966) discusses the relation between Aristotle and earlier Greek values on the basis of too rigid a dichotomy between competitive and cooperative virtues, and Radt (1971) 203 goes too far in calling Ar.'s ideal 'bourgeois' ('bürgerlich').

fortune (*eutuchia*) which is one of the poles of the tragic action.[35] We can conclude, therefore, that in Aristotle's perspective the heroism of the tragic agent is incorporated essentially in the fabric of status, for it is the vulnerability of prosperity, not of virtue, which the philosopher identifies as the proper subject-matter of tragedy, as I shall try to show in ch. VII.

If Aristotle's theory of tragedy makes it possible to dispense with traditional religious views altogether, its implications for the treatment of heroism are less drastic but no less significant: the tragic hero, in the philosopher's scheme, ceases to be the full paradigm of human excellence, since by ethical criteria he must be kept within range of the audience's sympathy and pity; while his external trappings of honour and status are precisely the human fortune whose instability it is tragedy's function to dramatise. Since, however, Aristotle's thinking modifies traditional Greek values without rejecting them altogether, it remains possible for him to accept the general characterisation of tragedy (and epic) as a portrayal of men 'better than present humanity'. It is only in the details of the theory that a vital qualification on this description emerges, a qualification which rests on the philosopher's own conception of the good life.

---

[35] The passage which perhaps best shows the Aristotelian separation of external goods, specifically designated as *eutuchia*, from intrinsic virtue, is *EN* 1124a 12-31, esp. 15f. and 30f. On this and other passages see further ch. VII pp. 204ff. and nn. 3-5.

VI

Tragedy and the Emotions

My previous chapter was concerned with internal constituents and features of tragic drama, though features which pertain to its mimetic status and so to its portrayal of reality. In the present chapter an attempt will be made to show how Aristotle's understanding of action and character is complemented by a theory of the emotional effect of tragedy on an audience or reader. Taken as a whole, the theory of tragedy expounded in the *Poetics* might be thought to devote less attention to the nature of a distinctively tragic experience than many later theories have done: in purely quantitative terms, it is certainly the case that more weight is placed on the structure and organisation of the dramatic poem than on the emotions which it is capable of arousing in its audience. A partial similarity can be observed in this respect with the *Rhetoric*, in which some effort is made to move away from what Aristotle considered to be the excessive interest shown by earlier rhetoricians in emotion and emotional manipulation.[1] But the parallel with the *Rhetoric* has a positive aspect too, and it will indeed soon emerge that it is this treatise which supplies us with our best evidence for interpreting the pity and fear of the *Poetics*. Neither a theory of drama nor a theory of rhetoric can avoid making strong assumptions about the relationship between these arts and their audiences. If Aristotle sometimes leaves the impression of a relative neglect of the affective response elicited by tragedy, this is paradoxically but precisely because, just as in the case of rhetoric, he perceives an integral connection between this response and the nature of the works which produce it. A properly conceived plot-structure implicitly calls for, and will inevitably evoke in the attuned audience or reader, the distinctive tragic experience of pity

---

[1] See esp. *Rhet.* 1354a 16ff., though Ar. returns to emotion in Book 2 in order to present a rational analysis of rhetorical arousal of emotion. Cf. pp. 172ff. and n. 5 below.

and fear; the nature of these emotions is such that they will be spontaneously felt in response to a dramatic action of the requisite kind. The *Poetics* therefore rests on interlocked and mutually reinforcing views about poetic composition and the emotional psychology of the audience of poetry, and such a position must be carefully distinguished from a truly rhetorical poetics, in which the audience is a major and *independently* determinant factor.

To see how this can be so, however, it is essential to grasp that Aristotle's notion of the emotional effect of tragedy must be read on the same level as the rest of his theory, which means that it is derived from the interpretation of existing and historical facts but in the light of certain philosophical beliefs. It is built on an understanding of what has been revealed by the natural evolution of poetry, as well as on a philosophical psychology of the nature of the emotions. The theory of tragedy articulates the best of which the genre has shown itself capable, and the corresponding assumption about the experience of such tragedy must be that it depends on an audience or reader able to appreciate what is embodied in the poetry. Hence the possible discrepancy between the ideal and the actual, intimated most obviously at the end of ch. 13 (53a 33-5), where the reference to the weakness of actual audiences implies that the prescriptions earlier in the chapter posit an audience of appropriate responsiveness. Elsewhere in the *Poetics* there are signs that such a discrepancy need not always exist, and it seems apt to suppose that in this as in other details of his theory Aristotle stands somewhat ambivalently towards the normal experience of the theatre.[2] To codify or sanction that experience at a vulgar level was evidently not the philosopher's purpose; but, equally, his view of tragic poetry needed to retain some

---

[2] For Ar.'s attitude to the theatre see Appendix 3. At *Poet.* 53a 26-30 he is prepared to appeal to theatrical success as, in certain conditions, a confirmation of his theory. This seems a little ironic in view of the subsequent censure of audiences (33-5), but there need be no real inconsistency: audiences are weak, according to Ar., and poets sometimes pander to them; but they can be induced to respond to a well-made tragedy, which will arouse the true tragic emotions. The reactions of audiences are also referred to for confirmation of points (albeit in obscure contexts) at 55a 26-9, 56a 18f. We get glimpses of a broader, cultural view of audiences at 61b 27-62a 14, as at *Pol.* 1281b 7-10, 1286a 26-31, 1341b 10-18, 1342a 18ff.: compared to Plato's (see Appendix 2 under 53a 34f.) Ar.'s attitudes may appear relatively tolerant, but their ambivalence is not without a colouring of disdain for the ordinary spectator. For an indication, nonetheless, of the necessary connection between a successful plot-structure and the appropriate emotional response, see 53b 3-7. On Ar.'s assumptions about the audience of tragedy see Butcher 211-13, and L. Golden, 'Aristotle and the Audience for Tragedy', *Mnem.* 29 (1976) 351-9.

roots in the proven sense of the emotions typically aroused by the tragedian's art. The resulting uncertainty in the *Poetics*, over the degree to which Aristotle's conception of the tragic experience is one of which existing audiences are capable, is part of its characteristic elusiveness.

This uncertainty has implications for the basic formula for the emotional impact of tragedy, pity and fear. Reactions to this collocation of emotions in the final clause of the definition of the genre have varied from acceptance of it as a central insight, to repudiation of it as superficial and inadequate. But such ultimate judgements, which are so often complicated by consideration of types of tragedy unknown to Aristotle, ought to be suspended until we have reached a confident sense of what the formula signifies within the full context of the theory. Here we must take immediate account of two facts: first, that the association of pity and fear was not original with Aristotle, but can be found as far back as Homeric epic, as well as in later sources such as Sophocles, Gorgias and Plato;[3] secondly, that remarkably little is offered in the *Poetics* itself by way of explicit elaboration of the character or function of these emotions. This inexplicitness is represented at a notorious extreme by the idea of tragic *katharsis*, which is included in the definition together with the first mention of pity and fear, but does not reappear in the surviving chapters of the work. If any plausible approach to the interpretation of *katharsis* is still feasible, it can surely rest only on the basis of a wider account of the role posited for the emotions in the experience of tragedy. But if *katharsis* appears at first sight to possess the opaqueness of the unique (though I shall later try to show that this appearance is somewhat deceptive), pity and fear, as indicated, may well have been identified before Aristotle's time as central to the experience of tragic drama. In turning to a closer inspection of these emotions, we can expect to find that they provide a delicate link between the *Poetics* and earlier views of tragedy.

After the start of ch. 6, pity and fear are not mentioned again in

---

[3] For Homer see Shankman's article, and for Plato see Appendix 2 under 49b 27. See also e.g. Soph. *Ajax* 121-6, *Trach.* 296-306, *Phil.* 500-6 (though these passages involve self-regarding fear: cf. Friedrich (1967)), Gorgias fr. 11.8-9, Apollodorus fr. 4 (Kock). On the nature of Aristotelian pity and fear, and their differences from Christian and humanitarian ideas, see the contentions of Schadewaldt 194-213, with qualifications by Pohlenz 562-73. Schadewaldt certainly underplays the ethical implications of the emotions for Ar., and his influential dismissal of Lessing (on whom see ch. X pp. 312ff. below) does not seem to me entirely justified.

the analysis of tragedy until the end of ch. 9. They are reintroduced, in other words, where Aristotle's discussion starts to move away from general dramatic structure and unity to the specific components and patterns of tragic plots, and particularly to the preferred form of the complex plot. It is the shape and effect of the latter which Aristotle clearly has in mind in the statement that tragedy 'is a mimesis ... of fearful and pitiful events, and this effect comes about when things happen unexpectedly but on account of one another' (52a 2-4). We may notice here at once the locution which Aristotle will later use a further five times in chs. 13 and 14: the adjectival phrase, 'fearful and pitiful events', in place of the direct mention of pity and fear. The force of this is to insinuate the close and necessary connection between the tragic emotions and the internal construction of the drama; the capacity to elicit pity and fear is an objective attribute of the poetic material as handled by the playwright. If the definition of tragedy alone might create the impression that pity and fear are characteristic of the genre in a diffuse way, the references later in the treatise to the emotions, or to the actions which arouse them, dispel this idea. Pity and fear need to be comprehended within the framework of a coherent tragic action; the effect which they represent is the result of a particular configuration of events, not simply of a pervasive generic style or tone (for which a better Aristotelian candidate would be the moral goodness of character designated as typical of tragedy). It is only after the broader principles of structure and unity have been laid down, that Aristotle focusses on the critical stages of the tragic plot; and it is in elucidating these that he once more has occasion to stipulate pity and fear.

The passage from ch. 9 quoted in the previous paragraph indicates an intimate link between the emotions of tragedy and the crucial transformation of fortune, the *metabasis*, which the *Poetics* locates at the centre of the tragic plot-structure. The notion of a great swing or change of fortune, especially the collapse from greatness to disaster, is a major theme of Greek heroic myth, and an inveterate preoccupation of Greek moralising. Isocrates remarks on one occasion that 'most, and the most preeminent, of our demigods suffered the greatest calamities' (9.70); and his use of the word 'demigods' marks the sense that human frailty and vulnerability are paradigmatically illustrated in myth and legend by the tragedies of those very figures who come closest to acquiring a status which is

higher than human. Just as Aristotle's characterisation of the agents
of tragedy as 'men better than present humanity' in *Poetics* 2 alludes
to (without precisely demarcating) certain aspects of the heroic
world, so his emphasis on great transformations of fortune is a
response to the central mythic motif of the insecurity and
impermanence of human power and prosperity. The way in which
these ideas are developed, and reinterpreted, in Aristotle's theory of
tragedy will be part of the subject of my next chapter, but it is
necessary to register here that pity and fear belong in close
association with the concept of the tragic *metabasis*, particularly in the
complex version in which reversal and recognition set the
transformation in stark relief. Again, this is not a wholly surprising
or original association. Here too a parallel can be conveniently cited
from Isocrates, one of whose forensic speeches includes in a list of
proper objects of pity 'those who experience a very great change of
fortune (*metabolê*)' (16.48). It is often acknowledged elsewhere in
Greek literature that pity is a natural and appropriate emotion to feel
towards cases of extreme disparity between past and present status,
and Aristotle's theory partly rests on this common attitude.[4]
Whether, and how far, the theory goes beyond or diverges from such
attitudes, still remains to be decided.

The relationship between Aristotle's understanding of emotions
and the ordinary Greek conception of the same emotions is not an
easy one to settle. This emerges especially in the observations on pity
and fear offered in the second book of the *Rhetoric*. Aristotle is there
concerned to define and clarify for the purposes of rhetorical
persuasion the nature of the emotions in question, and his analysis
ought therefore to be consistent with the data of normal experience.
But since normal experience may itself be not wholly consistent or
uniform, Aristotle's aim cannot be taken to be a mere transcription
of it; it is, rather, an attempt to discern the true or essential nature of
the emotions, and to produce an ordered theory of them. Aristotle's
discussion is consequently systematic and discriminating where
much of the raw data of experience might be thought to be partially
disordered and irregular. Yet the purpose of the discussion remains
to articulate the character of feelings which belong to the real world
in which the orator must know how to work on the sensibilities of his
audience. This tension, between a concern with normal psychology

[4] For some relevant passages see Dover 197.

and a desire for definitive philosophical clarity, suggests a typical Aristotelian stance, and it is directly comparable to the feature of the *Poetics* to which I have already drawn attention. Pity and fear, whether in poetry or in rhetoric, have their place within the framework of theory, but they are also meant to represent a real and practical possibility, not something wholly remote from the actual experience of tragedies or of rhetorical speeches.[5]

This general observation can be reinforced in more detail by examining some of the contents of the *Rhetoric*'s treatment of pity and fear. What is perhaps most important in both cases is the cognitive status which Aristotle attributes to the emotions. In making explicit and analysing the conditions under which these emotions are properly to be felt, Aristotle brings them into close relation to the perceptions and judgements of the conscious, cognizant mind. While it is unnecessary to raise here the separate issues which attach to this tendency in his philosophical psychology, it is of the highest significance for the understanding of the *Poetics* to give full weight to Aristotle's refusal to follow Plato in largely severing the emotions from the other faculties of the mind. Pity and fear (though, of course, not these alone) are to be regarded not as uncontrollable instincts or forces, but as responses to reality which are possible for a mind in which thought and emotion are integrated and interdependent. It is therefore to be observed how the cognitive basis of Aristotle's psychology comports with the notion of mimesis which lies at the heart of his aesthetic thinking. The experience of mimesis provides the cognitive ground in which the emotional response to works of art can grow. Aristotle firmly states in the *Politics* that our reactions to mimetic works are closely aligned with those which we feel towards the equivalent elements of reality (p. 196 below). This principle, which will later prove germane to the interpretation of *katharsis*, incidentally supplies further justification for using the *Rhetoric*'s analysis of pity and fear to illuminate the place of these emotions in the *Poetics*. But it also helps us to see how Aristotle conceives of the tragic emotions not as overwhelming waves of feeling, but as part of an integrated response to the structured material of poetic drama: the framework for the experience of these emotions is nothing other than the cognitive understanding of the

---

[5] On the *Rhetoric*'s treatment of emotion see Fortenbaugh's book and the same author's essay in Barnes (1979) 133-53. Cf. W. Lyons, *Emotion* (Cambridge 1980) 33-5.

mimetic representation of human action and character.[6]

Aristotle's conception of the emotions, then, whether these are felt in direct response to life or as part of the experience of mimesis, involves conditions which need to be satisfied if pity and fear are appropriately to be aroused; and these conditions principally concern cognitive perceptions of actual or imagined reality on the part of the mind which is the subject of the emotions. The fundamental requirement for pity is that it should be felt only towards suffering which is undeserved – something indicated in the *Poetics* itself, at 53a 4, as well as at *Rhet.* 1385b 14, but which cannot be held to have been a universal presupposition of Greek pity:[7] to some degree Aristotle can be seen to be circumscribing the emotion more tidily than ordinary attitudes needed to do, as well as articulating the implications of common experience. The requirement of pity, as a leading premise in the argument of ch. 13 of the treatise, rules out any serious culpability on the part of the central agent in Aristotle's complex plot. It is worth anticipating, however, a point which will be given fuller consideration in my next chapter, namely that this primary need for innocent suffering leads to a latent strain within Aristotle's theory, since he has other reasons for wishing to exclude arbitrary or unexplained misfortune from tragedy. The possibility of pity, in other words, raises questions of causation and responsibility, but the innocence which Aristotelian pity presupposes nonetheless has to be accommodated to the underlying demand for intelligibility in the tragic action, which I discussed in ch. III. The pity to be evoked by the complex tragedy is not an emotion felt without qualification for sheer human vulnerability, but, on Aristotle's theory, a precise response to a structure of action in which innocence can be identified within a clear context of human motive and agency. The seemingly simple prerequisite of unmerited suffering therefore opens up important issues in Aristotle's larger understanding of the mechanisms of tragic action.

[6] Hence the various ways in which pity and fear can be blocked or displaced by other emotions which Ar. does not consider proper or adequate to tragedy: indignation (52b 34-6), *philanthrôpia* (53a 2f., with ch. VII n.25), the satisfaction of poetic justice (53a 30-5), and sensational horror (53b 7-10). Compare *Rhet.* 1386a 22, b 8, 1387a 3, b 16-21, 1388a 27-30. For a precise formulation of the cognitive element in the tragic emotions see Packer's article, and cf. Eden for a comparison with forensic rhetoric.

[7] See Dover 199f., and cf. his comments on 58-61 for the difference between philosophical definitions (of virtues, emotions etc.) and ordinary conceptions.

But it is not only the degree of specificity which distinguishes the Aristotelian conception of pity. If pity or compassion may appear to be one of the most altruistic of emotions, the analysis of it given in the *Rhetoric* subtly and challengingly argues that it contains a necessarily self-regarding element. Pity is to be felt, according to this remarkable formulation, for undeserved suffering 'which a person could imagine himself, or someone close to him, suffering' (1385b 13-15). The emotion rests on a capacity to sympathise with the sufferer, but Aristotle does not derive this sympathy from an undifferentiated sense of humanity: instead, he takes it to be rooted in a felt or perceived affinity between the subject and the object of the emotion.[8] This has two complementary sets of implications. In the first place, with the emphasis placed on the subject, Aristotle contends that certain types of people (such as those with kin) are particularly given to pity, while others (such as those who have suffered much themselves) may be deficient in it. On the other hand, he suggests more generally that we tend to pity those who are like ourselves, and who can be said, with the accent now placed more on the object, to invite or attract our feelings. Careful thought needs to be given to the possible relevance of these points to the *Poetics*. Variations in the capacity or predisposition to feel pity may need to be reckoned with in connection with *katharsis*, when we come to consider it later in the chapter. That the relation between the subject and object of pity is pertinent to Aristotle's view of the emotional experience of tragedy cannot be doubted, and we will soon observe more detailed ties between the *Poetics* and the *Rhetoric* on this matter. For it must be said emphatically that, without committing oneself to an easy transference to the *Poetics* of all that is said on emotion in the *Rhetoric*, we cannot afford to neglect the help which the latter provides in the interpretation of tragic pity and fear. Those who believe otherwise drive an unnecessary wedge into Aristotle's thinking.

The relevance to the *Poetics* of the *Rhetoric*'s analysis of emotion is

[8] Note esp. the phrase 'to suffer with and feel pity for' at 1386b 14; at *Pol.* 1340a 12-14 Ar. posits an essential sympathy in the experience of all mimesis. On the sympathetic aspect of the tragic experience see Lucas (1962) esp. 54-7, and for Homeric and other material note Rutherford 158f. I prefer 'sympathy' to 'identification': the latter implies too close a feeling, which would obliterate pity as such, as *Rhet.* 1386a 18-22 (n.12 below) indicates. The language of e.g. Butcher 261f., 266 ('imaginative union with another's life' etc.) ignores this important point.

The self-regarding element in pity is complemented (and so confirmed) by the same element in pleasure felt at others' deserved good fortune: *Rhet.* 1386b 31-3 (where 'likeness' is indicated: cf. pp. 178f.).

confirmed above all by the association which both treatises indicate
between pity and fear. In the *Rhetoric* we are told that men tend to pity
those sufferings which they fear for themselves, and that their fears
share the same sorts of objects as their pity for others.[9] The association is nonetheless somewhat asymmetrical, since while it is evidently
possible for fear for oneself to be unaccompanied in a given case by pity
for others, Aristotle's definition of pity implies that the reverse is not
entirely true. This asymmetry brings us to a point of key importance
for the relation between the emotions of the *Rhetoric* and the *Poetics*. In
the former, Aristotle naturally takes fear to be in the first, and
defining, instance an emotion felt at one's own prospective experience.
It has appeared to some that this fact invalidates any attempt to use the
Rhetoric to elucidate the tragic emotions of the *Poetics*, but this could
hardly be so unless we were to make the improbable assumption (for
which the *Poetics* itself gives not the slightest support) that tragic fear is
meant to be completely different in kind from the ordinary fear which
Aristotle examines in the other treatise. The simple but essential fact
is that tragic fear differs from ordinary fear by virtue of being focussed
on the experience of others, but that this does not take it outside the
conception of the emotion expounded in the *Rhetoric*. Indeed, it is
worth noting that in the latter the first definition of fear (1382a 21f.)
does not stipulate that the emotion must be directly self-regarding,
though this is for the most part assumed. Aristotle's discussion of the
nature of fear, in other words, does not rule out the possibility that its
object can in some cases be the prospect of *others'* sufferings. For this to
be so, we can deduce, one condition must be satisfied: the prerequisite
of strong sympathy. Once this exists, we can feel fear for others
analogous to fear for ourselves, because, just as in pitying others we
are (if Aristotle is right) implicitly sensing an underlying fear for
ourselves, so the capacity to fear for others must rest on an imaginative
fear for ourselves.

    Aristotle does in fact provide in the *Rhetoric*'s treatment of fear one
explicit illustration of how contemplation of others' sufferings can
influence our emotions about ourselves, when he observes that an
audience (of oratory, but the case is suggestive for drama too) can be
induced to fear for themselves by being reminded of the misfortunes of
others greater than or like them.[10] This passage has a triple bearing on

    [9] *Rhet.* 1386a 27f. (cf. 1385b 14f., 1390a 19-22), 1382b 26f.
    [10] *Rhet.* 1383a 8-12, and cf. the implications of 1382b 15-18, to which 1383a 32-4 is
the negative corollary.

the *Poetics*: first, it confirms the interlocking nature of pity and fear (for the fear in this case is implicitly mediated through pity); secondly, it provides parallels to those places in the *Poetics* where the ideas of characters 'like us' or 'better than us' occur; and, finally, it furnishes a hint as to how the notion of tragic fear is to be interpreted. Tragic fear has both an object in the play (we feel it for one like us, 53a 6) but also a self-regarding element equally presupposed by our perception of a likeness between ourselves and the object of our fear. Moreover, this self-regarding fear is in part a concomitant of pity, since, as I pointed out earlier, Aristotle's definition of pity incorporates the sense that 'a person could imagine himself, or someone close to him, suffering' the same thing. So we see confirmed the fine intricacy of this strand of Aristotelian psychology, and its mutually illuminating implications for the experience of tragedy: our pity for others' undeserved suffering depends in part on our sympathetic capacity to imagine, and imaginatively fear, such things for ourselves; and fear for ourselves (though this is not the main element in tragic fear) can in turn be created by the sympathetic experience of others' misfortunes.

This intertwining of pity and fear, and of objective and subjective elements in Aristotle's conception of the tragic experience, should act as a strong caution against attempts to reduce this conception to an exclusively altruistic one.[11] This need not, however, prevent us from recognising that the notion is predominantly altruistic, and perhaps even concluding – though this is more contentious – that in Aristotle's theory of tragedy pity is the predominant emotion and is intensified by the secondary or dependent experience of fear. One factor which might seem to support such an inference is the observation in the *Rhetoric* that excessive fear will drive out pity.[12]

[11] Bywater 211 and 215 (on 53a 5) refers to 'disinterested fear' and tries to distance tragic fear from the fear analysed in the *Rhet.* I give my reasons in the text for demurring at the idea that Ar. would have accepted the possibility of *disinterested* fear: cf. also House 100-4. Bywater was reacting against Lessing's *Hamburgische Dramaturgie*, nos. 74-9, who represented the opposite extreme of taking tragic fear as wholly self-regarding – 'das auf uns selbst bezogene Mitleid': on the possibility that Lessing was influenced by Greek tragedy in this respect see Friedrich (1967). Lucas (1968) 274f. seems, somewhat casually, to acknowledge both subjective and objective fear in the experience of tragedy, though his dismissal of the evidence of the *Rhetoric* on p. 275 is illogical. Butcher ch. VI, having equivocated over, but finally conceded, the self-regarding element in the tragic emotions (257-9 and 259 n.1), proceeds to claim that *katharsis* involves the purification of the 'taint of egoism' (268): there are no grounds for this belief.

[12] *Rhet.* 1386a 18-22, cf. 1385b 32f., 1375a 7f. On this point cf. Macleod 3f.

But the fear Aristotle has in mind, as the context shows, is either fear for oneself or fear for someone so closely connected to one that it is virtually indistinguishable from wholly self-regarding fear. What this passage therefore allows us to see is that the sort of sympathy which pity entails requires a certain *distance* between pitier and pitied; if this distance is removed, the predominantly altruistic emotion of pity is obliterated by a practically complete affective identification between oneself and the other.[13] Hence, for the tragic experience of pity and fear, the altruistic must outweigh the self-regarding, though *some* degree of the latter is actually implied, we have seen, in the former. Yet the predominance of the altruistic does not in itself mean the predominance of pity over fear, since tragic fear is focussed in the first place on the fictional agents of the drama, not on ourselves. Moreover, tragedies of averted catastrophe, which Aristotle recommends in ch. 14, may even give more scope to fear than to pity.[14] But it seems prudent not to try to do what the *Poetics* itself avoids doing, namely to tilt the balance in favour of one of the two emotions in the compound of pity and fear; but instead to concentrate on the apparent inseparability of these two elements in Aristotle's theory of the experience of tragic drama.

This inseparability is strengthened when we return to the *Poetics'* own succinct requirements for pity and fear – innocence, and likeness to ourselves, in the characters of tragedy. These requirements are attached respectively to pity and fear, but it is probable that each of them is also at least a partial condition for the other emotion too. In the *Rhetoric*, at any rate, likeness is stipulated as a precondition for both pity and fear,[15] and it is reasonable to suppose that innocence in a tragic agent should help to induce fear on his behalf (even if innocence cannot be said to be a condition of all fear). In all this, what seems to matter most is, again, the possibility of sympathy – though the word must be understood with a stronger force than it now usually possesses in English. Tragedy's access to deep feelings of pity and fear in its audience presupposes a delicate tension whereby an affinity ('likeness') with the tragic characters can be experienced, but without the erasure of altruistic by

---

[13] Cf. the indivisible identification between the feelings of friends at *EE* 1240a 33-9, 1246a 15f., *Rhet.* 1379b 22f., 1381a 3-6.

[14] Fear specifically concerns prospects: *EE* 1229a 39f., *EN* 1115a 9, *Rhet.* 1382a 21f. But pity too can be felt for the prospective: *Rhet.* 1382b 27, 1386b 1.

[15] *Rhet.* 1383a 10 (fear), 1386a 25 (pity).

self-regarding emotion which *too close* an identification would produce. Both pity and fear are consequently affected by the way in which Aristotle combines (and qualifies) the need for likeness with the tragic standard of characters 'better than us'. In this connection it is worth recalling a passage which I earlier cited from the *Rhetoric* (1383a 8-12), where Aristotle claims that an audience can be moved to fear by a reminder of the sufferings of those greater than themselves, or of those like them. We have here an allusion to the same combination of ideas found in the *Poetics'* dual emphasis on the need for the characters of tragedy to be within the reach of an audience's compassion, but also on the elevation represented by figures 'better than present humanity'. I argued in the previous chapter that this duality should be read not as insouciance but in part as a reflection on the nature of tragedy itself. The heroes of tragedy (to use 'hero' once more in its Greek not in its Romantic sense) are, according to Aristotle, to be humanised so as to allow true sympathy with their misfortune and suffering, but without their being reduced thereby to the level of perfectly ordinary humanity. They are to be close enough in nature to the audience to elicit full pity and fear, yet they must remain sufficiently heroic to excite a special and heightened degree of these emotions.

But I also argued at the end of my last chapter that the heroic standing of the agents of tragedy is understood by Aristotle principally in terms of their great 'esteem and prosperity' (53a 10) not their ethical character. It is this preeminent status, and the external goods which define it, that constitute the basis of tragedy by providing a context in which human vulnerability can be dramatised and exhibited in an acute form. Moral goodness (up to a certain degree) is required in the agents, but Aristotle rules out extreme virtue in ch. 13, and the corollary of this is the stipulation of 'likeness' to enable true sympathy to be felt. The positive point which now needs to be stressed, therefore, in order to link the *Poetics'* dichotomy of virtue and status with the tragic emotions, is that Aristotle's theory places the weight of the experience of tragedy onto the transformation in the external fortunes of the agents rather than on the ethical nature of the characters and their actions. Tragedy is possible (though not commendable), as *Poetics* 6 acknowledges, without explicit characterisation, and this is so because in Aristotle's scheme it is the pattern of action itself, not the morality of those involved in it, which is the real focus of the emotions. The innocence and likeness which are the prerequisites of pity and fear might, after all, be interpreted as largely *negative* conditions, leaving the objective change of fortune to carry the main charge of tragic emotion. It is, then, the possession of exceptional human status or prosperity (but not ethical excellence) which opens up the possibility of the 'pain and destruction' and the most moving kinds of instability, of the type around which the ideal tragedy of the *Poetics* is built.

Yet to say this might appear to presuppose that the direction of a tragic action is necessarily from good to bad fortune, from heroic prosperity to catastrophe. While this is indeed the movement of the complex plot as Aristotle understands it in *Poetics* 13, there are several other passages in the work where the alternative of a transformation from bad to good fortune is recognised, or even, in ch. 14, preferred. The full implications of this alternative within the theory of tragedy will be brought out in my next chapter, but it is appropriate to ask at this point how it can be thought to satisfy the condition of pity and fear included in the definition of the genre. That Aristotle believed that it could is quite clear, not least from the fact that ch. 14's argument (starting effectively at 53b 14, after a digression on *opsis*) sets out to declare precisely which types of dramatic event will be productive of pity and fear. This condition is therefore paramount in the conclusion that plays such as Euripides' *Cresphontes* and *Iphigeneia in Tauris* (and an unattributed *Helle*) possess exemplary plots. Aristotle's choice of illustrations (two of them now lost) helps to establish how a final transformation from bad to good fortune can nonetheless achieve the effect of tragic pity and fear. Two prime factors can be recognised. The first is that the possibility of the final movement away from adversity entails in itself a preceding stage of sufficient suffering; the ultimate turn of fortune involves an escape from evils which constitute a serious impairment of status and prosperity. The second factor is more specific. In both the Euripidean plays mentioned by Aristotle – and in this respect they are intended to form a category – the final turn is directly preceded by a prospective catastrophe: someone, in Aristotle's own phraseology, is on the point of perpetrating an 'incurable' deed. The play of averted catastrophe, in other words, might follow the course of the tragedy of actual catastrophe until the moment of irreversible suffering itself: it is only at this point (the point at which, in the *Cresphontes*, the mother raises the axe above the sleeping body of her unrecognised son) that a sudden twist occurs in the dramatic action to prevent the terrible event. That the element of fear in the response to tragedy should be aroused in such circumstances is unproblematic; fear is by definition a prospective emotion, and Aristotle may even envisage fear predominating over pity in the response to such plots. That the necessary pity should also be evoked is more uncertain, but Aristotle evidently accepts that the immediacy of the impending evil in the cases he cites is sufficiently powerful to produce a proleptic pity even before the deed is done.[16]

This point can in fact be confirmed, again from the *Rhetoric*. The experience of pity, according to the analysis there presented, varies in intensity depending on the closeness of the sufferings which are its object. Hence, Aristotle observes, misfortunes in the distant past make only a weak appeal to our compassion, and the same is true of those which seem remote in the future. From this he concludes that the orator who uses dramatic means to reinforce his appeal for pity will be more successful: those who employ 'gesture, voice, dress, and all other aspects of delivery' bring the sufferings 'before our very eyes'.[17] The language which Aristotle uses here, while not inappropriate to rhetoric, seems even more applicable to poetry, or rather to the theatre and the actor. If, indeed, it suggests a stronger awareness of theatrical power than we usually associate with the *Poetics* (though it is closely related to the start of ch. 17), it still helps to intimate how drama, even outside the theatre, can by its immediacy and potency of mimetic representation captivate and move the feelings of a reader, even though its material may be drawn from the distant past or from the realms of legend. In the same passage of the *Rhetoric* Aristotle generalises his observation on the relation between pity and the proximity of suffering in such a way as to strengthen the conclusion of *Poetics* 14, for he states that the greatest pity is elicited by events 'which have recently happened or are soon about to occur'. From this principle we can extrapolate to the belief that a play such as the *Iphigeneia in Tauris* can fully satisfy

[16] On the lost *Cresphontes* see Burnett 11-13, 18-21. Burnett's opening chapter emphasises Ar.'s rejection of multiple plots, but she does not sufficiently ponder the relation between her own and Ar.'s categories. *Poet.* 53a 13 and 30ff. do not necessarily cover everything that Burnett counts as multiple reversal, while ch. 14 and 55b 3-12 make it clear that Ar. regarded Euripides' *IT* as a single 'complex' action, from bad to good fortune.

[17] *Rhet.* 1386a 29ff. The phrase 'bring before the eyes' should be carefully noted (cf. Morpurgo-Tagliabue 256ff.). It does not refer to physical vision but to *imagination* (see e.g. *De An.* 427b 18f., *Mem.* 450a 4, *Rhet.* 1411b 24ff.), which is why it occurs at *Poet.* 55a 23. (Compare the feeling of fear at *near* prospects, *EE* 1229b 10-17.)

the requirement of tragic pity by vividly presenting the audience with imminent, if finally averted, suffering of the most terrible kind: the action forces us to imagine the evils, to recognise and hence to respond emotionally towards their implications; and it is this imagination, not the physical actuality of the 'incurable', which Aristotle now appears to identify as sufficient for the experience of tragedy.

If it is paradoxical that Aristotle's emotional premises should produce in *Poetics* 14 a theoretical preference for a category of drama which involves a final twist from adverse to good fortune (or at least away from adverse fortune), what this underscores is the fact that the theory of tragedy as a whole is less concerned with the pure presentation of suffering than with the causation and the patterns of action which lead towards such suffering. Tragic causation, the causation which operates in and through human agency, is more important in Aristotle's scheme than is the tragic result, the ultimate evil itself. Thus the theory accentuates the pattern of change or transformation (to the point of allowing a change into misfortune to be incomplete, or only prospective) rather than the individual states which mark its extremes. It accords well with this theoretical slant that Aristotelian pity and fear have a clear cognitive content, and represent not mere impulses but the emotional consequences of perceptions that certain things are or are not so: that the sufferer, or prospective sufferer, is largely innocent, that he is sufficiently like us for it to be possible to sympathise with the nature of his plight, that we could imagine ourselves or those related to us in an equivalent position, and so on. The cognitive content of the emotions means that the tragic dramatist can aim to evoke them by the deliberate organisation and design of his material. It means also that such a design, a unified structure of dramatic action, is more important and effective than individual elements or scenes of suffering: hence the location of physical suffering, *pathos*, within Aristotle's theory as a discrete component of which a playwright may make more or less prominent use, depending on the total pattern of his tragedy. The precision of Aristotle's emotional psychology has the paradoxical result that it focusses tragic pity and fear on a movement towards misfortune, but does not require that movement, the *metabasis* of the plot, to be irreversible; pity and fear, so the theory posits, can be successfully aroused by a clear glimpse of 'incurable' suffering. This line of enquiry therefore leads us to the core of Aristotle's understanding of tragedy, and to the apparent tension between the two types of plot-structure which are recommended as ideals in chs. 13 and 14 of the treatise. To pursue this question further calls for a broader perspective than the tragic emotions themselves can provide, and I shall have to defer a complete consideration of it until my next chapter. But to have reached this point is adequate evidence that pity and fear cannot be regarded as a detachable element of the theory of tragedy, and that to scrutinise their function in the theory is to be brought to an evaluation of the plot-structures whose content and form are the specific causes of the tragic emotions.

If we take stock of what has so far emerged from my argument, we must first reiterate that pity and fear are tethered to the experience of the transformation of fortune which Aristotle identifies as the crux of tragic action. The supreme importance of this is that the emotions are thereby conceived not as a response to individual, discrete moments or states of suffering, but as a concomitant of the perception of movement and change in the status and prosperity of the chief agent or agents. Implicit in this is the premise that pity and fear depend on an intelligible conjunction of circumstances, and so, in the case of tragic drama, on a comprehensible sequence of actions and events, to satisfy the requirements of unity which I analysed in ch. III. Embodied in this chain of actions must be at least a partial movement towards innocent (though not arbitrary) suffering, and the prospect or actuality of this suffering must touch agents with whom an audience or reader can feel an essential sympathy. I have tried to show that this notion of sympathy, which underlies both pity and fear, is not a vaguely humanitarian instinct: it is the capacity to recognise a likeness between oneself and the object of one's emotions, a likeness which imports with it a sense that one could imagine suffering such things oneself. Such a recognition infuses an element of self-regarding emotion into the pity and fear which are focussed on others, and by expanding the clipped phrases of *Poetics* 53a 4f. with the evidence of the *Rhetoric* we can conclude that Aristotle's theory of the emotional experience of tragic poetry presupposes a strong sympathy which does not take the spectator or reader out of himself, but entails a deeper sense of the vulnerability of his own place in the world.

To have gone this far in bringing the *Rhetoric* to bear on the *Poetics* will be to have gone too far for some, but the ground remains firm for supposing that the *Poetics* cannot require what it shows no signs of supplying – a special psychology of aesthetic emotion – but instead assumes the philosopher's general view of the emotions, for which the *Rhetoric* happens to contain the most germane evidence. But what the *Rhetoric* certainly cannot furnish is a ready solution to the remaining and the most difficult issue concerning the tragic emotions – *katharsis*. To this I now turn.

*

It is not altogether without reason that the debate over *katharsis* has been described as 'a grotesque monument of sterility', and no-one with even a marginal acquaintance with scholarship on the *Poetics* will either need or care to be reminded how many discrepant interpretations of the idea have been advanced since the Renaissance. 'Every variety of moral, aesthetic, and therapeutic effect that is or could be experienced from tragedy has been subsumed under the venerable word at one time or another.'[18] So wrote Gerald Else, with pardonable exaggeration, though he went on, ironically and less pardonably, to add himself yet another new reading of *katharsis* to the list. I relegate to an appendix a critical attempt to see some order in the history of *katharsis* interpretations, and my aim in what follows is limited to the deliberately cautious and tentative examination of the context, both Aristotelian and pre-Aristotelian, within which it may be possible to make some minimal sense of tragic *katharsis*. Any confident interpretation of the issue can be regarded as suspicious on that ground alone. Evidence is acutely sparse, and we are in any case dealing with an area of Greek thought which is alien to prevailing modern views of art. This is one, though not the only, reason for resisting the temptation to produce a translation for *katharsis* – a point to which I will return at the end of the enquiry.

We can set out with moderate assurance, however, from the premise that Aristotelian *katharsis* is intended in some way to produce an answer to Plato's objections to the psychological effects of tragic

---

[18] My two quotations are from J. Morley, *apud* Lucas (1957) 35, and Else (1957) 439. For a survey of *katharsis* interpretations see Appendix 5. A refreshing example of the modesty which is all too rare in treatments of the issue comes from Twining 233: 'what was precisely his [Ar.'s] meaning, and the whole of his meaning, will never, I fear, be the subject of a perfect, stoical *katalépsis* to any man.' Twining's own analysis of the subject (231-42) has in many respects scarcely been improved on.

poetry.[19] If this is right, then *katharsis* is likely to represent not only an attempt to characterise the emotional experience of tragedy as such, but also to indicate a view of the *consequences* of this experience. But we cannot take this for granted, and must move slowly in considering whether it is an assumption validated by the meagre evidence. But that *katharsis* must, at the very least, be consistent with a rebuttal of Plato's charges, can scarcely be doubted, for the *Poetics* as a whole evidently accepts that the arousal of emotion is a legitimate aim and effect of the poet's art. By way of explicit justification of this stance against the Platonic case, however, the *Poetics* offers nothing but the solitary reference to *katharsis* in the definition of tragedy. Elucidation of the concept must therefore be sought outside the treatise, though it will be necessary to test any findings against the general view of the tragic emotions which I have sketched in the first half of this chapter. But on this point perhaps more than any other in the *Poetics* it is worthwhile to try to reconstruct the larger perspective which lies behind Aristotle's ideas. To do this it will be necessary not just to consider the earlier use of *katharsis* vocabulary, but also to take account of wider Greek ideas on the quasi-magical powers of music and language. Some of the primary evidence on these matters is to be found in Plato, and it will emerge paradoxically that certain elements in Aristotle's response to the Platonic charge against tragic emotion had been anticipated by Plato himself – a confirmation that, as I observed in ch. I, the relation between the philosophers' views of art is far from straightforward.

Pre-Aristotelian occurrences of the *katharsis* word-group can be seen to fall into a number of relatively well-defined areas of meaning. If we leave aside mundane and unproblematic references to the physical cleansing of objects, four main categories can be briefly delineated, all of which may have a contribution to make to the interpretation of tragic *katharsis*. The first is medical – a well-attested employment of the word-group, covering both the procedures and materials of purging used by doctors, and also the physical processes of discharge and secretion which may be the results of medical

---

[19] See esp. *Rep.* 606a-d. The response to Plato is clearly seen by Proclus in his reference to *katharsis* (quoted in Kassel 52 = Lucas (1968) 52: cf. ch. I n.2). Plato may not have been alone in being critical of the emotional experience of tragedy: note Isoc. 4.168, where it is wryly observed that the Athenians have more pity for poetic than for actual suffering.

treatment or the symptoms which call for such treatment. These types of *katharsis* are related by virtue of belonging to the sphere of the purely physical and physiological.[20]

A second area of usage, classifiable as religious and ritual, is large and complex.[21] For my purposes it is necessary to do no more than indicate the main applications of this concept or set of concepts, and to observe their chief implications. Ritual and religious *katharsis* normally concerns people, though it does have possible uses for inanimate objects: of these the most obvious is the purification of a place or area of land as part of its dedication to a deity or a sacred function. For individuals, purification may be called for in a variety of contexts. At one extreme it is a necessity for those who are dangerously unclean, particularly those who carry the pollution of blood-guilt: here the emphasis falls on what is removed by the ritual purification. But at the other end of the scale purification may have a more positive significance, as a means of preparing a person for participation in a religious ritual or ceremony: such forms of *katharsis* were an element in initiation into mystery religions, and their importance resides in the special state of purity which they produce. The category of ritual *katharsis* also sometimes overlaps with that of medicine, through the therapeutic use or value of purificatory procedures.[22] It will shortly become clear that this latter fact is of direct relevance to Aristotelian *katharsis*, but it can be more generally observed that religious purification appears to combine both a physical and a spiritual significance: unlike purely medical *katharsis*, in which all the phenomena are physical, it usually presupposes a mutual influence between the seen and the unseen, the material and the spiritual. In this respect, as well as in its coverage of both positive and negative types of purification, the notion of religious *katharsis* provides an important antecedent to Aristotle's choice of the term for the emotional effect of tragedy.

A third and narrower category of *katharsis* is Pythagorean. Little

---

[20] See LSJ s.v. *kathairō* I 3, *katharsis* II, and for surveys of this and other senses of the word-group see Susemihl & Hicks 643-50, Moulinier 149ff. Physiological uses of *katharsis* are by far the most common in Ar.'s own works: e.g. *Phys.* 194b 36, *HA* 572b 30ff., *GA* 727a 14f., b 14ff., *Met.* 1013b 1, and Bonitz s.v. *katharsis* and cognates for many further references.

[21] See Parker, esp. ch. 7, W. Burkert, *Greek Religion*, Engl. transl. (Oxford 1985) 75-84.

[22] Cf. G. Lloyd, *Magic, Reason & Experience* (Cambridge 1979) 44-9, Parker 215f. Plato *Crat.* 405a-b combines ideas of ritual and medical *katharsis*.

can be said about this subject, but that it cannot be altogether ignored is difficult to deny, especially in view of the fact that the earliest evidence for Pythagorean *katharsis* comes from a fragment of Aristoxenus, one of Aristotle's own pupils.[23] Aristoxenus asserts that the Pythagoreans used medicine for the purification of the body, and music (*mousikē*) for that of the soul. Whatever may have been distinctive about the former, it is the musical and spiritual type of Pythagorean *katharsis* which may represent an important precedent for Aristotle's use of the term. It is true that the Pythagorean *katharsis* which Aristoxenus attests might with some reason be called religious (or magical), and so be regarded as a sub-class of my previous category. But this possibility is less significant for my purposes than the fact that the Pythagorean application of music for cathartic effect must have differed appreciably from the ecstatic or frenzied type of Corybantic *katharsis*. Although Aristotle refers to the latter in *Politics* 8 as an extreme instance of musical *katharsis*, we will shortly see that he is concerned to extend the term to cover psychologically less abnormal experiences. We ought not lightly to dismiss the idea that the Pythagorean precedent was at least in this respect influential.

To medical, religious, and Pythagorean forms of *katharsis* we must finally add the more indeterminate class of metaphorical uses of the term and its cognates. To decide precisely how to separate metaphorical from literal senses of the terminology is difficult – the *katharsis* of the *Poetics* being itself a case in point. A germane illustration can be taken from Plato, who refers in the *Phaedo* to those 'who have been purified by philosophy' (114c). The phrase, which may contain echoes of Orphic and Pythagorean doctrines, has the flavour of a religious puritanism, grounded in a conviction of the sharp antithesis between body and soul and of the need to liberate the latter from the entrammelling and debasing nature of the former. Earlier in the dialogue, such a release or escape of the soul from the

[23] Aristoxenus fr. 26 Wehrli (1945): Wehrli 54f. regards Pythagorean *katharsis* as magical in origin. Cf. also Aristoxenus fr. 117 with Wehrli 84. On Aristoxenus' reliability as a source for Pythagoreanism see G. Kirk et al., *The Presocratic Philosophers* 2nd edn. (Cambridge 1983) 223f. Lienhard 51-61 speculates that in *Pol.* 8.7 Ar. alludes to a *katharsis* theory of Aristoxenus's own. For later evidence on Pythagorean *katharsis* see C.J. de Vogel, *Pythagoras and Early Pythagoreanism* (Assen 1966) 164f., 261-3. Since Pythagorean practice seems to have been allopathic, not homoeopathic, it would be wrong to argue for too close a link with Ar. For balanced discussions of the matter see Croissant 49-58, Rostagni (1955) 135-61, and for a much more elaborate but dubious case cf. Koller's book, esp. 92-104, 132ff.

body is described as *katharsis* (67c), and the philosopher is compared to the purified initiate of a mystery sect (69c-d). The adoption of the language of ritual purification for processes of philosophical enlightenment resists, when it is embedded in its suggestive Platonic context, an easy choice between the literal and the metaphorical. But there are at least hints of a self-conscious use of *katharsis* as an image, and elsewhere, in the *Sophist*, Plato certainly draws on an explicit analogy with medical *katharsis* in order to attribute a quasi-cathartic function to the procedures of philosophical cross-examination, *elenchos*.[24] Related metaphorical language is to be found in Xenophon's reference to 'those whose souls have been cleansed by philosophy', and Aristotle himself talks of the special 'purity' of philosophical pleasures.[25] Provided we do not identify the metaphorical with the non-physical, it should be uncontentious to recognise in these passages the extension of the language of *katharsis* to embrace a range of intellectual, psychological and spiritual phenomena – from the explicitly religious to the plainly metaphorical, and covering a number of varieties in between.

Even this cursory glance at the established pre-Aristotelian range of meanings for *katharsis* suggests a complex semantic background for the philosopher's adaptation of the term to describe the nature (or the result) of the emotional experience of tragedy. This complexity may in itself act as a caution against dogmatic or exclusive readings of the *katharsis* clause in the *Poetics*. But before we turn to the one other Aristotelian reference to artistic *katharsis* outside the *Poetics*, a further but more diffuse part of the larger perspective must be sketched. This consists of a set of attitudes, again fluctuating between the literal and the metaphorical, towards the quasi-magical powers of language and music. As early as Homeric epic we find the notion of 'bewitchment' by means of language appearing in a range of contexts: it is applied to poetry itself, but also to other powerful and potentially deceptive uses of words.[26] How widely such a notion was

---

[24] *Soph.* 230b-e, with the medical analogy at 230c 4-7. The passage is part of a larger enterprise, starting at 226d, to identify the whole genus of cathartic processes, and to subdivide them into physical, spiritual, etc. In the *Phaedo* note the indication of metaphor at 67c 3, and of allegory at 69c-d. Cf. also the *katharsis* metaphor at *Rep.* 411d 5. On the Pythagorean-Orphic background to *katharsis* in the *Phaedo* and other Platonic works see the speculative treatment of Boyancé 155-84.

[25] Xen *Symp.* 1.4, Ar. *EN* 1177a 25f.

[26] Hom. *Od.* 1.337 (Phemius' poetry), 11.334 ~ 13.2, 14. 387, 17.514, 521 (Odysseus' quasi-poetic narratives, both true and false), 3.264 (Aegisthus' adulterously seductive words), 12.40 (the Sirens' song). Cf. the idea of poetry and

disseminated, and how seriously it was taken, is impossible to say; but what is certain is that it was given new life by more than one writer in the classical period. Gorgias, in the same context of his *Helen* in which he refers to the power of poetry to arouse pity and fear, compares the art to incantatory magic, and to this he later adds an analogy between the effects of language on the mind or soul, and of medicine on the body – an analogy which recalls Aristoxenus's comment on the Pythagoreans, cited above.[27] These same ideas, as well as others germane to them, are found again in Plato, who frequently likens language to magic, and who also expresses the belief, perhaps specifically Pythagorean once more, in the analogous nature of medicine for the body and magical-cum-medical treatment for the soul.[28] Such ideas were probably also current in a more diluted form in popular uses of the language of *psuchagôgia* (literally, 'the conjuring of souls') for the emotional potency of poetry, rhetoric and other arts: Aristotle himself employs the image twice in the *Poetics*, once for the emotive force of reversal and recognition in the complex tragedy (50a 33), and once for that of theatrical 'spectacle' (50b 16); and parallels are to hand in a number of other authors.[29]

Alongside these notions of the magic of language existed comparable ideas about the power of music. Here we encounter attitudes which, if sometimes metaphorical, were at other times evidently subscribed to with full and literal conviction. We have already met the Pythagorean use of music for cathartic purposes, and touched on the role of music in religious rituals such as those of the Corybantes. In the Pythagorean case we can presume that the practice rested on special beliefs about both music and the soul; while in Corybantic ritual the explanation is likely to have been conceived in wholly religious terms. But outside these specific phenomena it is clear that there were more widely held views on the

---

song as pleasures which remove care, help us to forget sorrows, etc.: Hesiod *Theog.* 53-5, 98-103, Pindar *Nem.* 4.1ff. (with medical imagery).

[27] Gorgias fr.11.8-10 (pity and fear, sympathy for others' good and bad fortunes, poetic incantations and magic), fr.11.14 (analogy between *logos* and drugs): for commentary on these points see Lanata 192-204, Süss 83ff., 92ff., and cf. ch. II n.24 above. Close to Gorgias is Thrasymachus' claim, attested at Plato *Phdr.* 267c-d, to be able to rouse an audience to anger or to 'charm' its anger away.

[28] The 'magic' of language: e.g. *Phdr.* 261a, 267d, 271c, *Protag.* 315a-b, 328d, *Rep.* 601b, *Euthyd.* 289e-90a. On the general parallel between body and soul medicine (or magic: the language covers both) see *Charm.* 155e-158c, 175e-6b.

[29] See the references in ch. II n.24 above.

power of music to affect and shape the mind.[30] Our primary classical sources for these views are Plato and Aristotle. For Plato, the emotional force of music is problematic in the same way and for the same reasons as that of poetry, with which it is often combined in Greek culture: both arts are capable of embodying and communicating feelings which can permanently change the soul of the listener. Plato is prepared to apply the language of magic to music's power over the mind, and it is hardly surprising that he shows a particular interest, to which I shall shortly return, in the special function of music in Corybantic ritual.[31] But virtually all that has just been said of Plato can equally be said of Aristotle. In Book 8 of the *Politics* we find an exposition of the educational significance of music which presupposes its capacity to influence and shape the emotional faculty of the mind (and, through it, the character). The channel for this influence is mimesis, by which the emotions and ethical character enacted in the music are sympathetically experienced by the hearer too. Aristotle specifically attests that his discussion of these matters is indebted to the ideas of others, and he thus confirms that the context of the *Politics* in which he mentions *katharsis* is one in which he is not producing entirely new philosophical concepts but indicating a position in relation to existing issues and beliefs. This is not, however, to rule out an element of originality altogether. In his main reference to *katharsis* in *Politics* 8 (1341b 38ff.) Aristotle promises to explain more clearly the meaning of the term 'in my treatment of poetry', and the need for explanation perhaps implies a degree of his novelty in his adaptation of it. We must therefore turn to a closer inspection of this context in the *Politics* to see whether it is possible to discern more precisely the relationship between Aristotelian *katharsis* and the broad background of views on music and poetry which I have outlined.

Whether or not the reference in the *Politics* to a 'treatment of poetry' means the *Poetics* itself,[32] this passage puts it beyond

[30] On this whole intriguing but difficult subject see Anderson's book.

[31] For the magic of music in various Platonic contexts see *Symp.* 215c-e, *Rep.* 411 a-b, *Laws* 659d-e, 790-791, 840e.

[32] Notwithstanding the authority of scholars such as Vahlen (1911) 230-4 and Rostagni (1945) XLV, it seems to me unlikely that Ar. would have reserved an explanation of *katharsis* for the second Book of the *Poetics* (which is not to deny the likelihood of comic *katharsis*: see ch. IX n.33), since the matter calls for comment, if anywhere, after its mention in the definition of tragedy. Why it does not occur can hardly be divined (cf. ch. I pp. 31f.). See De Montmollin 174f., Lord (1982) 148-50, the latter following Finsler 8 in taking the *Politics*' promise as anticipating a later (lost)

reasonable doubt that there is a significant link, though not necessarily simple identity, between the *katharsis* of *Politics* 8 and tragic *katharsis*. This connection, which was perceived by Renaissance writers such as Vettori, and given renewed attention from Bernays onwards in the nineteenth century, is only, however, the first step in the unravelling of the problem. A careful scrutiny of this section of *Politics* 8 yields the inference that musical and poetic *katharsis* cannot be all of precisely one kind. This is entailed, for one thing, by the very existence of tragic *katharsis*, since, despite arguments to the contrary, it is intolerable to suppose that the latter could be wholly assimilated to the *katharsis* of those who suffer from abnormal emotional propensities, as indicated at *Pol.* 1342a 5ff.: an effect of this kind, which could operate only for an exceptional portion of a tragic audience, could never have earned a place in Aristotle's definition of the genre, the statement of its essence.[33] Moreover, the *Politics* text itself appears to assert the existence of a range of cathartic experiences available from music. At one extreme stands the orgiastic experience of 'sacred melodies', which allows those in need of it to find 'a medical cure, as it were, and a *katharsis*'. Alongside this there is the possibility of varying degrees of *katharsis* for those who are emotionally susceptible, but whose susceptibilities are less than pathological. It is likely that this range covers most members of the audience of music or poetry, and that some form of *katharsis* is considered by Aristotle to be the appropriate effect on entire audiences of those types of music or poetry which possess the power to produce it. The possibility of variation in the degree or quality of *katharsis* is strengthened by the evidence from the *Rhetoric* (p.175 above) on the differing emotional sensibilities of certain sorts of people. For, as Aristotle puts it just before mentioning orgiastic *katharsis*, 'the emotion which some souls feel strongly exists in all souls to a greater or lesser degree'. And, to reiterate a vital

---

section of that work itself.

Note that *katharsis* may represent an early element in Ar.'s response to Plato's critique of poetry (see ch. I n.2), which is one among other reasons for rejecting the view of Else (1957) 231ff. that the *katharsis* clause is a late addition to the *Poetics*. The date of *Politics* 8 is arguable: see Lord (1982) 25-8.

[33] On the existence of several kinds of Aristotelian *katharsis* see Bywater 152 and Lord (1982) 119-38. It is a flaw in the influential interpretation of Bernays that the orgiastic *katharsis* of *Pol.* 8 is treated as illustrating the whole of Ar.'s meaning. Hence the pathological inference: tragic *katharsis* is therapy for the overwrought ('eines beklommenen', Bernays 16).

consideration, if this were not so, it is difficult to see how tragic *katharsis* could belong in the definition of the genre.

We have, then, both encouragement to look to *Politics* 8 for some possible light on the notion of tragic *katharsis*, but also reason to resist the temptation to set up the extreme variety of orgiastic *katharsis*, as observed by Aristotle in a religious context, as the only model for emotional *katharsis* in general. It remains obvious, however, that orgiastic, Corybantic *katharsis* is mentioned by Aristotle as a well-known phenomenon which illustrates the fundamental type of psychological experience with which he is concerned, and its positive implications must therefore be noted with care. The first of these is that the process of *katharsis* is homoeopathic (though the term must be understood here without medical associations): the emotions involved, that is to say, are 'both the means and the object' of the experience, in Twining's phrase.[34] We can be confident that this holds for tragic *katharsis* too, since the relevant clause of the *Poetics*, '... through pity and fear accomplishing the *katharsis* of such emotions', directly expresses an identity of means and object. I shall return to the question of this homoeopathic relation below, but it can at once be seen that the force of the idea provides a strategy against Plato's claim that the arousal of emotion by tragedy has the effect of increasing the audience's susceptibility to such experiences. Aristotle's rebuttal of this charge may seem ironic in view of the fact that Plato's own account of Corybantic *katharsis* in the *Laws* itself posits a homoeopathic process underlying the phenomenon. Comparison with this Platonic passage helps also to bring out another feature of Aristotle's discussion in *Politics* 8, namely the emphasis on psychology rather than religion or ritual.[35] Plato had explained Corybantic practices as involving the use of one movement – physical and external – to counter and reduce another – internal

---

[34] Twining 233 and cf. 237.
[35] To call Aristotelian *katharsis* psychological is not to deny that Ar. believed emotional experiences to have a physiological substratum: see esp. *De An.* 403a 16-b 19, *EN* 1128b 15f. (and cf. *EN* 1147b 6-9 for a special case). But to say with Fortenbaugh 22 that through tragic *katharsis* the spectator 'is purged in so far as his bodily condition is altered' is simply reductive. Much the same is true of the fuller argument of Flashar's article, which shows how the emotions could be understood physiologically but does not establish that tragic *katharsis* is to be taken on this level. On the problematic relation of mind and body in Ar. see R. Sorabji, 'Body and Soul in Aristotle', in Barnes (1979), esp. 46-8, and E. Hartman, *Substance, Body and Soul* (Princeton 1977) 144-52.

and mental.[36] There is no trace of a religious aetiology in his account of the process, any more than there is in Aristotle's, who talks purely in terms of the arousal and relief of emotion.

But Plato and Aristotle have another detail in common; both employ the language of medical 'cures'. Whatever the significance of this in Plato, it is crucial to see that, contrary to the dominant modern interpretation of tragic *katharsis*, the medical reference in *Politics* 8 does not purport to provide a full explanation of the experience in question. This is immediately clear from the fact that Aristotle presents the point as an analogy: those involved find 'a medical cure, as it were, and a *katharsis*' (1342a 10f.). The qualification patently warrants the assumption that Aristotle does not believe the process or the effect to be properly medical, but only to have a result *comparable* to that of medical therapy. If we put this point together with that made in my previous paragraph, it can be proposed that *Politics* 8 presupposes the existence of both ritual and medical *katharsis*, and expects acquaintance with them both as part of the cultural background which gives force to Aristotle's application of the term to a range of emotional experiences provided by music and poetry; but, equally, that neither the extreme of orgiastic *katharsis* nor, *a fortiori*, the other forms of psychological *katharsis* hypothesised by Aristotle can count in his view as properly religious or medical. The status of medicine as an analogy is confirmed by Aristotle's explicit statements elsewhere that medical procedures entail treatment *by opposites*, and so are not homoeopathic – a factor which has been repeatedly neglected.[37] This enables us to conclude all the more firmly that in *Politics* 8 Aristotle takes his primary illustration from ritual *katharsis*, which he interprets in psychological terms and in turn compares for its therapeutic effects to medicine. This relationship between Aristotelian, religious and medical kinds of

[36] *Laws* 790d-791a: on the Damonian background to the passage see Anderson 38-41, 74-81. Compare Ar. *Rhet.* 1418a 14f. on conflicting motions in general.

[37] That the homoeopathic idea is taken from ritual *katharsis*, and in turn compared to medicine, is correctly perceived by E. Rohde, *Psyche* Engl. transl. (London 1925) ch. IX n.19; cf. Moulinier 410-19. (A homoeopathic procedure – blood to cleanse blood-pollution – is attested for ritual *katharsis* in Heraclitus fr. 5: cf. Plato *Laws* 870c 2f., 873a 1.) But medicine works by opposites: *EN* 1104b 17f., *EE* 1220a 36f., and cf. *EN* 1154a 27-31, 1154b 12-15, *EE* 1220b 30f., *Pol.* 1337b 41f., 1339b 17. *Contra* e.g. Susemihl & Hicks 641, Butcher 246 n. 3, there seems to be no satisfactory evidence for homoeopathic forms of medicine which Ar. could have known. Neither Pythagorean *katharsis* nor the ideas in Gorgias's *Helen* (nn.23 and 27 above) contain a homoeopathic element.

katharsis is surely unsurprising in the light of the philosopher's primary interest in the emotions: it is Corybantic ritual which, once it is stripped of its religious setting, supplies a striking instance of psychological homoeopathy (the arousal of the emotions to change the emotions), whereas the reference to medicine chiefly clarifies the objective phenomenon of an apparent treatment for a pathological condition. Once the idea is extended to less extreme or abnormal experiences, it is clearly psychology and not pathology which will be pertinent.

Since tragic *katharsis* must be supposed to be homoeopathic in the given sense, but cannot reasonably be thought to provide an experience of value only to the pathological, it is ritual *katharsis*, psychologically reinterpreted, which ought to give us the best clue to the poetic *katharsis* that Aristotle alludes to in the *Politics* and that we encounter without further explanation in its tragic variety in the *Poetics*. But before basing any inferences about tragic *katharsis* on this observation, another distinction must be introduced and explored. Where Aristotle talks in the *Politics* of the experience of orgiastic music, he refers to 'possession' and obviously has in mind an all-engrossing frenzy or delirium.[38] To suppose that something comparable holds for tragedy is out of the question, since it is incompatible with the conscious cognition which is essential for the appreciation of a dramatic plot-structure. Such cognition is not coldly cerebral, but forms the ground of the strong affective response evoked by tragedy. Nonetheless, this picture of the experience of tragic drama leaves no opportunity for anything comparable to 'possession', and for this reason too we must accept a separation of orgiastic and tragic *katharsis*, despite their common or analogous foundation in a homoeopathic psychological process. This argument adds support to the earlier claim that Aristotle recognises a range of emotionally cathartic experiences, and it strengthens the case for inferring that tragic *katharsis* must lie at a point on the scale where it is accessible to the type of audience presupposed by the *Poetics* as a whole, an audience capable of appreciating the substance of the ideal tragedy. Since tragic *katharsis*, as the definition intimates, is essentially and not just contingently entailed in the experience of tragic poetry, it must operate in conjunction with the full comprehension of all that is embodied in the mimetic structure of the dramatic work.

[38] On Ar.'s language here and elsewhere cf. ch. III n.5 above. Compare the language of Plato *Symp.* 215c-d, referring to the same phenomenon as *Politics* 8.

The perspective of *katharsis* which I have so far tried to construct involves using the assistance of *Politics* 8 in filling out the unelaborated doctrine of the *Poetics*, but also eschewing the direct transference of all that is said about *katharsis* in the former to the particular phenomenon of tragic *katharsis*. In order to try tentatively to advance a further step towards an elucidation of tragic *katharsis*, a paradox must now be proposed and confronted. In the context of *Politics* 8 as a whole, *katharsis* is only of marginal concern to Aristotle, and it is at one point explicitly contrasted with the main subject of the philosopher's argument, the use of music for emotional and ethical education. The importance of this latter theme is that it leads Aristotle to some general remarks about the power of musical mimesis, and these remarks, given the close association between music and poetry, can be taken to have wider implications for all mimetic art, as Aristotle's comparative references to the visual arts confirm. The power of music, and hence its significance for education, is here said to reside in its capacity to offer vivid representations of emotions which are correspondingly experienced by the hearer and can play a part in the training of his emotional sensibilities, whose ethical functions are important to Aristotle. The paradox which arises out of this is that it may be precisely Aristotle's account of this process of emotional and ethical habituation through mimetic art which can help to explain the concept of tragic *katharsis*, even though in *Politics* 8 itself *katharsis* seems at first sight opposed to, rather than part of, the education of the emotions.

But a solution to the paradox can perhaps be found by first observing that the *katharsis* which, at *Pol.* 1341a 23f., is contrasted with moral instruction is the kind available from orgiastic music. We have seen that this is an extreme form of *katharsis*, needed only by those with an excessive propensity to the emotion which Aristotle calls *enthousiasmos*. Moreover, even in this extreme case it is possible to regard the cathartic experience as involving at least a temporary restoration of the subject to a state or disposition closer to an emotional mean or norm, and we notice that the contrast drawn by Aristotle is accordingly comparative rather than absolute: '*katharsis* rather than instruction.' Once attention is shifted to types of *katharsis* connected with more common emotions and with those who do not experience them to a morbidly abnormal degree (and both these conditions are true of the tragic variety), it is possible to discern that *katharsis* may after all be in some cases compatible with the process which Aristotle characterises in *Politics* 8 as a matter of habituation in feeling the emotions in the right way and towards the right objects (1340a 16-18). Such emotional habituation is a contribution to the acquisition of ethical virtue, since it conduces to an alignment of the emotions with the perception of moral qualities in the world; and Aristotle accepts the possibility of such a development through the experience of mimetic art because he commits himself to the general (and Platonic) principle that 'to be accustomed to feeling pleasure and pain in the case of likenesses [i.e. mimetic works] is close to being disposed in the same way towards reality'.[39] Although this principle is expounded in the *Politics* for the sake of asserting a view of the function of music in the education of the young, the phrasing of Aristotle's generalisations communicates something about the possible nature of mature experience of mimetic art too: in this respect, it is worth comparing the discussion with ch. 4 of the *Poetics*, where statements about the origin of poetry and about the general experience of mimesis are conjoined (because necessarily related, from Aristotle's naturalistic viewpoint).

Simply to identify tragic *katharsis* with a process of ethical exercise and habituation for the emotions through art would be speculative and more than the evidence justifies. But to suggest that these two things ought to stand in an intelligible relation to one another (as the phrase 'for education and *katharsis*' at *Pol.* 1341b 38 encourages us to see them) is only to argue that tragic *katharsis* should be capable of integration into Aristotle's general philosophy of the emotions, and of their cognitive and moral importance, as well as into the framework of his theory of tragedy as a whole. When functioning properly, emotions such as pity and fear are consistent with reason and are a reflex of its judgements; if this were otherwise, the *Poetics'* whole emphasis on the artistic means for eliciting them would lose its point and force. In those passages where the tragic emotions are most explicitly and prominently drawn on as criteria of success in the

[39] *Pol.* 1340a 23-5. Just how close Ar. comes to Plato on this point can be seen from a comparison between *Pol.* 1336b 2f. and Plato *Rep.* 395c-d, 606b (note the verb *apolauein* in all three passages). Note also the connection drawn, regarding humour, between what one hears and what one will say oneself, at *EN* 1128a 1-32 (with Plato *Rep.* 606c 2ff.): cf. ch. IX n.31.

On the ethical importance of pleasures and pains (which includes the emotions), and of feeling them towards the right objects, see, in addition to *Pol.* 1340a 14-28, *EN* 1104b 11-13 (citing Plato), 1106b 16-28, 1152b 1-8, 1172a 21ff., *EE* 1220a 34-7, and compare Plato *Laws* 653b-c, 659d.

genre, chs. 13 and 14, Aristotle's argument presupposes that the audience of tragedy will respond emotionally as part of their apprehension of the facts of the play's action: its sequence of causation, the moral status of the agents, the discrepancy between intention and result in human action, the magnitude of the change in fortune shaped by the plot. It is with an experience of this order that tragic *katharsis* must somehow be reconcilable, unless we wish to posit a radical incoherence in the theory. Since pity and fear are not undesirable emotions in Aristotle's eyes, but represent a natural and appropriate reaction to certain situations, it will hardly do (despite orgiastic *katharsis*, for which this does hold) to suppose that tragic *katharsis* is no more than an outlet for overcharged feelings, a working off of emotional excess: the outlet theory suffers above all from the failure to explain the presence of *katharsis* in the definition of the genre. And once this possibility is discarded, it is difficult to resist the prompting to associate *katharsis* with the process described in the *Politics*, whereby the emotions become better attuned to the perception of reality, and, consequently, as Aristotle believed, better disposed towards virtue.[40]

The suggestion that *katharsis* may have an ethical dimension has met with much, though not universal, repudiation in modern times. A major reason for this has been the influence of Jacob Bernays and his interpretation of *katharsis*, which was formulated in conscious reaction against what was seen as the imbalanced moralism of earlier views. Thus it can be said, with a degree of simplification (to which Appendix 5 supplies a corrective), that there have been two dominant movements of opinion in this field since the Renaissance, the first heavily moralistic, the second 'clinical'. While, on account of the fundamental preconceptions of neo-classicism, the moralising tendency was often crudely reductive, it did at least furnish a

---

[40] On the relation of the emotions to virtue see esp. *EE* 1220b 7-10, 1234a 24-33. To say, without qualification, that pity 'is not a desirable thing at all', is highly misleading of Grube (1965) 75: it is not intrinsically desirable, of course, but Ar. certainly thought it ethically desirable when called for. Similarly, Kommerell 102 can only claim that Ar. thought pity 'ein Übel' by refusing to take *Rhet.* 1386b 11-14 seriously. On moderation in emotion see *EN* 1108a 30ff., *EE* 1233b 16ff. (where the emotions cited are related to pity and fear).

The best modern attempts to seek a connection between *katharsis* and the ethical habituation of the emotions are those of Finsler 107-23 (perhaps over-stressing Platonic precedents), Rostagni (1955) 89-161, House 108-11, Lord (1982) chs. 2-3, Wagner, and Janko 139-51 (rightly remarking, 149, the ethical emphasis of post-Aristotelian evidence on the subject).

framework within which a few outstanding critics – notably Vettori, Heinsius, Lessing and Twining – were in various ways encouraged to seek a link between *katharsis* and Aristotle's understanding of the emotions and their relation to virtue. It is this link which the thrust of much modern scholarship, following on Bernays, has tended to dislocate. But in order to do so it has placed an excessive weight, as I earlier tried to demonstrate, on the medical reference in *Politics* 8. It has also had the unfortunate consequence of tending to replace what Bernays unfairly characterised as Lessing's view of tragedy as 'a moral house of correction' with an alternative vision of it as a psychiatric clinic.[41] We need not wish, in rejecting this, to attribute to Aristotle any simple assessment of the moral value of tragedy, but it can hardly be thought extravagant to suppose that he saw a degree of ethical significance in the emotional experience of a genre concerned with some of the gravest matters of 'actions and life' (50a 16f.).

A further unfortunate consequence of the modern pattern of controversy over *katharsis* has been a distracting preoccupation with how the term should be translated. In particular a polarity has been set up between 'purification' and 'purgation' (and related words), and these versions have usually been aligned respectively with ritual and medical *katharsis*. But while both religious and medical phenomena are relevant parts of the background to Aristotelian *katharsis*, I have argued that it is misleading to try to identify the latter strictly with either of them. But there is a more fundamental fallacy which underlies attempts to force the issue between purification and purgation, and that is the assumption that we are faced with a mutually exclusive choice between positing a process of outlet and evacuation, or one of refinement. Various Greek forms of *katharsis* do indeed stress either what is removed or what is left by the process; but that is not a sufficient reason for excluding the possibility that Aristotle's notion of psychological *katharsis* combines an element of release with a sense of the improved or refined state of what remains: more concretely, that it entails both an expenditure of emotion, and an amelioration of the underlying emotional

---

[41] This is a juster riposte than the gibe against Bernays reported by Gründer 515. For objections to an ethical interpretation of *katharsis* see e.g. Bywater 160f., Schadewaldt 213-36, Söffing 57-65. Von Fritz XXVI, although holding to a Bernaysian line, mentions the need to complement it with a sense of the quasi-philosophical value attached to tragedy by Ar.

disposition.[42] That this is so is in fact favoured by the homoeopathic form of the process, in which the arousal of pity and fear (which must in the first instance be drained) effects a *katharsis* of the emotions themselves (which therefore ought in some degree to be changed).

To these points we must add the observation that translations of *katharsis* bring with them various connotations that only obscure further the comprehension of this enigmatic issue. For the inescapable fact is that we do not know enough, even with the help of the *Politics*, to find even a loose equivalent for the Greek term. The historical perspective which I tried to sketch earlier in this section may give us some sense of why Aristotle could choose *katharsis* as a suitable term for his purposes. But it has to be admitted that the perspective is itself in many respects an alien one, involving as it does a mixture of ideas from magic and medicine, a tradition of concepts and claims which shift between the literal and the metaphorical, and more than one source of esoteric beliefs about the nature of the soul and about the powers of language and music over the soul. As the reference to orgiastic rites in *Politics* 8 establishes, this complex tradition was not without its influence on Aristotle's thinking about mimetic art, though it is clear enough that there is no real trace of the esoteric in Aristotle's ideas themselves. The philosopher starts from what he takes to be the observable emotive effects of various forms of art, and his aim in invoking *katharsis* is to indicate the existence of a psychological account of these effects which will be his own, but which, given its description, may contain echoes of the theories of Pythagoreans, Gorgias, Plato and perhaps others too. It is our misfortune that, while we may still be able to detect some of those echoes, Aristotle's own voice is not wholly audible.

[42] At *GA* 738a 27-33 a moderate physical discharge is said to effect the *katharsis* of what remains. At *Soph.* 226d (cf. 227d) and *Rep.* 567c Plato conceives of *katharsis* explicitly as a process of removing the worse and leaving the better: cf. also *Laws* 791a. Butcher 253 n.1 notes the medical distinction between *katharsis* (partial removal) and *kenôsis* (evacuation), though Plato *Rep.* 560d 8 feels able to combine them.

On translations, note that virtually all Renaissance Italians used *purgar*, but they did not always mean the same things by it. Minturno, for example, uses both *purgare* and *expiare*: see Weinberg 739 n.37. Boswell reports Johnson as using 'purged or refined' non-disjunctively (April 12th, 1776). Twining 131-42 uses 'purgation', 'moderation', and 'correction'. Allan (1970) 159 accepts a combination of purging and purifying. Janko uses 'purged' on 143, 'purified' on 144. And so on. The issue should not be made a matter of translation, and interpretations should not necessarily be classified on this basis. The list of translations in Bywater 361-5 therefore gives an imperfect idea of the various understandings of *katharsis*: the generalisations of Keesey 193f. take insufficient account of this fact, despite his qualification in n.1 on 194.

If to settle on a translation for *katharsis* would give a false sense of familiarity to what remains a remote and obscure concept, the argument must nevertheless be brought to some sort of conclusion. The *katharsis* of the *Poetics* is a doctrine of the psychological nature and effect of the emotional experience of tragedy, and its presence in the definition shows that there is a strong affective dimension to Aristotle's theory of the genre. But tragic *katharsis* is not unique in Aristotle's thinking, and in addition to the types of musical *katharsis* referred to in *Politics* 8, there is the likelihood that he posited forms of *katharsis* related to epic and comic poetry.[43] In the extreme case of orgiastic *katharsis*, the experience is one only for those who suffer from severe emotional disequilibrium: for these, the homoeopathic relief from oppressive emotions by the frenzied expenditure of them fulfils the function of medical treatment. But *katharsis* of the kind mediated through tragic poetry is tied to a conscious, cognitive experience of a work of mimetic art, and the emotions involved, although potent, are properly and justifiably evoked by a portrayal of events which, if encountered in reality, would call for the same emotional response.[44] Since pity and fear are aroused, on Aristotle's theory, by elements of a carefully organised plot-structure, and since the theory emphasises above all else the principles of causal unity which give this structure its universal intelligibility, tragic *katharsis* cannot easily be supposed to be separable from the integrated experience of tragedy – an experience which is both cognitive and emotional, and which rests on the understanding of the universals embodied in the mimetic representation. I have therefore concluded,

---

[43] Epic *katharsis* ought to be entailed by Ar.'s own comparison between tragedy and epic at 59b 7-15; it was widely accepted in the Renaissance (though often for the wrong reasons), and has been in modern times by e.g. Rostagni (1945) LIV, Hogan 104-7. The consideration of Hubbard 132 n.3 against it seems to me to carry little weight. On comic *katharsis* see ch. IX n.33. It might be worth adding, speculatively, that *Pol.* 1342b 4-12 may imply the possibility of a dithyrambic *katharsis* of the more purely emotional kind, somewhat akin to the Corybantic.

[44] There has been much disagreement from the Renaissance onwards about whether pity and fear alone are the object of tragic *katharsis*. Bernays 24-30 thought that they were, as did Butcher 240 n.3. Others have dissented: e.g. Bywater 152, Pohlenz 574, Lord (1982) 159-64 (but drifting towards a quasi-Renaissance position in which the other emotions are stressed *more* than pity and fear), Adkins (1970) 195 n.1 (*all* the emotions), Janko 161 (but anger is incompatible with fear: *Rhet.* 1380a 32f., 1389a 28). On purely linguistic grounds, 'such emotions' at 49b 27f. certainly allows for others too: see the parallel usages at 54b 12 and 56b 1, and cf. *Rhet.* 1354a 17. But there seems little reason to look for other emotions, when Ar. mentions only pity and fear throughout the treatise.

with a minority of modern interpreters, that tragic *katharsis* in some way conduces to an ethical alignment between the emotions and the reason: because tragedy arouses pity and fear by appropriate means, it does not, as Plato alleged, 'water' or feed the emotions, but tends to harmonise them with our perceptions and judgements of the world. And because of this integration into the total experience of tragedy, *katharsis* must also be intimately associated with the pleasure derivable from the genre, for this pleasure, as I argued in ch. II, arises from the comprehension of the same action which is the focus of the emotions.[45] Tragic *katharsis* and tragic pleasure are both grounded in the understanding of the plot-structure, the 'soul' of tragedy: it is to the analysis of the components and significance of this structure that my next chapter will be devoted.

[45] *Poet.* 53b 12 favours a strong connection between *katharsis* and the proper pleasure of tragedy. They are regarded as identical by e.g.Schadewaldt 213ff., Janko 142. For objections see Rostagni (1955) 114, Lucas (1968) 275.

VII

Fallibility & Misfortune:
the Secularisation of the Tragic

The previous two chapters have shown how two prominent aspects of
Aristotle's theory of tragedy reflect the relevant areas of his ethical
and psychological philosophy – first, the relation between action and
character, which reproduces the general primacy of activity over
states in the moral life; secondly, the nature of pity and fear as
responses to the contemplation of certain types of misfortune,
responses which are the affective counterpart of ethical judgements
on those who encounter such misfortune. Together these arguments
confirm that the *Poetics* does not purport to seal poetry off from wider
concerns and values, but that it frames a conception of tragedy which
accepts the genre's serious engagement with 'actions and life', and
recognises the potential significance of this engagement for the
understanding of matters of major ethical import. Approached in
these terms, tragedy can be seen to give substance to Aristotle's
conviction that the appreciation of mimetic art is rooted in cognitive
experience, and to lend some force to the quasi-philosophical status
which he attributes to this experience in chs. 4 and 9 of the treatise.
In the present chapter this assessment will be carried a stage further
and clarified by consideration of the central tenets of the theory of
tragedy. I shall begin by asking more precisely how tragedy might be
thought to bear on the leading notion of Aristotle's moral philosophy
– 'happiness', *eudaimonia*, the goal and ideal of the good life. This will
call for closer scrutiny of the idea of extremes or poles of fortune
which is used to define the contours of tragic action in the *Poetics*.
And out of this will emerge a further pair of themes, which lie at the
heart of Aristotle's view of the genre: the implications of the tragic
dénouements set up as models in chs. 13 and 14 (including the
question of *hamartia*); and the relation between these models and the
religious dimension of Greek tragedy.

By its very nature the Aristotelian concept of 'happiness' (*eudaimonia*) is such that everything else in human life must be held subordinate to it. Happiness is the supreme moral good, but while Aristotle defines it as the perfect exercise of virtue, this rests on an entire theory of human nature within which virtues and vices are aligned with pleasure and pain. Happiness is, therefore, not a paradigm of self-sacrificing virtue, but entails a perfect, and perfectly fulfilling, harmony between the individual's will and the requirements of moral action: *eudaimonia* embodies, so to speak, a consummate equation between virtue and happiness. It was just such an equation which Plato had laid an obligation on tragic poets to affirm,[1] but Aristotle clearly felt unwilling to exact anything quite so uncompromising from them. This was in part because Aristotle was more prepared than Plato to concede the existence of an imbalance between virtue and external status or fortune in the world – at least below the level of perfect *eudaimonia*, though even here too in exceptional circumstances, as we shall see. But if tragic poetry cannot be expected to demonstrate the ethical ideal of happiness, the latter remains the supreme criterion of moral success, the standard by which less virtuous and happy lives are ultimately to be measured.

An indirect connection between tragedy and happiness may be specifically acknowledged in the *Poetics* itself. In the sentence following on Aristotle's description of the genre as 'a mimesis ... of actions and life', we encounter this: 'happiness and unhappiness both consist in activity, and the goal [of life] is a certain kind of activity, not a state; and while it is in their characters that people are of a certain sort, it is through their actions that they achieve or fail to achieve happiness.' (50a 17-20) Objections have been brought against the authenticity of this sentence, but the justification for some sort of reference at this juncture to Aristotle's wider principles of ethics should not be in doubt, and the link holds firm (as I argued in ch. V) between the primacy of plot in drama and the dependence upon action of moral success or failure.[2] A similar observation to the one just quoted can in fact be found earlier in ch. 6 of the treatise,

---

[1] *Rep.* 363e ff., 380a-b, 392a-b, *Laws* 660e-661c, 663c-d.

[2] Although a degree of textual corruption is possible, see H.-J. Horn, *Hermes* 103 (1975) 292-9 on the place of 50a 17-20 in Ar.'s argument. Belfiore 115 suggests that *eudaimonia* (if genuine) is here a synonym of *eutuchia*, but this is inapt: Ar. was not committed to the view that *eutuchia* is dependent on action (50a 2f. is not restricted to the sphere of *eutuchia*). Note that *kakodaimonia* does occur in *Protr.* B46 Düring (1961), though this may not be enough to prove the word genuine at *Poet.* 50a 17.

where we are told that 'it is in their actions that all men experience either success or failure' (50a 2-3). The language of this earlier remark does not refer us directly to the standard of *eudaimonia*, but it is clear enough from the connection made in the same context with moral purpose or character (*êthos*) that the success or failure in action which Aristotle has in mind is taken to possess an ethical dimension.

These passages confirm, then, what is more diffusely recognisable, that the types of human action encompassed by tragedy necessitate an ethical framework for their understanding. As a step further towards seeing how Aristotle supposes this to be so, we should now take account of a word-group (to which the language of 50a 2-3 is related) which, unlike *eudaimonia* itself, occurs repeatedly in the *Poetics*. The most prominent terms in this group are *eutuchia*, which can be translated, without prejudice to its place in Aristotle's argument, as 'prosperity' or 'good fortune', and its antithesis, *dustuchia* or *atuchia*, 'adversity' or 'misfortune'.[3] Prosperity and adversity, good fortune and misfortune, are the poles between which the action of tragedy moves. It is at first sight odd that the movement into and out of these conditions is not part of Aristotle's definition of tragedy, but reflection shows that it is in fact implicit in the phrase 'pity and fear', for these emotions will later be attached specifically to certain types of misfortune. The group of words in question are employed in the *Poetics* to define the curves of action, to mark the direction of events, which form tragic plot-structures. Prosperity and adversity constitute the grand dichotomy of tragic action in Aristotle's scheme, and it is worth listing some of the chief passages in which a transition or transformation of fortune (*metabasis*) appears in the analysis.

Ch. 7 (51a 13f.): the essential criterion of the appropriate scale of a tragedy is said to be the scope required for a change of fortune – in either direction – to occur according to the cardinal principle of probability or necessity. The fact of a transformation is here interlocked with the organisation and unity of the tragic action.

Ch. 11 (52a 31f.): the device of tragic recognition (*anagnôrisis*)

---

[3] At *Phys.* 197a 25-7 Ar. defines *eutuchia* and *dustuchia* as favourable or adverse fortune *of some magnitude*, and this qualification can be assumed in the *Poetics* (53a 10 makes it explicit); cf the phrase 'great *dustuchiai*' at *EN* 1153b 19. The good and evil fortunes of others are the objects of the pity and fear aroused by poetic *logos* at *Gorgias* fr.11.9: cf. ch. VI n.27.

involves the acquisition of knowledge which concerns or affects the success or failure (*eutuchia* and *dustuchia*) of the characters. Recognition is therefore one of the hinges on which the change of fortune in a complex tragedy turns, though it should be observed that here again Aristotle refers to the possibility of a change in *either* direction.

Ch. 11 (52b 2f.): prosperity and adversity are once more said to depend on the elements of the complex plot, recognition and reversal.

Ch. 13: there are here several mentions of a tragic transformation of fortune, and the change from good to bad which is caused by *hamartia* is part of Aristotle's definition of his ideal plot (52b 35-7, 53a 2, 4, 9f., 14f., 25).

Ch. 18 (55b 27f.): the change of fortune is here viewed as bounded by a structural section of the play, the dénouement (*lusis*).

The two questions which arise out of this clear insistence on tragedy's concern with the movement of human action between the poles of success and failure are: first, why does Aristotle make so much of this movement, and, secondly, what is the relation between *eutuchia*, good fortune, and *eudaimonia*, his ideal of virtuous happiness? It will be easier to take these in reverse order.

In more than one passage outside the *Poetics* Aristotle stresses that *eutuchia*, despite common opinion, is not to be identified with *eudaimonia*.[4] The latter derives from and consists in virtue; the former is a matter of what Aristotle calls 'external goods', things such as good birth, status, wealth, power and honour. In view of the fact that the word *eutuchia* can sometimes be translated as 'good luck', it is important to realise that neither in the *Poetics* nor in many other Aristotelian contexts does the emphasis of *eutuchia* fall on the pure randomness or fortuitous distribution of the goods in question, but on the fact that these goods are not intrinsic to virtue and are therefore not within the primary moral control of the individual agent.[5] *Eutuchia* consequently has affinities with traditional values of

[4] *Phys.* 197b 4f., *EN* 1099b 6-8, 1153b 21-5, *EE* 1214a 25, *Pol.* 1332a 25-7; cf. ps.-Ar. *Rh.Alex.* 1440b 18ff., and note Eurip. *Medea* 1228-30.
[5] The most important references to *eutuchia* are to be found at *EN* 1099a 31-b 8, 1124a 12-31, 1153b 16-25, *Pol.* 1323a 24-1324a 4, *Rhet.* 1390b 14-91b 6. Ar. sometimes speaks of *eutuchia* as the sphere of things of which chance (*tuchē*) is a cause, as at *Rhet.* 1361b 39ff. But this passage goes on to state what we could anyway infer from the range of goods covered by *eutuchia*, namely that chance is not their only possible cause:

status and success, including heroic values, as the *Poetics* itself seems to acknowledge;[6] but Aristotle's notion of external goods makes the components of material and social prosperity more contingent than they would be likely to appear in the eyes of the holder of a traditional outlook. The relation in the Aristotelian moral system between *eudaimonia* and *eutuchia* is that of the essential and primary to the subordinate and secondary. Whether it is also the relation between the indispensable and the dispensable is a little less certain. It seems to emerge at a number of points in Aristotle's works that happiness is to some unavoidable extent dependent on the support of good fortune: or, to put the proposition negatively, and perhaps more appropriately for my present argument, happiness can be undermined or impeded from fulfilment by misfortune. The main discussion of the relation between happiness and prosperity occurs in Book I of the *Nicomachean Ethics*. What is striking about this section of the work is the tension between Aristotle's concern to establish virtue at the centre of happiness, and his reluctant recognition (contrary to the Platonic view of the immunity of the good to change) of the vulnerability of even the virtuous man to the assaults of inescapable misfortune. Aristotle affirms unequivocally to begin with that happiness *requires* external goods (1099a 31ff.). Yet he also wishes, understandably, to deny that virtuous happiness is the gift of fortune (1099b 20ff.). Of the goods which fortune is said to control, some are indispensable while others are merely instrumentally useful (1099b 27ff.). But the negative caveat has yet to be expressed, for perfect goodness is the work of a complete lifetime (1100a 4f.), and there are many vicissitudes which can shake a life, even in its final stages. Aristotle here uses a word for changes of fortune, *metabolai*,[7] which

---

nature and human agency may also produce the fabric of *eutuchia*. Popular Greek belief, as alluded to at *Phys.* 196b 5-7, *Rhet.* 1391b 1-3, would add the gods as a source, perhaps *the* source, of *eutuchia*: see e.g. Aesch. *Cho.* 59f., Herod. 1.32, Isoc. 1.34. This fact may be obliquely reflected in the special type of *eutuchia* referred to at *EN* 1179b 22f., *EE* 1247a-8a, on which see M. J. Mills, *Hermes* 111 (1983) 282-95. *Eudaimonia* is not, for Ar., god-given, despite some equivocation at *EN* 1099b 9-18.

[6] See esp. 53a 10-12, with ch. V pp. 166f.

[7] 1100a 5, 23f., 1100b 1. In the *Poetics* Ar. applies *metabolê* to both reversal and recognition in tragedy (52a 23, 31), and he calls the change of fortune *metabasis* (52a 16, 18, 55b 29); but he uses the verb *metaballein* repeatedly in connection with the latter (51a 14, 52b 34f., 53a 9, 13f.), and comparison of 49a 14 and 37 shows that *metabolê* and *metabasis* are synonyms. This helps to indicate the special association in Ar.'s theory between reversal, recognition, and the tragic change of fortune (though it does

we find with its cognate verb several times in the *Poetics*, and the impression that he is treading on ground germane to tragedy is confirmed by the example of Priam's tragic old age which he cites from epic. He goes on to adduce the maxim of Solon's, which finds many echoes in Greek tragedy, that no man should be called happy before his death.[8] But after raising the obscure question of how happiness may be affected even after death, Aristotle returns to the subject of fortune. He now expresses misgivings about making happiness even negatively dependent on it, and attempts to restore the balance of his argument by giving more weight to the intrinsic stability and quality of permanence in virtue itself. In a tone which carries some Platonic resonances, Aristotle now stresses that the good man will, after all, know how to bear misfortune, to make a virtue even out of his external sufferings. Yet the balance is finally disturbed once again by a reiteration of the power of great adversity to damage happiness.[9]

Having sketched the relation between Aristotelian *eudaimonia* and *eutuchia*, and having seen how in his own exploration of this relation in Book 1 of the *Ethics* Aristotle's thought moves significantly towards a paradigmatic figure, Priam, we can now return to the *Poetics* itself and propose the hypothesis, in explanation of the accentuation on the *eutuchia-dustuchia* dichotomy in the treatise, that Aristotle's theory commits tragedy to an engagement not directly with the ethical centre of happiness, but with the external conditions or circumstances in which the quest for happiness takes place. The movements and patterns of tragic action concern, it seems, the fabric of material and social status (to allow that term to cover the full range of Aristotelian *eutuchia*) rather than the primary substance of virtue.[10] This inference must be qualified to some degree by the

---

not justify the use of 'reversal of fortune' which one still sometimes encounters as a translation of *peripeteia*).

[8] 1100a 10f. (~ *EE* 1219b 6f.). Cf. e.g. Aesch. *Agam.* 928f., Herod. 1.32.7, Soph. *OT* 1186-96, 1528-30, *Trach.* 1-3, Eurip. *Hkld.* 865f.

[9] 1100b 7-1101a 13. Cf. 1096a 1f., 1153b 16-25 and *Pol.* 1323a 24ff. for various acknowledgements of the need for a portion of external goods for *eudaimonia*. On the other side, note the great-souled man's relative indifference to good and bad fortune: *EN* 1124a 13-16. On this tension in Ar.'s thought see Adkins (1970) 207f.

[10] It is a weakness in Smithson's article that on the basis on 50a 16ff. he gives too simple an account of the moral implications of Ar.'s notion of plot (plot 'has as its objective the presentation of *eudaimonia*', 7) and ignores the emphasis on *eutuchia*. The distinction between happiness and fortune, and their varying vulnerabilities to change,

scope for ethical colouring provided by dramatic characterisation (*êthos*), and I noted earlier that at 50a 2f. Aristotle indicates a link between character and the success or failure in action which the action of a play portrays. If this link were straightforwardly causal, however, we would be left with the necessary entailment of happiness in virtue which Plato claimed, but which Aristotle's philosophy did not allow him to accept without reservation. While, therefore, we may see clearly that there should be a *general* integration and consistency of character and action in the type of tragedy envisaged by Aristotle's theory, we are faced with a radical problem about how the theory expects the tragic swings from prosperity to adversity, or the reverse, to be causally accounted for. We are still far from discerning just what sort of illumination Aristotle supposes that tragedy can shed on the vicissitudes of human fortune. Does the *Poetics'* emphasis on the extremes of fortune, and on the transformations that occur between them, imply that it is tragedy's business simply to exhibit the fragility and instability of fortune, and, if this should be so, why does Aristotle conceive so firmly of the figures of drama as active agents, and the substance of tragic plots as actions not passive states of suffering?

I warned earlier against the temptation to equate *eutuchia* and *dustuchia*, prosperity and adversity, purely with chance or luck. This caution is strengthened by Aristotle's choice of the misfortunes of Priam as an example in *EN* 1, since the Trojan King's sufferings were not wholly a matter of chance but were implicated in a complex series of human choices and actions (as well as, it should be added for future reference, divine actions). As the next stage in an attempt to elucidate the ethical implications of the *Poetics'* view of tragedy, I want to establish that Aristotle's whole theory of the genre requires and presupposes the exclusion of chance from the dramatic action.[11]

---

can be profitably compared to the general remarks at *Cat.* 8b 26-9a 13 on stable dispositions (*hexeis*, including virtues) and unstable conditions (*diatheseis*).

[11] Cf. Butcher 180-4, House 59, Stinton 231. Sorabji 295-8 argues that *hamartia* in *Poet.* could cover mishaps, *atuchêmata*. A serious difficulty here is that the same act can be sometimes described from more than one point of view: Sorabji 279f. and 298. In Oedipus' special case, to which Sorabji refers, there is the further question of whether, in view of the oracular background, normal standards apply. But Oedipus' case perhaps also makes it possible to see that an *atuchêma* (in Ar.'s secular terms) could be allowed *outside the plot*: it would then be catered for by what is said at 54b 6-8, 60a 27-30 (though this also alerts us to the problem of how *hamartia* enters into Sophocles' play: n.20 below). But Ar.'s whole theory rules out the impingement of chance within

If this is right, appreciation of the nature of tragic fortune can be advanced.

In the first book of his *Rhetoric* Aristotle describes chance events as those which happen 'for no reason, and neither always nor for the most part'.[12] This phrasing of the point conveniently shows how the idea of chance cuts right against the grain of the type of intelligibility which Aristotle repeatedly prescribes for tragedy in the *Poetics*, where again and again necessity or probability, which in Aristotelian terminology are equivalent to things which hold 'always or for the most part', are invoked as the principle of sequential coherence in the tragic action. Essentially the same diagnosis of incompatibility between chance and Aristotle's conception of tragic plot-structure can be made from other angles. According to the *Metaphysics* (1027a 20-2), for example, no knowledge is possible of the fortuitous or accidental: all knowledge is of that which exists 'either always or for the most part' – another occurrence of the formula that underlies necessity and probability. Yet if a tragic plot is to adhere to the latter principle and to embody the universals which ch. 9 of the *Poetics* declares to be the substance of poetry, it must exclude that of which we can have no knowledge. It is important that the ideas both of chance and of necessity and probability involved here concern not only individual events but also the relations between events, so that two occurrences whose causes are individually known may nonetheless stand in a meaningless or arbitrary relation to one another. A primary interest of Aristotle's in the *Poetics*, as I tried to show in ch. II, is in the sequential intelligibility of the tragic plot (which is also its unity), and it is not only particular impingements of chance which his theory requires to be eliminated, but fortuitous or irrational juxtapositions of events or actions. This much is clear from the most explicit reference to chance in the *Poetics*' analysis of plot, at the end of ch. 9. Aristotle says that the desired emotional effect of pity and fear will best be elicited by events which happen unexpectedly but on account of one another; and he goes on to suggest that a sense of wonder is more truly created by such things, reinforcing his claim by the remark that even chance happenings are more impressive if they *seem* to be causally significant (52a 1-10). The

---

the plot-structure. Lucas (1968) 302 takes a line similar to Sorabji's, though on p. 143 he correctly observes that an *atuchêma* would contradict probability.

[12] *Rhet.* 1369a 32-4, cf. *Top.* 112b 14-16, *Phys.* 197a 31f., *GC* 333b 6.

implication is that it would be a basic dramaturgical fault to portray actions or events which could only be perceived as standing in a chance relation to one another.

The exclusion of chance from tragedy, then, is entailed in the central Aristotelian requirement of unity of plot, which itself is a reflection of the need for necessary or probable clarity in the structure and logic of the dramatic action. It is the total coherence of a work, if Aristotle is right, which will be disturbed by even a single chance event within the sequence of action, as in the case of Aegeus' arrival in Euripides' *Medea*, faulted at 61b 19-21. Chance is one form, though not the only one, of 'the irrational', which the scheme of the *Poetics* explicitly rules out. The stress on connective unity, and the concomitant rejection of the irrational, are of wide application. They lead, for example, to the strictures in ch. 8 on plots, particularly epic plots, which concern one hero's life but do not make a unity of it: 'for many random events may happen to a particular individual' (51a 17). Similarly, it is the lack of any necessary or probable coherence in the data of history which means that the historian is not a maker of organised plot-structures comparable to the poet's (51a 38ff.). An individual life, the material of history, and an episodic tragic plot all have in common a deficiency of unity which impedes the possibility of generalised understanding or true knowledge. The standards of wholeness and cohesion are exacting indeed, too exacting for much that occurs in the real world. It is to these standards that we must refer the exclusion of chance from tragic action in Aristotle's ideal.

The relevance of these propositions to the theme of *eutuchia* is evident. They yield the conclusion that Aristotle's theory does not commit tragedy to the dramatisation of the crude and disconnected vicissitudes of life, even though it locates the genre's essential material in the transformations of fortune which affect those external goods that are the secondary conditions of happiness. This point is important, since there is no doubt, as Aristotle himself acknowledges elsewhere, that external goods can come under the control of chance. History may frequently demonstrate the random strokes of fortune, whether favourable or unfavourable, but it does not follow that the fabric of material and social status is solely or in all circumstances the province of chance. It is not to history that poetry's portrayal of human life approximates, but to philosophy, and it must therefore be that tragedy, on Aristotle's model, can seek to present some order and pattern in the transformations of fortune which it dramatises.

But in just what way does Aristotle believe that the requirements of tragedy's dominant themes can be reconciled with the need for a structure of dramatic events which can be rationally comprehended: is there a degree of tension between the stuff of tragic instability, without which tragedy would not be recognisably what it is, and 'the imperative of intelligibility',[13] without which, in the philosopher's terms, poetry is not fully itself?

Answers to these questions must be sought in the concentration of Aristotle's theory of tragic plot on the climactic stage of transition or transformation itself – the dénouement (*lusis*), as it is called in ch. 18,[14] or simply the 'change of fortune', *metabasis*. Aristotle appears to assume that a tragedy will involve a determinate turn in the status of the agent or agents, whether or not it has a transformation of the particular kind entailed in the complex plot to which he gives his preference. This assumption first occurs in the final sentence of ch. 7, and while there is some reason to believe that Aristotle allows the possibility that a change of fortune may extend so as to constitute the whole play (as, perhaps, in the *Prometheus Bound* or Euripides' *Trojan Women*), the more usual supposition is that the change will form a critical element or section within the play's structure. This is at any rate quite certain for the preferred type, the complex plot, to which the prescriptions for the best tragedy in chs. 13 and 14 apply. It is here that we must focus our attention to find further elucidation of the operations of fortune in Aristotle's theory, for it is here, if anywhere, that the paradoxical relation between tragic instability and

---

[13] Golden & Hardison 290.

[14] *Lusis* is defined at 55b 24-32; it is also used at 54a 37, 56a 9, and the cognate verb occurs at 56a 10. The antithesis of *lusis* is termed *desis* at 55b 24ff., and *plokê* at 56a 9. The standard English translations are 'complication' for *desis/plokê*, 'dénouement' for *lusis*. *Plokê* (literally, 'knotting') is cognate with Ar.'s term for the 'complex' plot. This is significant: if we combine the definitions of simple and complex plots in ch. 10 with those of *desis* and *lusis* at the start of ch. 18, we can infer that the simple plot's complication must be contained entirely in the events prior to the opening of the play, so that the play itself will constitute only a process of resolution or dénouement (Lucas (1968) on 55b 25 resists this inference in a self-contradictory note). It remains unclear whether Ar. thinks the same can happen with a complex tragedy, but since the *lusis* is in this case the structural counterpart of the recognition and/or reversal, Bywater on 55b 25 and Lucas (1968) on 55b 27 are certainly wrong to see the *OT* as an instance.

Ar.'s remarks on *desis* highlight an uncertainty over the importance of things outside the play. Ar.'s model of self-contained unity (ch. 7) would seem to make them negligible (see 55b 8 for an apparent example); and he is prepared to apply less stringent standards to them (53b 32, 54b 2-8, 60a 29). But the combination of *desis* and *lusis*, encompassing events both inside and outside the plot, would seem to view the matter from a different angle.

intelligibility of plot-structure must be reconciled. Around the central idea of a change of fortune there cluster, in the main chapters of the analysis (10-14), three related notions, all of them more specific than the *metabasis*, and each of them contributing a particular facet to the ideal model of a tragic dénouement. These are reversal (*peripeteia*), recognition (*anagnôrisis*), and a term which, even if translatable, it is prudent for the moment at least not to translate, *hamartia*.

Of these, the first two, which Aristotle virtually considers to be a linked pair, can be relatively firmly dealt with, particularly since their connection with the observable practice of surviving tragedy, and epic, is unproblematic. It is remarked towards the end of ch. 9 that the tragic emotions of pity and fear are best aroused by events which happen 'unexpectedly but on account of one another'. This phrase intimates Aristotle's adherence to his principle of unity, while also providing for dramatic elements of a sufficiently powerful kind to carry the charge of the desired emotions. But what the phrase also points to is the common requirement behind the three plot constituents – reversal, recognition and *hamartia*: namely, a disparity between the knowledge or intentions of the dramatic characters and the underlying nature of their actions; in short, tragic ignorance. This way of stating the inference is closest to Aristotle's own definition of recognition, which is said to be 'a dramatic change (*metabolê*) from ignorance to knowledge'; but it equally well covers his notion of reversal, according to which the outcome of events is the opposite of what is expected by those involved actively in them (and also, in a sense, by the audience). Aristotle's example in ch. 11 of a reversal from the *Oedipus Tyrannus* touches the fact that the expectation, aroused by the Corinthian messenger but shared by the other characters, that the King's fears of incest can be dispelled, actually leads to the recognition in which both Jocasta's and Oedipus's fateful ignorance is revealed.[15] It is not surprising that

[15] Much unnecessary argument has been spent on this reference to the *OT*: it is not difficult, given Aristotelian compression, to see at 52a 25 a *compound* reference first to *OT* 923ff., and then to the later part of the scene, 989ff. (Ar. may have had 1002f. particularly in mind). Cf. Hubbard 104 n.5. It ought also to be said, once and for all, that *contra* e.g. House 97 and Burnett 4, Ar.'s illustration has nothing to do with a reversal for the messenger himself.

On *peripeteia* in general an earnest debate continues. Schrier (who takes the point about the *OT* reference on 106f.) cites earlier contributions, but omits Glanville (1947), which remains in my view the most subtle treatment of the topic. Glanville 77f. acutely defines the sense in which the audience's expectations are involved, though her

Aristotle conceives of recognition and reversal ideally in combination.

It is of some interest that at a later stage in the *Poetics*, in ch. 24 (60a 13f.), the irrational or unintelligible is picked out as a source of poetic surprise and wonder, whereas in the passage from ch. 9 quoted above Aristotle attributes the effect of wonder to events which, however unexpected, do not sever the sequential coherence of the action or breach the exclusion of the irrational. The remark in ch. 24 is in fact explicitly made as a concession to epic, but it does help to demonstrate Aristotle's awareness of the need for dramatic poetry (which includes epic at its best) to achieve startling and emotive climaxes. In tragedy itself the most forceful devices available are precisely recognition and reversal: it is these which are called 'the most moving features of tragedy' at their first mention in the *Poetics* (50a 33-5). It is recognition and reversal, both of which, because of their involvement with the unexpected, might sometimes *seem* irrational or contrary to probability, that serve as tragedy's chief sources of wonder, which I argued in ch. II to be intimately related for Aristotle to the processes of understanding and learning.[16] Wonder here therefore combines a suggestion of emotional impact, concentrated in the specific tragic response of pity and fear, with an indication that the crucial constituents of the complex plot are to produce no emptily sensational effect, no mere *coup de théâtre*, but the culmination of the comprehensible design of the action. The moment or process of recognition and reversal represents the turning-point of the tragedy, the juncture at which ignorance has knowledge revealed to it, or at which action is confronted by its own unintended outcome. At the same time it is an integral part of the unity and order which the audience or reader perceives in the plot-structure (and hence in the causation of the action), and in which, through sympathetic understanding, its emotions are rationally engaged.

In its own terms this aspect of Aristotle's theory of tragedy seems sharply formulated (if, like everything in the treatise, compressed and

---

point – the alignment of *doxa* with probability – is not taken by e.g. Lucas (1968) on 52b 7. But to *restrict* the expectations to the audience, as Else (1957) 345-8 does, goes against the grain of 52a 22-6.

[16] 52a 4f. effectively refers to *peripeteia*, and so links it with wonder; this is confirmed at *Rhet.* 1371b 10-12 (a case of *peripeteia* overlooked by Lucas (1968) 130, final para.). On the link see Glanville (1947) 78, and on wonder cf. ch. II pp. 74f. Note also the connection between fear and the unexpected at *Rhet.* 1383a 10-12.

schematic). The critical factor is human ignorance, but ignorance implicated in action, and suffering (at least in prospect) the consequences of its action. The manifestation of this ignorance through the structural elements of recognition and reversal allows the momentous change of fortune which tragedy calls for, but without destroying the causal coherence of the action which Aristotle insists on for the sake of intelligibility. The root causes of the *metabasis*, the transformation in the status and fortune of the tragic figures, lie in the action itself, and are not the result of an arbitrary impingement of chance or any other irrational force. This much, at any rate, is what the theory ideally prescribes. But one cannot, I believe, reach or advance beyond this stage in the argument without raising a fundamental question about its validity.

The motifs of recognition and reversal are hardly an Aristotelian invention or discovery; they are prominent features of many major Greek myths, and they had been employed in certain archetypal ways in the Homeric epics.[17] Superficially at least, Aristotle's emphasis on these ideas is drawn from the best of existing poetic practice. But this observation holds good only if we regard recognition and reversal as discrete components or devices in tragic story-patterns. Once we reflect on their implications within Aristotle's theory, and compare these with their part in tragic poetry, new issues arise. The underlying theme of human ignorance, which I have identified at the centre of the complex plot of the *Poetics*, is, as a traditional tragic motif, the significant corollary and converse of divine knowledge; it is not a self-sufficient fact about the world, but one which Greek myth and poetry places within the framework of a larger religious view of things. The recognition and reversal of the *Oedipus Tyrannus*, to take a case which ostensibly fits Aristotle's model, represent not only Oedipus' discovery of his own and his parents' tragic ignorance, but also his recognition of the prescience and the mysterious agency of Apollo. Similarly in the *Trachiniae*, to cite the other surviving Sophoclean play to which the Aristotelian scheme of the complex plot appears most directly applicable, Heracles' discovery of the immediate cause of his suffering leads him not simply or even primarily to an awareness of his former ignorance, but to an overwhelming sense of the knowledge of Zeus, and of the way in which his own life's pattern has been both foreseen and effected

---

[17] See Rutherford's article for demonstration of this, but cf. ch. IX n.18.

without, until this final stage, his comprehension of it (if indeed he has fully acquired it even now). In both these works there is certainly, as the *Poetics* seems to require, a symmetry between the recognition-and-reversal within the play and the audience's understanding of the dramatic action. But the vital dimension of both plays which the theory of the complex plot does not allow for is the religious. In so far as the complex plot is regarded, as it is by some, as a purely formal or structural model, the neglect of religion may be thought to be irrelevant. But to attribute such formalism to the theory is to forget that the structure of a tragic plot is a structure of human actions, the ordered artistic enactment of 'actions and life': it is a construct which Aristotle's whole concept of mimesis demands should be apprehended as an image of possible reality.[18] If it is indeed the case that the complex plot posits a transformation of fortune without any divine involvement, then we are obliged to ask what the implications of this are for tragedy's representation of the universals of human existence.

But neither the conclusion, nor the consequent need for such a question, can be deemed to be properly established until we have examined the third component of the complex plot, *hamartia*. I have tried to prepare the ground for an approach to what has been in recent times the most controversial of the *Poetics*' ideas by paying closer attention than is often given to the other elements with which *hamartia* is associated in the ideal tragedy of ch. 13 (and 14: see below). For the first point which ought to be urged in the interpretation of *hamartia*, contrary to much traditional practice, is that it is not to be extracted from its context and treated as a concept or theory complete in itself. Both the disproportionate mass of criticism which has been produced on *hamartia*, and the striking range of different positions taken up within this criticism, reflect the assumption that *hamartia* is a self-contained or technical doctrine, a unique Aristotelian perception placed at the centre of the treatise. In the hope of avoiding the *longueur* of retracing all the old ground yet again, my analysis of the issue will concentrate on attempting to situate *hamartia* more closely, as well as more simply, in relation to the rest of the theory of the complex tragedy.[19]

[18] Else (1957) 328 rightly argues against the idea of the complex plot as pure structure, 'as if complex structure were an end in itself ...'; cf. also 353. Against formalism in general in the *Poetics* see ch. I pp. 4f. and ch. III p. 98.

[19] Radt (1976) is right to suggest that discussion of *Poetics* 13 has been obsessive over *hamartia*, though he exaggerates in calling the latter a 'Nebenergebnis' (279);

We must start, then, not by focussing intensely on ch. 13 itself, but by noting how it follows on from the preceding chapters (excepting ch. 12), as Aristotle says explicitly that it does. There is both a general and a specific connection with the earlier parts of the treatise: a general carrying over of the basic principles of wholeness, unity, and necessity and probability; and a specific continuation of what has already been said about the complex plot. Throughout ch. 13 (as again in his conclusions in ch. 14) Aristotle is considering the finest kind of tragedy (52b 31, 53a 12 and 19), not all tragic plots, and he stipulates that the best tragedies will be complex in his given sense. It is neither stated nor clearly implied that *hamartia* is or should be a feature of all kinds of tragedy – a fact which in itself makes dubious much of the '*hamartia* hunting' which has been pursued in attempted explication of Aristotle's doctrine. *Hamartia* is presented in ch. 13 as the substantive cause of the change of fortune in a complex plot whose other constituents are reversal and recognition. I suggested earlier that the common premise underlying reversal, recognition and *hamartia* is human ignorance, and it is on this level that the immediate sense of the combination can be seen. Reversal involves an unexpected yet explicably caused transformation, and one which must be unintended: it is consequently inevitable that some sort of human error or defect should be caught up in it. Recognition involves ignorance by definition, which again allows for – and once ignorance is part of action, necessarily leads to – positive error, as opposed to a merely passive state of erroneous belief. Though it remains to be seen more precisely how *hamartia* belongs in this scheme, its *prima facie* suggestion of a failure, fault or error obviously interlocks with the other implications of the complex plot. This is not to argue that the elements of such a plot simply coalesce, for at least one evident distinction is that Aristotle does not give *hamartia* the formal identity or the clear structural role which reversal and recognition possess; unlike them, it is not defined, simply because, I suggest, it is not a comparably technical term. Whereas there is no doubt about the place to be occupied in the pattern of a tragic plot-structure by these other components, we cannot immediately (if at all) deduce from the uses of the term in ch. 13 at what point or points in a play, or by what

---

similarly Smithson 12f. On the moralistic bias which has often marred understanding of the issue see von Fritz 1-112, Bremer (1969) 65-98.

mechanisms, *hamartia* is to function.[20] It is tempting to adduce the general dictum found in Book 2 of the *Nicomachean Ethics*, that 'it is possible to go wrong (*hamartanein*) in many ways' (1106b 28f.). This indeterminacy in the introduction of the concept of tragic *hamartia* will prove to be significant.

To indeterminacy must be added the fact that *hamartia* is presented as part of a largely *negative* argument in the first half of ch. 13. Aristotle's procedure here is to stipulate a set of conditions for the best type of tragic plot, and then to eliminate those patterns of possible dramatic action which do not fulfil the requirements. Since, however, he does not declare all his premises systematically, it is useful in trying to understand his conclusions to analyse schematically the quasi-syllogistic train of his thought. The three primary desiderata are:

(a)   a complex plot-construction: that is, a transformation entailing recognition or reversal, and preferably both;
(b)   a representation of fearful events;
(c)   a representation of pitiful events.

Conditions (b) and (c), by their implications of certain kinds of suffering, generate two further conditions:

(d)   tragic characters 'like ourselves': that is, not morally extreme;
(e)   undeserved misfortune.

These can be supplemented by another two requirements, one derived from the earlier stages of the theory, and the other an assumption which appears only in ch. 13 itself:

(f)   intelligibility, which presupposes, as I have argued, the exclusion of chance, and is grounded in the conception of unity;
(g)   dramatic concentration on a single, central tragic figure.[21]

[20] This is clear enough from Soph. *OT*, in which Oedipus' *hamartia* can only be his ignorance and the acts in which it is implicated. This means that it is not a discrete element in the plot-structure, but a pervasive factor in the events of the past (part of the 'complication', n. 14 above) as well as in the play's present.

[21] The point stands despite the objections of Jones 11-20: Romantically rich ideas of the tragic hero may be inapt, but *Poetics* 13 assumes the preeminent individuals of Greek heroic myth. However, 53a 11 and 19 anticipate a point which Ar. elaborates in

A final condition calls for special comment. It is:

(h) a change of fortune from good to bad.

The difficulty attaching to this final premise arises from the fact that it is abandoned in ch. 14, which I shall be discussing later. What needs noting here is that this discrepancy should not be treated as an isolated problem concerning the relation between the two sections of the work, still less as an oddity about ch. 14 in itself. The change of fortune which Aristotle's theory presupposes for tragedy has been mentioned several times before ch. 13, but invariably in a manner which leaves open the possibility of a change in either direction.[22] Moreover, not only does the preferred type of tragedy in ch. 14 involve a positive change from bad to good fortune, but in the one reference to this point later in the treatise, in ch. 18 (55b 28), the non-committal formula of a change either to favourable or to adverse fortune once more occurs. It is of course now ingrained in attitudes to tragedy that the genre is characterised by a dominant movement towards suffering and evil, and it is because ch. 13 of the *Poetics* accords with this that there is a tendency to attribute special authority to this part of the work. But while the analysis of ch. 13 itself must indeed proceed with the premise of a required transformation from prosperity to misfortune, it is vital to keep in mind that this is actually exceptional within the *Poetics'* total discussion of tragedy.

From the conditions set out above, then, Aristotle moves to a straightforward process of elimination. But since here too the presentation of his argument is not as systematic as it might be (though there are grounds for believing that he may have used a diagrammatic aid at this point)[23] it will be as well to tabulate all the relevant patterns of action that can be derived from the elements defined by the theory. (All are compatible with conditions (a) and (g).)

---

the following chapter, the familial context of many heroic tragedies. See pp. 223f., and cf. pp. 165-7 with nn. 33-5.

[22] 51a 13f., 52a 22f. (and note the double change in the *Lynceus*, 52a 27-9), 52a 31f.

[23] See the parallel passage at *EE* 1232b 31ff., esp. 1233a 1f. ('the man opposite to these is left ...'): the use of a diagram is indicated at 1233a 9. On Ar.'s use of

(1) An outstandingly virtuous character falls from good to bad fortune (52b 34-6):[24] although consistent with (e), this goes against (d) (and hence (b) too), and also against (c), since such a case, according to Aristotle, would be morally and emotionally repellent. In addition, this plot-pattern is implicitly contradictory of (f).

(2) An outstandingly virtuous character moves from bad to good fortune: although it is not mentioned by Aristotle, and might seem to be a very unpromising formula for tragedy, this case should be noted as a strong version of (4) below.

(3) A moderately virtuous character moves from good to bad fortune: this is Aristotle's preferred type (see below).

(4) A moderately virtuous character moves from bad to good fortune: this is not considered in ch. 13 (though it is alluded to negatively at 53a 14), but it is, with the relaxation of condition (g), essentially the kind of tragedy which is recommended as best in ch. 14.

(5) An evil character moves from good to bad fortune: this may appeal to humane sympathy[25] (which is weaker than pity), but it offends against (b), (c), (d) and (e).

(6) An evil character moves from bad to good fortune: 'most untragic' (52b 37).

However artificial it may seem to display Aristotle's argument in this way, the above scheme does fairly exhibit the process of thought embodied in *Poetics* 13. A final piece of schematisation can be used to analyse the tragic case which best satisfies Aristotle's requirements

---

diagrams cf. Allan (1972) 83-5, and for other arguments where he works by elimination see e.g. *EN* 1141a 3-8, 1142a 31-b 15, *Rhet.* 1385b 29-33.

[24] The qualification 'outstandingly' needs to be supplied for the following reasons: it is the only way of discriminating between this first, rejected case and the eventual ideal; it explains the vehemence of Ar.'s judgement ('repellent', *miaron*, 36); it balances 'extremely wicked' at 53a 1; and it matches what is again ruled out in the conclusion at 53a 8. The point was seen by Twining 232, and it is strengthened by 54b 11ff., where the characters of tragedy are said to be good (*epieikeis*) *but* with some failings (i.e. not outstandingly *epieikeis*).

[25] I take *philanthrôpon* at 53a 2f. in this sense, but without much confidence. On the dispute over the term see most recently Lamberton 96f. and Moles (1984b) 328f. For an association with pity see Bywater on 52b 38, and cf. Dover 201f. 56a 21 may lend some support, though the context is opaque (ch. I p. 32 and n.48), and 53b 18 seems to refer to a weak form of pity which *may* be germane to *philanthrôpia*. On the other hand, one would not have expected the extremely wicked man at *Poet.* 53a 1-3 to merit *any* positive feeling, but rather the pleasure to be taken in deserved suffering (*Rhet.* 1386b 26ff.).

(again, (a) and (g) can be presupposed). 'We are left', as Aristotle himself puts it, acknowledging the negative thrust of his procedure, with:

  i. a moderately good character (= (d))
 ii. who has enjoyed, but loses, great prosperity (= (h))
iii. and who does not deserve his adversity (= (c) and, given i, (b) too)
 iv. but who yet is also not the victim of arbitrary misfortune and whose downfall must therefore be the result of an intelligible causal factor (= (f)) which leaves his innocence intact.

It is stage iv in this argument which is the crucial one, for it is here that *hamartia* makes its appearance. I drew attention earlier to what seems to be a paradoxical feature of Aristotle's theory as a whole, its combination of emphasis on tragic instability, as embodied in the *metabasis*, with a pervasive insistence on unity and coherence, marked above all by the cardinal principle of necessity or probability. The crux of this paradox, as we pick our way through Aristotle's argument, turns out to be *hamartia*, and the paradox hardens in the juxtaposition of elements iii and iv in the above model of the complex tragedy. The effect of the direction of thought in ch. 13 is gradually to narrow down the circle which delimits the area of tragic possibility where essential moral innocence coexists with *active* causal implication in the suffering which is the upshot of the plot. It is, so to speak, somewhere in the space between guilt and vulnerability to arbitrary misfortune that *hamartia* ought to be located. But to look at the matter from this angle is not only to see the strong negative force of the argument, but also to recognise that *hamartia* is not, as much scholarship has presupposed, a discrete, technical term, designating a single, sharply demarcated formula of tragic potential, but rather an appositely flexible term of Greek moral vocabulary to signify the area opened up in Aristotle's theory by the exclusion both of full moral guilt and of mere subjection to the irrational strokes of external adversity.[26]

It is because my thesis leads to this last claim that I have avoided the procedure, common in modern discussions of *hamartia*, of setting

---

[26] Cf. Dover 152: 'not all errors are crimes or sins, but any crime or sin can be called 'error' [*hamartia*] in Greek.' For a survey of the word-group's usage see Bremer (1969) 24-60. *Hamartia* is misleadingly called a 'technical term' by e.g. Østerud 65, 68, 76.

out to show how my interpretation is to be aligned with Aristotle's treatment of responsibility and error in his ethical philosophy. If I am right to argue that the conclusions drawn in ch. 13 derive from a set of premises contained in the concept of the complex plot, as well as in the more general analysis of plot-construction proffered in chs. 7-10, then the quest for a precise relation between tragic *hamartia* and specific Aristotelian notions of ethical failure becomes unnecessary for my purposes. This is not to advocate the detachment of *hamartia* from the broad realm of Arisotle's understanding of moral action, but simply to suggest that there is no reason to expect it to conform to particular technical doctrines or definitions to be found in the ethical treatises.[27] However, two further and connected observations on the relation of *Poetics* 13 to the ethical works are in place, since both of them will strengthen my argument that tragic *hamartia* is not a discrete doctrine, but an element in Aristotle's theory necessitated by the negative implications of his approach. The first point is that the word-group to which *hamartia* belongs not only carries a wide range of meanings in Greek generally, but within Aristotle's own ethical philosophy covers virtually the whole gamut of moral failure and error, from voluntary wickedness at one extreme to innocent mistakes at the other.[28] The *hamartia*-group is therefore of very broad and varying applicability, and that the *hamartia* of ch. 13 is not meant to be tied to one specific kind of fault or error is strongly suggested by the phrase 'some sort of *hamartia*' (*hamartian tina*) at 53a 10. It does not follow from this that tragic *hamartia* can correspond to any of the range of things of which this word and its cognates are used in the ethical writings; the terms of Aristotle's theory rule out at least fully guilty action, as well as errors of a purely fortuitous kind. But the extent of application of *hamartia*-language in the *Ethics* does lend support to my interpretation of *Poetics* 13. This leads on to my second point, which is that, if closer scrutiny of the relation between tragic

[27] The basic affinity is illustrated by the occasional use of tragic *exempla* in Ar.'s discussions of voluntariness: *EN* 1110a 27-9 (Alcmaeon: cf. *Poet.* 53a 20, 53b 33, *EN* 1136a 11-13); *EN* 1111a 11f. (Merope: cf. *Poet.* 54a 5-7); *EE* 1225b 2-4 (the Peliads – a subject of plays by Sophocles and Euripides). But there is no encouragement here to try to fix tragic *hamartia* in a narrow or technical sense.

[28] For the broadest sense of the verb *hamartanein*, covering all failures to produce virtuous results, see e.g. *EN* 1106b 29, 1159b 7. Members of the word-group are applied to wickedness (*EN* 1110b 29), *mikropsuchia* (1125a 19), other character defects (1115b 16), *akrasia* (1148a 3), acts of passion which constitute injustice (1135b 22), acts done through ignorance (1135b 18f., 1136a 7), and the category which includes both the latter and mishaps or accidents (1135b 12).

hamartia and the relevant parts of Aristotle's moral theory should be thought necessary or valuable, I am content to note that my position is largely consistent with the findings of the most impressive and thorough re-examination of the whole issue by Stinton, who concludes that tragic *hamartia* could encompass one of a number of moral failings and errors defined elsewhere by Aristotle.[29] My conclusions have, however, been reached from a somewhat different direction, and it remains less important for my case that such a relation should be perceived to exist between *Poetics* 13 and the doctrines of the ethical treatises, than that the inherent indeterminacy of tragic *hamartia* should be seen to be the consequence of a tension within the theory of tragedy itself.

It is a relatively plain inference from the thesis I have so far offered on *hamartia* that no particular English translation evidently recommends itself for this term. It is especially difficult to commit oneself to a single equivalent in view of the fact that several of the possible candidates – error, fault, mistake, flaw – have been closely associated with various attempts to pin the word down to a restricted sense. In so far as it is impractical to proceed altogether without translations, the terms 'fallibility' and 'failing' seem to me perhaps the least prejudicial ones available. But it should be clear from the whole tenor of my argument that it would be futile to imagine that we could find a precise equivalent for the function of *hamartia* in the compressed context of Aristotle's theory. There is much to be said, somewhat ironically, for avoiding a consistent translation for the term.

But the understanding of *hamartia* in the *Poetics* may not, in any case, be confined to the actual occurrences of the word in ch. 13. For although *hamartia* is mentioned as such only in this one passage, it is one of a number of suppositions which are carried over and sustained in the following chapter. In order, therefore, to carry the argument a

---

[29] Stinton's central argument is detailed and powerful. Two marginal reservations: first, I cannot share his belief that Ar.'s doctrine is somehow vindicated by the discovery of multiple *hamartiai* in certain plays (esp. 248); secondly, I doubt his acceptance (244, but contrast 252) of the view that *hamartia* is consistent with the religious conception of *atê*. This view is argued for by Dawe; it is also discussed by Bremer (1969) chs. IV-VI, whose position is more elusive, though it seems to concede a basic discrepancy between Ar. and tragedy (esp. 111f., 184, 193). For scepticism see Radt (1976) 274f., Golden (1978) 5-12, Winnington-Ingram 323, Söffing 236 ('eine säkularisierte Fassung des Ate-Motivs'). In connecting *atê* and *hamartia* Armstrong & Peterson are led to the curious conclusion that Oedipus's *hamartia* in the *OT* is 'partly caused by ... success and high reputation at Thebes' (70).

stage further, and to try to open up the ethical implications of Aristotle's theory a little more clearly, it is necessary to take account of the evidence of ch. 14. It is, I believe, from a realisation of the degree of continuity between the two sections of the treatise that we must begin an assessment of *Poetics* 14, rather than from immediate puzzlement over the discrepancy between the types of plot recommended in the two chapters. There are certainly some inconcinnities in the juxtaposition of the chapters, including the jolt to the sequence of thought caused by the occurrence of some remarks on theatrical spectacle at the start of ch. 14; and, after these remarks, Aristotle can to some extent be said to be readdressing himself to questions he has already raised, but now approaching from a slightly changed angle.[30] There are doubtless some difficulties here, and ones which give scope for conjecture about Aristotle's original intentions. But such concerns are not as deep as is sometimes thought, and they should not be allowed to obscure an underlying, and in my view more significant, consistency between the two chapters.

One strand of continuity between 13 and 14 is supplied by the fact that in both Aristotle's method follows the negative procedure of considering a series of possibilities, and eliminating, or demoting to inferior status, all but one of them. It is therefore pertinent in both cases to ask what is excluded or devalued, and why. In ch. 14 two main issues are raised: first, what is the ideal relationship between the chief parties in a tragic plot; and secondly, which combination of circumstances – and the variables here are knowledge or ignorance on the part of the prime agent, and the possibility of a recognition before or after the committing of a tragic deed – will arouse the finest effect of pity and fear. Aristotle's answer to his first question is that the parties in a tragedy should be related by a strong tie, particularly that of kinship. If this can be taken unproblematically as a reflection

---

[30] It will be clear that I cannot share the common view that ch. 14 involves a new concentration on the *pathos*, the physical act or suffering (e.g. Twining 322-5, Vahlen (1914) 48-58, Radt (1976) 280, Moles (1979) 82-92, Söffing 33f., 122-9). Ch. 14 shows precisely that *pathos* in itself is of minor importance (53b 18) and even, in the ideal, dispensable (a fact which may help to explain the remarks on *opsis* at the start of the chapter: see Appendix 3 n.6). Cf. *EN* 1101a 31-3, which indicates that *pathē* may just as well belong to the antecedents of a play. Ar.'s focus in *Poet.* 14 continues to be on the plot-structure (compare 53a 3, 23, 53b 2, 54a 14), that is, in particular, on the *metabasis* which constitutes the setting of the *pathos* (actual or imminent) in the cases Ar. considers. Grube (1958) 28 n.3 is right, therefore, to say that there is 'no hint of a change of criterion'.

of the tendency of Greek tragic myth to portray events within the family or other closely related group,[31] it might also be thought to represent a shift from the perspective of ch. 13, in which a central figure is postulated for the ideal plot. It is important, however, to observe why this is so only to a limited extent. Certainly Aristotle is now taking explicit account of a factor which was only assumed in the previous chapter (particularly in the choice of illustrations at 53a 11 and 20-2), but it is essential with this as with other details to discern the underlying continuity of premises. Where this especially emerges – and in such a way as to reinforce the whole theory's stress on agency – is in ch. 14's primary criterion, the knowledge or ignorance of the *active tragic figure*. It is true that an uncertainty remains, since the active figure in a particular situation may not be the leading character in the play as a whole; but about the steadiness of Aristotle's focus on tragic agents, not victims, there can be no doubt at all.[32] Ch. 14's consideration of the familial settings of tragedy therefore need not undermine, even if it does modify a little, the idea of tragic individuals presented in the preceding section (condition (g) in my earlier scheme, p. 217).

But it is appropriate to ask also how the cases considered in *Poetics* 14 stand in relation to the other conditions which I earlier drew out of Aristotle's thinking. The results are as follows:

i.   An act intended in full knowledge, but not performed (Aristotle instances, somewhat curiously, Haemon's attempted killing of his father at Sophocles *Antigone* 1231ff.). Although such an action might lead to reversal, and so take the form of the complex plot, it fails to satisfy conditions (d) and (e), and therefore (b) and (c), in my earlier list. Instead of arousing pity and fear, the evil of the intended deed (presupposed by Aristotle) is morally repulsive (*miaron*).

ii. An intentional, knowing deed, such as Medea's murder of her children. Aristotle classes this as next-to-worst in his group of four; it is not hard to see why. Such a case (which is conceived of as entailing the *agent's* misfortune, it must be stressed)

[31] See Knox 21f. on this aspect of Greek myth, and cf. Else (1957) 349-52 on the importance of *philia* in Ar.'s argument from the start.

[32] In plays such as Euripides' *IT* and *Cresphontes* Ar. may have been attracted by the fact that both parties to the *pathos* were *actively* implicated in events, and neither could be regarded as a merely passive victim: even the sleeping Cresphontes was in the process of planning the King's death.

would presumably, as with type i, involve precisely the 'evil and wickedness' which was explicitly ruled out in ch. 13 (53a 8f.). At any rate, it flatly contradicts the possibility of *hamartia*, and makes it difficult if not impossible to feel pity and fear for the agent, though not necessarily for the victim(s). Neither reversal nor recognition would be feasible in such a plot-structure (unless in subordinate actions).

iii. A deed done in ignorance, followed by recognition, as in the *Oedipus Tyrannus*. It is not necessary to enter into detail for this case, since it appears to correspond to the ideal tragedy of ch. 13, which I have already examined. It remains, of course, to be asked why, if that is so, it is here classed only as second-best.

iv. An act about to be done in ignorance, but prevented in time by a scene of recognition, as in Euripides' *Iphigeneia in Tauris* and (lost) *Cresphontes*. This is Aristotle's new recommendation for the finest tragedy. I return to it below, but mention for the moment that it allows for a complex plot-construction, since recognition is essential to it and reversal is possible (and probably presupposed); that it entails pity and fear for the undeserved sufferings which are *in immediate prospect*[33] (though averted); and that its change of fortune from bad to good is consistent with everything in the *Poetics* other than the recommended model of ch. 13. On the status of this type of plot in relation to the criterion of intelligibility, I reserve comment for below: it is, I believe, of key importance for the interpretation of the new tragic ideal of ch. 14.

What clearly emerges from this brief analysis of the main argument of ch. 14 is that if we attempt, as we are obliged to do unless baulked, to read the movement of Aristotle's thought in the light of the principles and suppositions offered in the preceding sections, there is a substantial degree of coherence between the latest conclusions and what has gone before. The judgements passed on the kinds of tragic material considered in ch. 14 can largely be made sense of by reference to the set of conditions apparent in, or deducible from, the earlier stages of the theory. It is important to grasp this point before

---

[33] The notion of a prospective or imminent deed certainly strikes a new note in the theory: *mellein* is used for this purpose six times in ch. 14 (53b 18, 21, 34f., 38, 54a 6, 8) but otherwise only at 55b 9 (again referring to the *IT*). For the wonder aroused by sudden escapes from danger cf. *Rhet.* 1371b 11 (with n.16 above).

trying to deal with the anomaly between *Poetics* 13 and 14, for the temptation, to which many have succumbed, is otherwise to treat the first of these chapters as necessarily authoritative in itself, and then to measure the second as if it were simply aberrant from what has preceded.[34] But once it is seen that ch. 14 is at least as compatible with Aristotle's general requirements for tragedy as is ch. 13, the issue of a specific discrepancy becomes subordinate to a larger question, which I wish to approach, about the whole nature of Aristotle's view of tragedy.

In order to put the relation between chs. 13 and 14 more firmly in perspective, it has to be recognised that the recommendation of the type of plot illustrated by the *Iphigeneia in Tauris* does not straightforwardly contradict the earlier preference for works such as the *Oedipus Tyrannus*. For not only does the tragedy of averted catastrophe conform, as I have tried to indicate, to Aristotle's major conditions, but it also in a sense contains within itself, and goes beyond, the ideal tragedy of ch. 13. In putting the point this way I am not offering an independent evaluation of the two types, but comparing them by reference to the terms and standards of Aristotle's schematic theory. Apart from the shift from attention to a single character to attention to an encounter between two parties, which I have argued is only a moderate change of emphasis, the preferred tragedy of ch. 14 could be thought to incorporate all the significant elements of the ideal of ch. 13: the components of the complex plot; *hamartia*[35] (and hence the preservation of intelligibility); and even, in fact, the transformation from prosperity to adversity, since, to judge by the *Iphigeneia* at least, the final turn from adverse to favourable fortune is in effect an inversion of a preceding and contrary turn. To look at the relation between the two plots in this way is, of course, precisely to play down what differentiates them; but that, I suggest, is just what the combination of arguments in these two chapters warrants us in supposing that Aristotle's theory itself does.

---

[34] Jones 47 and Kaufmann 83f. rightly object to the common assumption, but Jones (n.1) overlooks the implicit presence of *hamartia* in ch. 14, and Kaufmann persuades himself (despite 52b 31f.) that reversal and recognition are ignored in ch. 13.

[35] Although the term *hamartia* does not recur (which hardly matters if, as I urge, we do not regard it as a technical term), ch. 14 stresses ignorance: in particular, 'through ignorance' (53b 35) is equivalent to 'through *hamartia*' (53a 9f.) – which is *not* to suggest that *hamartia* must be restricted to acts involving factual ignorance.

Having so far stressed the continuities between chs. 13 and 14, the *prima facie* incongruence must now be directly confronted. When in the course of ch. 14 Aristotle describes the kind of plot in which a terrible act, about to be committed in ignorance, is prevented by a scene of recognition, the phrase he employs for the act is 'to perpetrate something incurable' (53b 35). Aristotle uses the adjective 'incurable' nowhere else in the *Poetics*, and only once outside it, but it is an apt word in Greek for the ultimates of suffering and evil, and it is found with this force in a variety of authors.[36] It is mildly ironic that the term should occur at just this point in the *Poetics*, since it can apply only proleptically (and without fulfilment) to the case which Aristotle is considering – the tragedy in which the tragic deed, and therefore the *pathos*, the physical suffering, is prevented by recognition. Aristotle's averted catastrophe simply is not, in the end, a catastrophe at all; and if the requisite emotions of pity and fear are to be aroused by undeserved misfortune, then while the prospect of such misfortune may successfully elicit them, as Aristotle's argument presupposes, it cannot do so in quite the same way as the actuality. This is not a matter of an exactly calculable difference between the emotional response called for in the two cases; one can say, though of course from premises other than those which Aristotle implicitly accepts, only that the enacted tragedy subsumes and goes beyond the prospective but prevented tragedy. Nor is the difference purely one of emotion: the tragic emotions are aligned, on Aristotle's own theory, with the understanding of the whole pattern of dramatic action. What the type of play recommended in *Poetics* 14 lacks is precisely the finality of the 'incurable', the tragedy of collapse into irredeemable misfortune. Yet it is just this extreme degree on the scale of human fortune which characterises many of the major tragic myths from Homer onwards, and which involves the kind of suffering that, as Aristotle himself observes of the misfortune of Priam in the passage from the *Ethics* to which I earlier referred, makes any possibility of happiness inconceivable (1100a 8f.). Even if we allow the title of tragedy, then, to the drama of averted catastrophe, as on one level we must, it cannot, on Aristotle's own terms, be tragedy of the same irreversible intensity, and cannot carry quite the same significance, as the tragedy of a Priam or Oedipus: for the avoidance of the 'incurable' does not eliminate the possibility

---

[36] *Rhet.* 1399b 4; see e.g. Plato *Rep.* 619a 4 and LSJ s.v. *anêkestos*.

of happiness, in either the traditional or the Aristotelian sense. I think we are therefore justified in regarding *Poetics* 14 as a prescription, in the realm of dramatic theory, for the avoidance of the starkest tragedy. And to reach this conclusion is to evaluate Aristotle's view not by the criteria of some later or quite independent notion of the tragic, but by reference both to the dominant quality of the genre for which the *Poetics* offers its ideal, and to the philosopher's own ethical system of thought.

Yet such a conclusion might be taken by some to be a confirmation of the problem posed simply by ch. 14 itself, and so to bring us back round to the common opinion that this section of the work is aberrant within the theory as a whole. I have already argued, however, that this opinion comes up against the objection that the ideal tragedy of ch. 14 satisfies the requirements of the theory (including *hamartia*) as well as does that of ch. 13; and I want now to reinforce this objection, and to go on to contend that the avoidance of extreme tragedy discernible in ch. 14 has wider implications for Aristotle's view of tragedy in general. One fundamental observation, which I touched on earlier, suffices to show that *Poetics* 14 does not represent a departure from the rest of the analysis of tragedy, namely Aristotle's repeated provision, from ch. 7 to 18, for the possibility that a tragedy may not end in unmitigated misfortune: *all* the references to the tragic pattern of change, outside chs. 13 and 14 themselves, employ the dual formula of a transition from good to bad, or bad to good. So far, then, as the ideal tragedies of 13 and 14 are concerned, we have alternatives which are equally compatible with the general statements and principles of the theory. If this is so, then it is to ch. 13 that we must return, in order to question whether it is really as open to extreme tragedy as an initial reading might lead one to believe.

An answer to this question needs to take into account the fact that, as Aristotle himself clearly recognised, a serious conception of what I have called extreme tragedy cannot rest on the notion of misfortune alone. It is for this reason that the *Poetics* strives for a formulation of the integral relationship between states of fortune and the actions of those who experience them. But this relationship cannot be ethically invariable: if it were, Aristotle would have no reason not to commit himself to Platonic moralism, and to demand of tragedy the dramatisation of either merited prosperity or deserved unhappiness. On the other hand, Aristotle is partially constrained, as chs. 13 and 14 both indicate, by the desire to avoid too stark a disparity between moral worth and state of fortune, a disparity which he describes and rejects as *miaron*, repellent or outrageous. This judgement is applied to the first type of play considered in ch. 13, the downfall of the exceptionally virtuous man, and it signifies that the sufferings of such a figure would too deeply disturb our moral expectations (to which the emotions are, in principle, attuned). The vehemence with which Aristotle rejects such a subject for tragedy is in itself sufficient to establish that his criteria are not in any restrictive sense 'aesthetic', as is sometimes claimed:[37] no merely dramatic or technical factor would call for the expression of outrage or disgust. In fact, not only here but throughout the theory Aristotle's premises concerning the emotions elicited by tragedy rest on foundations which contain a necessary ethical element. Nowhere does he suggest that the conditions affecting these emotions in the experience of poetry differ at all from the conditions affecting them in life: as I pointed out on p. 196 above, Aristotle commits himself in the *Politics* to the principle that our feelings towards mimetic works are directly related to our feelings towards the equivalent reality. The downfall of the exceptionally virtuous man in tragedy is morally repellent for precisely the same reasons as it would be in life.

Aristotle's theory of tragedy therefore faces the dilemma of equally unacceptable alternatives – simple, Platonic moralism, and wholly arbitrary and unjustifiable misfortune. I have already tried to indicate that it is the function of *hamartia* to solve this dilemma by reconciling the requirement of tragic misfortune (actual or prospective, temporary or 'incurable', we can now add) with the human agent's active, if largely innocent, implication in the configuration of events. The indefiniteness of the doctrine of *hamartia* is a sign of its crucial role as the factor which allows tragic instability to be operative, but without breaking the chain of unity and intelligibility. Now it is clear that the man of outstanding virtue could fall into misfortune, on Aristotle's terms, only through something over which he had no control at all, the impingement of some accidental or quite external cause, for anything originating with the agent himself would constitute a defect in his practical

[37] E.g. Potts 77f. ('aesthetic rather than moral'), Goldschmidt (1970) 127 ('normes purement esthétiques'), Moles (1984a) 54 n.8 (cf. his (1984b) 334f., which I find more qualified). It is important to avoid polarising the issue between the purely aesthetic (whatever that might be) and the didactic: for criticisms of such polarities, which are not Ar.'s, see G.K. Gresseth, *TAPA* 89 (1958) 328-35, and I.A. Richards, *Principles of Literary Criticism* 2nd edn., reset (London 1967) 51-3. Cf. also ch. I pp. 3f. and n.4.

wisdom. Aristotle's rejection of such a case is consequently not just a matter of instinctive moral outrage. It can be traced back to the same premises which lead to the doctrine of tragic *hamartia*, and it is the fundamental premise of comprehensible causality – with its corollary, the exclusion of the 'irrational' – which now calls for further elucidation. Earlier in this chapter I tried to show how Aristotle's standards of necessity and probability rule out the play of chance from the tragic plot. This is not, however, the most significant negative implication of the principle of dramatic coherence, and I also earlier touched on the possibility that the theory of the complex plot, revolving as it does around human ignorance and fallibility, leaves little space for the central religious component in Greek tragedy. These two subjects, chance and divine agency, are in fact related, for while it was possible by Aristotle's day to make a clear separation between them, traditional Greek thinking had closely associated them, and this is especially pertinent to the world of heroic myth in which tragedy has its being.

The essential point for this traditional mentality about the idea of *tuchê* (customarily but sometimes misleadingly translated as 'chance') is that it represents a source of causation which lies beyond human comprehension or rational expectation. It is not surprising, therefore, that *tuchê* should to some extent coalesce with belief in divine causation, and indeed sometimes be simply identified with it.[38] The salient implication of this is that traditional Greek 'chance' need not be purely random: it does not exclude the possibility of a concealed order or pattern in events, only the immediate human ability to perceive one. Chance and the gods may be alternative and equivalent ways of accounting for the operation within human life of factors which cannot be explained in entirely human terms. If this is so, then it is indeed necessary to ask whether Aristotle's conception of tragedy rules out the traditional understanding of divine agency and responsibility, as well as more impersonal notions of the 'irrational'.

A preliminary doubt about this proposition might seem to be raised by the well-known passage in ch. 25 of the *Poetics* where Aristotle nonchalantly dismisses philosophical complaints about the

---

[38] Some passages in which *tuchê* and the gods are related: Hes. *Theog.* 360, Hom.*Hymn* 11.5, Pind. *Ol.* 8.67, 12.1ff., *P.* 8.53, *Nem.* 6.24, Soph. *Phil.* 1326, Gorgias fr. 11.6, Eurip. *HF* 309, *IA* 1136, *Cycl.* 606f., Plato *Rep.* 619c 5; for popular belief see Dover 138-41. Ar. himself acknowledges the point at *Phys.* 196b 5-7.

theological and moral inaccuracy of poetry's treatment of the gods. He identifies these complaints by reference to the early philosopher Xenophanes, but his point is also implicitly directed against Plato, with whose strictures on the religion of Greek myth Aristotle's negative attitude stands in sharp contrast. The line of defence, that 'it may be neither good nor true to say such things about the gods, but this at any rate *is* what men say' (60b 36f.), makes a simple appeal to conventional or popular beliefs the solution of the problem raised by the philosophers. This is remarkable evidence of Aristotle's tolerance of the character of traditional Greek religion, but it has, in fact, little bearing on the question of whether the major tenets of the *Poetics'* theory of tragedy leave space for the divine, since it is advanced only as an instance of how poets can be defended against certain types of criticism, and not as a positive injunction. For the latter we must turn elsewhere, particularly to ch. 15. Here we find a passage in which Aristotle explicitly denounces the use of the gods in the solution of dramatic action, giving as his examples the divine help which allows Medea to escape at the end of Euripides' play, and the intervention of Athena which helps to prevent the departure of the Greeks for home in *Iliad* 2 (a characteristically tangential choice). He goes on to specify that the *deus ex machina* may be employed for 'events outside the play ... since we allow the gods to see everything'.[39] It would be a mistake to suppose Aristotle here to be attending only to special divine interventions of the kind typified by the tragic *deus ex machina*. His choice of a standard mode of involvement of a deity in the action of the *Iliad* indicates what we might anyway infer from the repeated insistence on the principles of coherent plot-construction: that Aristotle's ideal of dramatic action does not readily permit the intervention of divine agency in any form, except 'outside the plot' – which is where, we note, the 'irrational' in general belongs.[40]

The point is in fact strikingly confirmed by another passage later in the treatise, and one which has peculiar relevance to the interpretation of Aristotle's theory, since it concerns the *Iphigeneia in Tauris*. In his summary of the plot of this play in ch. 17, Aristotle

[39] 54a 37-b 6. Else (1957) 470-3 emends away the *Iliad* example, but he ignores the prefix of *apoplous* (cf. 59b 7) and wrongly dismisses the implication of fr. 142 (Rose) from *Homeric Problems*. The relevance to Ar.'s attitude to the gods remains anyway unaffected (see Else 306, 474f., cf. 508 and n.63).

[40] See 54b 6-8 and 60a 28f.

remarkably claims that 'the fact that Apollo gave Orestes an oracular instruction to make the journey, and his reason for sending him, are outside the plot' (55b 7f.). This is contestable, as the two facts in question are not only mentioned in the play, but are essential to the causal sequence of the action. It must matter, for one thing, that Orestes has been sent by Apollo, for his journey would otherwise be, on Aristotle's own terms, an unintelligible coincidence comparable to the one in Euripides' *Medea* which he faults at 61b 20f.; the paraphrase at 55b 6f. ('the priestess's brother *happened* to arrive') fails to disguise this problem. It also matters why Apollo sent Orestes, since, to go no further, the parallelism between the god's aim of helping his own sister, and Orestes' rescue of Iphigeneia, is part of the interweaving of divine and human in the plot. Apollo's involvement in the action, then, although initiated prior to the start of the plot, is sustained within it:[41] without this, the play would lose a fundamental level of significance. Nor is it surprising that Aristotle fails to mention Athena's intervention in the final scene of the play, which is closely related to the Apolline strand in the story. Athena's appearance explains the divinely executed pattern in all the preceding action, and it is difficult to see how this could be regarded as a dispensable view of things, a merely optional or external perspective on the human events. To make the crucial recognition-scene wholly a matter of causally intelligible action on the human plane, as Aristotle's summary appears to do, is to substitute only a part for the whole, and to displace the religious with the secular. Some (especially those given themselves to a secular reading of Euripides) will wish to regard Aristotle's summary as an innocent outline; but it does effectively intimate his theoretical presuppositions.

The procedure exhibited in ch. 17 cannot be treated as a local aberration (though one notices that Aristotle is inconsistent enough to mention Poseidon's involvement in the *Odyssey* at 55b 18). If my argument is justified, the attempt to set out the essential structure of the *Iphigeneia* in rationally lucid terms is a symptom of the deeply-rooted preoccupation in the theory as a whole with coherently connected patterns of tragic action. For it is a consistent assumption of the traditional religious outlook with which tragic myth is impregnated that the gods, and other forces associated with them, represent at best only a partially intelligible cause of events. This

---

[41] See esp. lines 77-94, 711-23, 936-78, 1438.

assumption is pervasive and unavoidable, despite the many variations of detail in the presentation of the divine both between playwrights and even between plays by the same dramatist. It is not, then, with a clear or fixed religious doctrine that the *Poetics'* conception of tragedy comes into conflict, but with the general status of the gods in Greek myth, and hence in tragedy, as active forces which lie at and beyond the limits of human comprehension, and which therefore cannot be reduced to the level of steady and rational expectations. The discrepancy between such an outlook and the requirements of Aristotle's view of tragedy is ineliminable. Even if he was able to suppress his own philosophico-religious beliefs in order to accept the personal notion of gods operative in the fictions of poetry, as the sentence from ch. 25 suggests, Aristotle could hardly have reconciled his attribution of a quasi-philosophical value to poetry with a recognition of the possibility of a traditional religious world-view in the best tragedy. It was precisely this world-view against which some of Plato's strongest censures had been directed. The price of Aristotle's philosophical *rapprochement* with the tragic poets turns out, at the level of ideal theory, to be secularisation.[42]

If it is true that the theory put forward in the *Poetics* posits a type of tragedy from which divine agency is to be excluded, then we are now in a better position to frame a judgement about Aristotle's view of the ethical scope and potential of tragedy. I have tried to establish that the treatise puts human ignorance and fallibility at the centre of the genre, making these the active yet innocent causes of the great disturbances in fortune which furnish tragedy's characteristic subject-matter. But I have also tried to suggest that, contrary to the practice of the tragedians themselves, this fallibility is to be dramatised and made intelligible within a purely human framework,

---

[42] On Ar.'s neglect of the gods in tragedy see Goldschmidt (1970) 127, (1982) 406, Söffing 224f., 236, 265, Silk & Stern 157, 227, Østerud 76f., Lord (1982) 172, 174, 179. Kitto 125-7 links this aspect of the theory with fourth-century tragedy, Kannicht *Poetica* 8 (1976) 327f. n.5 with Euripides – both unjustifiably, in my view. Rees (1981) 33f. thinks that Ar. would have regarded the subject as irrelevant, while Gomme 209f. plays down the point (his argument, 210-12, against a determinist reading of Greek tragedy may be right, but it is a separate question). I find Glanville (1949) 54-6 elusive on the implicit religious significance of Ar.'s theory.

Ar. rejects a central element of traditional (poetic) religion, divine jealousy, at *Met.* 982b 32-983a 3 (compare *Rhet.* 1386b 16, which only concedes the popular view). Other passages which reflect his attitude to popular belief and poetic theology are: *Met.*1000a 9ff., 1074a 38ff., *EN* 1099b 11-13, 1145a 22ff., 1178b 8ff., *Pol.* 1252b 24-7 (a reminiscence of Xenophanes).

the framework of ethical intention and action. This is, in other words, one side at least of the world perceived and described by Aristotle's own moral philosophy, a secular and naturalistic world of human aims and failures. Moreover, being shorn of accident and the irregularities of 'the irrational', this world is, as Aristotle himself claims, closer to the general insights of philosophy than to the disconnected variety of ordinary life. It is a world whose causal connections demonstrate 'things as they might or should be', not as they simply are; but it is equally remote from the sense of the hopeless, the mysterious and the opaque which colours much of the tragic myth that we know. The universals which tragic poetry can handle are akin for Aristotle to the categories of the ethical philosopher, and they are categories made for the understanding of the fabric of man's state, his fortune and adversity, as these are influenced by his own actions and marred by his own shortcomings.

It would be fanciful to imagine that Aristotle supposed tragic poetry capable of exploring these matters with the thoroughness or cogency of philosophy itself; Aristotle no doubt believed that much which concerns the moral philosopher remains inaccessible to even the finest dramatist. For one thing, to cite a negative point which cannot be elaborated here, the *Poetics* gives no hint that tragedy's material can bear with any seriousness on the political dimension of ethics; the scope of action envisaged within Aristotle's scheme does not extend beyond the individual and his personal ties of kinship.[43] But tragedy's ethical potential is limited in other ways too. From the point of view of the positive thrust of the philosopher's own ethical system, these limitations are due above all to tragedy's necessary (though not exclusive) presentation of human adversity and suffering. This means for Aristotle that the genre centres around the changes in men's external states, rather than their virtues and vices. But the pressure to find some ethical significance in tragedy leads to the attempt to preserve some degree of alignment between character and fortune, or at any rate to avoid the more shocking cases of disparity between them. Having undertaken, as I have contended, to produce a theory of tragedy which proscribed direct divine participation, Aristotle was left with the acute problem of allowing for tragic instability without giving way to a vision of the sovereignty of

---

[43] The reference to the 'political' (which includes moral) use of rhetorical 'thought' in early tragedy at 50b 7 perhaps represents a certain qualification on this proposition; but Ar. makes nothing of this factor anywhere else in the treatise.

chance, which would have been alien to his whole philosophy. What can be conceded as a rare and exceptional possibility must not be made the ideal subject-matter for the most important of all poetic genres: hence, as *Poetics* 13 prescribes, tragedy must not exhibit that ultimate vulnerability against which, as Aristotle reluctantly accepts in the *Ethics*, even perfect virtue cannot protect.

This last point, it is true, can also be seen from a different angle. Since it is the perfectly virtuous man who will best be able to withstand external misfortune, the tragic emotions will be better aroused by the sufferings of ethically less elevated figures. Aristotle's theory does recognise the importance of external goods in the imperfect lives which most men lead, and he differs from Plato in allowing the impairment or destruction of these goods to be a proper object of pity, though only at the price, as I argued at the end of ch. V, of compromising the paradigmatic standing of traditional heroism. Where Plato is implacably hostile to the tragedians' care for the fabric of existence, Aristotle at least meets them half-way by acknowledging the real, if secondary, ethical value of external goods – the material and social conditions of status. But there also remains a degree of deep kinship between the philosophers in their rejection of the pessimistic side of the Homeric and tragic view of life. If the latter places man against the backdrop of a religious *Weltbild* which offers little if any consolation to the perception of ineradicable conflicts in nature, the configurations of events posited in Aristotelian tragedy are bounded by a more limited and less awesome horizon.[44]

This returns us again, and finally, to that telling but often misapprehended section of the treatise, ch. 14. Certain features of the theory of tragedy – its emphasis on coherence and intelligibility, its exclusion of the irrational, and the affinity with philosophy – combine to highlight a paradoxical strand of optimism in the *Poetics*, and one which can be seen to produce the preference in ch. 14 for the play of averted catastrophe. The paradox arises out of a desire to make misfortune accessible to reasoned understanding through the principle of necessity or probability, and so to turn tragedy's business

[44] There is no warrant in the *Poetics* for the Hegelianising vision of Butcher, marked by such phrases as 'human destiny in all its significance' (241), 'the fate of mankind' (266), 'the higher laws which rule the world' (270), 'universal law and the divine plan of the world' (271). Butcher was following where others had already led: Zeller 780 presumably borrows the phrase 'das Gesetz einer ewigen Gerechtigkeit' directly from Hegel. More recently, Tumarkin talks repeatedly and portentously of 'Schicksal': this is all alien to Ar.

into a kind of pathology of human fallibility: the mind that contemplates the tragedy, and is drawn into it by the pull of pity and fear, is led to recognise the mechanisms of human errors and their consequences in the heightened form made available by myth. This is not meant to entail, it is important to insist, a simple process of moral propaedeutic; it is not Aristotle's suggestion that we can straightforwardly transfer to our own practical lives what it is that we perceive in the causation of the tragic action.[45] But the central emphasis on the comprehension of tragedy does contain an element of reassurance and rational confidence: understanding, where the failures of action are concerned, may imply that in principle things might be effected otherwise, that they might be controlled so as to avoid suffering and misfortune. That part of the force of Aristotle's theory does push in this direction seems to be confirmed by the superficially, and only superficially, surprising verdict of ch. 14 in favour of tragedies such as the *Iphigeneia in Tauris*. For what this verdict suggests is that the experience of prospective suffering is sufficient to allow the human conditions and causes of misfortune to come within the range of intelligibility, without the physical fulfilment of the misfortune becoming necessary. But even this statement of the point is too negative for ch. 14, since in the terms of its argument 'incurable' suffering not only becomes dispensable in tragedy but can be shown to be averted – and without the assistance of beneficent gods.

Aristotle himself was certainly aware that a preference for a particular sort of tragic plot might derive from a desire to avoid facing up to the worst that tragedy can offer, since in ch. 13 he refers to the 'weakness' of audiences who appreciate best the play which ends with the equilibrium of poetic justice, both good and bad getting their deserts.[46] Aristotle wants nothing so morally or emotionally simple,

[45] It is all too easy, but unjustified, to translate the Aristotelian connections between tragedy and philosophy into didactic terms. This can be seen even from such a careful work as Lord (1982), which lapses into the conclusion that tragedy 'provides ... models of moral and political behaviour' (178). Eden's article offers a more measured statement of the ethics of poetry. Gulley 170-5 is right to oppose the more grandiose readings of Ar.'s treatise, but he seems to me to underestimate the implications of *Poetics* 9 for poetry's capacity to promote comprehension of human action and life, and he tends to set up the emotional effect of tragedy as a self-sufficient aim.

[46] 53a 30-9. Compare the weakness of the young (a propensity towards pity) at *Rhet.* 1390a 19f., and of rhetorical audiences at 1419a 18. I do not understand the claim of Bywater ix that Ar. 'is ready to make concessions to the weakness of the audiences' in

and my thesis is not designed to convict him of weakness but of a more subtle and deliberate philosophical reinterpretation of Greek tragedy. Yet, if my argument is right, his own theory is formulated in such a way as to eliminate from tragedy at least some of those events with which our moral hopes and expectations cannot easily cope. At the centre of the *Poetics*, I conclude, we see the results of a confrontation between a confident rationalism and the tragic vision of the poets.[47]

---

the fourth century. On Ar.'s reaction against contemporary taste see Lamberton's article (though the larger argument is questionable).

[47] Although I cannot endorse everything he says, there seems to me to be some justification for the claim of S. Booth, *King Lear, Macbeth, Indefinition & Tragedy* (New Haven 1983) 81-90 that Ar. attempts to set limits on tragedy against its true nature.

VIII
The Chorus of Tragedy

If the chorus and lyric poetry of Greek tragedy have scarcely been mentioned in this book so far, that is because they represent an aspect of the genre to which the *Poetics* itself devotes minimal attention. The present chapter sets out to ask why this should be so, and attempts to offer an explanation. The assumption which warrants such an enquiry is that Aristotle's scant treatment of the chorus cannot but be regarded as a significant omission or neglect, and that the effort of understanding what underlies it may therefore be able to contribute some illumination on the nature of the treatise. It ought to be a necessary part of the interpretation of any work of theory to consider what has been left out of account or displaced to the margins of the subject, and to try to relate such things to the theorist's positive concerns. Yet it appears that this principle is not universally accepted. One modern writer on the *Poetics* has suggested that 'we, [Aristotle's] readers, ... have been forced by our own ignorance ... to blame him for omissions which he would have thought it superfluous to supply.'[1] Such humility may be chastening, but it is hardly to the point, particularly since it seems here to be supposed that the explanations for explicable omissions are scarcely worth giving. I take some encouragement from the fact that in his posthumously published Oxford lectures on the *Poetics* Humphry House, who professes at the outset an attitude to omissions not unlike the one I have quoted, and who promises not to lecture 'about what Aristotle did not say', finds it impossible to avoid altogether the work's neglect of the tragic chorus, which he describes as 'striking' and 'rather startling'.[2]

The lyric element in tragedy is formally recognised in Aristotle's analysis first in the generic scheme of poetic media ('rhythm,

[1] Rees (1981) 24.
[2] House 11 and 40-2. On omissions I prefer the attitude of Butcher ix.

language and music', 47a 22), and this fact is then picked up both at the end of ch. 1 (47b 25-7) and later in the reference to varieties of 'embellished' or 'garnished' language in the definition of tragedy.[3] The choral component is categorised among the six 'parts' of tragedy as *melopoeia*, 'lyric poetry', and Aristotle asserts that the sense of the term is 'apparent' (49b 35f.). This has not, of course, prevented some modern reinterpretation of the meaning, which is now commonly translated as 'music' or 'melody' or the like, so as to eliminate the suggestion of poetry from the word and to support the belief that for Aristotle *melopoeia* would have been easily separable from 'poetry proper'.[4] Were such a separation quite so straightforward, however, we might have expected Aristotle to indicate this explicitly, as he does in the case of theatrical 'spectacle', *opsis*, and, more respectfully, in that of 'thought', *dianoia*, which he assigns to the province of rhetoric.

Melopoeia cannot, in fact, be so easily disposed of, and while Aristotle at times seems to think particularly of its musical dimension (which may be in itself telling), the term cannot in the *Poetics* be given a purely musical denotation. Two passages firmly establish the point. In ch. 6 Aristotle couples *melopoeia* with *lexis*, 'language' or 'style', and he defines the latter as 'the composition of the spoken verses'. *Lexis*, in other words, excludes lyric portions of tragedy, and if we were to take *melopoeia* as referring only to the music of these sections, it would follow that Aristotle had defined and analysed tragedy in such a way as to overlook the verbal component of lyric poetry altogether.[5] Quite apart from the intrinsic unacceptability of this conclusion (which would only make the problem of Aristotle's attitude to the chorus more acute, not solve it),

[3] For explanation of the translation 'garnished' see the passages cited by Lucas (1968) on 49b 25. Note also that although Ar. recognises the natural, mimetic potential of melody and rhythm at 48b 20f. (cf. ch. II nn.29 and 35), the only elaborations of this point later in the treatise concern the rhythms of the spoken verses of tragedy and epic (49a 21ff., 59b 31ff.).

[4] Bywater on 47a 8, referring to lyric in general; but his verdict on choral lyric, p. ix, is apter. *Melopoeia* is translated as 'music' *vel sim.* by e.g. LSJ s.v., Atkins vol. 1, 96, Kaufmann 60, Brink (1971) 260f., and in the translations of Bywater, Potts, Grube (1958) and Hutton. This sense is to be found at *Pol.* 1341b 24, but for the *melopoeia* word-group in reference to the full lyric compound of music and poetry (rightly defined for the *Poetics* by Vahlen (1911) 270f.) see e.g. Aristoph. *Thesm.* 42, *Frogs* 1250, 1328, Plato *Symp.* 187d, *Protag.* 326a. Butcher's 'song' or Hubbard's 'song-writing' avoid the restrictively musical sense.

[5] Allan (1971) 82 is certainly wrong to suppose that *lexis* in Ar.'s sense (50b 13-15) enters into the lyrics of tragedy.

we can see from the end of ch. 18 and the transition at the beginning of 19 that *melopoeia* is to be understood as embracing the full combination of musico-poetic elements in the choral portions of tragedy. At the start of ch. 19 Aristotle announces that all the parts of tragedy other than style and thought have now been discussed, but there is no section of the preceding analysis which could constitute a treatment of *melopoeia* other than the remarks at the end of ch. 18, and these are addressed not to music in itself (which is indeed ignored) but to the dramatic relation between the chorus and the plot-structure of tragedy.

It remains true, of course, that the musical dimension of *melopoeia* helps to account for the fact that Aristotle does not enter into a *full* examination of the choral aspect of the genre. In fact, *two* of the features of choral lyric, music and dance, belong to tragedy only in performance, and the second of these has connections with Aristotle's category of spectacle, whose extrinsic relation to the strict art of poetry is specifically stated at the end of ch. 6.[6] From this point of view the relative unimportance of *melopoeia* to the theory of tragedy can be readily seen, and can be regarded as a reflection of Aristotle's concern to make his conception of the genre independent of the requirements of theatrical staging (Appendix 3). But to allow this factor full weight is still not to provide a sufficient explanation of Aristotle's attitude to the chorus, since we have seen that the end of ch. 18 acknowledges that *melopoeia* needs to be reckoned with at the primary level of dramatic construction. The point can be clarified by the observation that although *melopoeia* and spectacle may to some extent overlap, their logical status in the eyes of a theorist of drama must be distinct. The separation of poetic drama from the conditions of performance is at least a theoretically defensible position, and the notion that, to cite Johnson's formulation, 'a play read affects the mind like a play acted' is not evidently incoherent, however deplorable some may find it. But any theory of Greek tragedy which lacks a conception of the chorus's role in the genre must be judged to be evading a major part of its essential nature; and it is for this reason that it is imperative to ask whether Aristotle's few references to the lyrics of tragedy adequately integrate this side of tragic drama into the theory as a whole.

The answer to this question must chiefly be derived from an

---

[6] For a fuller discussion see Appendix 3.

examination of two passages in the *Poetics*. Of these the fuller is that at the end of ch. 18, which I have already mentioned: here, in three sentences, Aristotle prescribes that the chorus should be treated as 'one of the actors', as happens, he claims, in Sophocles; and he reinforces this positive injunction with the complaint that tragedians since Agathon have used choral songs which bear no relation to the subjects of the plays in which they are inserted. He calls these songs *embolima*, supposititious odes. It is this passage which needs detailed consideration, but some account must also be taken of the statement in ch. 4 that Aeschylus reduced the choral portions 'and gave the leading role to the *logos*' (49a 17f.). These passages apart, there is scarcely anything in the *Poetics* which declares or implies a positive view of the tragic chorus. In a number of places Aristotle simply mentions lyrics without elaboration as an ingredient in the genre; in ch. 12 we are given perfunctory and somewhat questionable definitions of the structural parts of tragedy, choral sections included; on three occasions Aristotle allows himself the briefest acknowledgement that lyrics can provide some kind of aesthetic pleasure.[7] In total all this comes to only a few lines of the treatise, and there is nothing here which purports to be a contribution to the theory of poetry or of tragedy. Nowhere in the *Poetics*, except conceivably in one place,[8] does Aristotle quote from a tragic chorus, and, so far as I can see, not one of his nearly forty citations of particular plays tells us anything at all about the dramatic significance of the chorus in these works.

It is, then, to the two passages in chs. 4 and 18 that we must turn for some intimation of Aristotelian thinking on the nature and importance of the tragic chorus and its poetry. In ch. 4 the claim that Aeschylus diminished the role of the chorus and subordinated it to the spoken verse of the actors follows on the suggestion that tragedy went through a complex period of growth and change before acquiring its fully mature form or 'nature'. This context prompts one to combine the implications of the passage with those of the section at the end of ch. 18, in order to reconstruct a single scheme of dramatic development whereby the initially dominant chorus gradually

[7] For passing references see 49b 33-6, 50a 10, 14, 59b 10. On ch. 12 see Taplin App. E and Janko 233-41. On the pleasure of lyrics see 49b 28-31, 50b 15f., 62a 15-17 (with ch. II pp. 64, 67-9).

[8] 57b 29f.: the quotation could be made to scan as part of a trimeter without a normal caesura, but this is improbable; a lyric source is almost certain, though not necessarily a tragic chorus (cf. Kassel 79, *Index Locorum*).

became secondary to the spoken scenes, until the point of perfect
balance and integration was reached with the work of Sophocles,
only to be followed by the degeneration which set in with Agathon
and led to the irrelevant choral interludes of the fourth century.

Since such a scheme has sometimes been thought by modern
scholars to be approximately right (though reservations have recently
and rightly grown), it has occasionally been thought that we have
here the basis for an explanation of Aristotle's neglect of the chorus:
Aristotle witnessed the debasement of the chorus, so the argument
runs, and was consequently tempted to underestimate its possible
significance.[9] It is hard to see how, against the background of *Poetics*
18, such a consideration could be anything but deeply paradoxical.
Since Aristotle specifically deprecates the choral practices of his own
day, then if we hypothesise that his theory has also been influenced
by them, we necessarily both impute gross insouciance to him and
strip his commendation of Sophocles of all conviction. In fact, there
are internal reasons for suspecting such a lack of conviction;
elsewhere in the *Poetics* Aristotle does nothing to give substance to his
recommendation of Sophoclean choral practice. Yet ch. 18 would
appear to imply that most other tragedians had handled the chorus
less than perfectly, and this ought to necessitate some explication of
the correct principles of *melopoeia* in the manner in which other
departments of dramatic technique are analysed. While the chorus is
required to make a contribution to the plot-structure, nothing else in
the treatise, it must be said, gives the slightest grounds for believing
that the plot-structure has need of the chorus. And if the extreme
redundancy of interlude songs is firmly criticised, this hardly seems
to constitute an essential flaw in a tragedy, since by Aristotle's
definition such songs are not really part of the play at all, but a
pleasurable 'garnishing' to it (50b 16). In short, the *Poetics* taken as a
whole supplies no compelling reason for preferring a Sophoclean
chorus to no chorus at all,[10] and the passage at the end of ch. 18 is
left suspended in something of a theoretical vacuum.

But if such a judgement has any real weight to it, as I believe that

[9] E.g. Webster 308, Lucas (1968) on 56a 29. But for reservations on the linear
development of the chorus see e.g. A. Pickard-Cambridge, *The Dramatic Festivals of
Athens* 2nd edn. (Oxford 1968) 232f., Taplin 207-9.

[10] Cf. Else (1957) 60 and n. 240. It is intriguing to speculate whether Ar.'s reference
to the Sophoclean chorus bears any relation to the treatise 'On the Chorus' attributed
to Sophocles (see Lanata 142-4) – though this is not a work in which everyone
believes.

it has, then it is surely insufficient to appeal to fourth-century tragedy to explain this feature of the work. If an explanation is to be found, it is not outside the *Poetics* that it should be sought, but inside the theory of tragedy itself. Why this should be so will emerge from a closer scrutiny of the remarks in ch. 18, which are, I suggest, more problematic than is usually realised. It will not do to understand Aristotle here simply to be drawing a broad contrast between the relevance and irrelevance of choral odes to the action of a play, for just as the interlude songs represent more than incidental irrelevance – *embolima* are intentionally independent and separable songs – so the putative integration of the Sophoclean chorus into the plot-structure, which is what treating the chorus as 'one of the actors' entails, should mean something more than thematic appropriateness. It ought, that is, to involve positive participation in the events structured according to the principle of necessity or probability, which gives the plot its coherence and intelligibility. This is confirmed by the specific formula that the chorus should be 'a part of the whole' (56a 26) – a phrase often omitted or ignored when reference is made to this passage. We are entitled to assume that Aristotle is here using the term 'the whole' in the strong and special sense which he took care to define in chs. 7 and 8. In that earlier context we were told that the unity of a tragedy's plot-structure (*muthos*) consists in its parts being so disposed that no element can be either displaced or removed without damaging the total organisation: any component which does not satisfy this criterion cannot be 'a part of the whole' (51a 32-5). Once this important connection is taken into account, the requirement for the chorus at the end of ch. 18 becomes stringent indeed, and can be seen to prescribe (if taken seriously) no mere thematic pertinence, but indispensable involvement in the action of the plot.

This interpretation naturally raises the dual questions of just what form Aristotle conceived of such choral involvement as taking, and of whether Sophoclean tragedy can be reasonably judged to conform to the rigorous Aristotelian standard of unity. It is a commonplace for modern writers on Sophocles to cite Aristotle's approval of the playwright's choral practice, and for them both to presuppose that Aristotle had something definite in mind, and to concur in his evaluation. But one rarely encounters such a reference to the *Poetics* which is accompanied by a recognition of what Aristotle meant by the phrase 'a part of the whole'. The result of this mollification of the philosopher's prescription is that it is always possible for the individual critic to cite Aristotle in support of a particular interpretation of the Sophoclean chorus, but while the interpretations may differ, Aristotle's blessing on them, as it were, remains constant. It is not therefore surprising that critics can even disagree over such a fundamental point as whether Aristotle's remarks are intended to apply to choral odes or to more practical forms of choral participation. There are, in fact, several different ways of translating the principle laid down at the end of *Poetics* 18 into the terms of known dramatic technique and method, and while these do not all necessarily exclude each other, it is worthwhile to consider each of them briefly in turn.[11]

The broadest possible interpretation of our passage is to take Aristotle to mean that a tragic chorus should be a definite party within the action of the play, as are, for example, the sailors who collaborate in Neoptolemus's intrigue in the *Philoctetes*.[12] In each of Sophocles' surviving seven plays the chorus's identity and its relationship to the plot is clear and intelligible, but there are several reasons for refusing to believe that this was the basis for Aristotle's reference to the playwright at the end of ch. 18. One reason is that a defined status does not determine everything that a chorus may say or do in the course of a play. In the *Philoctetes*, the stasimon of pity for the life of the wounded and isolated hero (676 ff.) is not directly related to the chorus's involvement in the intrigue; it has no effect on the subsequent action (the chorus seem to forget their pity at 827 ff.) and the removal of it could hardly be thought to constitute damage to the unity of the drama as this is understood by Aristotle. Moreover, it is difficult to see why, if this were all that he had in mind, Aristotle would have singled out Sophocles and warned against the example of Euripides. Even in a play such as Euripides' *Phoenissae*, in which the chorus's identity has no pertinence to the action, particular choral lyrics may be just as significant as those of choruses which have a better justification for being part of the scene. Certainly, many other Euripidean plays, and all the surviving works of Aeschylus, are directly comparable to Sophoclean practice in this respect.

A more specific interpretation of the chorus-as-actor principle is to treat it as referring to particular actions, decisions and interventions

---

[11] Cf. G. M. Kirkwood, *Phoenix* 8 (1954) 1ff.
[12] See G. Müller in *Sophokles*, ed. H. Diller (Darmstadt 1967) 212ff.

by which the chorus influence the course of a plot.[13] Such an interpretation comes much closer to satisfying the requirement of 'a part of the whole', and Sophoclean instances are not hard to find: the councillors' belated success in changing Creon's mind at *Antigone* 1091 ff.; the chorus's intervention in the argument between Oedipus and Creon at *Oedipus Tyrannus* 649 ff.; the warning of Aegisthus' approach in the *Electra*, 1428 f.; or the attempts to defend Oedipus and Antigone at *Oedipus Coloneus* 822 ff. But again there are several reasons for dissatisfaction with this interpretation. In the first place, it is not easy to suppose that such interventions were especially a feature of Sophocles' work. To judge by the extant plays, there are at least as many, and probably more, instances to be found in Aeschylus, particularly in the plays in which the chorus is a necessary party to the action throughout, the *Suppliants* and *Eumenides*; and Euripidean examples too can be collected.[14] It is unlikely that in such a matter our sample of tragedies is unrepresentative, since we should expect choral interventions to be most obviously a factor in early tragedy, in which the chorus had not yet, in the terms of *Poetics* 4, been subordinated to the spoken scenes. Moreover, the prescription at the end of ch. 18 appears to concern the general handling of the chorus, yet even in Sophoclean tragedy the opportunities for integrating choral participation into the plot-structure are inevitably limited, and leave much of the lyric poetry of the plays necessarily untouched. This leads on to a third objection to this interpretation of *Poetics* 18, to which I shall return after mentioning a further possible reading of the passage.

A very simple, and ostensibly appropriate, way of understanding Aristotle's phrase 'as one of the actors' is to refer it to the choral share in spoken dialogue where, strictly speaking, only the chorus-leader would be employed. Objections to this, however, are conclusive. For prominent choral engagement in spoken dialogue one turns not to Sophocles but to Aeschylus, in whose plays it is abundant and includes long stretches of stichomythia. More than a few lines of such dialogue at a time is found only rarely in either

[13] Cf. H. Kitto, *Greek Tragedy* 3rd edn. (London 1961) 193f., R. Burton, *The Chorus in Sophocles' Tragedies* (Oxford 1980) 20 and 253-73 (esp. 265). See also J. Rode in *Die Bauformen der griechischen Tragödie*, ed. W. Jens (Munich 1971) 115 n.100.

[14] For Aeschylus see e.g. the Danaids' suicide threat (*Suppl.* 455ff.), the women's attempt to dissuade Eteocles at *Sept.* 677ff., the persuasion of Orestes' Nurse at *Cho.* 767ff. For Euripides, e.g. *Hkld.* 75ff., 961ff., *Suppl.* 271ff., *Ion* 747ff., *Bacch.* 519-75 (with Dodds' edn., xxxvi and 142).

Sophocles or Euripides, and the difference of proportion between the two playwrights is not striking.[15] For extended iambic speech by the chorus-leader we would again look most immediately to Aeschylus, and in this respect it happens that our surviving plays preserve more Euripidean than Sophoclean material. But the clinching refutation of the present interpretation is more specific: after the reference to Sophocles and Euripides at 56a 27, Aristotle goes on to complain about 'the lyric sections (or 'songs') of other playwrights', in such a way as to indicate that the preceding principle for the treatment of the chorus must encompass *odes* and cannot be restricted to contributions to iambic dialogue. This same factor supplies a further objection to the previous interpretation which I considered, since choral interventions in the action of a tragedy are rarely embodied in full odes.[16] While, therefore, we cannot rule out the possibility of a partial reference in *Poetics* 18 to other elements of choral technique, it is evident from the wording of the passage that Aristotle's point must be applicable to formal odes, and does indeed seem to pertain primarily to these. In addition to the interpretations so far cited, we must consequently note that it is also insufficient to suppose Aristotle to have in mind those tragic sections, lyric either in whole or in part, in which both chorus and actors participate together (and which, again, are commonest in Aeschylus's work).

To acknowledge that the final sentences of *Poetics* 18 must be relevant to the role of the choral ode in tragedy is not to have progressed very far, yet it at once brings us up against major impediments to understanding. If we ask whether, given the spareness of Aristotle's conception of a dramatic plot-structure, the phrases 'as one of the actors' and 'a part of the whole' are readily comprehensible in a way which would allow Aristotle to leave their application to choral lyrics to be self-evident, it is impossible to give an affirmative answer. Despite the confidence with which Sophoclean critics use *Poetics* 18 to support claims about the playwright's choral methods, the sense of the passage remains inevitably obscure and paradoxical. The paradox is obvious once one realises that 'one of the actors' and 'part of the whole' are formulas which derive their significance from Aristotle's own theory and analysis of the tragic plot-structure. Yet, as I earlier commented, there is nothing in this

---

[15] See Dale 214.

[16] Soph. *Phil.* 391ff. (and perhaps 507ff.) is a rare example: the ode is part of the deception against Philoctetes.

analysis itself to explain or hint at what contribution could be made to the *muthos* by a chorus and its lyrics, and since *Poetics* 18 simply asserts the need for a strong choral integration without in any way elucidating it, we are left with an unexplained challenge to the fundamental distinction between the chorus and the actors of tragedy. Aristotle's position seems all the more questionable in view of the fact that Aeschylus is ignored in his recommendation for the chorus, even though it is probably in the earlier playwright that some of the most cogent instances of choral participation in the action could be found.[17] But Aristotle was committed to regarding Aeschylus, so it appears from *Poetics* 4, as working with a still less than perfectly mature dramatic form. If this is so, then the further paradox emerges that it is only when the chorus has been reduced in status and subordinated to a plot-structure of spoken scenes that the question of its proper integration into the design of the play can arise.

It is important to reinforce the observation which I have already made that the *Poetics'* criteria of unity will not make it acceptable to understand the end of ch. 18 purely in the terms of thematic relevance. Aristotle's commendation of Sophocles is sometimes justified by what is commonly thought to be the drift towards irrelevance in the late choral odes of Euripides.[18] But no amount of putative Euripidean irrelevance will make it much easier to see how Sophoclean practice conforms to the stringent requirements of the Aristotelian plot-structure. We might turn, for example, to the *Oedipus Tyrannus*, cited in the *Poetics* more often than any other play by its author. Do this work's stasima really bear out the idea that the chorus is used throughout as 'one of the actors', and that it is an indispensable 'part of the whole'? We cannot say that they do, I suggest, simply on the basis of the fact that the play's lyrics explore and enlarge religious and emotional themes which arise out of the

---

[17] See Taplin 87, 114, and 207-9. On Ar.'s attitude to Aeschylus see ch. III n.20.

[18] In fact, it is worth noting that Ar.'s reference to Euripides at 56a 26f. does not imply that his odes are simply irrelevant: so, rightly, against the common view, Twining 102 n.2, Else (1957) 554, Grube (1965) 90. For an example of the kind of condescension to which Euripidean choruses are treated see Knox 256, *à propos* the chorus of the *IT*: 'What has it to sing about? Nothing. And that is what it does sing about, very beautifully, ... nothing at all.' In fact, it sings about some very important subjects, such as the nostalgia for the loveliness of the country from which they think they are, with Iphigeneia, exiled for ever. To suppose that such themes are 'nothing at all' is to take a very reductive view of poetic drama. For a defence of Euripidean odes against the charge of irrelevance see Vickers 9-23 (though his references to the *Poetics* are not entirely accurate).

action. To warrant Aristotle's principle, we would need, rather, to be able to show that the choral odes belong to the *muthos* in such a way that the latter would be disturbed by their removal. To propose that this cannot be demonstrated is not to imply that the chorus of the *OT* is dispensable, but only that the criteria of indispensability put forward at the end of *Poetics* 18 are inapplicable.[19]

The problematic nature of the relation between the tragic chorus and Aristotle's conception of the plot-structure can be exposed further by reference to the other play most frequently mentioned in the *Poetics*, Euripides' *Iphigeneia in Tauris*. Here we can draw on the fact that in ch. 17 Aristotle gives an outline of what he regards as the essential framework of the play. It is hardly surprising that there is no place or necessity in this outline for a chorus or its lyrics (though in the play itself the chorus are at one point a party to the action)[20] – the enterprise excludes this dimension of the play virtually by definition. This is not a reflection on the supposed irrelevance of the Euripidean chorus, since substantially the same would have to be said about most of Sophocles' surviving plays. It is, on the contrary, a symptom of the incompatibility between an identification of the Aristotelian plot-structure as 'the whole' of a drama (as it is at 56a 26) and the distinctive character of choral lyrics as these are employed in much of the work of all three major tragedians. *Melopoeia* is not reducible to the elements and standards of a play's action. The choral odes of the *Iphigeneia in Tauris*, as of virtually all our tragedies, belong to an altogether different mode and level of poetry from the spoken verse of the acted scenes: no 'functionalist' assessment of them could do justice to the imaginative qualities which they share with a long tradition of Greek lyric poetry. Aristotle's notion of tragic plot, which carries with it twin concepts of structure and unity, makes no allowance for tragedy's use of the lyric mode or imagination, nor for its independent potential as a complex means of enriching the significance of drama without itself being a wholly integrated part of the dramatic plot. Against this background the brief remarks at the end of *Poetics* 18 can be properly seen as no more than a gesture towards the recovery and revaluation of an aspect of tragedy which has been otherwise left conspicuously out

[19] For variations in the Sophoclean chorus, and the embarrassment of critics who try to ignore them, see the comments of Knox 188-90 (and cf. 168f.).

[20] At *IT* 1056ff. the chorus becomes a party to Iphigeneia's plan, in a manner characteristic of Euripides.

of account. If we had to reconstruct from the *Poetics* alone the nature of Greek tragedy, we should have scarcely any idea of the substantial and precious part played in it by choral lyrics.[21]

It is worth lending some further weight to this judgement by surveying some of the main theoretical emphases of the *Poetics* with the question of the tragic chorus in mind. To consider first the six 'parts' of tragedy listed in ch. 6, it is apparent that four of them – plot, character, language and thought – form an interrelated group, while the remaining two, lyrics and spectacle, seem to make a pair not only by virtue of being to some extent explicitly associated, but also because of the fact that they are presented as the least important of the six – as pleasurable accessories, rather than essential components of the genre.[22] Character, language and thought are all, as defined by Aristotle, facets exclusively of the actors' scenes, elements within the framework of the plot-structure. The placing of these constituents in the theory of tragedy helps to highlight the negative implications of Aristotle's attitude to lyric poetry, for we can observe by way of contrast that the treatise gives no advice at all on the characterisation of the chorus (which might be thought to be germane to treating it as 'one of the actors'), and directs no attention to the distinctive features of lyric style and thought. It is precisely because such radical differences exist between these elements in the lyric and non-lyric sections of tragedy that Aristotle's unequal treatment of them can be viewed as a telling fact about the *Poetics'* priorities.

But beneath this specific discrepancy there can be detected a more fundamental point about Aristotle's presuppositions. One of the central concepts of the *Poetics* is that of action, *praxis*. Tragedy is defined as 'the mimesis of a *praxis*', and the characters of tragedy can be designated as 'the agents', those responsible for the action. In addition, the structural relations within the action are predominantly understood by Aristotle in causal terms. Yet this compound emphasis on action and causality makes highly problematic, and may even exclude, the scope of choral lyric within tragic drama. It is an important fact about most tragic odes that they are divided from the action of the play precisely by the *impossibility* of their having any

---

[21] A contrast can usefully be drawn with the contest in Aristophanes' *Frogs*, where tragic lyrics bulk large: esp. 1248ff.

[22] *Opsis* and *melopoeia* are listed together at 50b 15-20, 59b 10, and perhaps also at 62a 16.

causal bearing on the course of the action. Choral lyrics, for the most part, can no more help to shape the events of a drama than epic similes can determine the poem's direction. Whereas the characterisation, language and thought of the actors' scenes are contained within the framework of the *muthos*, and are difficult to disengage from the latter except conceptually, this is to a large degree not true of the choral lyrics. Furthermore, if we go back to the start of ch. 2 of the *Poetics*, where Aristotle commits himself to the assumption that mimesis entails the representation of 'men in action', or to ch. 3, where the two basic modes of poetic mimesis are specified as narrative and enactment, it can be seen that from those seminal early chapters a concept of dramatic mimesis is elaborated which leaves little room for the special nature of lyric poetry, since the latter is not straightforwardly reducible to a notion of action at all, nor to the two modes in question.[23] In this context it is pertinent to notice a connection between the *Poetics'* neglect of the tragic chorus and its neglect of other genres of lyric poetry, which I shall be discussing in my next chapter. Since the *Poetics'* concept of mimesis is intended to hold for all poetry, these two negative aspects of its theory can be to a considerable extent explained in the same terms. The point can be summed up in the case of the tragic chorus by saying that we frequently find in its lyric odes a mode of utterance which has affinities with the personal 'voice' of much lyric outside drama, as well as with the manner of the didactic or elegiac poet.[24] This style, or range of styles, particularly in its tendency towards reflective and moralising utterance, is difficult to accommodate to the *Poetics'* central stress on plot and action.

I am contending, then, that the fundamental premises of Aristotle's theory of poetry and tragedy virtually dictate the devaluation and neglect of choral lyric. If that is right, then it is reasonable to conclude that the end of ch. 18 is an inchoate attempt at rationalisation, an attempt to bring *melopoeia* into line with the thrust of the theory as a whole, but one whose formulation effectively confirms that the treatise's chief principles implicitly slight the lyric dimension of the tragedian's art. Once the prescription that the

[23] It is interesting that ps.-Ar. *Probl.*918b 29 states that the chorus engages in mimesis (*mimeitai*, here in a strongly enactive sense) less than the actors, and 922b 26 calls the chorus *apraktos*, i.e. not an agent in the drama. On lyric poetry generally in Ar.'s scheme of mimetic modes cf. ch. IX n.45 below.

[24] For Ar.'s rejection of the poet's speaking 'in his own person' – which can include narrative, and *a fortiori* personal statements of any kind – cf. ch. IV p. 126.

chorus should be integrated into the plot-structure is seen to be, at most, a very partial and belated consideration, no function is left for lyric poetry in tragedy other than to be an ornament or embellishment, as indicated at the end of ch. 6. But if this is so, it remains to be briefly asked why Aristotle's failure to offer an assessment of the chorus commensurate with its importance and status in Greek tragedy should have been so readily tolerated, or even overlooked, by many readers and interpreters of the treatise.[25] My argument purports to have shown that it is certainly superficial to believe that Aristotle in any sense took the chorus of tragedy for granted, or presupposed, but declined to provide, an analysis of its function which would square perfectly with the rest of his view of the genre. But once such ideas are put aside, the reason for a lack of concern about this feature of the *Poetics* must be looked for in the nature of later European drama, which has so often predisposed Aristotle's readers to view the work in the light of their own immediate experience of drama. The fact that a chorus has only occasionally been employed in tragic drama since the Renaissance (and then usually in an enervated neo-Senecan fashion), and the absence of an illuminating or instructive modern analogue to the fusion of spoken and lyric drama in Greek drama (the comparison sometimes drawn with opera being unhelpful), have combined to prevent many readers of the *Poetics* from feeling disquieted by the small amount of attention paid to choral lyrics. Even those – a minority – who have approached the work in the hope of finding specific insight into Greek tragedy, rather than permanent critical truths which could supposedly be applied to later poetry, have scarcely been troubled by this major deficiency in the treatise's frame of reference, and here too I think we must discern the influence of an underlying sense of the chorus as alien to the dominant post-Renaissance experience of drama.[26] The *Poetics* itself has impregnated dramatic theory and criticism throughout this period with a notion of drama as structured action, enriched by

[25] For rare acknowledgements of the significance of Ar.'s disregard for the chorus see Bywater ix (but implying fourth-century influence), Solmsen 193, Else (1957) 60.

[26] The chorus was not greatly discussed by neo-classical critics and theorists, and when it was, it was sometimes found problematic: for English instances see e.g. Ben Jonson's *Sejanus*, preface 'To the Reader', Herrick 90, and E.N. Hooker, ed., *Critical Works of John Dennis* vol. 1 (Baltimore 1939) 437 note. Ar.'s injunction for the chorus was also known through the somewhat softened version found in Horace *Ars Poetica* 193-201, on which see Brink (1971) 254ff.

characterisation; and the prevailing nature of drama produced in this era has fostered this mentality's disregard for the potential of the lyric mode within drama.

It is perhaps, therefore, the most disappointing fact about the *Poetics* that it does nothing to enrich for us the significance of lyric poetry in Greek tragedy, and that it may even obstruct, or distract from, the difficult effort now needed to recover this significance. The chorus of tragedy remains often inaccessible to our common intuitions about drama, and the problems entailed in coming to terms with it are reflected in the demonstrable inconsistency of modern attitudes on the subject. If the chorus of tragedy can be described by one major student of the genre as 'that most wonderful of Greek dramatic instruments', to another it is 'relentlessly undramatic'; and if one finds the chorus to be 'most intensely actionful', another concludes that it is 'an essentially non-active group'.[27] Both in the extent of the disagreement apparent here, and also in the terms of the disagreement themselves, it may not be implausible to discern part of the legacy of Aristotle's *Poetics*.

[27] G. Murray, *Euripides* 2nd edn. (London 1946) 4, Knox 196, Jones 60 n.3, Taplin 87.

IX

Epic, Comedy and Other Genres

'The subject of the treatise is the art of poetry in general, and the potential of each of its types ...' The opening of the *Poetics*, with its characteristic promise of a compendious scope and an analytical method, may arouse some misleading expectations. While the announcement of a concern with generic categorisation and with questions of poetic structure is later sufficiently fulfilled, the impression given that all the various kinds of Greek poetry will be individually examined turns out to be less than precise. The *Poetics* in its surviving form is dominated, of course, by the treatment of tragedy, and it is noticeable that at more than one point in the course of this treatment Aristotle either digresses from his strict attention to the genre in order to offer generalisations about all poetry ('the art of poetry in general'), or else comments on tragedy in such a way as to imply that his observations are of wider applicability.[1] Tragedy stands in many respects, it seems, as a paradigm of the art as a whole. This implication is reinforced when we reach the discussion of epic in the later chapters of the work, for this discussion is both much briefer than that of tragedy and also dependent on it in many important details. The relationship between these two sections of the treatise additionally reflects a view, indicated by Aristotle in ch. 4, of the historical or quasi-historical relationship between the genres themselves. Tragedy is temporally later than epic but develops into a higher poetic form: it therefore merits prior and fuller consideration within the philosopher's teleological frame of reference.

After epic Aristotle had previously declared an intention to analyse comedy, and this fact, together with some fragments of relevant evidence, gives us adequate reason to believe that the *Poetics* has been

---

[1] The chief passages are ch. 8, 51a 19-35 (general principles of poetic unity, with references to epic), ch. 9 as a whole (philosophical generalisations on poetry), and the chs. on *lexis* (see Appendix 4). For epic references in the chs. on tragedy see n.8 below.

incompletely preserved.[2] There are few if any grounds, however, for believing that the work ever went on to turn its attention to the remaining genres of Greek poetry: in particular, lyric poetry (both choral and monodic), elegiac verse, and didactic poetry. This latter group of omissions has often been acknowledged by writers on the *Poetics*, but it has rarely been thought problematic or of any consequence. In the final section of this chapter I shall propose a different view of the matter, by asking whether it may not be possible, as in the case of the tragic chorus, to discern a significant relation between the omissions and the nature of Aristotle's theory of poetry. In the first two sections, however, I shall attempt separate consideration of the evidence, in the one case explicit, in the other consisting only of hints, for Aristotle's views on epic and comedy. Here too it will necessarily be an important part of my aim to try to see what place these genres may have occupied in the Aristotelian picture of poetry as a whole.

*

The essence of Aristotle's conception of epic poetry can be stated very concisely: epic (Homeric epic, at any rate) is a genre which has much in common with dramatic tragedy (as well as a certain amount with comedy), and which can at its best be regarded as a form of proto-drama and proto-tragedy; but, in the 'natural history' of poetry, it has been improved on and superseded by tragedy, which possesses all the capacities of epic, but has more besides.[3] One strand at least in this conception was not original with Aristotle. The idea of Homeric epic as a type of tragedy is to be found in more than one passage of Plato's dialogues, where Aristotle must have been familiar with it.[4] But whereas Plato elevates Homer to the status of 'the finest of poets and the first among tragedians', Aristotle, while fully acknowledging Homer as incomparably the greatest of epic poets, is also unequivocal about the inferiority of the epic genre to dramatic tragedy. This judgement is expressed more than once in the preliminary section of the treatise. In the sketch of poetic evolution given in ch. 4, Aristotle suggests, after claiming that Homeric epic

---

[2] See Janko 63ff.

[3] Ar.'s treatment of epic is discussed in Koster 42-80, and more specifically his view of Homer in Hogan's article.

[4] *Theaet.* 152e, *Rep.* 595c, 598d, 602b, 605c, 607a.

created the prototypes for later tragedy and comedy, that when the possibility of these genres became discernible (when tragedy and comedy had 'been glimpsed', 49a 2), poets specifically turned to them instead of to epic, 'on the grounds that their forms were greater and more highly thought of than those of epic' (49a 5f.). The point is corroborated in *Poetics* 5, where Aristotle draws some comparisons and contrasts of detail between the two genres, before observing: 'and so, whoever is able to evaluate the merits and defects of tragedies is also equipped to evaluate epic, for tragedy embraces all the attributes of epic, while the reverse is not the case.' (49b 17-20) The final chapter of the treatise will make the comparison once again, and in fuller form; but the ultimate verdict will be the same.

The Aristotelian assessment of epic, as can be seen from the passage in *Poetics* 4 cited above, entails a claim about the putative historical relationship between the two genres. Aristotle shows a firm conviction that the development of tragedy was actively influenced by the major Homeric epics, but equally that at a certain stage poetic energies were rechannelled from the older to the newer genre. This connected pair of claims gives rise in turn to two related issues: firstly, the problem of just how strictly historical Aristotle's views purport to be; and secondly, the question of how close in any case these views are to what can be reconstructed of Greek literary history. On the first of these issues I have already made some observations in an earlier chapter, where I suggested that the whole of the framework of ostensible literary history in *Poetics* 4 and 5 is so theory-laden, so heavily grounded in *a priori* and philosophical assumptions about poetry, that it can only be judged to offer a historical account in a severely qualified sense of that term.[5] Such a conclusion clearly has a bearing on the secondary and contingent question of how accurate Aristotle's data can be believed to be, if only for the reason that our independent information about the origins of Greek tragedy is so pitiful as to make it essential to decide on the reliability of Aristotle's references to the subject. My purpose in mentioning this controversial matter is not to embark on a fresh enquiry into it, but to make an opportunity to emphasise how very little there is in Aristotle's version of the transition from epic to

[5] Cf. ch. III pp. 93f.

tragedy which can be separated from his theoretical preconceptions.[6] It should be especially noticed that when the transition is first described, no detail at all is given. Homer – emerging from the primitive cultural mist in which men engaged their mimetic instincts in hymns, encomia, and invective – established the epic form of proto-tragedy, and showed the way for further development; and then, 'when tragedy had appeared' (or 'been glimpsed'), the argument runs on, poets began to turn from the old to the new. The line of cultural influence is picked out clearly, but only because the background of historical texture is missing.

It is only later in ch. 4, after the fundamental configuration of genres has been fixed, that Aristotle introduces what appear to be historical elements in the origins and growth of tragedy: the prior existence of dithyramb, the occurrence of associated improvisatory performances, the appearance of the first actor, and the many other changes referred to at 49a 14. The arrangement of the chapter is significant. The crucial relation between epic and tragedy is posited and affirmed before less clear-cut and coherent factors in the development of tragedy are mentioned. Negatively, the striking feature of this argument is the lack of any explicit indication of how the details of dithyramb and improvisation, whatever their status, are to be brought into intelligible combination with the larger claim about the prefiguring of tragedy by Homeric epic. But this is only a reflection of the positive fact that Aristotle is far less concerned with history on the contingent and documented level than with insights into the essential relationship between genres as this can be discerned from the point of view of a philosophical understanding of poetry. The assertion of this relationship, in other words, is to be taken in the same spirit as the statements made later in *Poetics* 4 about the 'nature' of tragedy and the natural life-cycle of its growth. This is abstract cultural and literary theory, supported by a network of Aristotelian assumptions at least as much as by uncited reserves of evidence (though these too may have existed).

Aristotle's claims about the historical connection between epic and tragedy turn out, therefore, to lead on directly to, and not to be properly separable from, a second aspect of the *Poetics'* comparative placing of the two genres, namely a judgement on their intrinsic

---

[6] A subtle critique of Ar.'s position is to be found in Pickard-Cambridge 121-31. For a strongly anti-Aristotelian thesis see G. F. Else, *The Origin and Early Form of Greek Tragedy* (Cambridge Mass. 1965).

poetic form and potential. Here Aristotle builds on the basis of the principle that epic and tragedy have most of their features in common, and that many of the same criteria are applicable to both. But an evaluative bias is lent to this principle by the fact that whereas epic has the historical priority, it is tragedy which receives the prior and more elaborate analysis in Aristotle's theory, and the concepts and standards elaborated in this analysis are then largely carried over to the much shorter treatment of epic. It is worth listing the points which fall into this category, as they occur in chs. 23 and 24.

59a 18f.: epic plot-structures (*muthoi*) should be 'dramatically' constructed, as they are by Homer, on the same principles as tragedy's (cf. 48b 35f. and 60a 7-11 for Homer's dramatic qualities).

59a 19-21: epic plots should present a single 'action' (*praxis*) (cf. 51a 30ff.), which should have the unity of wholeness and completeness (cf. e.g. 50b 24), with beginning, middle and end (cf. 50b 26-31), and the pleasurable coherence comparable to that of a living creature (cf. 50b 34ff.), the pleasure effected being that 'proper' to the genre (cf. esp. 53b 10ff.).

59a 21-9: the construction of epic is to be contrasted with that of history (cf. 51a 38ff.), in which unity is merely that of a temporal period or sequence, and in which events may be randomly connected (cf. ch. 8).

59a 30ff. (and 59b 19): an epic plot should be, as Homer's are but others' are not, compact enough to be grasped as a whole unit (cf. 51a 4 for terminology, and 51a 22ff. for the back reference).

59a 37-b 2: many poets err by believing that the story of a single hero necessarily lends unity to a poem (cf. 51a 16ff.).

59b 8f.: epic shares with tragedy the four plot-types – simple, complex, character-based (*êthikê*) and *pathos*-centred (*pathêtikê*)[7] (cf. 55b 32-56a 3).

59b 9f.: epic shares the six parts of tragedy, except for spectacle and lyrics (cf. 49b 16f.).

59b 10f.: epic like tragedy makes use of the three special components of plot (implicit in the plot-types listed above): reversal, recognition, and *pathos* (cf. esp. chs. 10-11).

60a 26-9: epic should conform mostly to the criterion of probability

---

[7] For these terms see Lucas (1968) 186f.: as he rightly argues, there is no good reason to divorce them from the regular sense of *êthos* and *pathos* in the *Poetics*.

(*eikos*: cf. e.g. 52a 20f.), and any unavoidable element of 'the irrational' should at least be kept outside the plot-structure (cf. 54b 6-8).

It is obvious from the above catalogue how dependent Aristotle's conception and treatment of epic are on the theory of tragedy which precedes it in the treatise. Nor do the specific echoes of terminology and principle exhaust the interconnections between the genres. Aristotle states, as we have seen, that all but two of the six parts of tragedy – and those the two least important by his own standards – are also to be found in epic. Most of the above references clearly concern the most fundamental of these, plot-structure (*muthos*). If we ask what Aristotle has to offer on the remaining three – characterisation, thought and language – the answer, so far as the explicit material of the section on epic is concerned, is nothing but one or two allusive hints. On thought, *dianoia*, this is not troubling, since it was relegated to the province of rhetoric at 56a 34ff. For the other two, however, it is legitimate to ask why more is not said. The obvious answer is that it is precisely because these elements are shared with tragedy: the remarks which have been made on characterisation and language in tragedy can be assumed to be directly transferable to epic. That this is indeed so receives some confirmation from the fact that examples from epic were cited in the sections on these topics, just as, in fact, some illustrations from tragedy occur in the chapters on epic itself.[8] There is, in other words, some discreet interweaving of the analyses of tragedy and epic which helps to bind the genres more closely together in Aristotle's theory.

Despite the accumulated force of the association for which Aristotle argues between epic and tragic drama, there is of course some attempt to bring out the differences as well. Yet what is striking in this respect is how marginal the differences appear alongside the emphasis on the common ground. Metre and scale provide two factual generic features about which Aristotle naturally needs to say little, though it must be observed that the exceptional size of the *Iliad* and *Odyssey* cause him a little uneasiness.[9] Besides these, we find

[8] Epic references in the sections on tragedy: 51a 19-30, 53a 32, 54b 2, 14f., 26-30, 55b 16-23, 57b 10f., 58a 7, 58b 25-31. Tragic references in the chs. on epic: 60a 29-32.

[9] Ar. is not prepared to allow unlimited length to epic (59a 32f.), though it may cover unlimited *fictional* time (49b 12-16, with Lucas (1968) ad loc.). This accords with his general aesthetic of form: 50b 34ff. Yet he must acknowledge epic's greater scope in this respect: 59b 17ff., cf. 62a 18ff. It is in this latter connection that he

three main points of distinction which emerge in the course of these later chapters. The first two, 'grandeur' and freedom in the deployment of episodes, are related by virtue of both being consequences or symptoms of epic's scale.[10] The third, epic's capacity for the marvellous, is derived by Aristotle from the fact that epic is not performed on stage, so that anomalies which might show up in the theatre, but do not in recitation or reading, therefore become permissible.[11] This latter point remains unsatisfactory and somewhat obscure, partly because of the choice of a far from cogent example, the pursuit of Hector in *Iliad* 22. It is not clear, in fact, why the marvellous, which Aristotle does not define but which he elsewhere thinks of in terms of emotive power and a challenge to the understanding, should have greater scope in epic than in tragedy. But if it does, Aristotle's negative explanation of the phenomenon is inadequate, if only because it relies on a factor – the stage performance of drama – which is elsewhere regarded as inessential to tragedy's poetic nature. A further problem concerning the ascription of the marvellous to epic will be mentioned below.

---

recommends (59b 20-2) a length which is much shorter than that of the Homeric poems, but closer to 'other' works in the epic cycle. I cannot follow Solmsen 194f. in finding a contradiction between 59b 17ff. and 49b 13ff., still less in inferring from this and other points that ch. 24 is a later stratum of the work.

[10] Grandeur: 59b 22-9, 34-7. Episodes: 55b 15-23, 59a 35-7, 59b 28-30. The term *epeisodion* and its cognates have caused unnecessary anguish among interpreters, who sometimes appear to forget that Greek words, even in Ar.'s hands, were not surgical instruments but belonged to a living language. The basic sense of *epeisodion* is a 'dramatic scene' or portion of a play: *Poetics* 12 gives a stricter if unsatisfactory definition, but, *pace* Taplin 472, there is nothing else which the word can mean at 49a 28 and 56a 31. The term is easily extended to cover portions of the action of an epic poem too. Now the essential requirement for Ar. is that 'episodes', whether in tragedy or epic, should be integrated into the design of the plot-structure: 51b 33-5, 55b 13. But, of course, his concept of *muthos* permits some things to be regarded as more indispensable than others: hence at 55b 23, 59a 35-7, and 59b 30 there are suggestions of episodes as scenes which flesh out or expand or give variety to the main scheme of action. This does *not* turn episodes into mere frills. If they do become that, then a poem is flawed, and described derogatorily as 'episodic', i.e. disjointed (51b 33, with *Met.* 1076a 1, 1090b 19f.). The verb *epeisodioun* does not refer to 'mere stuffing' (House 53 n.1) at *Rhet.* 1418a 33: Hubbard 167 appropriately translates the metaphor as 'divide the speech into acts'.

For a good discussion of the issue see House 51-7, and for the difference between epic's and tragedy's use of episodes see Friedrich (1983), though cf. ch. III n.39 for a reservation. *Epeisodion* may have been used in a special sense in fifth-century comedy: see Cratinus fr.208 and Metagenes fr.14, with G. Norwood, ' "Episodes" in Old Comedy', *CP* 25 (1930) 217-29.

[11] 60a 11-19. On wonder or the marvellous see ch. II pp. 74f. with nn.40-1.

Whether the other two features which Aristotle suggests as characteristic of epic are much more satisfactorily presented may also be thought doubtful. As for 'grandeur' or 'gravity', the point is again made in part by an awkward contrast with the limitations imposed on drama by the conditions of performance (59b 22-8), and so on a theoretical level the objection mentioned in the previous paragraph applies here too.[12] Aristotle does hint at positive metrical and linguistic factors which conduce to lend a characteristic tone to epic, but he does so with such brevity that his claims are practically impossible to assess. Similarly, in the case of epic's use of episodes, if there need be no doubt that this is an important issue in the comparison between the two genres, Aristotle's handling of it amounts to no more than a passing remark about the capacity of epic to incorporate a greater variety of material than is possible in the narrower confines of tragedy. The standards by which these attempts to suggest the distinctive qualities of epic might be judged thin and undeveloped are, it must be emphasised, those of Aristotle's own treatise. It is the contrast between the brevity and the obviousness of much of the discussion of epic, and the strong theoretical thrust of the earlier analysis of tragedy, which ought to strike a reader of the *Poetics*. The explanation for this must be sought, as already indicated, in the fact that the section of the treatise on epic is dominated by a determination to stress not only the substantial common ground between the two genres, but also the ultimate inferiority of epic to tragedy. Neither of these premises gives Aristotle much inducement to explore the distinctive powers of epic in any detail.

But there is, perhaps, a little more to the matter than this. The scale of Homeric epic, and the concomitant feature of episodic complexity, raises a serious question about the validity of the whole attempt to subject epic to the same criteria of artistic unity as those elaborated for tragedy. To demonstrate this, one need only juxtapose two passages from the *Poetics* itself. In the first, in ch. 23 (59b 2-4),

---

[12] A further and important objection is that Ar. ignores the role of the messenger-speech (an 'epic' element) in tragedy. More speculatively, Ar. might have seen that, stage conventions allowing, a change of scene *would* make possible the dramatisation of more than one scene of fictionally contemporaneous action. Soph. *Ajax* 719ff. and 815ff. could even be argued to be an instance of this (though no positive prompting is given to take the scenes in precisely this way). Nor need changes of scene have always been as unusual in the Greek theatre as is sometimes imagined: for evidence on this see Taplin 49 n.2 (post-classical tragedy), 416f. (lost Aeschylus).

Aristotle illustrates how close the two major Homeric poems come to the ideal of tragic unity by suggesting that only a single play (or perhaps two: already a compromise on the principle stated at 59a 19) could be derived from each of them. This is said to be in contrast to other epics, which deal with too much material to be cohesive. Yet in ch. 26, at 62b 7-11, we are offered the alternative judgement that both the *Iliad* and the *Odyssey*, while still the most unified of epics, nonetheless dramatise more than a single action: they are said to have 'many parts', which was precisely the criticism levelled at inferior epics in the earlier passage.[13] What we have here, I think, is no casual inconsistency, but a sign of the tension caused by the direct application of tragic standards to epic; it is not accidental that the limiting judgement on the Homeric poems occurs in the final chapter of the treatise, where Aristotle is trying to establish epic's inferiority to tragedy.

That this is not the only tension in the *Poetics'* treatment of epic has already been noted in my earlier chapter on mimesis, where I showed that Aristotle is involved in a significant equivocation over the mimetic modes used by epic.[14] This equivocation is evidently the result of his desire to assimilate Homeric epic, but not the genre as a whole, to drama. Only Homer, it seems, satisfies the requirement that epic plots should be 'dramatically' constructed. Only Homer, of epic poets, made works of 'dramatic mimesis', we are told in ch. 4, and in the same context Homer is said to have 'made dramatic poetry' out of the humorous material of the comic epic, *Margites* (48b 35-8). It is important to observe that the terminology used in these places is not found elsewhere in Greek before Aristotle, and Aristotle himself applies the adjective 'dramatic' only to *epic*. The concept of 'the dramatic' as such, in other words, appears only as a touchstone by which the earlier but subordinate genre of epic can be tested. And while the recognition of quasi-dramatic qualities in Homer might be reckoned to intimate a fine literary sensibility on Aristotle's part,[15]

---

[13] Cf. also 56a 11ff., where the *Iliad* is covered by the description of epic as *polumuthon*. There is probably sone variation in what Ar. counts as belonging to the *muthos* of a poem; otherwise, it is difficult to reconcile this passage (where a tragedy based on the plot of the *Iliad* is offered as an absurdity) with 59b 2-4: it helps if we suppose the former to mean all the material of the *Iliad*, including less integral episodes.

[14] See ch. IV pp. 128f.

[15] In fact, the contrast with the epic cycle may not have been difficult to see. A fragment such as *Thebais* fr. 2 suggests a flat narrative style and the coverage of much mythic material in a small compass (the very opposite of Homer). For a valuable

my immediate concern is to point out the theoretical consequences of his attempt to translate this recognition into part of his formal understanding of the nature of epic. Epic poetry other than that of Homer is not only deemed to be inferior, but relegated to a level where its very status as poetry can be called into question, as it is in ch. 24 (60a 7-9).

That Aristotle's conception and discussion of epic is dominated by Homer can be readily explained and defended by reference to the towering status of the *Iliad* and *Odyssey*, and to the consequent fact that within the context of classical Greek culture no theory of epic needed to look beyond these unique achievements. But that is a relevant qualification on only part of the above argument, for it does nothing to justify Aristotle's effective conviction that epic aspires to the condition of tragedy. There remains a major question to be raised about the whole of Aristotle's view of epic, and it is one which perhaps applies most forcefully to his treatment of the Homeric epics themselves. Even if we can accept the validity of the connections which Aristotle constructs between epic and tragedy, and can understand the model of a unified plot-structure which is central to his comparative enterprise, we may still feel that there is a significant lacuna in the later chapters of the treatise. The most evident symptom of this is the lack of a definition of epic to correspond to that of tragedy. While it would be possible to infer large parts of the missing definition both from passages in the early chapters and from the later comparisons with tragedy, one major element is not readily apparent, and that is the distinctive emotional experience at which epic should aim, and with which the 'proper pleasure' of the genre (59a 21, 62b 13f.) would have to be associated. This question is exacerbated by the allusiveness of Aristotle's references to the marvellous in epic, since in the case of tragedy he seems to imagine this factor operating in conjunction with the generic emotions of pity and fear. Part of the indeterminacy of this aspect of the theory of epic derives from uncertainty over whether the marvellous in epic operates in connection with other emotions, or is an independent effect and pleasure.[16]

---

contrast between Homer and the cycle see J. Griffin, 'The Epic Cycle and the Uniqueness of Homer', *JHS* 97 (1977) 39-53.

[16] 60a 11-18 both suggests a link with tragic wonder (11f.) but also seems to envisage a much wider play of it in epic. 60a 35ff. (if this is a case of the irrational which could produce wonder) points more towards 'niraculous' aspects of the *Odyssey*

Yet there appears to be one passage towards the very end of the *Poetics* where Aristotle does indicate the purpose of epic. In claiming in ch. 26 that tragedy is superior to epic in 'its artistic effect', Aristotle adds the parenthesis: 'for these arts ought not to produce an arbitrary pleasure, but the one which has been mentioned' (62b 13f.). Many commentators have taken this to refer us back directly and exclusively to the concept of the proper pleasure of tragedy, described in ch. 14, 53b 12, as 'the pleasure deriving from pity and fear through mimesis'.[17] It should be noted, however, that this is not the inevitable sense of the passage in ch. 26, for the phrase 'the one which has been mentioned' could in this context be understood to have a plural force, and to refer us back both to the proper pleasure of tragedy and to that of epic, which was separately mentioned at 59a 21. If interpreted in the latter fashion, however, the point remains mysterious, since Aristotle has simply not specified an independent pleasure or emotional effect for epic. This adds to the already considerable reasons for preferring the first interpretation and for inferring that the Aristotelian theory of epic aligns it with tragedy in this crucial respect as in others. Chief among these reasons is the assertion in ch. 24 (59b 7-9) that the same four plot-types can be used in epic as in tragedy. Three of the implicit components of these plots – reversal, recognition, and physical suffering (*pathos*) – all necessarily entail pity and fear. In addition, Aristotle goes on specifically to categorise the *Iliad* and *Odyssey* with his two main types of tragedy, the simple and the complex, thus confirming his earlier designation of Homeric epic as proto-tragedy. While it is difficult to see why the *Iliad* should not be classed as a complex tragedy, the general implications of these remarks for the nature of the genre are unequivocal. There are, in fact, several other passages in the treatise where either or both of the Homeric poems are viewed as tragedies, and what is most remarkable is that, with one partial exception, the

---

of the kind which need not be linked with pity and fear, but this is something to which Ar.'s theory does not otherwise look hospitable. The case of Hector's pursuit presumably involves the tragic emotions as well as wonder: the term used at 60b 25 (*ekplêktikon*) is also used of tragic recognition at 54a 4 and 55a 17; and note that Plato *Ion* 535b cites the pursuit of Hector (also with a reference to *ekplêxis*) as an outstandingly emotional scene.

[17] E.g. Vahlen (1914) 234f., Bywater on 62b 12, Lucas (1968) on 62b 13. Cf. Else (1957) 651-3, apparently not fully harmonised with 573. On the connected issue of epic *katharsis* see ch. VI n.43.

Odyssey is as consistently regarded in this way as is the *Iliad*.[18]

If this argument is acceptable, then we do after all have the necessary information to piece together a comprehensible definition of epic on the model of that of tragedy: precisely on this model, indeed, since the only obvious adjustments which would have to be made in it to cater for epic concern metrical form and, less straightforwardly, the mode or modes of mimesis. In this way the assimilation of epic to tragedy can be carried through to an extreme which seems to accord with Aristotle's intentions. If this assimilation can be admired and endorsed from one point of view – namely for what it involves in the positive apprehension of Homeric qualities – three important reservations must nevertheless be recorded in conclusion. The first is that Aristotle's approach to epic cannot be treated as disinterestedly critical. It is in part the carrier of a theory of poetic and cultural development, according to which epic needs to be seen as the precursor of a later genre, and needs correspondingly to be judged by standards which have only been fully realised by the growth to maturity of this genre. Aristotle's views cannot, in other words, be simply translated into an understanding of the influence of Homer on Attic tragedy, and that is why we must not accommodate them to our own sense of Greek literary history by emphasising Aristotle's insight into Homer the dramatist, while taking less seriously the verdict with which the *Poetics* comes to a close: that the *Iliad* and *Odyssey*, if preeminent among epics, nonetheless fail to match the highest standards of dramatic tragedy.[19] Closely related to this is a second reservation which I have already discussed and now simply reiterate: the *Poetics*, in its desire to bring epic and

[18] The *Iliad* is called 'simple' at 59b 14. Why? It is certainly possible to identify *peripeteia* and *anagnôrisis* in it: cf. Rutherford 146. The quasi-tragic nature of the *Odyssey* is indicated, explicitly or implicitly, at 48b 3ff., 51a 24-30, 54b 26-30, 55a 2-4, 55b 16-23, 59b 2-4, 14f. Even 53a 30ff. suggests that the *Odyssey* represents the second-best type of tragedy, though it *assimilates* its pleasure to that of comedy.

[19] Else (1957) 648 exaggerates in attributing 'embarrassment' to Ar. Else has earlier gone too far in his presentation of Ar.'s attitude to Homer: e.g. 499-501, 534 ('the epic is and has something more than tragedy ...', flatly contradicted by *Poet.* 49b 18-20), 572 ('idolatry'), 582 n.32 ('divinity'). The last two references are a little naive. Ar.'s praise of Homer as 'divine' (*thespesios*) at 59a 30 echoes Homeric passages such as *Il.* 2.599f. and *Od.* 8.43 (cf. Pindar *Isth.* 4.43), but it may also have been a current idiom: see Plato *Ion* 530b 10, *Phaedo* 95a 2, and cf. Aristoph. *Frogs* 1034, Plato *Meno* 81b 2, 99c-d (referring to female and Spartan idioms: cf. Ar. *EN* 1145a 28f.), *Theaet.* 151b 6, 154d 3, *Protag.* 316a 1, *Rep.* 331e 6, *Laws* 629b 9, 682a 3, and Ar. himself at *Met.* 1074b 9. But Ar.'s use of 'divine' in connection with virtue is of a different kind and force: *EN* 1099b 16, 1145a 20, 1177b 26ff., 1178b 25-7.

tragedy into the closest relations, fails to do justice to the distinctive attributes of the former. We may be left pondering in particular whether Aristotle's canons of unity and cohesion are not too artificially exacting, as his own equivocations seem to suggest, even for the great Homeric epics, and whether the formula of pity and fear can match the scope of the material handled in the *Iliad* and *Odyssey*. Finally, if the major tenets of Aristotle's theory of tragedy are to be applicable to epic as well, then the problems and objections to which this theory is vulnerable must also be carried over to the interpretation of epic. Above all, if the core of the analysis of tragedy, with its stress on the causal structure of the complex plot, entails, as I argued in ch. VII, a movement towards secularisation of the world of tragic myth, it is hard to see how Aristotle's treatment of epic could be exempted from a similar judgement.

A brief comment must be appended, however, on a level of Aristotle's attitude to epic which does something to counterbalance the preconceptions I have tried to point out. It is paradoxical that some of the most important glimpses which we receive of the philosopher's practical handling of poetic interpretation should come in the crabbed and rebarbative ch. 25 of the treatise. This chapter summarises Aristotle's larger work, *Homeric Problems*, in which he dealt with a mass of criticisms against the poet's work, and a wide range of interpretative difficulties.[20] If many of these criticisms appear captious, and the difficulties trivial or fatuous, that is largely a reflection on others, not on Aristotle himself. Once we have struggled through the fine, abbreviated detail of *Poetics* 25, and the remains of the larger work, we can see, in fact, that Aristotle emerges from the whole subject with credit: not only because it gave him opportunities to display linguistic, historical, technical and critical erudition, but also because it enabled him to work out certain essential principles of poetic interpretation, whose validity extended beyond epic, and whose thrust was intended to counteract the more severe aspects of Platonic moralism. These principles do not amount to the aestheticism which is sometimes ascribed to Aristotle on the

[20] For a thorough reappraisal of ch. 25 see Rosenmeyer's article. For the *Homeric Problems* see frs. 142-79 Rose: the range of subjects covered includes heroic behaviour, problems of consistency and probability, points of morality, social custom and politics, and various technicalities. Cf. G. L. Huxley, 'Historical Criticism in Aristotle's *Homeric Questions*', *Proceedings of the Royal Irish Academy* (c) 79 (1979) 73-81. Fr. 142 of the work refers to the same point as *Poet.* 54b 2, and for other similarities compare e.g. frs. 160, 164, 166 with *Poet.* 61a 1-4, and fr. 168 with 54a 26ff.

basis of this chapter, but they do sufficiently show an awareness of the need to grant to poetry aims and methods distinct from those of morality or of other human activities. Interpretation of individual details must take account, Aristotle indicates, of context and of the relation of parts to the whole. Standards appropriate to the particular genre must be applied, and poetry must not be subjected to judgement in terms of inflexible ethical or technical criteria. While not implying that moral or rational considerations can be dispensed with in the understanding of poetry (61b 19-20), Aristotle's treatment of Homeric 'problems' has a positive spirit which is favourable to the independence of the art. By rebutting most of the existing criticisms of Homer, he not only vindicates this poet's status, but also combats a reductive attitude to the reading of poetry in general, and advocates attention above all to the specific aims of works of art, with which his own larger theory is designed to deal.

*

Some of the issues which collect around Aristotle's view of comedy can be said to be, at least at the *prima facie* level, extrinsic to the *Poetics*. This is for the simple reason that our texts of the treatise do not contain the discussion of comedy which is promised at the beginning of ch. 6 (49b 21f.) and which we would expect to follow the section on epic. The question of whether any independent evidence survives for the contents of this discussion lies outside the scope of this book.[21] In the present section my purpose is chiefly to survey the small amount of material on comedy in the surviving *Poetics*, and to offer some concise remarks on its relation to the main contents of the work.

Given the immediate cultural conjunction of tragedy and comedy in the dramatic festivals of classical Athens, we would naturally anticipate that any theorist of poetry would consider both their common features and their significant differences. Plato not infrequently mentions the two genres together for the purposes of contrast or comparison, and in the *Poetics* too there are signs of an awareness of the special relationship between them, as well as some

---

[21] Janko's book offers a new, incisive and informative treatment of the whole issue, building on Cooper (1922) but with a good deal more acumen. I cannot, however, accept his major claims about the Aristotelian origin of the *Tractatus Coislinianus*. See also nn.30-1 below.

apparent echoes of Plato's views on comedy. Within the general scheme of Aristotle's analysis of poetic mimesis, tragedy and comedy can obviously be aligned in certain basic respects. They share, in the first place, as ch. 1 of the treatise acknowledges, the same set of poetic media – language, rhythm, and music; and this simple fact could be elaborated, though Aristotle is not interested in doing so in what survives, into a much more detailed comparative treatment of their technical forms and structures. In their common use of these media and of the dramatic mode, tragedy and comedy can with equal validity be categorised under the formula of 'the mimesis of men in action' (48a 27f.). Both, furthermore, should embody the enactment – mimesis in the strong sense – of designed and unified plot-structures of generalised significance (49b 8f., 51b 11-15). It is evidently a point of major import that the *Poetics*' canons of unity, which are central to Aristotle's conception of poetic significance, should apply to comedy as well as to tragedy; and this will later be corroborated.

But it is in terms of the third differentia of mimesis, the status of its human objects, that tragedy and comedy have to be fundamentally distinguished. Aristotle announces the point in ch. 2 by describing tragedy as the mimesis of 'men better than present humanity', comedy as that of 'men worse than it' (48a 16-18). This dichotomy was later to harden into a critical commonplace, and one often translated (perhaps as early as Theophrastus) into narrow and inflexible terms of the social rank of the typical characters portrayed by the two genres.[22] Social rank may not be wholly irrelevant to Aristotle's conception of the generic distinction, particularly since in the dramatic tradition with which he was familiar tragedy normally took its material from heroic myth and saga, while comic plots were frequently built around fictitious figures from the ordinary world. But Aristotle's point certainly cannot be confined to such criteria, both because he needed to allow for considerable variation in the status of comic characters (who might even, in burlesque plays, come from heroic myth itself), but also because the language in which he draws his distinction between tragedy and comedy, and the context in which it first occurs, have moral implications which are later strengthened by the terms in which character (*êthos*) is defined for tragedy. The genres are separated, in Aristotle's theoretical

---

[22] See Janko 49f., McMahon *passim*, Spingarn 61-7.

formulation, primarily by ethical character and tone, which may be associated with aspects of social rank, but are not, *au fond*, categories of this kind. I have argued earlier in this book that the *Poetics'* categorisation of the characters of tragedy as 'better than us' involves an amalgam, though not an entirely stable one, of ethical values and heroic standards of external status.[23] A clearer idea of what is involved on the *comic* side of the Aristotelian disjunction of the genres will have to be sought from hints later in the treatise, but it is certainly not possible to project back onto the *Poetics* the bland neo-classical contrast between the deaths and disasters of kings, on the one hand, and the frolicks and nuptials of plebeians, on the other.

It is appropriate to glance first at the references to comedy in ch. 4, where analogies with tragedy again present themselves. Two independent issues are here raised. In the first place, it appears from the sketch of poetry's evolution that comedy just as much as tragedy can be derived from the basic roots of man's natural mimetic instincts. If this is so, and if my earlier analysis (in ch. III) of Aristotle's argument was correct, then it follows that comedy too must provide an experience which is in part cognitive and a source of understanding. We can take this point, moreover, to be closely related to the need for unity on which I have already touched, since the understanding of comic plot-structures will depend on their internal coherence. One fundamental question, therefore, though it is not one to which we can confidently expect to find an answer, is how Aristotle may have conceived of this cognitive dimension of the experience of comedy.[24] A contribution to the answer might be made by a firm interpretation of the second issue which arises from

[23] On tragedy see ch. V pp. 153f., 165-7. The terms used to characterise the baseness and inferiority of comic agents are specifically juxtaposed with those for tragedy at 48a 2-4, 17f., 48b 25f., and compare 49a 32f. with 49b 10. These passages alone strongly favour the assumption of an essential ethical scale, though connotations of social inferiority are probably involved too, and 49a 32-7 makes it clear that a wide range of failings and deficiencies could find their place in comedy. Moreover, the contrast between seriousness and humour at *EN* 1177a 3ff. and *Rhet.* 1419b 2-9 indicates that the ethical difference between the genres is associated with, and productive of, a strong divergence in mood or tone. For a narrower ethical interpretation see Held 171ff.

[24] Lord (1982) 174-7 speculates within too restricted a sphere, in my view. The cognitive experience of comedy need not be supposed, any more than that of tragedy, to carry a reducible moral lesson. Plato had accepted, rather late in life, that comedy might help us to understand virtue from its opposite: *Laws* 816d-e. It should be noted that at *Rhet.* 1412a 17-b 23 (cf. 1410b 10-21) even the pleasure of individual witticisms is attributed to understanding and learning (*mathêsis*).

Poetics 4. Here we encounter once again a subject which I have had more than one earlier occasion to discuss in connection with tragedy and epic, namely the historical status and reliability of some of the propositions advanced in this part of the work. With comedy the point is at least as important as with the other genres, and it is perhaps even more difficult here to reconstruct out of the material mentioned by Aristotle a plausible account of origins and development. The problem concerns not only how much weight, and what kind of weight, to give to the claim of an affinity between epic precedent (in this case the *Margites*) and the later dramatic genre, but also how to relate Aristotle's distinction between invective and 'the comic' to the concrete data of generic form and style. What are the boundaries of these latter categories on the historical map of comic epic, iambic poetry, 'phallic songs', and the types of dramatic comedy developed separately in Sicily and Attica? Aristotle's allusive utterances have been picked over by historians of comedy, but it may be doubted whether attempts to effect a reconciliation between the theoretical concepts and the historical data can make much sense, since it is the concepts which show that Aristotle is here, as with tragedy, primarily interested in tracing a pattern of natural poetic evolution, and not in accounting for a contingent sequence of events.[25] Although the 'nature' of comedy and the natural status of its development is not explicitly stated, as it is for tragedy, the parallel form of the argument in *Poetics* 4 and 5 intimates that these same premises must be supplied for comedy just as much as for tragedy.

Poetics 4 makes it at any rate clear that the truly comic or ridiculous has come to separate itself, or be refined out of, the iambic character of invective, and it is primarily in relation to this antithesis that we must try to piece together Aristotle's other hints about the genre, including the formulation of its object as 'men worse than ourselves'. The contrast with iambic invective is to be noted not only for its negative implications, but also for its indication that there is a degree of affinity between the two modes. Comedy, like invective, has a critical force, and needs an object or target against which this force of laughter can be directed. That is a premise accepted by

---

[25] For a properly sceptical appraisal of Ar.'s evidence on comedy see Pickard-Cambridge 225-40. Lord (1974) 197-204 gives a very strained account of this section of the treatise. In particular, the claim (201 n.14, 223) that Ar. regarded Crates as the true founder of comedy *tout court* goes right against the grain of 48a 33f. and 49b 2ff. On Epicharmus cf. n. 32 below.

Aristotle, and it explains why he takes care, here and elsewhere, to draw the distinction between the comic and the iambic.[26] Since the comic rationale, as *Poetics* 5 allows, is to portray various faults, errors and deficiencies in men, and since such a rationale is consistent up to a point with invective, a further demarcation is required. The opening of ch. 4 itself supplies part of this, by excluding outright evil from the sphere of the comic, and limiting the latter to 'error and deformity which involve no pain or destruction' (49a 34f.), a phrase which for Aristotle could denote a wide spectrum of ethical, physical and other failings. The one instance given, that of the distorted comic mask, happens to be physical, but we are expected to deduce comparable cases for other human attributes and aspects of behaviour. Although it is only the merest hint, this passage is sufficient to show that the baseness posited as the generic feature of comic characters is not of a single kind, and that we have here some sort of comic counterpart to the combination of features, both moral and non-moral (in the philosopher's own terms), which Aristotle's theory predicates of the agents of tragedy. That is not, however, to hypothesise a precise or neat parallelism between the genres – an unwarranted assumption which has vitiated much writing on Aristotle's view of comedy.

The weaknesses and foibles with which comedy typically deals are restricted to the relatively light and harmless – they must stop short of the point of real vice, and also of 'pain and destruction'. It is probably implied that invective, by contrast, might direct itself against matters of such gravity, even with extremes of evil (certainly, much Greek invective did purport to handle such subjects).[27] But there is another, equally important differential between comedy and the iambic mode. Both in ch. 5 and later in ch. 9 Aristotle indicates

[26] Another reason is that, despite Crates' pioneering style (49b 7f.), iambic elements had not entirely disappeared from Attic comedy in Ar.'s day: see Meineke 272-6. This is acknowledged by Ar. himself at *Rhet.* 1384b 9-11, where comic poets are interestingly described as slanderers (*kakologoi*) who publicise the faults (*hamartiai*: n.34 below) of their neighbours or fellow-citizens. Note also the association of iambus (evidently performed: n.36 below) and comedy at *Pol.* 1336b 20, as at Plato *Laws* 935e. For Ar.'s acceptance of some degree of mockery (*skôptein*) in all laughter see esp. *EN* 1128a 4-35, *Rhet.* 1381a 33-5, and note that at *Rhet.* 1389b 11f. wit (*eutrapelia*) is described as 'cultured insolence' (*hubris*, for which cf. 1379a 31f.).

[27] There can be no doubt that at the centre of the era of invective mentioned at 48b 30ff. Ar. would have placed Archilochus: note the verb *psegein* of the latter at *Rhet.* 1418b 27. On Ar. and Archilochus see H.D. Rankin, *L'Antiquité Classique* 46 (1977) 165-8.

that he regards invective as dealing with the individual and the particular, whereas comedy proper offers a mimesis of generalised action and characters. Comedy is brought, in other words, within the prescriptive definition of poetry put forward in *Poetics* 9, and can be said to stand in a relation to invective which is analogous to that between tragedy and history: the movement of thought in this section of the work conveys this point unmistakably. Here we get a glimpse of how a number of details already mentioned – the pleasure of understanding mimetic works, the unity of action, and now the generalised content of plot-structure and characterisation – coalesce into a single theory. The same principle of probability which holds for tragic plays holds equally for comic, so that the critical force directed against 'error and deformity' must be integrated within the design of a coherent and intelligible action. It is because of conformity to these fundamental Aristotelian principles of poetry that comedy can be accommodated to the cognitive theory of mimesis, and of the pleasure derived from it, as adumbrated in *Poetics* 4. The 'proper pleasure' of comedy (53a 35f.) is another species of the pleasure grounded in the understanding and emotional experience of mimetic works.

But to reach this point in the reconstruction of the Aristotelian theory of comedy is already to face the prospect of an impasse. The passage just cited from ch. 13, where the pleasure peculiar to comedy is referred to, gives us the only other substantial clue to be found in the treatise, but it is desperately difficult to interpret. In judging a double plot such as the *Odyssey*'s, 'with contrasting outcomes for good and bad', to be less than the perfect tragedy, Aristotle likens the pleasure which it yields to that required by comedy, and proceeds to elaborate on the latter by giving the example of a hypothetical play in which even the greatest of enemies become reconciled at the end, 'and no one is killed by anybody else'. There is a disorientatingly compressed movement in Aristotle's thought at this point: firstly, because the double plot is said, in quick succession, to be the second-best type of tragedy and yet to give not a tragic but something more like a comic pleasure; and, secondly, because the type of comedy which Aristotle then cites does not reproduce the configuration of the double plot mentioned before it. To make sense of all this, we need to grasp that Aristotle's focus is here on the morally comfortable, on the type of play, whether tragedy or comedy, which conforms to our best moral expectations. For a tragedy to do this is, he asserts, less than ideal; but the pleasure of the morally reassuring dénouement is legitimate and proper to comedy. Whether or not Aristotle has in mind a particular type of burlesque comedy (the reference to Orestes and Aegisthus may, but need not, mean that),[28] he is suggesting a general point about the way in which comedy can make light of potentially serious matters, and can solve, or dissolve, matters which in life might prove more untidy, more problematic, and more unjust in the outcome. But the contrast is not so much with ordinary life as with tragedy. 'No one is killed by anybody else' reminds us of ch. 5's specification that comedy should leave alone matters of pain and destruction, for these are precisely the realm of tragedy.[29] Comedy must stay within the bounds of the morally and emotionally unthreatening in order to elicit our laughter, and laughter is incompatible with serious ethical or other failings, and with their consequences.

Two primary conclusions can fairly be drawn from the considerations so far adduced. The first is that the *Poetics* indicates that dramatic comedy is to be situated and analysed within the same framework of interlocking concepts – mimesis, unity, necessity and probability, and universals – which is employed for the treatment of tragedy and epic. Comedy, just as much as the more serious genres, must satisfy Aristotle's basic criteria of poetry. The second conclusion – which is really a corollary of the first – is that Aristotle holds to a notion of the comic which distinguishes the genre's human subject-matter both from the moral gravity and tone of tragedy, but also from the personal specificity of iambic invective (even in dramatic form, as 49b 7-9 shows). The comic, on this theory, retains a critical basis and thrust; its nature involves the dramatic presentation of various types of human deficiency. But it must not expose these in their individually identifiable instances; it must aim

---

[28] Hubbard 108 n.1 shrewdly suggests that Ar.'s reference to Orestes and Aegisthus is a humorous hyperbole, not a citation of an actual comedy. But I am not so sure that we can rule out a burlesque play on this theme: in addition to Alexis' *Orestes* (e.g. Bywater ad loc.) we know of fourth- and third-century *phlyakes* called *Orestes* by Sopater and Rhinthon, and such works may have influenced Ar.'s choice of illustration. I do not think that Else (1957) 405f. clinches the case for excision of 53a 36-9.

[29] In addition to the definition of tragic *pathos* at 52b 11f., the point is confirmed by various references to pain and destruction in the *Rhetoric*'s discussion of pity and fear: esp. 1382a 22, 1385b 13f., 1386a 5ff. Cf. also the idea that good humour or wit (*eutrapelia*) will avoid causing *pain* to its butts: *EN* 1128a 7, 26, and, with more qualification, *EE* 1234a 21f.

at the intelligibility which arises not only out of the unity of a dramatic plot-structure, but also out of the generalised status of the agents and their actions. If this conformity to the Aristotelian concept of poetry threatens to ascribe too sober a value to comedy for some tastes, the passage at the end of *Poetics* 13 may stand as an acknowledgement that Aristotle still allows to the genre plenty of scope for the indulgent and sentimental dissolution of seriousness into make-believe.

But this remains only the barest outline of a theory of comic poetry, and one which leaves many pressing questions both unanswered and, in my view, unanswerable. In the first place, it is uncertain to which period or type of existing comic drama Aristotle would have thought his theory best applicable; we lack for comedy, as we do not for tragedy or epic, any sure way of elucidating and testing the theory against the prime instances of the genre. In *Poetics* 3 Aristotle cites Aristophanes, alongside Homer and Sophocles, as a representative of his genre, but it is difficult to separate Aristophanic comedy altogether from the later strictures on the 'iambic mode' which an older tradition of comic drama is supposed to have inherited from the iambic genre itself.[30] Furthermore, despite the subtlety of certain modern readings of his plays, it is extremely doubtful whether Aristophanes' work could have satisfied the philosopher's criteria of unified and probable plot-structures. The reference to comedy in *Poetics* 9 seems primarily to concern fourth-century plays, and it is clear that in an important passage of *EN* Book 4 Aristotle associates 'new comedies', which must here designate those of the mid-century, with his ethical standard of cultivated, moderate humour or wit.[31] It is above all this passage in the *Ethics*

---

[30] On the relation between Old Comedy and the iambic genre see R. M. Rosen, *Old Comedy and the Iambographic Tradition* (Harvard Dissertation, 1983). Attempts to make Ar.'s comic ideal fit Aristophanes (particularly Cooper (1922) 18-41) seem to me doomed to failure; and to find an allusion to Aristophanes at 53a 30-6, as Lamberton 98f. suggests, is out of the question. *Pace* Janko 66, *Poet.* 48a 27 tells us little: Aristophanes' name is a convenient one to represent the genre, because he was well-known and historically prominent; but this does not make him into Ar.'s ideal. What remains decisive is that Aristophanes' plays are mostly pervaded by the personal invective which the *Poetics* excludes from the truly comic: Janko 205f. skirts round this point. I note, *à propos* of this and of *Poet.* 49b 7-9, that the fragments of Crates contain an extremely low number of personal references in comparison not just with Aristophanes but also with the remains of other Old Comedians: cf. Meineke 59ff. It is also worth recalling that at Horace *Sat.* 1.4. 1ff. (which plays with Peripatetic ideas, according to Janko 103 and 208) Aristophanes is unequivocally classed as a poet of invective.

[31] *EN* 1128a 22ff. The difference between cultivated wit (*eutrapelia*) and buffoonery (*bômolochia*) is not, *contra* Janko 244, a contrast between two extremes, but between a *mean* and one of its corresponding vices (the other being boorishness): the point is clear

which gives grounds for supposing that a strong degree of decorum and restraint was central to Aristotle's comic ideal. This remains our most cogent reason for believing that the philosopher was more sympathetic to recent and contemporary developments in the genre than to the robust and personal style of comedy dominant in the previous century. But Aristotle's other references to comedy are too casual and allusive to allow a conclusive inference to be drawn about his views of existing plays, or for us to be sure that he regarded any particular type of comedy as fully embodying the ideal. We ought at least to keep open the possibility that he did not accept that the natural evolution of the genre had yet reached its final maturity.[32]

But more fundamental than this uncertainty is our inability on surviving evidence to reconstruct the core of the Aristotelian theory of comedy. Apart from the passing mention of a possible burlesque play in which the dénouement brings an accord between great enemies, Aristotle has left no indication in the remaining parts of the treatise of the types of plot available to comic drama. Similarly, although he acknowledges in this same passage that comedy, like other genres, has its proper pleasure, and although this seems to be bound up with the avoidance of 'pain or destruction', we are not told on what emotional basis, if any, this pleasure rests. The specific issue of whether Aristotle would have posited a comic as well as a tragic *katharsis*, is only one, if a peculiarly obscure, aspect of this whole question.[33] Energy has been spent on attempting to create a

---

enough, but even clearer at *EN* 1108a 23-6, *EE* 1234a 4-23. *Eutrapelia* is aligned with, and illustrated by, the style of humour in 'new comedies' (1128a 23). This is one reason for rejecting the strong division between ethics and art posited by Cooper (1922) 121-3. The other is that in this passage of *EN* Ar. explicitly links what one will say oneself with what one is prepared to hear from others (which includes comic drama): hence, importantly, the fact that he is ready to envisage restrictive legislation on stage-comedy (1128a 30f., cf. *Pol.* 1336b 14ff.). In all this, Ar. is close to Plato, esp. *Laws* 934d-936; and for the underlying principle cf. ch. VI n.39.

[32] For a survey of Ar.'s references to comic poets see Cooper (1922) 150-61, from which it is obvious that Epicharmus was well-known and important to him (for Plato's estimate see *Theaet.* 152e). This might mean that Ar. favoured mythological subjects for comedy: as well as *Poet.* 53a 37f. (n.28 above) note his references to Strattis and Anaxandrides, poets who seem to have had a penchant for mythological burlesque, though admittedly so did others (cf. R.L. Hunter, *Eubulus: The Fragments* (Cambridge 1983) 22-30). 51b 13f. evidently refers to non-mythological comedies, but it does not entail this as a necessary element of the comic ideal.

[33] It may be worth illustrating how opinion is divided on comic *katharsis*. Believers include Vahlen (1911) 233f., Bywater xxiii and 152, Rostagni (1945) LIV, Stark 91f. Unbelievers: Zeller 772, Gudeman 145, 166, Else (1957) 447, Olson (1968) 36, Lord

hypothetical Aristotelian theory of comedy, on the assumption that this theory will have closely followed the detailed shape of the theory of tragedy. Such an assumption is unwarranted, and it certainly receives no support from the use in *Poetics* 5 of the term *hamartêma*, cognate with tragic *hamartia*, for the species of 'error' or 'failing' which is the characteristic object of comedy.[34] *Hamartêma*, which like *hamartia* itself is capable of a wide range of meaning, is introduced in explication of the general ethical nature and tone of comedy, as part of the definition of the baseness which the agents of comedy typically display. But this represents a broad contrast with tragedy, whose characters are 'better than present humanity', and it can have little or nothing in common with tragic *hamartia*, which is a specific component of the 'complex' plot, to which we have no sufficient reason for positing a comic analogue.

To rule out, as I believe we should, the possibility that the theory of comedy will simply have been a reverse image of that of tragedy (that 'the *Poetics* can be metamorphosed into a treatise on comedy'),[35] is not to deny that Aristotle was interested in individual points of contact and contrast between the genres. The passage at the end of ch. 13 remains evidence that Aristotle grasped the mixed nature of the relationship between tragedy and comedy, but also that he was aware of the peculiar challenge to a theory of the genres posed by their tendency towards convergence in recent dramatic history – in the movement initiated by Euripides towards the tragic melodrama of the happy ending, and in comedy's apparently

---

(1982) 175f. with n. 54. Agnostics: Cooper (1922) 63-90, Lucas (1968) 287-9. The decisive consideration, I believe, is that the Platonic charge (esp. *Rep.* 388e-9a, 606a-d) calls for comic just as much as for tragic *katharsis*, and this is corroborated in the neo-platonic evidence on the subject, cited by Janko 146 in what is now the major discussion of comic *katharsis* (136-51), though he overestimates, in my view, the value of the *Tractatus Coislinianus* on this point.

It is difficult to say what emotions Ar. would regard as aroused by comedy. Plato, *Phileb.* 49b-e, makes *phthonos* fundamental, expressing our superiority over the self-ignorant agents of comic drama. But Ar.'s view of *phthonos* at *Rhet.* 1387b 22ff. and 1388a 35-8, is different, and can hardly be so relevant to comedy, despite Cooper (1922) 60-98, who tentatively suggests anger and envy as the comic emotions. Lucas (1957) 45 thinks of *Schadenfreude* and the like: improbable. Janko 143 does nothing to justify the peculiar claim that laughter was an emotion for Ar.

[34] Janko 208-10, rightly citing *Rhet.*1384b 10 for the parallel use of *hamartiai*, acknowledges the difference.

[35] Cooper (1922) 17. Cooper's enterprise, as the quotation intimates, is often mechanically parasitic on the *Poetics*. A freer critical attempt to erect a theory of comedy on Aristotelian foundations is that of Olson (1968), esp. 36ff. and 45ff.

increasing sentimentality and potential seriousness. It is with reference to this passage that I wish, in conclusion, to note a paradox in Aristotle's own attitudes. The paradox hinges in part around the *Odyssey*, which is here said to belong to the second-best type of tragedy, in which both good and bad receive their deserts. But a liking for this kind of tragedy, according to Aristotle, displays 'weakness', and the pleasure which it affords is 'more suitable to comedy'. The equivocation discernible here – whereby the *Odyssey* is simultaneously taken to be a legitimate, if imperfect, example of tragedy (as it is regularly implied to be throughout the *Poetics*) and yet to provide an experience which has something in common with that of comedy – cannot be dissociated from the deeper uncertainty in Aristotle's theory over whether the final movement of the action in a tragedy should be towards or away from misfortune, an uncertainty which is of course crystallised in the tensions between chs. 13 and 14 of the treatise. The *Odyssey*, it seems, has two faces – the long history of the hero's suffering, and the final *metabasis* to good fortune – and because of this can be classed either as a complex tragedy, as it is in ch. 24, or as at least akin to the spirit of comedy. The later critical cliché that tragedy and comedy are distinguished by their respectively unhappy and happy endings is not straight-forwardly anticipated in the *Poetics*. The implications of this may be deeper for Aristotle's view of tragedy than of comedy: the primary significance for the latter, so far as we can now see, lies in the confirmation that Aristotelian comedy is ultimately to bring us round to a conclusion conformable to moral equilibrium.

*

In the programme announced in its opening sentence, as well as in various later parts of the work, the *Poetics* purports to offer a theory of the whole art of poetry. Yet to the genres which receive explicit treatment, tragedy and epic, we can add only the lost analysis of comedy (and perhaps also iambus)[36] in the second book of the treatise. This still leaves a large range of archaic and classical Greek

---

[36] I doubt whether we can be quite as sure as Janko e.g. 61, 69 that Ar. regarded iambus as unmimetic and so as 'not poetry at all'. Despite his objections to iambic invective, and despite *Poetics* 9's stress on universals, Ar. does seem to allow for mimesis of individuals and particulars at 48b 23-49a 6: cf. ch. II n.15. Moreover, since at least some iambic poems were *performed* in Ar.'s time (*Pol.* 1336b 20f.), it is hard to see how Ar. could have denied them poetic status altogether.

poetry untouched. In one case, that of dithyramb, which is twice included in a list of relevant genres in the opening chapter, Aristotle does seem to provide by implication an explanation for the fact that no formal analysis of the genre is forthcoming. In ch. 4 we are told that tragedy came into being 'from those who led the dithyramb' (49a 10f.), which presumably intimates the view that dithyramb has been artistically superseded by tragedy, and therefore does not call for independent discussion.[37] If the neglect of dithyramb, and the kindred genre of *nomos*, can be accounted for in this way, all we have left in the *Poetics* by way of consideration of genres other than epic and the two forms of drama is a handful of minor references and quotations: several mentions of iambus; one of hymns and encomia; one of elegy, as well as one possible quotation from elegy; one or two apparent allusions to burlesque epic; a reference to prose mimes and Socratic dialogues; two small quotations which might, but are not especially likely to, belong to non-dramatic lyric; two references to the somewhat mysterious 'mixed rhapsody' of Chairemon; and finally, a number of quotations from a writer whom the *Poetics* argues should not be called a poet at all, Empedocles.[38] There is no trace of the poetry of (to cite the most obvious cases) Hesiod, Archilochus, Sappho, Solon, Theognis, Simonides or Pindar.

It should be stressed at once that the issue I am raising is not why Aristotle chose to concentrate on tragedy and epic, but why, in a work which promises and evidently aspires to theoretical comprehensiveness, he should have omitted such a large amount of Greek poetry altogether. That Aristotle had good reason to pay most attention to tragedy, the major poetic genre in classical Athens, and to Homeric epic, whose preeminent cultural status in the Greek world had long been established, is not in doubt. But we must beware of sliding from this recognition into the supposition that other genres and other poets were unfamiliar or negligible. Gerald Else has suggested that Aristotle was concerned to deal with the poetry which

---

[37] It is reasonable to suppose that Ar. did not think highly of dithyramb, whose poets are called 'bombastic' (*psophōdeis*) at *Rhet.* 1406b 2; cf. the comparison between dithyrambic preludes and epideictic exordia at 1415a 10f. *Poet.* 61b 30-2 probably refers to the antics of dithyrambic performers.

[38] Iambus: 47b 11 (by implication), 48b 30ff. (with 49a 4), 49b 8, 51b 14f.; cf. 58b 9. Hymns and encomia: 48b 27. Elegy: 47b 12-14, 58a 29f. (with Athen. 452B). Burlesque: 48a 12-14, 57a 35f. Mimes and Socratic dialogues: 47b 10f. Non-dramatic lyric (?): 57b 29, 58a 29f. Chairemon: 47b 21f., 60a 2 (see Collard 24f.). Empedocles: 57b 13f., 24, 58a 5, 61a 24.

would have seemed important to the 'Athenian on the street'.[39] But
the *Poetics* is not a treatise for the man on the street, and even in these
terms some of Aristotle's omissions remain difficult to explain. If we
look to fourth-century sources, including Aristotle's own writings,
we find that most if not all of the poets I earlier listed were still
familiar and important. All, for one thing, are quoted by Aristotle
himself elsewhere. It is unnecessary to dwell on the status of each of
these writers, but it is pertinent to indicate that the fourth-century
standing of Hesiod, to take the strongest instance, was comparable to
that of Homer. Plato on several occasions cites Homer and Hesiod
together as the two great figures of Greek poetry, and he refers to
Hesiod more often than to any other poet except Homer himself.[40]
Aeschines significantly quotes lines of Hesiod's to popular Athenian
juries in the 340s and 330s – on one occasion citing the *Works and
Days* as the sort of poetry which the Athenians learn for life in their
childhood.[41]

A number of extrinsic reasons have been put forward to account
for the *Poetics'* neglect of large areas of existing Greek poetry. It has
been hypothesised, by Bywater among others, that lyric poetry is
excluded on the grounds that it was held to be more a branch of
music than of poetry. This argument is related to an explanation
which I mentioned and discarded in the previous chapter for the
scant attention paid to lyrics within the analysis of tragedy.[42] While
it need not be disputed that Aristotle would have wanted to separate
off the musical element in all lyric poetry as an independent art, this
can hardly provide us with a satisfactory reason for the almost total
failure to assess the poetic status of the various lyric genres. The

[39] Else (1957) 15 n.56.

[40] *Apol.* 41a, *Ion* 531a ff., *Crat.* 402b, *Rep.* 363-4, 377d, 600d, 612b, *Tim.* 21d, *Laws*
658d. Cf. *Protag.* 316d.

[41] Aeschin. 3.135, cf. 1.129, 2.144, 158. Some other classical references to Hesiod:
Aristoph. *Frogs* 1033f., Xen. *Mem.* 1.2.56, Isoc. 12.33 (where the description of those
who recite Homer and Hesiod in the Lyceum and 'drivel about them' is too early
(c.342-339) to refer to the Peripatetics, though sometimes taken this way). For Ar.'s
own references to Hesiod see Bonitz s.v. At *Met.* 984b 23ff. Hesiod is cited alongside
Parmenides as a source of philosophical ideas; cf. also 1000a 9, *Phys.* 208b 29ff., *Cael.*
298b 28f. (where the verb *phusiologein* connects with *Poet.* 47b 19), Plato *Symp.* 178b,
195c, and Plut. *Mor.* 402e-f. It is quite likely that Ar. would have said of much of
Hesiod's work something analogous to his comment on Empedocles at 47b 17-20. For
Hesiod in philosophical company see also Heraclitus fr. 40.

[42] Bywater on 47a 8 (but the passages cited there do *not* support a separation
between *melopoeia* and 'poetry proper'), Ross 290, House 41, Atkins vol. 1, 75. Cf. ch.
VJII pp. 238ff. above.

widespread involvement of music in Greek poetry, and the dominance of the verbal over the musical component in lyric forms, would have made it a very strange procedure to overlook lyric poetry purely on the grounds of its musical dimension, which is in any case allowed for in the scheme of poetic media set out in ch. 1 of the treatise. Nor is it any more adequate to argue that Aristotle chose to leave aside poetic genres which were no longer actively practised in his own day.[43] Such a view founders on the twin facts that the *Poetics* cannot be simply taken as a manual of poetic composition, and that one of the two kinds of poetry which it does examine, epic, was no commoner in the fourth century than were those which Aristotle omits.

Two further explanatory factors bring us closer, I believe, to the heart of the matter, though still not all the way. The first of these is the strongly evaluative aspect of Aristotle's theory of poetry. Not only does the *Poetics* communicate judgements of relative merit on individual instances of particular genres, but it is also prepared, most obviously in the case of tragedy and epic, to assess whole genres in relation to one another. Tragedy is a superior genre to epic, and by implication to dithyramb too; comedy is superior to iambus; and presumably such rankings would hold for other types of poetry too. The second factor is itself an element in Aristotle's evaluations, namely his belief in the natural dynamics of poetic and cultural evolution. It is specifically this sense of progressive evolution which leads to the comparative rating of tragedy, epic and dithyramb. These two related factors combine to express an Aristotelian conviction that it ought to be possible to define the character and attributes of poetry at its best. Poetic genres are not truly independent; they are parts of a single, evolving art. Thus Aristotle betrays in a number of places an ultimate interest in 'the art of poetry itself', an abstraction which he nowhere feels any pressure to justify.

It seems initially plausible that this feature of the *Poetics* should supply the explanation for the omission of a number of kinds of poetry. The genres which Aristotle does include could be said to be representative of the art, and of the art at its best; further material need not be examined. That there must indeed be an evaluative

---

[43] E.g. Finsler 65-7, Lucas (1968) on 47a 13 and p. 267. Note, for comparison, that Plato often refers to a wide range of genres in his discussions of poetry: e.g. *Ion* 534c (dithyramb, encomia, hyporchemata, epic, iambus), *Laws* 700a-b (hymns, *thrênoi*, paeans, dithyramb, nomes).

ingredient in the neglect of these other genres is an important truth, but there are two simple reasons why the factors indicated above do not amount to a sufficient account of it. The first is that the Aristotelian model of poetic evolution cannot in itself allow us to understand why lyric, didactic and elegiac poetry receives virtually no attention. If the version of poetic history found in chs. 4 and 5 contains many problems where epic, tragedy, dithyramb and comedy are concerned, there is no conceivable way in which the three areas of poetry mentioned above could have been imagined to be subsumed within those on which the treatise concentrates. In the second place, and more generally, simply to infer that genres on which Aristotle is largely silent were ranked by him as inferior to those which he discusses, is hardly to provide a proper explanation of the silence. It remains to be asked on what such an assessment might have been based, and to consider what sort of relation exists between the main principles of the theory of poetry and the types of poetic material which are left out of the analysis.[44]

The central tenets of the *Poetics* do, I think, make it possible to understand why large tracts of lyric, elegiac and didactic verse are excluded from, or hardly touched on within, the theory of poetry contained in the treatise. At the very centre of the theory, as we saw in earlier chapters, is the concept of mimesis. It is by virtue of mimesis, Aristotle declares in ch. 9, that the poet *is* a poet. But I have tried to show that the Aristotelian notion of poetic mimesis, which is so basic to the theory and yet is nowhere elucidated in a sustained manner, can be seen to involve more than one type of perception of poetry, and that these various perceptions have not been entirely integrated or harmonised. The strongest thrust, however, behind Aristotle's interest in mimesis is towards a heavily *dramatic* or enactive characterisation of the nature of poetry. The particular poetic genres cited by Aristotle in the opening section of the book all point in this direction, and the first categorical indication of it comes

---

[44] A variety of other reasons have been offered for Ar.'s omissions. Among them, Potts 67 ('the Greeks seem to have regarded personal poetry as a kind of rhetoric') must rank as the most curious. House 41 goes too far in suggesting that Ar. regarded lyric as absorbed by drama (and the neglect of tragic lyrics only compounds the problem). The explanation of T. Gomperz, *Greek Thinkers* vol. 4, Engl. transl. (London 1912) 407, that Ar. 'had no sense whatever for lyric poetry', is too subjective. Nor does it help to suppose, with A. Weir Smyth, *Greek Melic Poets* (London 1900) xxiv, that dithyramb in the *Poetics* (cf. n. 37 above) is representative of lyric poetry as a whole: see Bywater on 47a 14 for the correction.

with ch. 2's premise that the object of mimesis is 'men in action'. If the scheme of mimetic modes given in ch. 3 seems at first sight to be supple enough to cover most genres, this calls for two qualifications.

First, the mode of 'report' or 'narrative' (*apangelia*) will not, unless taken very nebulously, suit the full range of genres other than epic.[45] Lyric, elegiac and didactic poetry depend considerably on modes of discourse other than enactment and narrative, though all may make use of these too in one way or another. Modes such as exhortation or protreptic, moralistic gnomes or other kinds of generalisation, prayer and the invocation of deities, and the direct statement of feeling and belief – all these and others can find no secure or clear place in Aristotle's framework of poetic mimesis. Secondly, the narrative mode in any case comes to hold a dubious status in the theory, being deprecated even for epic in contrast to the mode of enactment which represents the poet's true art. But if even the narrative mode can be described, and devalued, by the significant phrase, 'to speak in one's own person' (60a 7),[46] it is evident that all the poetic genres neglected by Aristotle would fail this test of poetic character. This is most blatantly true of didactic and elegiac verse, in which the author's own person – understood, it should be stressed, as a 'voice' or mode, not necessarily an autobiographical reality – is a dominant generic feature. But the controlling use of a first-person mode of utterance, explicitly or implicitly representing the poetic subject, is also widely found in the various types of lyric poetry which the *Poetics* leaves out of account. It hardly matters that the 'mimesis of men in

---

[45] Teichmüller vol. 1, 22-7, thinks lyric is covered here. It is true that Plato gives dithyramb as the prime instance of *apangelia* at *Rep.* 394c 2f., and 398d 4-6 refers back, for lyric generally, to the earlier scheme of modes. If Ar.'s *apangelia* inc' :des the various styles of lyric, however, the fact remains that the *Poetics* gives not the slightest hint of this. It is certainly strange of Russell 19 to claim, presumably with reference to *Poetics* 3, that Ar. emphasised the narrative aspect of lyric poetry (107 skirts round the status of lyric in the treatise).

[46] Ar.'s awareness of the difference between authorial statement and the dramatic utterances of characters (cf. fr. 146 Rose, from *Homeric Problems*) does not prevent him outside the theoretical confines of the *Poetics* from the ordinary, unreflective habit of citation whereby even dramatic sentiments are seemingly ascribed to the author: see esp. *EN* 1136a 11f. (Euripides), 1155b 2 (Euripides, alongside Heraclitus and Empedocles), *Pol.* 1252b 7ff. ('the poets' and Hesiod), fr. 94 Rose (Euripides). Ar. was also sometimes prepared to draw biographical inferences from poetry: *Pol.* 1296a 19f. (Solon), fr. 515 Rose (Theodorus). For an equivalent discrepancy between Ar.'s theoretical definition of poetry in the *Poetics* and his casual, non-theoretical references to poetry elsewhere, see the passages cited by Janko 124, adding *Rhet.* 1407a 35, where Empedocles is treated as a poet, and 1405a 8, where 'verses' is synonymous with poetry.

action' plays *some* part in these and other genres:the essential factor is that mimesis, so understood, could not be claimed to be of primary importance in the work of any of the 'missing' poets whom I listed earlier. The whole system of analysis offered in the opening chapters of the work appears to be designed for a small group of poetic genres, and leaves obscure the question of how other kinds could be accommodated to it.

I shall return to the notion of the poet speaking in his own person in the conclusion to this section, after first considering the neglected areas of Greek poetry in relation to one of Aristotle's other central concepts, that of the poetic *muthos* or plot-structure. The premise that this concept is basic to poetry is insinuated in the first sentence of the *Poetics*, where the construction of *muthoi* seems to represent an aspect of the art as a whole. This is at once striking, and anticipates the development of the association between mimesis and action. While there is an ostensible precedent for the notion of *muthos* in Plato's general use of kindred terminology for the activities of poets, there is no precedent at all for the specialised sense of *muthos* which the *Poetics* goes on to elaborate.[47] Yet plot-structure turns out, it hardly needs to be reiterated, to be fundamental to Aristotle's theory not just of drama and epic, but of poetry as a whole. It is in ch. 9, one of the passages where the argument broadens out from tragedy to generalise about all poetry, that we find the conclusion that 'the poet ought to be a maker of *muthoi* rather than of verses' (51b 27f.). The plot-structure, in the new view of the poet-maker's craft, is the poet's true artefact, the design and structure which it is the essence of his art to make and shape. Yet this doctrine presumes, just as it helps to illuminate, the *Poetics'* principle of mimesis, and the crucial involvement of action in the latter means that a poetic *muthos* cannot be taken to be *any* sort of unified poetic construction, but only the special product of the mimesis of agents. Plot-structure, that is, like Aristotelian poetic mimesis itself, is an essentially dramatic concept, and it therefore makes no provision for precisely the same kinds of material as have already been seen to be excluded by the theory of mimesis. Even human themes will not provide suitable substance for a poetic *muthos* unless they are organised into a single structure of action. Such things as the role of myth in epinikian lyric or of fable (another sense of *muthos*) in iambic poetry will not bring these genres

47 On *muthos* see ch. II n.16.

within Aristotle's framework of analysis.

Since I have commented sufficiently on Aristotle's rejection of certain modes as inappropriate to poetry, two other implications of the concept of poetic plot-structure deserve to be emphasised. The first is unity. 'Just as in the other mimetic arts a unified mimesis is a mimesis of a single object, so a *muthos*, since it is the mimesis of an action, should be the mimesis of a single, entire action' (51a 30-2). The unity of the Aristotelian work of art reflects the unity of its object, and, where dramatic poetry is concerned, the logic of poetic unity depends, as I tried to show in ch. III, on the logic and intelligibility of causality in human affairs. Whatever the virtues of Aristotle's single-minded and repeated insistence on unity may be, his specific and strict understanding of the nature of unity leads him to find fault with much in the existing practice of both tragedy and epic. Even with reference to the genres in which Aristotle is most interested, and to which the applicability of his standard of unity is most direct, there are remaining difficulties concerning the degree of preconception in the theory. But in the case of the genres which are not discussed in the treatise, the problems are altogether more fundamental and inescapable. It is virtually impossible to see how the mixed and often paratactic structure of Hesiodic didactic, or the oblique and shifting techniques of much Greek lyric, or the varied moralising and exhortatory threads of elegiac poetry, could be brought into relation with the criterion of unity presented in the *Poetics*. In all these other genres, we have to deal with particular conventions and expectations which affect the types of unity that are possible and desirable. If, as Aristotle seems to claim, a plot-structure is indispensable to a true work of poetry, and if the plot-structure brings with it the canon of unity which the *Poetics* assigns to it, then the Aristotelian theory of poetry becomes very inhospitable to these other genres and to their rather different conceptions of what gives the individual work its cohesion and integrity.

Connected with Aristotle's doctrine of unity is his view of scale or size, and while what he says on this subject is less rigid than his pronouncements on unity, its implications may nonetheless be worth brief scrutiny. Two passages do in fact lend some support to the suspicion that Aristotle's attitude to artistic scale tends towards an absolutist position. The first is the section of ch. 7 where he seems to suggest that there is a naturally determined beauty of size, a universal standard of proportion. The problematic character of this submission is obscured by the way in which Aristotle cites the extremes of the massive and the minuscule, thus leaving uncertainty over how judgements are to be made on all that falls within these limits.[48] A passage in ch. 24 (59b 20-2), where the appropriate length for an epic poem is specified as the equivalent of three tragedies, leaves no doubt that Aristotle was prepared to make drastic criticisms of the scale of poems in the light of his sense of natural proportion, even where, as in the case of the Homeric epics, the special scale of the works is inextricable from their distinctive conception and design. But it is the question of insufficient, rather than excessive, length which appears to be most pertinent as regards those genres neglected by the *Poetics*. If we leave didactic aside, the majority of works in the categories of lyric and elegiac poetry are much shorter than the standard length of tragedies; and it may be justifiable to speculate whether on this ground alone Aristotle might have thought them too small to be unified or beautiful, or to allow profitable contemplation.

The notion of appropriate scale remains, however, inchoate, and dependent on that of unity. Unity in turn forces us back to Aristotle's basic understanding of poetry as the mimesis of men in action. It is ultimately at this fundamental level, as I have argued, that the explanation lies for the concentration on tragedy and epic, and the neglect of didactic, lyric and elegiac poetry. The goal of poetic mimesis, for Aristotle, is the dramatic, and the antithesis of this is summed up in the idea of the poet speaking in his own person (60a 7f.). It may be suggestive to end this chapter – and with it my substantial critique of the *Poetics* – with a reflection on this contrast in relation to the standard Greek view of the poet as a teacher. It was this view of the poet's didactic status and function against which Plato had reacted, and which led him to regard poetry and philosophy as locked in an 'age-old quarrel' (*Rep.* 607b). Aristotle's response to this issue can now be seen to be paradoxical. On the one hand, he assimilates poetry to philosophy more than once in the *Poetics*, most significantly in ch. 9. He does this by trying to elevate the art above an interest in particulars, and by attributing to it the power to dramatise general truths about human action. On the other hand, and perhaps as part of the same intention, Aristotle denies that

---

[48] On Ar.'s characteristic hyperbole in this passage see Vahlen (1885) on 51a 2. For recognition of the *relativity* of scale see *Cat.* 5b 15ff., and for the connection between size and unity see ch. III pp. 98f. and n.27.

the poet is truly a poet when he speaks in his own person. From this latter point of view the *Poetics* could be said to represent a denial of the poet's status as a teacher, while in the former respect Aristotle may be thought of as reintegrating a potentially enlightening element into his theory of poetic mimesis. Part of the price to be paid for the redistributed emphasis of this new perspective is a virtually exclusive attention to dramatic poetry, and an apparent insensitivity to some of the very different achievements of other genres.

X

Influence & Status:
the *Nachleben* of the *Poetics*

If one ventures at all far into the interpretation of the *Poetics*, one is likely to be enticed in various ways into the history of the work's reception and influence. Although this history is in certain respects an independent cultural phenomenon which the reader of the *Poetics* can afford, if he chooses, to leave aside, it is not entirely so, for apart from producing lines of enquiry and thought which are still with us, it has also helped to shape the formation of fundamental concepts and issues in the modern tradition of literary, and especially dramatic, theory and criticism. These concepts are apt to seem inescapable, so deeply embedded are they in common attitudes to poetry and drama. Though we no longer live in an age of neo-classicism, it would take a more radical and drastic break with the past of European culture than even the more brutal forms of modernism have effected to efface altogether the traces of the *Poetics*' continuing presence and insidious influence. Since the interpreter of the treatise is, therefore, whether he likes it or not, partially constrained from the start by interests and presuppositions which the work itself has been instrumental in creating, some intelligent awareness of the ways in which the treatise has been read and misread over the centuries, and of the more complex ways in which these readings and misreadings have insinuated themselves into the broader field of criticism, should be regarded as a necessary part of an aspiration to see the *Poetics* fully in perspective.

Yet to execute this task with anything approaching completeness would be an excessive ambition even for a whole volume, let alone a single chapter such as this. My aim here must therefore stop short of a detailed history of the *Poetics*' *Nachleben*. A number of contributions to such a history have been made by others, as well as various shorter attempts to map out the extent and contours of the relevant territory.[1] This chapter is designed only incidentally to provide another such outline; my chief intention is to offer an interpretative essay on the patterns and trends to be discerned in some of the more important areas of the subject. In the interests of selectivity, certain themes and topics prominent in the accounts of others will not be laboriously retraced here. I think especially of the all too familiar doctrine of the Three Unities, the classic case of a literary principle speciously foisted upon the *Poetics* (and therefore a pointed reminder of how little the treatise was actually *read*, as opposed to being simply appealed to, even in the most self-consciously neo-classical circles). It will also inevitably be impossible to pursue the wider ramifications of the *Poetics'* influence, such as the infiltration of its ideas into the criticism of the visual arts. Finally, this chapter does not constitute a survey of scholarship in the narrower sense, though it will include some observations on this within the larger framework of attitudes to the reading of the treatise.

*

The immediate fate of the *Poetics* after Aristotle's death, and its fortunes during the following two and a half centuries, are enshrouded in a general mist of obscurity which surrounds the history of Aristotle's entire *oeuvre* in the Hellenistic period. To enter into the wider debate on this subject would serve little purpose, though incredulity seems to me the appropriate response to ancient anecdotes repeatedly cited as evidence.[2] Where the *Poetics* is concerned, the problem is complicated beyond the hope of a clear solution by the fact that Aristotle had published more than one work on poetry (most pertinently, the dialogue *On Poets*, and *Homeric Problems* in several books), and while our ignorance of these is considerable, it seems beyond doubt that they shared some matter with the *Poetics*.[3] Interpretation of the evidence for knowledge of Aristotle's literary views and theories is therefore hazardous, and it is made only more so by the difficulties of reconstructing the work of early Peripatetic writers such as Theophrastus, Satyrus and Neoptolemus, who are likely both to have borrowed from Aristotle

---

[1] For surveys of some of the relevant material see Cooper (1923) chs. VII-XIII, Fuhrmann (1973) 188-308, Hutton 24-34. More specialised works are cited in the notes below.

[2] On the fate and knowledge of Ar.'s esoteric works in the Hellenistic period see P. Moraux, *Der Aristotelismus bei den Griechen* (Berlin 1973) 3-94.

[3] See ch. I n.2, ch. IX n.20, and cf. Appendix 1 §2.

and to have qualified or altered his ideas. It was one of these writers, Neoptolemus, who appears to have been the intermediate source by which some Aristotelian material became available to Horace for the *Ars Poetica*. Now that both Neoptolemus' own work and so much other Hellenistic criticism has been lost, we are left not only with the impossibility of defining the transmission of Aristotelian ideas to Horace with any precision, but also with the paradox, so full of significance for the status of the *Poetics* in Renaissance literary theory, that while the *Poetics* as such was certainly not widely known in the Hellenistic and Roman periods, Horace's poem stands out as a major document which incorporates and reworks much that had originally been formulated in the *Poetics*.[4]

Most readers of the *Poetics* and *Ars Poetica* in the Renaissance and the subsequent era of neo-classicism were oblivious to this paradox; to them the relation between the two works was transparent and unproblematic: Horace was Aristotle's 'premier interprète', as René Rapin was representatively to put it, and their views of poetry were entirely complementary.[5] To such an ahistorical point of view, seeing all classical ideas in a single dimension, the radical shifts in presupposition and emphasis between Aristotle and Horace were lost to sight. Even if we leave aside the strong differences of tone and presentation between treatise and literary epistle, a gulf divides the poet from the philosopher. From one angle this can best be seen in terms of cultural context. Two related factors had dominated the background to the *Poetics*: the first was the standing of Homeric and tragic poetry; the second was Plato's hostile reaction against this cultural force. Aristotle was extremely close to, if not entirely of, the Athenian society in which Homer and the tragedians had acquired such central importance. On the positive side, therefore, these genres were of paramount concern. Aristotle's existence as a philosopher

[4] A bold but excessively confident attempt to find traces of the *Poetics*' influence in the ancient world is made by Rostagni (1955) 188-237. Brink (1963), esp. 79-119, takes a more temperate view in connection with Horace and his sources. For sketches of the Hellenistic developments in criticism see Fuhrmann (1973) 121-34 and Russell ch. 3. On the Peripatetics in general see A.J. Podlecki, 'The Peripatetics as Literary Critics', *Phoenix* 23 (1969) 114-37. There is no doubt that in time, and through various filtering channels, many Aristotelian ideas did become commonplace: see, for example, the echoes of his terminology and principles in the Homeric scholia, illustrated most recently by N. J. Richardson, 'Literary Criticism in the Exegetical Scholia to the *Iliad*', *CQ* 30 (1980) 265-87. Cf. also n.7 below.

[5] *René Rapin: Les Réflexions sur la Poétique de ce temps etc.*, ed. E.T. Dubois (Geneva 1970) 20.

gave him an essential framework within which to view poetry, and against which to measure its claims. I have tried in this book to show that, while he was not led to endorse the philosophical condemnation of poetry that Plato and others before him had reached, his approach to the subject was nonetheless philosophically conditioned for that. To grasp the full force of the *Poetics'* doctrines, we need to take some account of such matters as Aristotle's philosophy of action, of knowledge and pleasure, of emotion, and of art's relation to nature. But in this sense Horace's view of poetry can certainly not be called philosophical, despite a streak of philosophical ethics in the Horatian outlook as a whole. Nor was Horace in a position to give the intense concentration to epic and tragedy which the *Poetics* provides. Although these genres receive as much attention as any others in the *Ars Poetica*, the work is not built around them, nor are we left with an overriding sense of their cultural importance, as is the case with the *Poetics*. That this should be so, in a Roman literary epistle, is hardly a cause for surprise.

But the fundamental change which has occurred between Aristotle and Horace is not primarily a matter of Greek and Roman; it is rather a reflection of the domination acquired over literary criticism during the Hellenistic period by rhetoric. In contrast to Aristotle, for whom rhetoric is one component element within tragedy and epic, and for whom the poetic production of emotion is not a matter of manipulating an audience but of constructing a literary artefact with certain objectively emotive properties (ch. VI above), the Hellenistic age saw the establishment of a thoroughly rhetorical view of poetry, or even, for some, of language in general. Such a view, which may already be discernible in Aristotle's successor Theophrastus, has a tendency to drive a wedge between style and content, and to emphasise the former at the expense of the latter. One consequence of this is a concern with discrete linguistic effects rather than coherent structures; another is a penchant for compositional formulae and rules. These features can all be found in the *Ars Poetica*, a work whose opening subject is unity, but which notably fails (or refuses) to give central value to this principle, and which mirrors this fact in its own epistolary avoidance of obvious cohesion. This is not to convict the poem of being addicted to rhetorical theory, or to deny Horace his special purposes in dealing with such matters, nor is it to argue that the *Poetics* itself has no affinities with rhetorical theory, but simply to suggest that the dominant colouring of Horace's poem and doctrines, for all their superficial resemblance to Aristotle's, is that of the rhetorical preoccupation with the conditions imposed by an audience. I would contend that it is also a symptom of this preoccupation, as Hellenistic criticism had developed it, that we find in the *Ars Poetica* the classic polarisation of the poet's functions ('aut prodesse volunt aut delectare poetae', *AP* 333). While the roots of this argument lie far back in Greek culture, the polarisation of the issue was a Hellenistic phenomenon, and in particular it contrasts with the way in which Aristotle had declined to force the question of poetry's ethical significance into a crudely reductive dichotomy.[6]

These considerations on the relation between the *Ars Poetica* and the *Poetics* broach matters which will later recur in discussion of neo-classicism's treatment of Aristotle's ideas on literature. Between Horace and the Renaissance there is little to note.[7] Only a handful of cursory references or allusions to the *Poetics* can be found in the works of late antiquity, and even some of these can hardly be relied upon; certainly few need imply first-hand familiarity. Although we do not know at what date the treatise lost its second book, in which comedy was analysed, the fact of this damage to the work can be taken as evidence of its neglect and of the small number of copies of it which must have existed. Some neo-platonist commentators on Aristotle had knowledge of the *Poetics*, but scarcely any real interest in it; its subject had started to acquire the remoteness which would only increase in the course of the Middle Ages, and it is not altogether surprising that the neo-platonists found reason to classify both the *Poetics* and the *Rhetoric* as appendages to the Aristotelian system of logic.[8] This view was to be perpetuated by the Arabic philosophers who encountered the work from the tenth century onwards in a translation (or possibly more than one) made in turn from a Syriac version of perhaps a century earlier. The significance of this involvement of the *Poetics* in the general movement of Islamic Aristotelianism is that it produced, among other works, the

---

[6] For relevant Hellenistic material see Pfeiffer 166f. On Ar.'s position see ch. I pp. 3-6 above.

[7] For late ancient references (real or possible) to the *Poetics* see Bywater 261f., Janko 64f., 88f., 115, 172f., the passages quoted by Kassel 50-2, and cf. n.4 above.

[8] See R. Walzer, *Greek into Arabic* (Oxford 1962) 129-36, P. Moraux, *Les Listes Anciennes des Ouvrages d'Aristote* (Louvain 1951) 179ff., and Dahiyat (next note) 12-20.

twelfth-century 'middle commentary' of Averroes.[9] This was translated into Latin by Hermannus Alemannus in 1256 in the revival of Aristotelianism which occurred in this period, and which was also marked by a second Latin translation, composed by William of Moerbeke, friend of Aquinas, in 1278. The latter version, made directly from the Greek by one of the very few Europeans of the day with knowledge of the language, was lost until the present century, and was consequently without influence.[10] But Hermannus' translation of Averroes, incorporating the many basic misunderstandings which arose from study of the alien work at several removes from the original, was to be printed with further garbling in 1481, and again during the sixteenth century. Before that, there is some evidence to suggest that Hermannus' work was used in the fourteenth century, probably at Paris, for the teaching of the *Poetics* as a contribution to Aristotelian logic.[11] That this should have been so, and that Averroes' paraphrase should have continued to be read even in the Cinquecento, when far superior versions had become available, stands as a reminder that the Renaissance did not mark an immediate or complete break with medieval culture.

The preservation of the Greek text, minus the second book, was due to the literary culture of Byzantium, where some of its ideas found their way, though not without considerable dilution, into pedagogic treatises on poetry.[12] This precious if limited interest was sufficient to ensure the survival of two independent manuscripts, the earlier and more important of which was widely copied in fifteenth-century Italy. It was from one of these copies that the first

[9] On the earlier Arabic work on the *Poetics* see I.M. Dahiyat, *Avicenna's Commentary on the Poetics of Aristotle* (Leiden 1974): Dahiyat argues on pp. 4-9 for a second tenth-century translation from the Syriac. For Averroes' work consult C.E. Butterworth, *Averroes' Three Short Commentaries on Aristotle's Topics, Rhetoric and Poetics* (New York 1977), and on its dominant ideas and their influence see Hardison (1970).

[10] See L. Minio-Paluello, ed., *Aristoteles Latinus XXXIII: De Arte Poetica* 2nd edn. (Brussels 1968).

[11] On Hermannus' translation see W. F. Boggess, 'Hermannus Alemannus and Catharsis in the Medieval Latin *Poetics*', *CW* 62 (1969) 212-14: Boggess shows that Hermannus himself should be exonerated from some of the faults of the later printed version, on which see Weinberg 352-61. For the early Renaissance see E.N. Tigerstedt, 'Observations on the Reception of the Aristotelian *Poetics* in the Latin West', *SR* 15 (1968) 7-24, and Boggess, 'Aristotle's *Poetics* in the Fourteenth Century', *SP* 67 (1970) 278-94.

[12] For an example see the treatise edited by Browning. I would also place the *Tractatus Coislinianus* somewhere in this category, despite the indefatigable arguments of Janko to the contrary.

printed text of the *Poetics* was established at Venice in 1508.[13] This
Aldine text was reused in several of the editions of the treatise
produced in Italy in the course of the same century, in the period
which represents not just the Renaissance rediscovery of the work,
but the most intensive concern with the *Poetics* shown at any time
between the death of Aristotle and the concentrated endeavours of
philologists in the second half of the nineteenth century. To this
remarkable Cinquecento movement of interpretation of the *Poetics*,
which laid the basis for so much of later neo-classicism, a large part
of any account of the treatise's influence must be devoted. My
primary interest here is in the main lines of approach to the *Poetics* in
the sixteenth century, but in order to attempt an analysis of these it
will first be useful, for orientation, to provide a concise outline of the
major documentary material.[14]

Although, as already mentioned, the text of the *Poetics* was
frequently copied in the fifteenth century, very few traces of active
study of the work have survived from this earlier period. Yet it was at
this time that the general spread and intensification of classical
humanism prepared the ground for a new reading of the treatise. The
strength of the revived interest in ancient texts led in turn to the rise
of a critical and theoretical concern with poetry, which crystallised in
the reappearance of formal poetics on the model, above all, of the *Ars
Poetica*. Here was the primary precondition of a fruitful and fresh
study of the *Poetics*. Yet in this area as in most others, the imbalance
of humanism on the side of knowledge of the Latin language and its
literature was a critical factor. So too was the deep colouring of
attitudes to poetry by fundamentally rhetorical assumptions. Both

[13] See E. Lobel, 'The Greek Manuscripts of Aristotle's *Poetics*', *Supplements to the
Transactions of the Bibliographical Society* IX (1933).
[14] For the basic bibliographical data see Cooper & Gudeman (1928) §§I-IV, F.E.
Cranz, *A Bibliography of Aristotle Editions 1501-1600* 2nd edn., rev. C.B. Schmitt
(Baden-Baden 1984) Index 215f. s.v. 'Poetica', and Weinberg 1113-1158. Weinberg
also provides an exhaustive analysis of Cinquecento criticism, chs. IX-XIII dealing
specifically with the *Poetics*. It should be noted, however, that Weinberg's own view of
the *Poetics* reflects that of the Chicago Aristotelians, on whom see p. 317 and n.48
below. Spingarn's book (which reflects the influence of Butcher) is still worth reading
for a short but incisive sketch, including French and English material; and
Hathaway's offers a critique of the Italian material on five major topics. Reprints of
many sixteenth-century commentaries and treatises can be found in the series
'Poetiken des Cinquecento' (Wilhelm Fink, Munich), but, for convenience, most of
my references below are to secondary works which quote the originals. Finally, for the
wider perspective of Renaissance Aristotelianism see C.B. Schmitt, *Aristotle and the
Renaissance* (Cambridge Mass. 1983).

these points will need to be explored further. Emblematic of the first is the place of Latin translations in renewed awareness of the *Poetics*. Giorgio Valla's version of 1498 (reprinted in the following century) was the first of a series. An anonymous Latin translation appeared six years later, and then, most importantly, a version by Pazzi was posthumously published with the Aldine text in 1536. Pazzi's translation must have some claim to being the most widely known form of the *Poetics* not only for the rest of the sixteenth century, but also for part of the seventeenth as well. It was frequently reprinted (as late as 1668) and its significance is increased by the fact that it was included in both of the first two Renaissance commentaries on the treatise, those of Robortello (1548) and Maggi (1550). But the general reliance on Latin versions was not limited to Pazzi's. Others produced in Italy, by Vettori (1560) and Riccoboni (1579), also went through several editions; and the pattern was continued in the following century, most notably by the translations of the Dutch scholar Heinsius (1610) and the Englishman Goulston (1623), both of which were used outside their native countries and the latter of which was included, in a revision, in the edition produced by Tyrwhitt as late as 1794. Although three vernacular Italian translations appeared in the sixteenth century (by Segni (1549), Castelvetro (1570), and Piccolomini (1572)) it is certain that of these only that of Castelvetro was disseminated and known to anything like the same extent as most of the Latin versions I have mentioned.

But translations alone were in any case inadequate for the comprehension of most readers of the *Poetics*. Exegesis and elucidation were needed too, and this was forthcoming from Italian humanists in two forms: either by direct commentary on the treatise, or as part of a more general discussion of poetic theory and practice. For the first of these, in addition to the commentaries of Robortello and Maggi, the cited translations of Vettori, Castelvetro, Piccolomini (in the second edition of 1575) and Riccoboni (especially in the expanded edition of 1587) were all accompanied by annotation of greater or lesser bulk. Translation and interpretation were therefore fully intertwined, and the Cinquecento had established, with remarkable fervour, the foundations of a tradition which has continued unbroken up to modern times, qualified only by the new philological rigour of the nineteenth century. The ramifications of this tradition were widened by the use and treatment of the *Poetics* in sixteenth-century treatises on poetry such as those of Trissino, Giraldi, Minturno and Scaliger. With the latter's posthumously published *Poetices libri septem* of 1561, as with Castelvetro's edition of nine years later, we have already reached the stage at which Aristotle's views on poetry could be subjected in places to stern criticism: by Scaliger because, for all his acknowledgement of the 'omnium bonarum artium dictator perpetuus', his diffuse and desultory work does not share a single major literary value with Aristotle; and by Castelvetro, because, above all else, of the critic's vigorous independence.[15] Yet this is hardly a sign of waning influence, and with the diffusion of knowledge of the *Poetics* outside Italy in the seventeenth century, above all in France, and, largely via France, in England, a new wave of neo-classicism was to occur, characterised notoriously by the doctrines of the Rules and the Unities (to keep the now appropriately ironic capitals). To continue the sketch of publications relating to the *Poetics* in this period is largely unnecessary, though some later comment will be reserved for the misuse made of Aristotle's ideas by French *savants*. It is sufficient for the moment to indicate that the Italian editions and translations of the preceding century, as well as the more general works of poetic theory, were reprinted and reread at this time, and that some of their interpretations were also disseminated through the perhaps even more influential edition of Daniel Heinsius, which contained in its second edition of 1611 the essay *De tragoediae constitutione*.

This mere catalogue of some of the major documents in the Renaissance's revival of interest in Aristotle's *Poetics* must now be put in the broader perspective of cultural context. It should be stressed at once that, since my remarks will be selective, much must be taken for granted; and, since my tone will be mostly critical, let it be firmly acknowledged that the positive achievement of the best Cinquecento commentators and translators – above all, Robortello, Vettori and Piccolomini – in making sense of an obscure Greek document which had for long been neglected and scarcely comprehensible, was a very remarkable one.[16] In the late stages of a tradition of interpretation,

---

[15] Some older claims about Scaliger's Aristotelianism need to be severely qualified. His work represents two dominant features of literary humanism: the influence of Latin literature (overwhelmingly of Vergil, in this case), and the preoccupation with *style*. Cf. B. Weinberg, 'Scaliger versus Aristotle on *Poetics*', *MP* 39 (1942) 337-60.

[16] In addition to the relevant sections of Weinberg's book, see F.W. Cerreta, 'Alessandro Piccolomini's Commentary on the *Poetics* of Aristotle', *SR* 4 (1957) 139-68.

when there is much already to build on, it is easy to be glib about the
shortcomings of those who laid the foundations of the tradition. But
in a delineation of the larger movement of critical thought in the
period, it is regrettably necessary to subordinate such an
acknowledgement to more qualified observations. Two essential
components of the context in question, the predominantly Latin
weighting of classical humanism and the close association between
poetics and rhetoric, have already been touched on, but now call for
elaboration. These aspects of Cinquecento literary culture are indeed
not wholly independent of one another, and to them must be at once
added a factor which participates in them both – the domination of
theory and criticism in this period by Horace's *Ars Poetica*, a work
which had been known much longer and more widely than the
Poetics. The *Ars Poetica* was for most readers a more accessible work
both linguistically and in terms of its main points of reference.
Having been the primary document of ancient criticism available to
the humanists of the fifteenth century, Horace's poem had become
firmly fixed as the central classical source of literary principles, and
one which could be much more comfortably combined with the
pagan texts at the core of the Renaissance – Vergil, Seneca, Roman
Comedy, Ovid – than Aristotle's treatise could ever have been. To
make such an observation is not to commend the approach to the *Ars
Poetica* which became standard in the new movement of classicising
theory: its supposed doctrines were extracted by neat surgery from
the subtle and shifting texture of the poem, and were turned into
invariable canons of literary success and propriety. Horace's work, in
its tendency towards aphorism and to the crisp formulation of
existing issues of critical controversy, undoubtedly gave some
prompting to such attitudes, though it is ultimately not to the *Ars
Poetica* itself but to the craving of classical humanism for a corpus of
authoritative regulations that we must look for an explanation of the
phenomenon.[17] At any rate, Horace's epistle was fundamental to an

[17] It must be remembered that the fusion of Horatian-Aristotelian literary and
rhetorical principles extended to the visual arts, for which a whole set of analogical
issues developed: see R.W. Lee, *Ut Pictura Poesis* (New York 1967). This phenomenon is
a symptom, among much else, of the close-knit society of Italian Academies and
humanist circles, in which the ideal of *l'uomo universale* thrived. Witness, for example,
the case of Trissino, both literary theorist of Aristotelian tendencies and influential
patron of Palladio: see R. Wittkower, *Architectural Principles in the Age of Humanism* 4th
edn. (London 1973) 57-69. The application of classical aesthetics to both literature
and the visual arts, for which both Aristotle and Horace provided explicit

enterprise of prescriptive theorising which had already acquired its
defining characteristics by the time of the awakening of interest in
the *Poetics* from around 1530 onwards.

It has been cogently shown by others that of these characteristics
the most important was the rhetorical emphasis of the new poetics.[18]
The conjunction of Horace with explicitly rhetorical texts, above all
Cicero, exacerbated the drive towards a sharp definition of essential
rules of literary composition, and rules which focussed on the
relation between the literary work and its audience. If, as indicated,
the *Ars Poetica* was consequently treated to some naive reading on
this score, its character was not entirely distorted, since the
coalescing of rhetoric and poetics was already a feature of the work
and of its background. It is vital to insist that the same cannot be
said of the *Poetics*, despite the common misconception that the stress
of Aristotle's tragic theory on pity and fear implies a rhetorical point
of view. The point can be put both negatively and positively: first, by
observing that the acceptance of an emotional effect for a poem is not
intrinsically rhetorical, since it is impossible to attribute any
significance to a literary work without implying the potential
experience of an audience; secondly, by drawing attention to the
critical fact that the accent of Aristotle's theory falls on what he
regards as the objective emotive properties of the well-constructed
plot, not on the audience as such (a fact corroborated by his desire to
make drama independent of the theatre). There is in the *Poetics* an
explicit divergence between what should be the case and what the
weakness of actual audiences may in practice make acceptable.[19] A
sharp contrast can be seen between this and the stance which Horace
adopts in addressing the would-be poet: 'tu quid ego et populus
mecum desideret audi' ('listen to what I, and with me the public,
want' – *AP* 153). The difference can be broadly characterised as one
between a primary Aristotelian concern with the internal or formal
organisation of the poem (though without any formalist implication
of a purely autotelic status for the work of art) and a
rhetorical-Horatian tendency to locate the chief attributes of the

---

encouragement, is a major strand leading to the eighteenth-century conception of the
fine arts: see Kristeller on the whole cultural process.
    [18] See Weinberg chs. III-IV and M.T. Herrick, *The Fusion of Horatian and Aristotelian
Literary Criticism 1531-1555* (Urbana 1946), with the review article of the latter (but also
covering later material) by A.H. Gilbert and H.L. Snuggs in *JEGP* 46 (1947) 233-47.
    [19] See *Poet*. 53a 30ff., with ch. VI pp. 169ff. above.

poem in its effect on a reader or audience.

Yet the persistent thrust of Renaissance and neo-classical literary theory was towards the obliteration of this major discrepancy between Aristotle and Horace. The general presumption of the uniform authority of classical sources made it imperative to regard the principles of the two writers as fully compatible, and it is only a small detail representative of this feeling that men such as Robortello and Heinsius should have seen fit to publish work on the *Poetics* and *Ars Poetica* in the same volume; many others too worked on both documents. Robortello was not alone either in asserting the near identity of poetry and rhetoric. Scaliger goes further – and shows the tendency of rhetorical thinking to extend its *imperium* wider and wider – by his claim, in the opening section of his treatise, that philosophy, rhetoric and drama all aim at persuasion: 'unus enim idemque omnium finis, persuasio.' It is not possible here to trace all the implications and consequences of this process, but it is necessary to appraise the central effect on the interpretation of the *Poetics*. This effect was largely one of simplification and coarsening, grounded as it was in a willingness to fragment Aristotle's ideas and to assimilate them to the formulations of doctrine found in the *Ars Poetica*. At the most fundamental level, Aristotelian mimesis lost its significance as a philosophical notion of poetry's potential to embody general conceptions in the portrayal of particulars: mimesis was blandly reduced to the 'imitation of nature' (but without the original content of this Aristotelian principle for all *technê*), and its universalising capacity was turned into the much more emollient notion of idealisation, which plays a more limited role in Aristotle's thinking.[20] The idealisation propagated by neo-classical theories owes something to a neo-platonist tradition which gave art an aspiration to elevated metaphysical truth, and it was often associated with the conversion of 'wonder' or surprise into the *admiratio* which the best poetry was thought to elicit;[21] but such a tendency could only shift the view of poetry away from the Aristotelian focus on human action and its dynamics. Action, as has been shown earlier in this book, is one of a set of interlocking concepts in the *Poetics*, the

[20] On the original Aristotelian idea of art's imitation of nature see ch. II p.47 above, and on idealisation cf. ch. IV n.39.

[21] One of the roots of this belief in *admiratio* lies in Averroes' treatment of tragedy as the poetry of panegyric: see Hardison (1970) 71. Another is the neo-classical drive to find poetry as edifying as possible. On the shift from wonder to *admiratio* see J. E. Gillet, *MLR* 13 (1918) 233-38, Herrick 74f.

other principal ones being plot-structure, unity and probability. The tightness of relation between these was dissolved by most neo-classical interpreters of the *Poetics*, and the nature of the individual concepts was damaged in the process.

The loss of Aristotle's concentration on action and unity, and hence on plot-structure, is demonstrated most obviously by the downgrading of 'unity of action' to the same level as the newly invented Unities of time and place.[22] Castelvetro, who was chiefly responsible for making the doctrine of the Three Unities explicit, goes even further by actually subordinating unity of action to the others. One reason for common neglect or trivialisation of Aristotle's criterion of unity was the severance of it from the notion of probability as applied to the design of the dramatic action. Aristotelian probability, though not unconnected with ordinary and rhetorical ideas of the credible or plausible, was, as I argued in ch. III, chiefly a principle of structural coherence and continuity, and therefore of the intelligibility of the plot-structure. But Renaissance and neo-classical theorists typically turned probability into a jejune notion of the merely believable or convincing (the 'proxima veris' of Horace *AP* 338) – a notion which, whatever else can be said of it, has no essential bearing on artistic *structure* as such, and is therefore radically different from probability in the *Poetics*.[23] The application of the canon of rhetorical credibility or *vraisemblance* was a diffuse matter, carrying few implications for unity of action in any serious sense. The importance of the latter was further diminished by a widespread inclination to regard epic as a superior genre to tragedy, while Aristotle himself had acknowledged that the unity of epic could never be as tightly knit as his ideal for drama required. On this point, the issue ramifies in a direction in which it is not possible to follow it, into Cinquecento debates about the relation between epic and romance.[24] But it is the effective loss of Aristotle's understanding of unity of action which is fundamental. That understanding may be thought to have severe limitations in what it expects of the poet, but

---

[22] On the evolution of the doctrine of the Unities see Butcher 289-301 and Kommerell 286-308.

[23] Cf. Weinberg's essay, 'From Aristotle to pseudo-Aristotle', in Olson (1965), esp. 196. The stress on verisimilitude led some critics to the unAristotelian conclusion that truth to history is a positive poetic virtue: see e.g. H.B. Charlton, *Castelvetro's Theory of Poetry* (Manchester 1913) ch. IV.

[24] For an extensive discussion of these debates, and of the *Poetics'* involvement in them, see Weinberg chs. XIX-XX.

without a strong sense of its centrality to Aristotle's treatise interpretation of the *Poetics* inevitably entails misrepresentation. Corneille, in the first of his *Discours* of 1660, was both reacting to the indefiniteness of neo-classicism in this respect, and evincing at the same time the acute quality of his own attempt to reach a *rapprochement* with the predominant doctrine of the Rules, when he commented on the difficulty of knowing what unity of action was supposed to involve.[25]

Deprived of its foundation in the concept of a unified structure of human action, the plot-structure of Aristotle's theory was all too easily converted, and reduced, to the *fabula* of the *Ars Poetica. Fabula* and its vernacular equivalents were accepted as the standard substitute for *muthos*, with the consequent loosening of the texture and rigour of the idea. This indeed lies at the heart of the deformation of the Aristotelian theory of poetry. Individual and discrete elements of the *Poetics* were often enough repeated and agreed with, but understanding of, or consent to, such details was not adequate for a general comprehension of the nature or purpose of the treatise. And what was so often lacking was an appreciation of the place of form and structure in Aristotle's conception of a poem. Instead, the rhetorical bias of criticism tended to make the poem as *fabula* (with its fluid suggestion of fictional but credible material, rather than structured action) into the locus or occasion of a particular impact on reader or audience. For the whole of the sixteenth and seventeenth centuries, and beyond, poetic theory readily and boldly advanced to the task of specifying what this impact should be. It would be superficially false to say that there was universal agreement, since the issue was argued over the dichotomy between pleasure and learning. But at a deeper level the very acceptance of this dichotomy – classically formulated in the *Ars Poetica*'s 'aut prodesse ... aut delectare' (333), together with its resolution, 'qui miscuit utile dulci ...', mixing profit and pleasure (343) – is a symptom of the rhetorical assumptions shared by most theorists. It is for this reason, I wish to argue, that it may be necessary to judge diametrically opposed views of Aristotle's notion of the purpose of poetry to be equally misguided.

The forced dichotomy, pleasure or edification, as well as the naively compromising combination of the two, in origin represents

---

[25] For a text of the *Discours* see H.T. Barnwell, ed., *Pierre Corneille: Writings on the Theatre* (Oxford 1965) 1-79.

the configurations of Hellenistic literary criticism, though an occasional earlier hint of similarly reductive views can be found. I have already insisted, earlier in this book, that we should not expect to be able to locate the *Poetics* on such a drastically simplified scale of judgement. In particular, Aristotle's attempt to define the peculiar pleasure of tragedy (and of other genres) cannot be taken to imply that he is championing a hedonist theory of art against contrary moralistic theories. While Aristotle qualifies the outright moralism of Plato, his own position is more complex, and to understand it we need to take account of factors some of which are not explicitly stated in the *Poetics*, but which belong to its essential philosophical background. Far from taking such a wide view of the matter, interpreters of the treatise in the sixteenth and seventeenth centuries approached it with the Horatian dichotomy firmly fixed in their minds, and they looked for an answer to the question, on which side does Aristotle stand. Prevailing assumptions made the most natural answer to this question that Aristotle must be found to concur with Horace; two such classical authorities could not be at odds on this most grave of issues.

But while this conclusion was widely reached, it did not militate against a common moralistic bias (to which the *Ars Poetica* too gave encouragement). This centred above all on *katharsis*, for there was little else in the *Poetics* which could be construed as attributing a directly didactic function to poetry. *Katharsis* appeared to offer scope for those who wished to find an Aristotelian commitment to the 'utile' in tragedy, and perhaps elsewhere too. But some important discriminations need to be made here. In the first place, there was no more unanimity on this point than on any other, and great credit ought not to be denied to those Cinquecento theorists, above all Vettori and Piccolomini in their editions of the *Poetics*, who realised that *katharsis* should be related to the Aristotelian ideal of the mean, and must concern, or have implications for, habituation to feeling the emotions of pity and fear to the right extent. That *katharsis* has an ethical aspect is therefore true, even if the details of Aristotle's conception remain obscure. But it was in the belief that *katharsis* entailed a straightforward form of moral protreptic that a majority of interpreters reduced the idea to an inappropriately basic level of didacticism. Whether the emphasis was placed on acquiring fortitude or resistance against the assaults of misfortune, as it was by Robortello; or on the administration by tragedy of a conscious moral lesson, as it was by Segni and Giraldi; or on pity and fear as a means of helping us to avoid *other* dangerous emotions (anger, lust, greed etc.), as it was by Maggi and others – in all these cases, a much more direct and explicit effect is posited than anything which can reasonably be thought to have been Aristotle's meaning. The common significance of these various interpretations is that they evince a combination of moralism with rhetorical preconceptions. *Katharsis*, that is to say, was generally aligned not only with the poet's ethical function, but more precisely with the achievement of a persuasive effect to behave, or avoid behaving, in certain ways. It is a testimony to the tenacity of these attitudes that even Castelvetro, who went further than anyone else in denying that Aristotle wished to assign a didactic potential to poetry (and who consequently went to the opposite extreme of making pleasure its sole purpose for the philosopher) nonetheless found it impossible to deny altogether an element of 'utility' in the theory of *katharsis*.[26]

Katharsis is a facet of the *Poetics* for whose interpretation the continuity of approach between sixteenth-century Italy and seventeenth-century France is most evident. Corneille, although sceptical about the reality of the phenomenon, nevertheless took it in the second of his *Discours* to mean that tragedy should lead us to moderate or eradicate those passions which we see to be the cause of misfortune. René Rapin, in his treatise of 1674, seems to have wavered in his interpretation, but that he took the effect to be directly moral is beyond doubt; and it is with *katharsis* also in mind that he decrees as the aim of poetry in general the 'purification of morality by salutary instructions'.[27] And in his 1692 translation of the *Poetics*, Dacier combines, in the manner of some of his Italian predecessors, the idea of acquiring emotional resilience with that of learning to moderate potentially tragic passions. But such continuity does not justify the belief that French neo-classicism simply perpetuated the theories of the Cinquecento. In a number of respects French criticism represented a narrowing of vision and a more intense concern with a small number of central ideals than had characterised Italian criticism of the preceding century. In the new

[26] For details of Castelvetro's and other sixteenth-century interpretations see Hathaway 205-300, Kostić's article, and cf. Appendix 5 below. The prevailing view of *katharsis* as a didactic or edifying effect helped to promote the common idea that Aristotle's *hamartia* was a moral flaw in the tragic figure: on this and other interpretations of *hamartia* see Bremer (1969) 65-98.

[27] *Réflexions* (n. 5 above) 21.

movement of rigorously legislative poetic theory which arose in Paris in the 1630s, the canons of the Unities, of *la bienséance* (Horatian and rhetorical *decorum*), and of *vraisemblance* – codified for dramatic poets as *les règles* – rapidly established themselves as definitive principles of the French theatre.

The genesis of this stringent neo-classicism is a complex matter beyond my expertise.[28] Although the influence of Italian poetic theory will not furnish a complete explanation of it, what matters for my purpose is to note that the impetus behind the interpretation of the *Poetics* certainly passed from Italy to France, and in the process became more closely associated than before with the production of new tragedies. If a dominant classical influence on the tragedies of the sixteenth century had to be identified, whether in Italy or in France (or in England), Seneca's entitlement to this status could not be disputed. The Senecan model, dominant from the very beginnings of Italian neo-classical tragedy in the early fourteenth century, had easily coalesced with both the precepts of the *Ars Poetica* and the pervasively rhetorical colouring of contemporary poetic theory. Senecan influence did not end with the turn of the sixteenth century, and its strength can perhaps best be gauged by the extent to which it infiltrates the work of even such a relatively Aristotelian theorist as Daniel Heinsius (himself an editor of Seneca's tragedies and the author of neo-Senecan plays).[29] But Seneca did recede somewhat into the background for the dramatists of the new French neo-classicism, even if he was to be replaced by the Greek tragedian with whom he had most in common, Euripides. The waning of neo-Senecan tragedy complements the increasing emphasis on Aristotle's *Poetics* as 'l'unique source d'où il faut prendre des règles', and as the classical document which represented, in the words again of Rapin, 'la nature mise en méthode, et le bons sens réduit en principes', nature made methodical and sense reduced to principles.[30]

[28] See R. Bray, *La Formation de la Doctrine Classique en France* (Paris 1927).

[29] See for example the citations of Senecan plays in chs. 6 and 11 of Heinsius' *De tragoediae constitutione* (1611, 2nd edn. 1643). There is a reprint of the 1611 edn., including the treatise: *Aristotelis De Poetica Liber* (Hildesheim 1976). A translation of the 1643 edn. of the treatise is available in P.R. Sellin & J.J. McManmon, *Daniel Heinsius: On Plot in Tragedy* (Northridge Calif., 1971). For aspects of earlier Senecan influence see the essays in E. Lefèvre, ed., *Der Einfluß Senecas auf das europäische Drama* (Darmstadt 1978), and G. Braden, *Renaissance Tragedy & the Senecan Tradition* (Yale 1985).

[30] Rapin op.cit. (n.5 above) 9-10.

Yet it will call for little substantiation here to reiterate the familiar fact that this spirit of French neo-classicism involved a considerable element of intellectual delusion. One fundamental factor is not difficult to identify. The first French translation of the *Poetics* was not produced until 1671, a generation after the foundations of the movement were laid; and the widely read version by Dacier did not appear until 1692. Most of the French *savants* were familiar with one or more of the Italian editions, as well as with the works of the Dutchmen Heinsius and Vossius. But they tended to use these publications not so much as a means of access to the *Poetics* itself, as by way of a pool of ideas and interpretations to be selected and tendentiously reorganised. The point can be made most effectively in connection with Heinsius' treatise on tragedy (1611), which has been argued to have been perhaps the prime source of the Aristotelianism of French critics.[31] If so, this ought to have led to a deeper understanding of the *Poetics*, since the earlier chapters of Heinsius' essay presented probably the purest and most illuminating statement yet achieved of some of the chief ideas of Aristotle's work. Yet it is remarkable how little difference this made during the seventeenth century. While Heinsius had provided an exemplary discussion of *katharsis*, relating the concept properly to Aristotle's general theory of the emotions, my earlier references to Corneille, Rapin and Dacier illustrate how little impact this had on French writers. Equally clearly, Heinsius has nothing to say of the three unities as such (which the French derived directly from Italian sources); he mentions that of time briefly, ignores that of place, and follows Aristotle in regarding the unity of action as all-important. And of *vraisemblance* and *bienséance*, neither of which is authentically Aristotelian, Heinsius has virtually nothing to say: his paraphrase of the *Poetics'* conception of poetry's concern with general truths, not particulars, is not to be confused with the much looser notions of verisimilitude current in the later decades of the century; and on decorum, it is plain that Heinsius would hardly have agreed with Rapin's etiolated judgement that it was 'la plus universelle de toutes les règles'.[32]

[31] E.G. Kern, *The Influence of Heinsius and Vossius upon French Dramatic Theory* (Baltimore 1949), and P.R. Sellin, *MP* 70 (1973) 199-215. For Heinsius' influence in England see the latter's *Daniel Heinsius and Stuart England* (Leiden 1968) esp. 123-99.

[32] Rapin *Réflexions* 67. Heinsius' discussion of *katharsis* is in ch.II of his treatise, and his treatment of various aspects of plot in chs. III-X contains much that is both Aristotelian and freshly perceived. Where Heinsius most diverges from Ar., and shows

Neither Aristotle himself, then, nor the best of his earlier interpreters could validly be described as 'l'unique source' of the canons of French neo-classicism. Instead, its foundation consisted of the composite, hybrid structure of Renaissance humanism, in which elements were amalgamated from Horace, Aristotle, the rhetoricians and the poetic practice of a range of ancient authors. Superimposed on this were the more specific requirements developed by the French critics from the 1630s onwards – the rational rules of poetic art. It has often been supposed that, even where they diverged from authentic Aristotelian doctrine, the spirit of their critical enterprise was still kindred to that of the *Poetics*. But even this is arguable. Certainly most neo-classicists were broadly aligned with Aristotle as regards the ancient debate over the relation between 'art' and 'nature' in poetic composition; as a system of principles implying a conception of the poet's productive powers, and opposed to neo-Platonic notions of inspiration, 'les règles' were comparable in status to Aristotelian *technê*. But a distinction still needs to be drawn between the legislative aspirations of the neo-classic critic and the philosophical detachment of Aristotle. The latter's own use of prescriptive formulae is deceptive, since there is little evidence to suggest that he aimed at, still less achieved, any practical influence on practising poets. Aristotle was able to look back on supreme poetic achievements, at least in epic and tragedy, and in many respects his theory was designed to codify the dynamics of those achievements. But French critics looked back to the challenge of classical culture, in a context where a direct impact could be made on contemporary dramatists and their audiences: the establishment of the Rules is closely correlated in date and effect with the founding of the first permanent theatres in Paris. In the tightly knit world of *salons*, classicising criteria of dramatic propriety came to be accepted as largely valid by playwrights and their audiences alike. It is against this theatrical and social background that the authority of neo-classical critics must be viewed. Some, such as Georges de Scudéry, critic of Corneille's *Cid*, were prepared to affirm not only the necessity but also the virtual infallibility of rules. The extremity of

---

the inescapable rhetorical slant of contemporary thought, is in his exposition of style, character and 'thought' in tragedy, chs. XIII-XVI: here Roman sources (Horace, Quintilian, Terence, Seneca) are dominant. One other notable feature of Heinsius' work was his attempt to reorder the text of the *Poetics*: on this cf. Bywater xix-xx.

such an attitude led to the tensions which Corneille finely responded to in his remark, 'il est facile aux spéculatifs d'être sévères';[33] but the force behind the new poetic canons could at any rate not be simply ignored. Knowledge of the *Poetics* may have played some part in helping to create a sense of the critic's voice as more knowing than that of the poet himself, as well as a characteristic tone of disdain for popular taste. But the emphatically prescriptive manner of the neo-classicists, and their rationalist faith in the rules as the basis for all poetic achievement, goes well beyond anything learnt from Aristotle, and belongs to a different cultural climate.

It is perhaps fortunately beyond the scope of this chapter to discuss in any detail the impact of the *Poetics* as such on the playwrights of seventeenth century France. The task would in any case be a somewhat unrealistic one, since meaningful claims of influence can only be made where confirming evidence exists, and we necessarily lack the directness of relation which can exist, or be seen not to exist, between the *Poetics* and other critical texts. But some very brief remarks can be made on the two major tragedians of the period, Corneille and Racine, both of whom undoubtedly knew Aristotle's treatise (in Racine's case, in the original).[34] It was Corneille who was chiefly responsible, after the criticisms of *Le Cid* in 1637, for putting into practice the Unities and the other neo-classical canons of decorum, regularity, and a *vraisemblance* which nonetheless tilted towards moral idealisation. Corneille's first-hand acquaintance with the *Poetics*, however, is likely to belong to his period of withdrawal from the theatre during the 1650s, after most of his major works had already been written. It was not so much as a dramatist as a dramatist-turned-critic, in the *Discours* written for the 1660 edition of his *Théâtre*, that he confronted Aristotle, and, through him, the literary theorists of his own day. It is indeed the awkward relation between these two sources of authority which is Corneille's main subject. He should certainly not be read as a disinterested interpreter of the *Poetics*: on some points, such as *katharsis* or necessity and probability, he either follows a false lead from the Italians, or else reveals a rather tenuous understanding of the Aristotelian principle.

[33] Corneille's third *Discours,* in Barnwell (n.25 above) 79.
[34] For Corneille and Aristotle see Kommerell, esp. 37-50, 63-78, Fuhrmann (1973) 236-50, and P. J. Conradie, 'Pierre Corneille and the *Poetics* of Aristotle', *Acta Classica* 18 (1975) 47-59. The evidence for Racine's knowledge of the *Poetics* can be found in E. Vinaver, ed., *Racine: Principes de la Tragédie en marge de la Poétique d'Aristote* (Paris 1951).

But what is most striking is the general evidence of the *Discours* that the *Poetics* had meant little or nothing to Corneille in the way of a positive guide to playwrighting. He expresses uncertainty over the central Aristotelian requirement of unity of action, and he claims, supposedly in contradiction of the *Poetics*, that most tragic subjects do *not* possess verisimilitude. And on an even more fundamental point, the design of tragic plots, Corneille states open dissent from Aristotle's views. But in these cases of disagreement, just as much as on the details where Corneille professes acceptance of *les règles*, we receive the impression of a dramatist facing and answering his *contemporary* critics: the *Poetics* is a vehicle of the argument, rather than its true object.

Racine's interest in Aristotle was more active and positive; we still possess the copies of Heinsius' and Vettori's editions which he annotated, and in which he attempted his own translation of parts of the treatise. Coming to the theatre when the battle over the Rules had long ago been fought, Racine was able to accept more uncompromisingly the challenge of the neo-classical ideal. Above all, in his two Greek plays from the 1670s, *Iphigénie* and *Phèdre*, he made more use of Attic originals than Corneille had ever done, and his references to the *Poetics* in the prefaces to them both show that he wanted to harmonise his Euripidean material with his understanding of Aristotelian principles. To some extent, this has been achieved only at the cost of departing from Euripides' version, and introducing elements from Seneca (in the case of *Phèdre*) and other classical sources. Thus the miraculous rescue of Iphigeneia is avoided, as well as her death, by the discovery of an alternative victim, Eriphile. But it is legitimate to wonder whether, in his desire both to preserve *vraisemblance* and to avoid the morally shocking, Racine has not been led simply into an alternative form of improbability. It is pertinent here to observe both the intrinsic tensions of an attempt to reuse classical myth, and also the reflection of these tensions in the relation between the myth and the *Poetics*. Racine refers in his preface to the traditional detail of Iphigeneia's miraculous metamorphosis, which, he says, might have received 'quelque créance du temps d'Euripide', but would now be found 'absurde et trop incroyable'. But this specific point only raises a much larger issue about the conflict between the rational requirement of probability and the religious nature of Greek tragic myth. I have tried to show earlier in this book that this conflict is present, and unresolved, in the *Poetics* itself (see ch. VII). It is at least some testimony to the seriousness with which Racine took both Aristotle and Euripides that he faced a similar problem.

A closely related point arises in connection with *Phèdre*, where Racine purports to satisfy Aristotle's demands for 'le héros de la tragédie'. He interprets this essentially in a negative way, as meaning the avoidance both of complete guilt and of complete innocence. If this appears a somewhat compromising ideal of tragedy, it does nonetheless have much in common with ch. 13 of the *Poetics*. Racine, however, acknowledges two other factors. The first is the role of destiny and divine anger: Phaedra's crime 'est plutôt une punition des Dieux qu'un mouvement de sa volonté', more a punishment from the gods than an act of will. But in the revealingly moralising conclusion to his preface Racine also mentions, not without Jansenist overtones, the human disorder caused by the passions. In exposing this the tragedian is fulfilling a moral function, emulating the Greek dramatists who worked in 'une école' where virtue was taught as clearly as by the philosophers.[35] The attempt to see an essential identity both between himself and the Greek tragedians, and between the latter and the principles of the *Poetics*, cannot obscure the uncertainty at the heart of Racine's elucidation of his purpose. Are the tragedies of Phaedra and Hippolytus matters of destiny and divine causation, or are they terrible demonstrations of the disruptive power of passion? Or can they be both? It is tempting to argue that for Racine as for Aristotle the concept of destiny is no more than a mythical premise whose effect can be allowed vaguely to hang around the drama, but which must not interfere with the probable dynamics of human action and passion. Racine is certainly in tune with the spirit of the *Poetics* when he explains that he has detracted from Hippolytus' virtues in order to make his death produce pity rather than indignation. But here too one may be aware that the Aristotelian impetus is towards containing tragedy within rational limits, and protecting it – for different reasons in Racine's from Aristotle's case – against the religiously objectionable aspects of the original (Euripidean) myth.

These short remarks are not intended to derogate from the brilliance of *Phèdre*. They raise a question about the difficulties in the Aristotelian view of tragedy as comprehended by Racine. I have

---

[35] Similar phrases are later found in Dacier, Voltaire and Lessing: see Robertson 371 and n.2.

chosen to touch on this side of things rather than on the more general and familiar issue of the neo-classical development of unity of action, buttressed by the unities of time and place. Racine is also worth singling out because he was probably the only major dramatist of the sixteenth or seventeenth centuries who read the *Poetics* with a view to assimilating its ideas into his own creative intentions. It is too much, as well as inappropriate, to expect that he could have achieved a completely dispassionate reading of the treatise. His reference to Attic tragedy as a school of virtue, and to Aristotle's codification of this ethical function, reflects all too clearly the pervasive moralism on whose contribution to humanism and neo-classicism I have already said something. Yet despite this, Racine tried with exceptional seriousness to apply the tragic requirements of the *Poetics* to his own art, and to hold them in balance with other pressures weighing on his work: in doing so, he advanced beyond the pedestrian rule-bound mentality which disfigured so much literary theory of his time.

*

As regards the status and influence of the *Poetics*, the Cinquecento in Italy and the seventeenth century in France can be regarded as a largely coherent period, marked by certain consistent concerns and recurring emphases. The same cannot be said of the following two centuries, during which it becomes much more difficult to pick out the interpretation of Aristotle's ideas as an identifiable cultural thread. This is in part simply because, while works specifically devoted to the *Poetics* are fewer, the range and complexity of the relevant material in this period is much greater than before, and to pick any single thread out at all becomes less realistic. But it is also because attitudes to the *Poetics* lose much of their stability, and we need to allow for a full gamut of overlapping views and judgments, from outright rejection to attempts to make completely fresh approaches to the treatise. I will have to be severely selective once more in trying to evaluate some of the more significant features of this intricate pattern.

The neo-classical tradition itself was perpetuated beyond the end of the seventeenth century, not only in France but also in Germany, and, above all, in England.[36] Dacier's French translation of the *Poetics*

---

[36] For England see Herrick chs. 2-4 (as well as ch. 1 for sixteenth- and seventeenth-century documentation which I have not had space to consider in the text); for Germany, Fuhrmann (1973) 252ff. and the same author's 'Die Rezeption der

(1692) was in turn anonymously translated with its notes into English in 1705, and this edition, which reproduced the orthodoxies of the previous half-century, was widely used. It may be unnecessary to dwell on the more extreme consequences of the influence of French on English dramatic theory, as manifested in the doctrines of Thomas Rymer; but the naive dogmatism of Rymer's insistence on the Unities, on poetic justice, and even on the necessity of the chorus, cannot be altogether isolated from the general movement of English attitudes in this area. Even in the case of a more moderate and balanced writer such as Dryden, for whom a real problem existed in the relation between modern and ancient literature, the force and influence of French neo-classicism could certainly not be shirked. But what can be observed both in Dryden and increasingly in the first half of the eighteenth century, is a new sense of the need to qualify the excessive rigour and simplicity of some earlier formulations of classical principles. Attitudes to the *Poetics* were inevitably caught up in, and largely conditioned by, this broader current of thought and feeling. If it is impossible to demonstrate the process in detail here, we can at any rate illustrate its lineaments from a major mid-century document, Johnson's *Preface to Shakespeare* of 1765.[37] The *Preface* is an interesting test-case for more than one reason, but particularly because Shakespeare represented at its strongest the challenge posed to neo-classicism by the 'irregularity' of English drama. In Johnson this challenge is confronted by a critic who owes a general allegiance to rationalist and moralistic standards of criticism, but also has a sharp sense of Shakespeare's native genius.

The resulting conflicts are there to see beneath the remarkable poise of Johnson's prose. While rejecting the dross of neo-classicism, in the form of the Unities, Johnson nonetheless sets out to judge Shakespeare by the essential criteria established in the sixteenth century's fusion of Aristotle and Horace, and hardened by the

---

aristotelischen Tragödienpoetik in Deutschland', in W. Hinck, ed., *Handbuch des deutschen Dramas* (Düsseldorf 1980) 93-105.
[37] Johnson had earlier written a *Rambler* essay (no. 139, 16 July 1751) in which he measured *Samson Agonistes* against 'the indispensable laws of Aristotelian criticism' and above all the 'law of poetical architecture' that a plot should constitute 'a regular and unbroken concatenation' of events: he found Milton's play to have a proper beginning and end, but to lack an organised 'middle'. (For a different view of the play see Rees (1972b) 13ff.)

French orthodoxy of the following century: a general fidelity to 'nature', approved by the traditional image of the 'mirror of manners and of life'; the aspiration of poetry to universality or generality (Shakespeare's characters are species, not individuals); the primacy of plot in drama (Shakespeare's power lies in 'the progress of his fable') and the necessity for unity of action; the observance of probability; the tragic requirements of 'terror and pity'; and the most fundamental principle of all, the aim of combining pleasure and instruction. Yet it is entirely appropriate that Johnson's attempt to bring such standards to bear on Shakespeare should produce unresolved ambiguities. Most obviously, Johnson seems to have contradictory impulses both to find unity of action in Shakespeare ('he has well enough preserved the unity of action ... his plan has commonly what Aristotle requires') and to find it lacking (his plots are often 'loosely formed ... and ... carelessly pursued'). A different and less obvious kind of tension, but one which equally stems from the nature of Johnson's neo-classical presuppositions, emerges between the claim that Shakespeare's work is a true mirror of life – that he exhibits 'the real state of sublunary nature' – and the judgement that he 'is so much more careful to please than to instruct, that he seems to write without any moral purpose'. The incompatibility between moral purpose, which entails a 'duty to make the world better' by enforcing poetic justice, and the capacity to be a 'faithful mirror', is left unbridged. And through this presentation of unreconciled perceptions we can discern an underlying unease in Johnson's *Preface*: it is one which inheres in the neo-classical enterprise of seeking a complete order of reason and morality in art.[38]

While this enterprise was not, as should by now require no reiteration, purely Aristotelian, it took an important part of its momentum from the *Poetics*, and the general strain that was increasingly placed on classical canons of criticism in this period was therefore felt specifically in the reading of the treatise. Johnson's ambivalence towards Shakespeare must stand in the present context as a single but prominent English example of what could be more widely instanced. We can see in it some of the elements involved in the eighteenth century's confrontation between classicism and newly emphasised values of imagination and originality – values which

[38] But Johnson saw the point and had second thoughts, as Bremer (1969) 86 n.8 points out.

were able to find their own centre of classical sanction in (pseudo-)Longinus' *On the Sublime*.[39] Johnson's own comparison of Shakespeare to a forest, as opposed to the formal garden of 'a correct and regular writer', may be thought to have a proto-Romantic quality to it, and it certainly implies a recognition of poetic values which cannot be contained within the confines of peremptory rules and precepts. Another of Johnson's remarks can also be used to point towards a literary fact of great significance to the status of the *Poetics*. Johnson comments on Shakespeare's mixture of genres, his failure to adhere to a strict distinction between tragedy and comedy. The *Poetics* had always been enlisted, together with the *Ars Poetica*, in support of a strict classical doctrine of genres, with the concomitant principle of appropriate *Stiltrennung*. In fact, as in other respects, Aristotle was a little less clear-cut on this point than some other authorities, and while he himself complained about a possible blurring of tragedy and comedy, critics such as Giraldi and Corneille had not failed to notice Aristotle's own acceptance, in *Poetics* 14, of the 'happy ending' as valid for tragedy. Nor had Aristotle differentiated the genres stylistically as sharply as later theorists (a point where the rhetorical tradition made a deep impression). Yet his authority was invoked for neo-classical standards of this kind, and his authority consequently suffered in the face of challenges to generic purity. But more than this, Aristotle had only treated drama and epic in detail. He had ignored lyric, the importance of which grew with the eighteenth century's increasing interest in subjectivity; and he had lived before the invention of pastoral, satire and the prose romance. Recognition of the status of these genres necessarily clashed with the conviction that Aristotle was, or could be, the source of a complete poetic and literary system. The

[39] On the rise of Longinian ideas in the eighteenth century see S.H. Monk, *The Sublime* 2nd edn. (Michigan 1960), and Abrams 72-8, 132-8. For a sketch of a comparable transition in the theory of visual art see R. Wittkower, 'Classical Theory & Eighteenth-Century Sensibility', in *Palladio and English Palladianism* (London 1974) 193-204.

It may be worth attempting a brief set of contrasts between the *Poetics* and *On the Sublime*: Ar. is exclusive and deliberately narrow, Longinus is wide-ranging and open-ended (covering lyric, history, rhetoric etc.); Ar. regards poetic skill (*technê*) as sufficient, L. as necessary but limited; Ar. largely ignores inspiration, L. acknowledges it; Ar. regards genius (Homer) as the natural perfection of poetic principles, L. as a force which overrides principles; Ar. is dry, laconic and philosophical, L. communicates his own enthusiasm; Ar. prefers definition and analysis, L. emphasises intuition and taste; Ar.'s chief concern is with intelligible structure, L.'s with the achievement of individual effects.

development of the romance into the novel posed a peculiar difficulty for literary orthodoxy. If Fielding's notorious attempt in the preface to *Joseph Andrews* to present his work as a comic prose-epic, meeting Aristotelian standards, cannot be taken entirely seriously (though it was not without precedent),[40] it nonetheless gives some idea of the problem of accommodating new literary achievements to the rigid framework of existing criticism.

But the standing of the *Poetics* itself could be rescued from the general reaction against neo-classical rigidity. To show how this could be done was precisely the intention of Lessing in the *Hamburgische Dramaturgie* of 1767-8.[41] Lessing rejected French classicism both in itself and in Gottsched's claims for it earlier in the century as a model for the German theatre, and he paved the way for German Romanticism by his elevation of Shakespeare as the paradigm of dramatic genius and imagination. Yet the paradox arises that Lessing also became a major advocate of the *Poetics*, which he was even prepared, in a manner ironically reminiscent of some of the French themselves, to call infallible. The resolution of the paradox lies in the complete severance which Lessing set out to make between Aristotle's original principles and the French abuse of them: 'gerade keine Nation hat die Regeln des alten Drama mehr verkannt, als die Franzosen', he wrote near the end of the *Dramaturgie* (nos. 101-4). In putting forward what he considered, sometimes wrongly, to be entirely fresh interpretations of the *Poetics*, Lessing certainly did not aspire to completeness. Both the journalistic nature of his enterprise and some of his own presuppositions led to a significant selectivity. In particular, it is hardly surprising that Aristotle is not mentioned in the portion of the work which concentrates on dramatic characterisation, since Lessing here places a stress on natural, psychological motivation which is not shared by Aristotle; while the latter's extreme concern with plot-structure is not mirrored in Lessing's thinking, despite one passage in which the importance of self-contained poetic unity is acknowledged (no. 79). Despite this, Lessing both picks out and elucidates with remarkable force some of the central tenets of the

---

[40] For analogues of Fielding's thesis cf. some of the arguments used in the Cinquecento debate over Ariosto's *Orlando Furioso*: see Weinberg 954ff.

[41] For informative and wide-ranging assessments of Lessing's relation to the *Poetics* see Robertson chs. XI-XII, Kommerell *passim*, and F.J. Lamport, *Lessing and the Drama* (Oxford 1981) 129-44. I take a higher view of Lessing's interpretation of Ar., however, than all these writers.

Poetics. On the broader level, it is Aristotle's contrast between poetry and history, and his formulation of poetic generality, which Lessing attends to in more than one article. Part of the importance of this lies in the reaffirmation of strict Aristotelian doctrine against the various neo-classical confusions over the use of historical material in poetry (such as Castelvetro's self-contradictions on the point). Lessing here recognises a vital element in the *Poetics*, Aristotle's attempt to free poetry from the need to portray factual reality (in the face of the Platonic charge of parasitic copying), but yet to preserve the possibility of truth in its treatment of human action.[42]

But Lessing's chief interest in the *Poetics* was in what he saw as its correct identification of the essence of tragic drama in the power to arouse pity and fear. He sought to reach a more precise understanding of the relation between these emotions, and also to provide a new answer to the vexed question of *katharsis*. On the latter, Lessing was both acute and, in my view, arguably close to the truth, so far as this is now recoverable. His interpretation, which was built on a recognition of the place of the emotions in Aristotle's concept of virtue, deserves more credit than it has recently received, though it was not as new as Lessing seems to have believed: in essentials, it reproduced the view put forward a century and a half earlier by Daniel Heinsius.[43] But where Lessing did represent an advance on Heinsius was in making explicit the difference between the oblique ethical significance which his interpretation of *katharsis* entailed, and the blander neo-classical faith in the moral value of poetry, to which *katharsis* had previously been so often assimilated. It is a failure of discrimination in some later critics that Lessing should sometimes have been considered a crude moralist on *katharsis*. On the tragic emotions themselves, Lessing's analysis must be treated more equivocally. By taking tragic fear to be purely self-regarding ('das auf uns selbst bezogene Mitleid') he allowed a component in Aristotle's psychology to be exaggerated beyond its true status. The result is the virtual absorption of fear into pity, and the redefinition of tragedy as 'ein Gedicht ... welches Mitleid erreget'. Fear, on this reading, loses its distinctive part as a strongly anticipatory emotion in

[42] See esp. *HD* nos. 19, 89, 94 (with a long quotation from the English writer, Richard Hurd).

[43] Lessing's treatment of the emotions and of *katharsis* is to be found in *HD* nos.74-9; cf. also the attack on Corneille in nos. 81-3. Lessing nowhere in *HD* refers to Heinsius by name; the latter's possible influence on him is therefore a moot point: see Robertson 358 n.2, 361 n.4.

the response to the events of tragedy (hence Lessing's preference for
'Furcht' over 'Schrecken'); its object becomes less the substance of
tragedy itself than the hypothetical experience of the spectator.
Lessing's interpretation of the tragic emotions has been criticised
from other angles, and it has been argued that its tone is too
humanitarian or philanthropic. But Lessing follows Aristotle in
differentiating between *philanthrôpia* (a weaker feeling of sympathy)
and pity; and it is precisely the insistent amalgamation of fear with
pity in his theory which prevents the latter from being too altruistic.
The combination of the emotions, as presented in the *Dramaturgie*,
has a darker force than some have allowed, and it is to be
remembered that one of Lessing's complaints against French drama
is its failure to achieve true tragic depth and intensity. If, in the last
analysis, Lessing's observations on pity and fear cannot be accepted
as an objective commentary on Aristotle's, they still approach this
central concept of the *Poetics* with more earnest attention than
perhaps anyone had earlier done. And if they ultimately fail to bring
the treatise's theory of tragedy into proper focus, they do at least
show, for the first time, that there is such a theory there to be
grasped.[44]

Neo-classicism had used the *Poetics* principally as the source of a
general definition of poetry and its functions. In the process, it had
produced two main types of work which addressed themselves to the
treatise: first, the commentary (often accompanying a translation)
on the text itself; secondly, the independent work of poetic theory or
criticism, in which elements of the *Poetics* were set out and explored
in conjunction with ideas from other sources. Although Lessing's
Hamburgische Dramaturgie could be said to belong to this latter
category (with occasional moments in the manner of the former), its
concentration on the *Poetics* as the carrier of a distinctive theory of
tragedy meant that the treatise could now be clearly seen to be
approachable from three main angles: that of scholarship, primarily
devoted to the elucidation of the work in its own terms; that of
general *Poetics*, for the purposes of contributing to new theory or
criticism; and that of the theory of tragedy. These categories cannot,

---

[44] Lessing makes clear his dissent from the traditional moralistic interpretation of
katharsis at the end of *HD* nos. 77 and 78. In his attempt to show that Lessing is
unoriginal in the matter, Robertson 368-80 fails to make some necessary
discriminations: in particular, Dacier's view of *katharsis* is not as close to Lessing as he
suggests : cf. Appendix 5, §§1 and 3.

of course, always be kept distinct, and they have certainly overlapped in practice. But it is useful to bear them in mind in attempting to find some minimal order in the mass of material pertinent to the status of the *Poetics* during the nineteenth and twentieth centuries. In the remaining part of this chapter I shall offer some necessarily brief remarks on each of the three approaches to the treatise I have mentioned.

The third volume of George Saintsbury's *History of Criticism and Literary Taste in Europe* contains the index entry, 'Aristotle, *passim*'. This is accurate yet potentially misleading for the nineteenth century, covered by the volume, and would be equally so for the present century: potentially misleading, in that it might disguise the fact that the *Poetics'* reputation has fallen in modern times from its neo-classical dominance to the rank of one among a multitude of critical texts, and is no longer a pervasive influence; but strictly accurate, in that the treatise continues to be sporadically cited, whether for the purposes of agreement or dissent, in a wide variety of contexts. There had always, of course, been individuals like Castelvetro or Saint-Évremond capable of rejecting or severely qualifying the precepts of the *Poetics*, but neo-classical reverence had kept such attitudes mostly in check. But with the progression of the eighteenth century, Aristotelian literary authority was placed under increasing strain, and with the rise of Romanticism the possibility of an open devaluation materialised. Perhaps the most important statement of this challenge to authority was made by August Wilhelm Schlegel, spokesman of the *Frühromantik*, as part of his attempt to define the difference of spirit between ancient and modern art. In his *Lectures on Dramatic Art and Literature* of 1808 not only do we find a refusal to accept individual doctrines such as *katharsis*, for so long established orthodoxy, but Schlegel further and forcefully argues that there is a fundamental deficiency in Aristotle's understanding of poetry. The philosopher's fault is to have tried to dissect and analyse the mystery of poetry, which is a matter of beauty, imagination and feeling, not of rational comprehension. So, while concurring that unity of action is indispensable to drama, Schlegel criticises Aristotle's notion of it as too superficial, and calls instead for 'a deeper, more intrinsic and more mysterious unity'.[45]

---

[45] See *A Course of Lectures on Dramatic Art & Literature*, Engl. transl. by J. Black, 2nd edn. rev. by A.J.W. Morrison (London 1846) 232-45 for Schlegel's main treatment of the *Poetics*. *Katharsis*, together with Lessing's interpretation of it, is rejected on p. 68.

The terms in which Schlegel characterises the classical-romantic dichotomy now seem all too familiar and partial. When he cites Aeschylus and Sophocles alongside Shakespeare to illustrate his concept of unity, and when he expresses approval of Plato's intuition of the nature of true beauty and art, we are reminded that the distinction is certainly not a straightforwardly historical one. But there remains no doubt that Schlegel is representative of an important shift in ideas and values, and one with major implications for attitudes to the *Poetics*.[46] Characteristic Romantic preoccupations with genius, imagination and subjectivity were inevitably irreconcilable with much of Aristotle's aesthetic thinking.

Schlegel himself can be seen to be an opponent both of Aristotle's own ideas and of the French classicism which had used the Greek treatise to sanction its literary authoritarianism; but he was well capable of separating the two. This is clearest in his assault on the Unities, of whose pseudo-Aristotelian status he was directly aware. But the estimation of the *Poetics* in modern times has varied partly according to the degree to which the separation between Aristotle and neo-classicism has been perceived. As a striking instance of the failure to make, or a lack of interest in making, the distinction, one can cite Brecht's antithesis between Dramatic and Epic Theatre, the former supposedly Aristotelian through and through, the latter often characterised negatively as 'nicht-aristotelisch' and marked by an 'alienation effect' which is conceived as the contrary of *katharsis*. Brecht was certainly not interested in understanding the *Poetics* as such, but in using its reputation and historical associations as an emblem of the traditional, and particularly the naturalistic, theatre, and of the views of those who claimed knowledge of the 'eternal laws of the theatre'.[47] Brecht's case may seem a special one, but it is in its attitude to the *Poetics* largely typical of those who cannot dissociate the treatise from its exploitation by earlier theorists and critics, and who consequently see it only as a symbol of an outmoded literary

[46] Many aspects of this shift are explored by Abrams' book. On the Romantic acceptance of both Shakespeare and Greek tragedy see G. Steiner, *The Death of Tragedy* (London 1961) 186ff.

[47] For a selection of Brecht's writings in translation see *Brecht on Theatre*, ed. and transl. J. Willett, 2nd edn. (London 1974): the well-known list of differences between Dramatic and Epic Theatre can be found on 37, and the references to 'eternal laws of the theatre' occur on 161. One oddity of Brecht's position is the connection which he apparently draws between *katharsis* and the dramatisation of fate: see 57, 78, 87, 181. Brecht's relation to the *Poetics* is discussed by H. Flashar, 'Aristoteles und Brecht', *Poetica* 6 (1974) 17-37.

ideology. Such a point of view has to some extent been stimulated by continuing attempts to extract a valid general poetics from Aristotle's work. Of these the most important has been that of the Chicago school of neo-Aristotelians, who have harnessed interpretation of the *Poetics* itself to the application, or adaptation, of its ideas to a wide range of later literature. But if such an enterprise sounds like neo-classicism revived, its tenets must be sharply differentiated from the earlier movement. The Chicago critics emphasised Aristotle's principles of poetic structure and unity, and they were concerned with the internal features and the autonomy of literature rather than with moral or other larger issues relating to works of art. The resulting reading of the *Poetics* was, in the narrow sense, aesthetic and formalist, and, despite reactions against the critical stance of the Chicago school, their interpretation of Aristotle has, I believe, done much to spread the dominant modern belief that the *Poetics* embodies a clean separation of poetic and ethical standards.[48]

The contrasting examples of the previous paragraph demonstrate the extremes in the modern status of the *Poetics*. In between lies the diffuse area of sporadic citation, both positive and negative, which I have already noted. No real order can be imposed on this multifarious material, but a generalisation can be attempted. The fall in authority of the *Poetics* which came with the reaction against neo-classicism largely did away with wholesale acceptance of the continuing validity of the work, but it did not prevent or stop the piecemeal reinterpretation of individual sections and tenets. The upshot of this has been the common fragmentation of Aristotle's conception of poetry, by the selective quotation of particular dicta on mimesis, *katharsis*, character and action in drama, the unity of poems, the place of universals in poetry, the relation of poetry to history, and the importance of metaphor – to mention only the most salient themes. The removal of ideas and pronouncements from their context allows the characteristically eclectic modern theorist or critic to gesture towards Aristotle's significance as a pioneer in the

---

[48] For examples of the Chicago critics' work see my Bibliography under R.S. Crane, R. McKeon and E. Olson. There are critiques of the movement in W.K. Wimsatt, *The Verbal Icon* (London 1970) 41-65, and, more specifically, J.M. Gray, 'Aristotle's *Poetics* and Elder Olson', *CL* 15 (1963) 164-75. The Chicago school's interest in genres was carried much further, and further from Ar., by N. Frye, *Anatomy of Criticism* (Princeton 1957): for the basic Aristotelian acknowledgement see esp. 14f., 33f., 357, and for a comparison of Frye and the *Poetics* see L. Golden, 'Aristotle, Frye and the Theory of Tragedy', *CL* 27 (1975) 47-58.

field, but without incurring any suspicion or taint of real Aristotelianism. Many other historical texts are treated in similar fashion, of course, so that *aperçus* from the *Poetics* are regularly found in mixed company, to be used as a starting point for thinking which is likely to move far afield from Aristotle's concerns, or simply as a foil to an alien argument. The relationship between the *Poetics* and contemporary literature, which has always had anomalous and strained elements in it since the sixteenth century, has not so much been solved as dissolved by this modern device of substituting *disiecta membra* for a coherent engagement with the treatise as a whole.

To go any further with analysis of this phenomenon would carry us into broad cultural issues beyond the scope and competence of this chapter, but I have drawn attention to the critical fragmentation of the *Poetics* in order to suggest that, as far as the work itself is concerned, this form of token respect and acknowledgement may be more harmful than complete neglect, since it impedes a serious and rigorous attempt at historical understanding of Aristotle's theory, and is often content to tolerate loose paraphrase instead of a careful attention to the problems of translation. Paradoxically, the status of the *Poetics* in modern literary criticism and theory can after all be judged largely as the tail-end of neo-classicism, which had itself often atomised the precepts of the treatise and reordered its priorities to construct out of them a dogmatic orthodoxy. If the dogma has now long been abandoned, the ahistorical selectivity which first appeared in the theorists of the Cinquecento has left its diminished legacy in current criticism's nodding acquaintance with the *Poetics*.

A partial exception to this generalisation might seem to be provided by the place of the treatise in the treatment of tragedy, where Aristotle's views have their greatest *prima facie* claim on the critic's attention. It is certainly true that discussions of tragedy form the likeliest context for modern references to and interpretations of the *Poetics*, and that the continuing interest in Greek tragedy helps to maintain the obligatory recognition of Aristotle's book by those dealing with the genre. But even here there has been a discernible tendency towards fragmentation of the theory, and a number of underlying reasons for this can be traced. In the first place, once more, is the reaction against neo-classicism, which brought with it an inevitable aversion to the supposed gospel of French classical tragedy. One specific factor was the importance of Shakespeare to the Romantic movement, and the way in which his work was understood as the antithesis of French regular tragedy. Despite attempts such as those of Johnson and Lessing, earlier illustrated, to show that Shakespeare was consistent with the spirit of the *Poetics*, the treatise unavoidably suffered from the devaluation of neo-classical drama at the hands of critics such as Schlegel and Coleridge. In the course of the nineteenth century, this effect was broadened by the development of various kinds of 'bourgeois' tragedy far removed from the grand mythological and historical themes which had formerly been prevalent in the genre. Whether, in fact, such plays are necessarily further from Aristotle's theory than neo-classical tragedy is not as simple a question as it at first seems. But there remains no doubt that this phase of dramatic history made it impossible for the *Poetics* to keep its earlier esteem.

A further displacement of the treatise from the centre of interest in tragedy was caused by the existence of new and rival theories of the genre. The attention paid to tragedy by German writers, from Schelling onwards, was of a very different sort from Aristotle's. Although in Schelling's case there are some ostensibly close points of contact, and while some affinities with Aristotle can be discerned in Hegel too, these are greatly outweighed by the metaphysical preoccupations of the German theorists, in whose writings dramatic tragedy as such is often of less concern than a tragic philosophy of life itself.[49] Aristotle's theory does not belong on this level, and if it is not as straightforwardly pragmatic as some other traditional definitions of the genre, it nonetheless is firmly focussed on tragic drama and poetry, and has little or nothing to offer in the way of an existential view of the tragic.[50] Without venturing into further comparison between Aristotle and the more ambitious modern theories of tragedy, it can at any rate be said that the latter have played a leading part in transforming the framework within which

[49] For a critical survey of theories of tragedy see M. Weitz, 'Tragedy', in *The Encyclopedia of Philosophy*, ed. P. Edwards (New York 1967) vol. 8 155-61. The main German theories are also examined in Silk & Stern ch. 9, and see 225-39 for a comparison of the *Poetics* and *The Birth of Tragedy*. For a general contrast between Ar.'s and modern theories of tragedy see Lesky's essay.

[50] The traditional ancient view of tragedy, attested by late grammarians, but deriving from Theophrastus, emphasises the rank of characters (heroic) and the nature of the dénouement (catastrophic): the evidence is set out, and the influence traced, by McMahon, who, however, exaggerates the Aristotelian colouring of the conception (deriving it from the *On Poets*). Ar. is more qualified both about characters and about the outcome of tragedy: on the former see ch. V pp. 165-7, on the latter ch. VII pp. 226ff.

large questions and issues concerning tragedy are now usually
raised, and consequently in reducing the dominance of the
categories and ideas about the genre found in the *Poetics*. Aristotle's
treatise has, however, clung tenaciously to its important position as
one of the central reference points in controversy over the nature of
tragedy, and it may well be that it has been assisted in doing so by
its very lack of obvious metaphysical content. Despite occasional
aspirations, such as Butcher's, to detect quasi-Hegelian resonances
in the *Poetics*, the more restricted focus of the work's theory of
tragedy has in general been well appreciated by more empirically
minded critics, even if it has not always been grasped that, as I tried
to show in ch. VII, Aristotle deliberately diminishes the religious
dimension of the tragedies which he knew, and therefore cannot be
assumed to offer a wholly authentic view of Greek tragedy. The
limitations of what Aristotle has to say on the agents of tragedy, and
on the forces operative in tragic action, as well as the degree of
uncertainty which continues to attach to the terms *katharsis* and
hamartia, may lead the modern critic either to reject the *Poetics*
outright, or alternatively to exploit the limitations and uncertainty
by incorporating Aristotelian terminology selectively into his own
approach. The latter is probably a more common strategy than the
former, but the result of it, essentially as with literary criticism in
general, is usually not to advance the understanding of the *Poetics* as
such, or even to disseminate the best reading of its contents currently
available, but simply to give fragmented and undigested elements of
it their place in syncretistic criticism of the genre.

It is, then, finally to scholarship that we may turn in the hope of
finding a more consistent and integrated view of the *Poetics* than I
have argued is any longer easily to be derived from the literary
theorist or critic, whether of tragedy or of other genres. But some
reflection on the movement of modern scholarship may suggest that
this hope is not entirely or readily to be fulfilled.

The scholarship of the sixteenth-century commentators on the
Poetics had been, in its own way, a considerable achievement. If
defective in some respects (particularly textual) it had within little
more than a generation prepared the ground for a cohesive reading of
the work, where before there had been none to speak of. But after
Heinsius' edition of 1610 and the essay on tragedy of the following
year. which incorporated many of the best features of the Italian
editions of the preceding two generations and added to them the

fruits of a fresh and intelligent reading of the text, there was little new interpretative work of note until the later eighteenth century. Standard views and options were well established, together with inveterate misconceptions; and most later neo-classical references to the *Poetics* relied on casual familiarity with sometimes imperfect translations, or even just second-hand information. Dacier's heavily annotated version of 1692 stands as a summation of the orthodoxies of the preceding period, but it is hardly a work in which much new ground is broken. It is not until the translation of Thomas Twining in 1789, and the posthumous edition by Thomas Tyrwhitt five years later, that the philological tradition can be said to have been seriously revivified. The text was now examined with fewer conventional presuppositions, and the interpretations of earlier critics were subjected to similar scrutiny. A genuine knowledge of the Aristotelian corpus and of relevant works elsewhere was brought to bear; historical data displaced much idle fancy and sheer guesswork. Twining and Tyrwhitt both represent the application of a new precision to the study of the *Poetics*, but their works also make an interesting contrast, and one which helps to explain why Twining, the less technically assured but more adventurous of the two, has not always been given full credit for his achievement. Twining's book, with its two dissertations and its wide-ranging, often expansive notes, in some ways stands for an older style of 'amateur' interpretation. Tyrwhitt's, on the other hand, is more narrowly textual, and its *animadversiones* are written in a more clipped style: in these respects, it looks forward to the professional philology of the following century, and to the series of critical editions of the *Poetics* which it would produce. It is tempting to think almost exactly a century ahead, and to see this contrast between Twining and Tyrwhitt reproduced in the works of two other English scholars, Butcher and Bywater, whose first editions of the *Poetics* appeared in 1895 and 1897. Although both these men were devoted to the exegesis of the details of Aristotle's text, they were divided, as a perusal of the preface to Bywater's later commentary (1909) confirms, in their views of the feasibility and desirability of a broader treatment of the philosopher's understanding of poetry, and of the place of the *Poetics* in his thinking as a whole.

Without projecting back precisely this disagreement onto Twining and Tyrwhitt, it is nonetheless legitimate to discern in the contrast between their works the early signs of a possible divergence of scholarly approach to the treatise. In fact, despite occasional later attempts such as Butcher's at constructing a larger framework of interpretation, there is no doubt that nineteenth-century scholarship as a whole settled for the narrower method and the finer tools of the critical edition, the commentary and the learned article. It preferred, that is, the closer but piecemeal handling of the *Poetics*, and was able to justify this preference by reference to the peculiar nature of the work. The benefits of this approach, both for the establishment of the text and for its exegesis, are not to be slighted, and while no technical account of the period can be given here, it is impossible not to mention the exceptional work of Johannes Vahlen, whose abundant writings on the *Poetics* from the early 1860s up to 1914, including an edition of the treatise, constitute the outstanding modern contribution to the understanding of the *Poetics*. Vahlen, in fact, went much further than most other scholars towards a cohesive general interpretation, but the dominant trend of philology has largely relinquished such an endeavour, and has instead concentrated on specific issues and cruces. This is not unnatural, since the *Poetics* is an especially crabbed work, elliptical in style, missing its second book, and possibly lacunose in other places too: hence, among other things, the revival in the last century and a half of attempts to identify considerable portions of the text as interpolation, or to improve its coherence by internal transposition. But few of the results can command much approval, and it is difficult to see how, in the nature of the case and without external evidence, they are ever likely to do so. In other respects – notably the understanding of the textual tradition, and the elucidation of many fine details – progress may confidently be claimed. Yet it is still possible to feel that specialised attention to individual questions, while entailing a refinement of exegesis for which one must be grateful, has also unnecessarily narrowed attitudes to the *Poetics*. This is particularly regrettable in conjunction with the fact that modern Aristotelian scholarship as a whole has mostly neglected the work, so that its philosophical roots are still not properly investigated by those best equipped to reveal them. The paradoxical upshot of the philological approach to the treatise, then, is a greatly strengthened grasp of detail, but a loss of some of the vigour and the engagement which had characterised the best neo-classical treatments of the *Poetics*.

One partial exception to scholarship's reaction against neo-class-icism's concerns is the issue of *katharsis*, on which there have been far more modern contributions than on any other in the *Poetics*.[51] It is likely, in fact, that one relevant factor is precisely the legacy of the neo-classical conviction that *katharsis* exposes the heart of Aristotle's theory, though to this one ought to add two further elements of explanation: first, the sheer obscurity of the matter, which gives endless scope both for conjecture and for elaborately inconclusive lucubrations; secondly, and insidiously, the suspicion (congenial in a Freudian age, but probably quite misleading) that *katharsis* may turn out to contain a deep psychological insight.[52] Whatever the reasons for the obsession with *katharsis*, there has been a strong tendency to follow the lead set by Bernays in the mid-nineteenth century, and to reject the idea that *katharsis* is a doctrine with any ethical import. As the question has been discussed earlier in this book (ch. VI) it will not be reopened here; but it is still worth observing that, despite the connection noted above, the new orthodoxy on *katharsis* is emblematic of the broad difference between the scholarly consensus of the last century and a half and the prevalent moralism or didacticism of the sixteenth and seventeenth centuries. Aristotle's treatise on poetry was once regarded by almost all readers and critics as affirming the fundamental ethical value of literature. The dominant modern view is that the *Poetics* is essentially formalist and, in the unfortunately narrow sense, aesthetic in its spirit. The former of these attitudes was certainly carried by a large degree of preconception, but if it now seems taken for granted that we cannot attribute a reductively moralising theory of poetry to Aristotle, it may well be that we should also be on our guard against some distinctively modern preconceptions too – preconceptions which may too blandly encourage us to mistake the absence of moralism for pure aestheticism. The serious reader of the *Poetics* has indeed a great many preconceptions, historical and contemporary, to resist. If he cannot altogether escape from the various, fascinating influences of the ways in which earlier readers have taken and interpreted the work, he must at any rate persevere in struggling to put Aristotle's words back in their distant context, and to comprehend them there.

[51] Sections V and VI of Cooper & Gudeman's Bibliography (covering 1860-1927) includes almost one hundred items whose titles indicate a primary concern with *katharsis*, and there is no doubt that many others too touch on the subject.

[52] On Freud and *katharsis* see Lucas (1968) 289f., Gründer 516-19, and A. Momigliano, *Quinto Contributo alla storia degli studi classici e del mondo antico* vol. 1 (Rome 1975) 144f. Freudian interest in the *Poetics* is not limited to *katharsis*: witness Devereux's unfalsifiable analysis of the work in terms of art's replication of the structure of the psyche.

Appendix 1
The Date of the *Poetics*

Aristotelian chronology is a minefield from which the prudent keep their distance. The aim of this moderately imprudent appendix is not so much to assign a date to the *Poetics* as to set out the limited evidence which might be thought to bear on the question. This has not, to my knowledge, been properly attempted before, and many of the standard editions contain no more than allusions to the chronological issue. I hope that others may be able to supplement or refine what I present here.

Even those who do not accept the details of Jaegerian *Entstehungsgeschichte* may agree that many of the treatises are likely to contain material dating from more than one period. The *Poetics* need be no exception to this, though it must be said that the principal modern attempts to detect chronological strata of composition (those of Solmsen, Lienhard, De Montmollin and Else (1957)) have failed to command much assent, and rightly so in my view: inferences in this area are too often based on evidently disputable premises. The possibility of textual dislocation in the work makes matters harder, and it is not easy to envisage comparative methods which could usefully be applied to so short a treatise. But the likelihood remains that the *Poetics* received Aristotle's attention at more than one date, and this will be borne out by the material discussed below.

I start by demonstrating the distribution of opinion on this issue. If there is hardly a settled consensus, the following references will show that the majority view places the *Poetics* in Aristotle's third period.

First Athenian Period (367-347): see Webster 307f. and *Art and Literature in Fourth Century Athens* (London 1956) 54ff., Düring (1961) 287 (first draft), (1966) 49f., 126, 163 (cf. *RE* Suppl. XI (1968) 228), Burkert, Söffing 8 n.5, J. Bremer *TLS* Jan. 4, 1985 p.13 (alleging general agreement for this date).

Middle Period (347-336): see De Montmollin 203-6, Else (1938) 203f., (1957) e.g. xi, 11, 131, 637f. Both De Montmollin and Else posit later additions by Aristotle.

Lyceum Period (335-323/2): see e.g. Bywater viii ('... some seventy years ...'), Solmsen *Gnomon* 5 (1929) 409 n.1, Rostagni (1945) XX-XXXI, Ross 19, J. Hardy, *Aristote Poétique* (Paris 1952) 13-16, House 32-5, Jones 11 (but cf. 50), Lucas (1968) xiif. (and cf. on 48a 31), Allan (1970) 158, Fuhrmann (1982) 150-55. Many more references could be given to document the prevailing preference for this final period.

The above range of opinion naturally reflects the paucity of good evidence. What there is can perhaps best be considered under four main categories.

1. *The relation of the Poetics to other surviving Aristotelian works*

(a) *Cross-references*: these are listed in ch. I n. 3 above. Taken at face-value (as by Thielscher, esp. 230-32, 239, 265), these would yield a relative position for the *Poetics* between the *Politics* and the *Rhetoric*, the dates of which are themselves highly controversial: on the *Pol.* see Lord (1982) 25-8, and on the *Rhet.* cf. 1 (b) vi below. But the reliability of cross-references has often been questioned (e.g. Lucas (1968) on 56a 35) and some would deny that, even if authentic, they need carry chronological implications (e.g. Hutton 36 n.17). It should be noted, however, that the parts of the *Politics* and *Rhetoric* from and to which the cross-references occur concern ideas which there are some independent grounds for attaching to the early part of Aristotle's career: see 1 (b) vi below on *Rhet.* 3 (with Burkert's article), and 2 (a) on *katharsis*.

(b) *Doctrine*: this is the most hazardous aspect of the whole chronological issue. Although parts of this book have been greatly concerned with the relation between the *Poetics* and the wider philosophical system, it is a very different matter to attempt to translate such arguments into inferences about date of composition. The following is only a selection of possible considerations, and of varying weight.

i.   50b 8-10, 54a 17-19: the definition of *êthos* by reference to *prohairesis* may well presuppose the doctrines of Aristotle's mature ethical thought, in which *prohairesis* is prominent (e.g. *EN* llllb 4ff.); but there is little agreement on the chronological significance of 'mature' in such a proposition.

ii.   53a 35f., b 11, etc.: the concept of 'proper pleasure', belonging to a particular experience, seems to be an application of the mature philosophy of pleasure found in *EN* 10, where just this notion repeatedly appears (cf. ch. II n.25).

iii. 55a 4-6: although the term *sullogismos* may have a wider scope (as 55a 7 shows), Aristotle's main example (though inaccurate) seems to involve a proper syllogistic deduction in the technical sense. The same terminology, however, is used in its looser senses elsewhere in the treatise, including 48b 16 (where House 118 and Goldschmidt (1982) 402 can hardly be right to discern the strict logical sense).

iv.   chs. 7-9: Webster 307f. argues that *Met.* 1090b 19f. ('nature is evidently not episodic like a bad tragedy') presupposes the doctrines of this portion of the *Poetics*. He follows Jaeger in believing this section of the *Metaphysics* to belong to the start of Aristotle's second period, and he accordingly takes the poetic principle to have been worked out before 347. This is flimsy. Aristotle also uses 'episodic' in the sense of disjointed, without reference to tragedy, at *Met.* 1076a 1, and this helps to suggest, what is anyway likely, that the usage had some existing currency (cf. also *Rhet.* 1418a 33, where the verb *epeisodioun* is used metaphorically: see ch. IX n.10).

v.   ch. 20: some of the linguistic definitions given here are close to those in the *De Interpretatione* – esp. 57a 10-12 ~ *Int.* 16a 19ff., 57a 23f. ~ *Int.* 16b 26f. The *De Interpretatione* is customarily regarded as an early work. Note, however, that *Poet.* ch. 19, 56b 8-19, is discrepant with *Int.* 17a 5f., and there are other differences. There is evidence here, then, for an early origin for *limited parts* of ch. 20.

vi.   chs. 21-2: the discussion of *lexis* (style) is closely related in parts to the section of *Rhet.* 3 (chs. 1-12) on the same subject; the relation is corroborated by the fact that four of the *Rhet.*'s six cross-references to the *Poetics* (1 (a) above) occur in this section. The dating of the *Rhet.* is controversial: for evidence of more than one draft see G. Kennedy, *The Art of Persuasion in*

Greece (London 1963) 103ff., and P.D. Brandes, *Speech Monographs* 35 (1968) 482-91; but Burkert's article argues forcefully that Book 3 is early, and see more generally Düring (1966) 118ff. Burkert's argument from this for an early date for the *Poetics*, however, fails to take into account an important factor. The *Poetics'* chapters on *lexis* not only form a self-contained unit, but they cannot be said, even on the most generous interpretation, to be closely knit with the rest of the treatise: although purporting to be part of the analysis of tragedy, they have little to say on the genre as such. Although, then, there are strong grounds for seeing material of early origin in chs. 21-2, it would be rash to suppose that this entails an early origin for the work as a whole.

2. *The relation of the Poetics to lost Aristotelian works*

(a) *On Poets:* the fragments of this work (71-7 Rose) show some possible connections with the *Poetics*; in particular, fr. 72 seems close to *Poet.* 47b 9ff. Moreover, if we accept that the neo-platonist texts quoted in Kassel 52 refer not to the lost book of the *Poetics* itself but to the *On Poets*, then there is a case for believing that the doctrine of *katharsis* has early origins in Aristotle's career: cf. ch. I n. 2. The link with *On Poets* is strengthened by *Poet.* 54b 17f., usually taken to be a reference to this work. There is a consensus, based on the use of dialogue-form, that *On Poets* belonged to Aristotle's period in Plato's Academy, though Rostagni (1945) XXIV (followed by House 29-32) dates it as late as the mid-330s, and Fuhrmann (1982) 154 puts it close to the *Poetics*, which he regards as late. Against such a date see De Montmollin 193ff. The earlier period remains more plausible, but it must again be said that to recognise an early origin for some of the ideas attested in the *Poetics* is not to establish such a date for the work as a whole (*pace* Else (1957) 501 and n. 44).

(b) *Homeric Problems:* for the *Poetics'* connection with this work, confirmed by some of the surviving fragments, see ch. IX n.20. It is customarily accepted that the larger work must have been the earlier: *Poetics* 25 has the look of being a compressed summary of an already worked out scheme of problems and their solutions. But I am not aware of any clear evidence for the date of the *Homeric Problems*:

Zoilus' attacks on Homer, to which Aristotle is normally thought to have been responding, cannot be dated with any precision (no closer than to, say, twenty years either side of the mid-century: see J. E. Sandys, *A History of Classical Scholarship* vol. 1, 2nd edn. (Cambridge 1906) 108f.). *Pace* Rostagni (1945) XXIVf. and Fuhrmann (1982) 153, little if any reliance can be placed in the tradition of a link between Aristotle's work on Homer and his supposed tutorship of Alexander: see Pfeiffer 71f. The *Homeric Problems*, containing a mass of material on a very large number of issues, would in any case appear a peculiarly suitable work to have been compiled over a protracted period of time.

(c) *Didascalic researches*: it is usually assumed that *Poetics* 4 and 5 owe something to Aristotle's work on the Athenian theatrical tradition, and the latter is often and plausibly assigned to his last period (e.g. Pfeiffer 81). Such a date receives support from the fact that Aristotle was probably engaged on his documentary research into the Pythian games in the early 320s: for this redating, based on inscriptional evidence, see D.M. Lewis, *CR* 8 (1958) 108 (the old date is uncorrected in Pfeiffer 80). It must be admitted that nothing in the *Poetics* indubitably presupposes the *Didascaliae*, but some passages do hint at a detailed knowledge of chronology and related points: see esp. 48a 33f., 49a 14ff., 49a 28-31, 49a 37-b 9.

3. *Internal references*

(a) 48a 31 refers to 'the Megarians here', i.e. on the mainland as opposed to in Sicily. This is sometimes taken to imply that Aristotle is addressing an Athenian audience (e.g. Rostagni (1945) XXII, Lucas (1968) on 48a 31). As a strict linguistic point, this remains arguable, though the Athenian setting cannot seriously be doubted anyway (4 (b) below), and indeed this passage of the *Poetics* does *as a whole* seem to presuppose it (48a 28-b 2).

(b) The *Poetics* contains a variety of references to fourth-century writers, of whom the most pertinent to the question of dating are Astydamas, Carcinus and Theodectes (on Chairemon see Collard 22 n.1). Carcinus is known to have been competing as a tragic poet in the mid-370s, but the large number of plays attributed to him means that his career is likely to have stretched into the second half of the century (for the evidence see Snell 210). Theodectes, a friend and pupil of Aristotle's, was writing plays in the mid-360s, and he probably died no later than about 340 (Snell 227ff. gives the evidence, which is inconsistent). Finally, Astydamas is known to have been active from the 370s, but also as late as 340 (Snell 198f.). This material is, therefore, not quite as unambiguous as is claimed by Burkert 72. On balance, the individual plays by these authors cited by Aristotle are more likely than not to belong to the 360s and 350s, during Aristotle's first period in Athens, though it is not impossible that Astydamas was still active when Aristotle returned to Athens in 336/5. In any case, hasty inferences should be checked. Aristotle mentions only a handful of fourth-century works, and for special points. It would be unwarranted to assume that he chose the very latest plays that he happened to have seen or read; and once he had examples for his purposes, he may well have gone on reusing them (as some lecturers do).

4. *General considerations*

(a) Else (1957) 36-9, 133, 402, 637f. argues that the *Poetics* contains signs of Aristotle's use of, or close engagement with, Platonic techniques and concepts. His individual points seem to me weak. Aristotle's relation to Plato is anyway, in this sphere, a complex mixture of borrowings and criticisms (see pp. 19-27 and Appendix 2). Whatever may hold in other areas of philosophy, it is difficult to see how Aristotle could have ignored Plato's views on poetry at any stage of his career, and he would expect his audience of students to have some familiarity with them too. Fuhrmann (1982) 152f. deduces a late date for the *Poetics* from Aristotle's rejection of the Platonic critique of poetry.

(b) Aristotle's concentration on Attic tragedy puts it beyond all doubt that the *Poetics* was produced against the immediate background of, and for an audience presumed to have a strong acquaintance with, Athenian literary culture. This is in itself equally compatible with an origin for the treatise in either Aristotle's first or his third period.

Of the various pieces of evidence catalogued above, most are ambiguous or indecisive. The strongest case for early elements in the *Poetics*, deriving from Aristotle's time in Plato's Academy (pre-347), must be based on the connections with the *On Poets* (2 (a) above) and *Rhetoric* Book 3 (1 (b) vi). The best pointers to Aristotle's second period in Athens, after 336, are the putative links with his didascalic researches (2 (c)) and the hints of his mature ethical thought (1 (b) i-ii). It seems unlikely, in view of the Athenian background (3 and 4 *passim*), that the *Poetics* will have been of much importance to Aristotle during his time away from Athens, 346-336. On these grounds, then, I would tentatively suggest that the *Poetics* has its roots in Aristotle's early thought, the period of his direct contact with the wonderful stimulus of Plato's passionate moralism, and that it actually contains some material first drafted before 347; but that it also received later attention from the philosopher, and that it is perhaps most likely, as it stands, to represent the first book of a treatise used for instruction in the full course of study and enquiry offered in the Lyceum during the last decade and a half of Aristotle's life. This conclusion complements my contention, in ch. I pp. 35ff., that the *Poetics* shows traces of resting on the foundations of a theory of poetry already worked out in part elsewhere.

Appendix 2
The *Poetics* and Plato

The general relation between Plato's and Aristotle's thinking on poetry has been raised at a number of points in this book. The purpose of this appendix is to supplement these passages by providing in convenient form a collection of possible parallels – whether positive or adverse, on Aristotle's part – between the *Poetics* and Plato's dialogues. The list is intended to give some idea of those areas where Aristotle's treatise touches specifically on Platonic ideas and terminology, but the material assembled is not all of precisely the same kind. As well as noting standard references, I have cited some details of a more speculative nature: inclusion should therefore not be taken to signify a definite echo of Plato in every case, especially since some points are likely to have been more widely shared. Concepts or terminology which appear more than once in the *Poetics* are usually mentioned at their first occurrence.

Ch. 1

47a 9   the construction or composition of *muthoi*: cf. *Rep*. 377d 5f.
            poetic *muthoi*: cf. esp. *Phaedo* 61b 3f. (further refs. in ch. II
            n.16)

47a 9f.   for the phrasing cf. *Rep*. 598e 3f.

47a 16   general poetic mimesis: see the refs. in ch. IV n. 23

47a 16-18   the analysis of mimesis according to media, object and
            mode: cf. *Rep*. Bk. 3, esp. 392c 7f., 394c 7f., 398b 7f.
            (compare also the tripartite analysis of *mimêmata* at *Tim*.
            50c-d)

47a 18f.   mimesis in 'colours and shapes': cf. e.g. *Rep*. 373b 5f.,
            601a 2, *Laws* 668e 2f., 669a 1

47a 18ff.   comparison between poetic and visual mimesis: cf. e.g.
            Rep. 373b, 377e, 596c ff., *Crat*. 423d, *Polit*. 288c, 306d,
            Laws 669a

47a 20f.   *technê* (cf. ch. II n. 3): for visual art cf. *Ion* 532 ff., *Gorg.* 450c 9f., *Laws* 669a 1; for poetry, *Symp.* 223d 5, *Laws* 719c 5 (but note the denial of *technê* at *Ion* 533e ff., and its insufficiency at *Phdr.* 245a); and for general mimesis, *Rep.* 601d lf., *Crat.* 423d 8f., *Soph.* 219a-b, *Laws* 667c 9ff.

47a 22   'rhythm, language and music': for the same and similar phrases see e.g. *Rep.* 398d lf., 601a 8, *Laws* 656c 4f., 669b 2f., 800d 2f., 840c lf.

47a 26-8   choreographic mimesis: see *Laws* 655d, 814e ff.

47a 28ff.   lack of mimetic terminology: cf. *Soph.* 267d

47b 13ff.   poetry not defined by metre: Plato sometimes seems to assume the reverse, esp. at *Gorg.* 502c, *Phdr.* 258d, *Rep.* 393d 8, *Laws* 811d 2f., e 2-4. But Plato allows 'poetry' to cover some prose writings at *Laws* 810b.

Ch. 2

48a 1   mimesis of 'men in action': cf. *Rep.* 603c 4

48a 1ff.   ethical division of agents in poetry into good/bad, better/worse than us: cf. *Laws* 659c 3f., 798d 9, 814e (referring to mimetic dance)

Ch. 3

48a 19ff.   triple division of mimetic modes: see *Rep.* Bk. 3, esp. 392d-394c. On the terminology cf. ch. IV n. 34

Ch. 4

48b 5ff.   the natural human propensity for mimesis: cf. the implication of *Rep.* 395d lf.

48b 12ff.   pleasure in learning through contemplation of mimesis: cf. *Rep.* 475d-e, *Laws* 667c

48b 15-18   the need to know and recognise the object of the mimesis: cf. *Crat.* 430e (the same example of a portrait), *Phaedo* 73e-4e (esp. 74d 9-e 4), *Rep.* 402b-c, *Laws* 668c-669b

48b 18f.   sensual pleasure from mimesis: see *Phileb.* 51b-e (*pure* sensual pleasure contrasted with that of art), and cf. *Laws* 667d-e

48b 20f.   natural instinct for melody and rhythm: *Laws* 653e-654a, 664e-665a

48b 25-7   the dichotomy of poetry: cf. e.g. *Laws* 810e 8f., 816d (serious v. comic), 829c 3 (encomia and invective). For hymns and encomia see *Rep.* 607a, *Laws* 801e, and for early poetry in general *Laws* 700a ff.

48b 34   Homer the precursor of tragedy: *Theaet.* 152e, *Rep.* 595c, 598d, 605c, 607a

48b 36-8   distinction between comedy and iambic abuse: cf. *Laws* 935d-6a

Ch. 5

49a 33   the comic excludes complete evil: compare *Rep.* 452d (the comic is simply the evil). But *Phileb.* 49b-e contrasts the comic and the hateful.

49a 34f.   comic faults: cf. *Phileb.* 48a-e (types of self-ignorance), *Laws* 816d (faults of body and mind)

Ch. 6

49b 27   pity and fear: cf. *Ion* 535b-c, e, *Phdr.* 268c 8, *Rep.* 387b-d, 605c-6b

49b 28   *katharsis*: for the term in Plato see ch. VI pp. 187ff. and nn.22 and 24. For the homoeopathic psychological principle see *Laws* 790d-791a. But Ar.'s *katharsis* rebuts a Platonic belief that art increases emotional susceptibilities: see esp. *Rep.* 387c, 388d, 606b-d.

50a 15   plot as a 'structure of events': for the terminology cf. *Phdr.* 268d 4f.

50a 17   'a mimesis of life': cf. *Laws* 817b 4

50a 29-33   the inadequacy of a series of set-speeches: cf. *Phdr.* 268c-d

50a 39ff.   visual analogy: cf. *Polit.* 277b-c

Ch. 7

50b 24ff.   poetic unity: see *Phdr.* 268d 4f., and cf. *Crat.* 425a. For general canons of order and unity see *Gorg.* 503e-4a, 506e, *Parm.* 137c.

50b 26f.   beginning-middle-end: *Phileb.* 31a, *Parm.* 137d, *Laws* 715e

50b 30   necessity as connective principle: *Phdr.* 264b (cf. *Theaet.* 149c, *Tim.* 40e for coupling of necessity and probability)

50b 34ff.   analogy with living creature: *Phdr.* 264c, cf. *Gorg.* 506d, *Rep.* 401a, *Tim.* 32d-33a, 87c

51a 10f.   principle of scale: cf. *Rep.* 423b on the size of a city (cf. ch.III n.27)

51a 13f.   fortune and misfortune: cf. *Rep.* 392c 2, 603c 5-7, *Laws* 814e (in dance)

Ch. 8
51a 30f.   mimesis of a single object: cf. *Laws* 669d 2

Ch. 9
51b 5ff.   comparison of poetry and philosophy: contrast Plato's references to, or expressions of, rivalry between them at *Rep.* 607b-c, *Laws* 817a-b, 967c, *Phaedo* 61a 3f. A limited affinity is allowed, but with a strong devaluation of poetry, at *Rep.* 475c-e (cf. 411a-e? and *Crat.* 406a).
51b 6f.   poetry and universals: Plato alleges a concern with particulars at *Rep.* 597b ff.

Ch. 13
52b 34-6   tragedy should eschew the exceptionally virtuous man's sufferings: for various relevant Platonic passages see esp. *Laws* 660e-661c, with *Rep.* 380a-b, 387d-e, 392a-b, 603e ff. *Rep.* 399a-c (*à propos* of music) envisages the drama of the good man's resistance to misfortune.
53a 4   pity for undeserved suffering: cf. *Laws* 936b
53a 10   *hamartia*: contrast Plato's use of the term at *Laws* 838c, referring to (putatively) culpable tragic acts. *Rep.* 396d may cover various types of tragic error.
53a 34f.   pandering to audiences: cf. *Gorg.* 502b-c, *Rep.* 493d, *Laws* 659b-c (Sicily), 700-701a
53a 35f.   the proper pleasure of tragedy: cf. *Phileb.*48a, *Rep.* 605c-e (cf. ch.I n.25)

Ch. 15
54a 16f.   goodness of character: a general Platonic requirement for poetry (e.g. *Rep.* 397d, 398a-b, 401b, cf. *Laws* 817b)
54b 1f.   avoidance of the theatrical 'machine': cf. *Crat.* 425d
54b 14f.   Achilles' character in Homer: contrast Plato's complaints at *Rep.* 391a-c

Ch. 17
55a 32-4   poetic madness: cf. e.g. *Apol.* 22b-c, *Meno* 99c-d, *Ion* 533e ff., *Phdr.* 245a, *Laws* 682a, 719c. See pp. 83f.

Chs. 20-21 passim

for related grammatical terminology cf. esp. *Crat.* 424c ff., *Soph.* 261-2

Ch. 23

59a 30 'divine' Homer: see *Ion* 530b 10, *Phaedo* 95a 2, with ch. IX n. 19

Ch. 24

60a 5ff. Homer's use of direct speech: cf. *Rep.* 393a-b

Ch. 25

60b 9-11 three possible objects of mimesis: cf. *Rep.* 598a 5 (for the first two), 392d (past, present, future), 598b (mimesis of appearances). See next item.

60b 13ff. artistic 'correctness' separated from moral, technical etc.: for Plato's identification of mimetic correctness with accurate image-making see esp. *Rep.* 598b ff., *Laws* 667d, 668b, 669a-b, and cf. *Phaedo* 74a-e, *Crat.* 430b-431c. For a freer principle note *Crat.* 432b-d. The identity of artistic with moral standards is apparently affirmed at *Laws* 655b, 669b 1, and often implied elsewhere. Artists' technical ignorance is mentioned at e.g. *Ion* 536e ff., *Rep.* 598c 1.

60b 25f. the poetic effect of terror (*ekplêxis*): cf. *Ion* 535b, with the same reference to *Iliad* 22.

60b 33ff. the charge of falsehood: see e.g. *Euthyph.* 6b-c, *Rep.* 364, 377d ff., 391b-e (*Poet.* 60b 36 looks like an echo of 391e 1), *Crat.* 408c, *Laws* 886b-c. Cf. ch. I n. 17.

61a 4ff. relevance of context, character etc. to judgements on art: *Laws* 719c-e seems to deprecate ironically the need for poets to give characters appropriate utterances.

61a 31ff. poetic self-contradiction: cf. *Protag.* 339b ff. (portraying Protagoras' criticism), *Laws* 719c 7.

61a 35ff. false presuppositions in criticism: cf. *Protag.* 341a-b, 343d

61b 12f. idealisation in visual art: cf. *Rep.* 472d, 484c, 500e-501b, with ch. IV n. 39

61b 23 the charge of 'harmful' against poetry: see e.g. *Rep.* 391e 4, *Laws* 656a 7 for just this.

Ch. 26

61b 26ff.   comparison of epic and tragedy: cf. *Laws* 658a-e

61b 29   a mimesis of everything: see the similar phrases at *Rep.*
397a 3, 398a 2 (and cf. 596c ff., *Soph.* 233d ff.)

Appendix 3
Drama in the Theatre:
Aristotle on 'spectacle' (*opsis*)

It is one of the more paradoxical aspects of the contrast between Plato's and Aristotle's views of drama that while the former's hostility encompasses a strong sense of the importance of public performance, Aristotle, the first major theorist of dramatic poetry, seems to sanction a clear separation of the playwright's art as such from its embodiment in the theatre.[1] A cursory reading of the *Poetics* is likely to leave the impression that its author's interest in theatrical production was slight; but closer attention to certain passages will prompt some qualification on such a conclusion. The argument of this appendix is that there is indeed an equivocation to be discerned in Aristotle's attitude to drama in the theatre, and I shall attempt both to demonstrate this and to offer a brief explanation.

It is first necessary to raise the question of what *opsis*, conventionally translated as 'spectacle', means for Aristotle. Is it, as Thomas Twining thought, 'the whole visible apparatus of the theatre', the '*Mise en scène*' of Potts' translation?[2] Or does it more narrowly denote the appearance of the actors (masks, costumes, and the players' physical contribution) and perhaps the chorus too?[3] When Aristotle introduces 'the arrangement of spectacle' as a

---

[1] Cf. Goldschmidt (1970) 112f., and see Janko 229, whose whole rehabilitation of Ar.'s attitude to *opsis* is well-balanced.

[2] Twining 74, note, Potts 24 etc. Cf. Butcher 146 ('the visible spectacular effect'), Rostagni (1945) on 49b 30-4 ('l'apparato scenico'), M. Walton, *The Greek Sense of Theatre* (London 1984) 20 ('the entire visual dimension'), Taplin 478 ('the entire visual aspect').

[3] Bywater on 49b 33, Else (1957) 233f., 278f., Grube (1965) 76, Lucas (1962) 56 (but less clear-cut in his 1968 commentary on 49b 33). Taplin 478 n.2 appears to assume that limiting *opsis* to the actors entails limiting it to costume. That is not so: it will still cover everything which focusses on the actors' persons (movements, gestures, actions, physical sufferings, etc.), as opposed to independent props, *skēnographia* etc. For *opsis* in reference to personal appearance see e.g. Ar. *Rhet.* 1381b l, Xen. *Mem.* 3.10.8. If we take *opsis* to include the chorus, this need not bring in choreographic *schēmata*, which Ar. might have categorised separately (and cf. n.8 below).

337

necessary part of tragedy, he deduces its function from the fact that tragic mimesis is performed by actors, and this favours the second of the two possibilities.[4] Of the six remaining direct references to *opsis*, four afford no help at all in settling the question (50a 10, 13, 59b 10, 62a 16).[5] The other two both tilt the balance towards the interpretation of the term as centring on the appearance of the actors, the first (ch. 6, 50b 16-20) because it specifically mentions actors and the mask-maker, the second (ch. 14, 53b 1-10) because it concerns the visual achievement of pitiable and fearful effects (or a spurious substitute for them), and it is difficult to see how, for the sort of Greek tragedies we know, this could concern anything other than the stage-figures themselves: we might think, for example, of the handling of the last scene of the *Oedipus Tyrannus*, in which the self-blinded king reappears, and more generally of the sphere of *pathos*, physical suffering.[6] To set against these passages there are only two details in the *Poetics* which positively suggest a wider conception of *opsis*: ch. 4's notorious reference, whose authenticity has in my view been wrongly impugned, to Sophocles' introduction of 'scene-painting';[7] and ch. 17's observations (see (c) below) on the poet's visualisation of his scenes (though here too the actor is the centre of attention). These passages may make us hesitate to conclude that other visual effects would necessarily be excluded from *opsis*, but they are insufficient to disturb the impression that in so far as Aristotle envisages 'spectacle' as part of drama, he is thinking

---

[4] 49b 31-3. Else (1957) 233f. wrongly takes *prattontes* here to mean the dramatic agents (cf. ch. V n.2). If they were, the deduction of necessary *opsis* would not follow, since *opsis* is not found in epic: see 59b 9f., which Else 597f. is compelled to treat as an interpolation; 62a 16 (with next note); and cf. 60a 14.

[5] 50a 13 is unfortunately corrupt, but appears to reinforce the necessary element of *opsis* in tragedy. On 62a 16 see Janko 228f. Bywater 250f. would also introduce the term at 56a 2 to designate a species of tragedy.

[6] The connection between *opsis* and *pathos* (on which *Rhet.* 1386b 1-4 has some bearing) is strengthened by the position of the remarks on the former at 53b 1ff.: I would argue that, taking ch. 14 as a whole, we have a positive emphasis on plot-structure set against the dispensability of *both* spectacle *and* the actuality of the tragic deed/suffering (*pathos*). *Pathos* would call for specific effects of *opsis*: note the examples (Ajax's suicide and Ixion's torment) of 'tragedies of *pathos*' at 55b 34f. I would also suggest that at 53b 6f. Ar. may have Oedipus' blinding particularly in mind: in this connection see *OT* 1224 (contrast between hearing and seeing), 1238 (*opsis* is missing), 1294 ff. (strong stress on *seeing* what has happened), 1296 (pity at the sight). On *pathos* cf. also ch. VII n.30.

[7] 49a 18f. Brown 1-8 has revived the case for an interpolation. While I cannot accept his arguments, I should say that retaining the reference to scene-painting need not commit one to believing that Ar. thought it of much importance.

principally of the various visual aspects of the actors, rather than the stage setting as a whole.

With this in mind, we can now proceed to a summary of the main points which emerge from the *Poetics'* treatment of *opsis*, when combined with the relevant implications of Aristotle's general conception of drama and of the theatre.

(a) The dramatic genres are species of poetic mimesis, whose media are language, rhythm and music (47a 22). At this fundamental level of his theory of poetry, Aristotle appears to make little or no allowance for performance: of the three media, only music seems to require it, though there is some uncertainty even here;[8] in any case, music has no bearing on the visual aspect of theatrical performance. Here, then, we have the basis for a theoretical divorce between dramatic poetry and the theatre.

(b) To set against (a) there is the fact that Aristotle acknowledges the place of performance in the *history* of poetry: in the improvisatory nature of the proto-dramatic forms (48b 23f., 49a 9-13), and in the reference to details in the development of drama concerning the actors and their performances (number of actors, masks, scene-painting).

(c) More sharply against the grain of (a), Aristotle includes *opsis* as a necessary part of tragedy (and the same would certainly hold for comedy): 49b 31-3, 50a 9f. By doing so he appears to envisage performance as the appropriate and essential embodiment of dramatic poetry.[9] The point is confirmed by several later passages: in

---

[8] It is just conceivable, though unlikely, that *harmonia* could be encompassed by poetic recitation without music: cf. purely vocal *harmonia* at 49a 28 and *Rhet.* 1403b 31, 1408b 33. If *opsis* were indispensable to dramatic poetry (as 49b 31-3 seems to concede), Ar. should have included a visual medium (cf. *schêmata* at 55a 29). On poetic recitation cf. ch. II n.30.

Note for comparison that by including dance under the same generic media as poetry at 47a 26f., Ar. finds himself mentioning choreographic *schêmata* only in parenthesis (27f.). This is interesting and significant. Dance could be viewed from the point of view of its cultural association with music and poetry, or as a kinetic equivalent to the visual arts (or, of course, as both); Ar.'s clear preference for the former categorisation implies that he regards dance as primarily *rhythm*: the visual dimension is conceptually played down, as with drama.

[9] Note, however, the term *kosmos* at 49b 33. As with linguistic *kosmos* (57b 2 etc., but undefined) it may imply something optional or additional, beyond the necessary: cf. e.g. *Top.* 157a 7ff., *EE* 1233a 34-6.

ch. 17, 55a 22-32, where Aristotle urges the composing dramatist to visualise his scene as vividly as possible, and in particular to imagine the gestures which will accompany his text; in ch. 24, 59b 24-6, where a point about the nature of tragedy is tied to the theatrical setting and the presence of actors; and in ch. 24, 60a 14, where he comments on the extra freedom allowed to epic, in contrast to tragedy, by the fact that we do not actually see the agents in the action. The first of these passages is particularly important for its suggestion that *opsis* (though not so named here) must be fully reckoned with by the poet when conceiving and elaborating his plot-structure.[10] It seems here again to be accepted that the poet properly aims at a theatrical performance of his drama.

(d) But the passages cited in (c) must now in turn be qualified by those in which Aristotle distinguishes between the art of the poet and the art(s) of those responsible for the visual management of a performance. The main statement of this principle occurs at the end of ch. 6 (50b 16-20), where although the emotional potency of *opsis* is acknowledged (see (e) below), Aristotle separates the potential of tragedy from 'performance and actors', and adds that 'the art of the mask-maker is more effective in the creation of visual effects than the poet's'. Part of this passage is often translated as saying that spectacle is 'unartistic':[11] but what Aristotle clearly means is that it is not part of the *poet's* art, but someone else's. So we are dealing with a typically Aristotelian analysis of skills and functions, the result of which is evidently to make the dramatic poet's art independent of the theatre *in principle*. Further passages which touch on the point are 49a 7-9, where a distinction is made between tragedy 'in itself' and 'in relation to the theatre'; 51a 6-10, where the intrinsic criterion of poetic scale is distinguished from one determined by theatrical conditions; 53b 3-7 and 62a 11-18, where Aristotle argues (though

[10] Ch. 17 in general perhaps shows a more practical concern with theatre than other parts of the treatise: Solmsen 200. Taplin 477 unnecessarily restricts the force of the passage, and 55a 24 shows that Allan (1971) 84 is wrong to take Ar. to be urging the dramatist to visualise the production *rather than* the actual events. Close to 55a 22ff. is the rhetorical principle at *Rhet.* 1386a 28ff. (cited in ch. VI p. 181). Cf. also ch. III n.10.

[11] 50b 17 (cf. 53b 8). For this or similar translation see e.g Butcher 29, Bywater 23, Brown 6, Potts 27 ('crudest'). *Atechnos* can mean 'outside the art', i.e. a given art (e.g. *Rhet.* 1355b 35, 1375a 22), though it is true that it seems to have a stronger evaluative force at *Poet.* 54b 20, 28f., 31. Ar. would regard the mask-maker's and actor's arts as subordinate to the poet's: for this hierarchical view of *technai* see *EN* 1094a 9ff., *Pol.* 1256a 3ff. In addition, mask-making would be considered banausic.

under pressure of combatting the charge of theatrical vulgarity) that tragedy can be appreciated and effective in reading as well as in performance. To understand the force of these last two passages in particular, but also Aristotle's position in general, it is important to remember that what is meant by reading here is probably what we would consider a kind of recitation, as the references to 'hearing' at 53b 5f. indicate: Aristotle's point is therefore not quite on a level with Johnson's 'a play read affects the mind like a play acted', though this, together with Johnson's 'a dramatic exhibition is a book recited with concomitants ...', does have something in common with the spirit of the *Poetics*. Aristotle should not be paraphrased as advocating the superiority of reading to performance; his principle is that dramatic poetry, and the poet's art, cannot strictly be tied to the conditions of production or be judged by theatrical standards.

(e) Objections to the position summarised in (d) often slide into the vague complaint that Aristotle was insensitive to the visual experience of dramatic performance. This slur is difficult to sustain, provided we do not expect the effusions of the theatre-critic from the philosopher (Aristotle's taste is very discreet). At the end of ch. 6 (50b 16) he acknowledges the emotional potency of *opsis* with a term which he uses elsewhere in the *Poetics* only of the special power of the elements of the complex plot, reversal and recognition (50a 33).[12] Such small details, in a work like the *Poetics*, are telling. We have also seen (in (c) above) that in ch. 17 (55a 22-32) Aristotle supplies an image of the poet in the act of composing which incorporates the vivid anticipation of the visual embodiment of his poetry by an actor. Finally, in ch. 14, 53b 1-14, he indicates that *opsis* can be a source of the true tragic emotions, pity and fear, even though he goes on to stress the dispensability of this visual reinforcement to the dramatic poem as such, and to frown on the misuse of spectacle to achieve an effect of 'the portentous' or 'the sensational'. The negative accent of the passage should not prevent us from still giving some attention to what it clearly if unelaborately concedes, which can fairly be taken to imply that the ideal performance will harness *opsis* to the realisation of the dramatist's aims.[13]

---

[12] For this term, *psuchagôgikon*, see ch. II n. 24.

[13] Some would see a reference to such congruence at 53a 28: in objecting to this, Bywater ad loc. (repeated by Lucas (1968)) misses the point that Ar. is emphasising

The above outline is not intended to vindicate Aristotle's understanding of theatrical spectacle and performance against all possible objections, but to show first that his attitude is not as straightforwardly anti-theatrical as is sometimes alleged, and secondly that there is an ineliminable equivocation in his statements on the importance of performance for the realisation of dramatic tragedy's effects (an equivocation crystallised in (c) and (d) above). Aristotle's views certainly deserve not to suffer reductive paraphrase. We have seen that he was fully aware (how could he not be in Greek culture, and as a historian of the theatre himself?) of the essential *cultural* status of drama as performance. We have seen too that this cultural fact influences the analysis of the 'parts' of tragedy, among which *opsis* is included as necessary; and that the *Poetics* also contains clear acknowledgements of the force of the visual in drama, and of the need for the poet to take imaginative account of this when composing. Yet with all this we cannot but contrast the unambiguous separation of the poet's art from those used in theatrical performance, as well as the fact that drama is treated within a larger framework of poetic analysis which makes no theoretical allowance for the visual.

A combination of three factors will give us, I suggest, at least the basis of an explanation for this instability in Aristotle's position. Two are theatrical. The first is the likelihood (though some would contest it) that in the Athenian theatrical tradition which forms the main background to the *Poetics* the visual was subordinate to the rhetorical and vocal nature of the actor's art.[14] If this is right, Aristotle's tendency to separate the poet's art from the theatre is easier to understand, since the primary art operative in performance itself would be the actor's, with which the poet's could hardly be identified: they might even, indeed, carry contradictory require-ments (51b 35ff.). But to this we need to add a more particular fact about the theatre of Aristotle's own century, its apparently increasing break-up of an older convention by which dramatists had been directly involved (even sometimes as actors) in the productions of their own plays. The departure from tradition was marked by three

---

how audiences who normally prefer a different sort of play (53a 33-5) can be brought to appreciate the type in question, provided it is effectively staged.
   [14] I shall explain and justify this claim in a paper on 'Greek Tragic Acting' which I hope will be published in the near future.

phenomena: first, the re-staging of old plays, now inevitably removed from the guiding designs of the playwrights; secondly, the establishment of the independent 'producer', and the clearer demarcation between his and the poet's functions; and, lastly, the growing availability of dramatic texts in a culture which had previously relied predominantly on performance for its access to drama. These circumstances encourage one to believe that Aristotle's attitude to *opsis* was in part a reflection of the more recent stages of the Greek theatrical tradition: that he was responding, that is, to the loosening of the bond between text and performance, but also perhaps reacting against the dominance of producers and actors in the contemporary theatre, which he himself attests in the *Rhetoric*.[15]

But I do not think that we here have a complete explanation. The third main factor to be considered lies firmly within the *Poetics'* own terms of reference. As with the other neglected, and closely associated, 'part' of tragedy, *melopoeia* or 'lyric poetry' (see ch. VIII above), it is to the inner character of the theory of poetry itself that we must ultimately look for an understanding of Aristotle's views on the theatre. If, as this book has consistently tried to argue, we read the *Poetics* as a text which belongs to a philosophical system, with all the pertinent presuppositions of that system latent in it, we should not have any difficulty in seeing the significance of Aristotle's attempt to turn the poet into an artist who is the maker not of materials for the theatre (though he may be incidentally that in practice) but of poetic constructs, *muthoi*, the experience of which is cognitive and emotional, but not directly dependent on the senses, as it would have to be if drama could only be fully realised in acted performance. It is this philosophical enterprise which accounts for the strong thrust in the *Poetics* towards a theoretical separation of poetry from performance, drama from the theatre. The equivocation which is still to be discerned in the treatise should perhaps be attributed to the clash between this impulse and the unavoidable recognition that Greek tragedy had been born, had grown and had flourished in performance.

---

[15] *Rhet.* 1403b 32f. Marzullo's article sees in Ar.'s attitude to *opsis* a reaction against the contemporary theatre and a defence of an older style of dramaturgy.

Appendix 4
Aristotle on Language (*lexis*)

Lexis is the last of the six 'parts' of tragedy to be analysed by Aristotle, but his discussion of it in chs. 19-22 means ostensibly that more space is devoted to it than to any other element apart from plot-structure. That, however, is a crude measure of the status of this section of the treatise. Chs. 19-22 are not only abstruse and difficult in many places (creating a dry impression which produces noticeable ennui even in most commentators), but the inescapable fact is that, while formally belonging to the theory of tragedy, they have precious little to say about the genre. One reason for this may be that most of the material here was composed early in Aristotle's career, perhaps as a general study of language and style, and that Aristotle later saw no reason to pursue its implications for tragedy as such in more detail.[1] But that speculation still leaves something more to be said about this section of the treatise, and about Aristotle's attitude to the poetic language of tragedy.

A certain amount has been already intimated about the philosopher's conception of language in tragedy even before we reach the chapters on *lexis*. From the start of the work there are hints of a view of poetic language as a combination of elements: *logos* (which is essentially 'meaning', or the common factor in all language), to which are added the accessories or embellishments of metre and music. This seems to have been a view which was held by others. Gorgias had defined poetry as 'language (*logos*) with metre', and similar ideas occur in his pupil Isocrates, as well as in Plato.[2] Where Aristotle certainly differed from these thinkers was in his theoretical refusal to make metre the defining criterion of poetry (47b 14ff., 51a 38ff., 51b 27), but this does not affect the underlying notion of

---

[1] For the early date of material in this part of the *Poetics* see Appendix 1, § 1 (b) v-vi.

[2] Cf. e.g. Plato *Rep.* 398d, Gorgias fr. 11.9, Isoc. 2.7, 9.10f., 15.45-7. On Ar.'s casual acceptance of metre as the criterion of poetry outside the *Poetics* see ch. IX n.46.

language. Thus, certain prose genres are described as using 'bare language' (47a 29, i.e. without rhythm or music), tragedy and epic are said to have in common the use of 'language (*logos*) with metre' (49b 10, very close to Gorgias's formulation), and the medium of tragedy in the definition of the genre is 'language garnished in various ways in the separate parts [of the play]' (49b 25f.). Aristotle elaborates this element of the definition by referring to the spoken verses and the lyrics of tragedy, and it is the former alone which is covered by *lexis*, 'the composition of the spoken verses' (49b 34f.). A further definition of *lexis* is offered at 50b 13-15: 'I mean by *lexis* ... the verbal expression, which has the same meaning for compositions in both verse and prose.' The relation between *lexis* and the chief task of the playwright is aptly crystallised in the dictum of ch. 9, 'the poet ought to be a maker of plot-structures rather than of verses' (51b 27f.). The poet's principal work, in other words, is the intelligible design of the poem, its essential framework; and the language is something then used to fill in this structure and to give it a continuous fabric. The combination of the primary poetic artefact – the structure of action – with the verbal expression which fleshes it out is recapitulated in a phrase at 55a 22f., where the poet is said 'to construct his plots and to finish them off with language'.[3]

When we reach the analysis of *lexis* itself at 56b 8ff., we may reasonably expect this relationship between structure and language to be clarified, and the distinctive nature of poetic language to be illuminated. Neither expectation can honestly be said to be fulfilled. After dismissing certain technical Protagorean criticisms of Homer's linguistic usage as having no serious import for the study of poetry, Aristotle proceeds himself in ch. 20 to provide a grammatical analysis of language of the kind of which there are hints in Plato, and which Hellenistic writers – particularly the Stoics and Alexandrians – were later to develop in various ways.[4] (Part of ch. 21, 58a 8-17, contains

[3] Ar. may here be thinking in terms close to those of his visual comparison at 50a 39ff., since language very similar to that of 55a 22f. is used of *painting* at Gorgias fr. 11.18, Plato *Protag.* 312d, *Rep.* 548d, *Soph.* 234b, 235e, 236c, *Laws* 656e.

[4] Note that Ar. *does* allow the relevance of Protagorean linguistics to poetics at *Int.* 17a 5f. For a treatment of *Poetics* 20 see Morpurgo-Tagliabue 13ff., 39ff. (who regards small parts as spurious; but earlier rejections of the whole chapter are unfounded). The chapter is put in the context of the wider evidence for Ar.'s views on language by R. A. Zirin, 'Aristotle's Biology of Language', *TAPA* 110 (1980) 325-47. For a sketch of later Greek linguistics see Robins ch. 2, and details on many points in Pfeiffer's book (esp. 266ff.).

a brief note on grammatical gender which belongs in this same category.) We approach closer to matters of style in ch. 21, where we find a classification of word-usage (ordinary words, dialect terms, metaphor, etc.) which prepares the ground for the remarks on style proper (that is, on general patterns of word-usage or types of vocabulary) which follow in ch. 22.

The first reason why even ch. 22 is likely to disappoint modern expectations is that it is curiously desultory. Apart from general references to the style of the minor writers, Cleophon and Sthenelus (58a 20f.), Aristotle cites the following examples: a recherché image from the poetess Cleoboulina; some parodies of epic metrical licences by an unidentifiable Eucleides; one line each by Aeschylus and Euripides; two lines from the *Odyssey* and a phrase from the *Iliad*; and some ordinary tragic phrases parodied as abstruse by Ariphrades (perhaps a comic poet). This somewhat jejune collection of material reflects the fact that much of the chapter is devoted to negative or apologetic remarks and observations: criticisms of basic stylistic faults, and the defence of major poets against a kind of parody which Aristotle (with youthful earnestness?) appears to take more seriously than it merited. This means also that the few positive principles of style which are advanced remain undeveloped and on the level of rather bland generality.

Nonetheless, the gist of the generalisations is unmistakable: 'the virtue of style is to be clear without being commonplace' (58a 18: 'the common word exact without vulgarity'?). Ch. 22 briefly elaborates this maxim in terms of the categories listed in the previous chapter, so that the stylistic mixture and balance commended – transparently an Aristotelian mean (esp. 58b 12f.) – is formulated as a moderate and appropriate infusion of metaphor, 'ornament' and other special word-types into the stock of current, normal and so *clear* vocabulary. As far as tragedy is concerned, Aristotle's primary assumption is that the style or vocabulary of the spoken verses 'imitates ordinary speech as much as possible' (59a 12), though it is also plain from references to dignity of style at 58a 21 and, much earlier, at 49a 19ff., that this cannot be taken to entail the reproduction of the simplest register of language. It is the unresolved or unrefined relation between the two principal requirements – clarity and dignity – which is perhaps the salient feature of Aristotle's view of poetic style.

Some light is cast on the point by the first twelve chapters of

Rhetoric Book 3, which are closely related to this part of the *Poetics*.[5] In discussing the style of rhetorical prose, Aristotle argues that fifth-century prose-style (such as Gorgias's) developed under the influence of ornate poetic style, but that such a style is inappropriate to rhetoric and has indeed been subsequently modified even in some poetry, including tragedy. Although Aristotle nowhere sets out his view in full, it is evident that he believed in a process of stylistic evolution: so much is explicitly indicated, in fact, at *Poet.* 49a 19-24. Where tragedy is concerned, however, a serious uncertainty remains. At *Rhet.* 1404b 25f. Euripides is said to have been the first to demonstrate how an appropriate stylistic blend of the normal or natural and the surprising or unusual could be attained. This appears to be a style which Aristotle approves of for tragedy, and it harmonises with his belief that the iambic metre is the closest to the rhythm of ordinary speech. Yet it also appears to be the style above all of *contemporary* tragedy. On this point, if on no other, it may be necessary to infer that fourth-century trends strongly shaped Aristotle's thinking.[6]

To this possibility (it can scarcely be demonstrated) must be added the significant if paradoxical tendency of Aristotle to assimilate the style of poetry to prose. The paradox resides in the fact that while asserting their difference (*Rhet.* 1404a 28f.) Aristotle defines their respective virtues, in the *Poetics* and *Rhetoric*, so similarly as to suggest a clear convergence; and this is confirmed at *Poet.* 59a 12f. specifically for tragedy. A distinction in the degree to which they depart from, or produce embellishments on, ordinary spoken language, remains intact, and where genres other than tragedy are concerned Aristotle does not pretend that any confusion is possible (though *Rhet.* 1404a 34f. claims an approximation to prose-style for contemporary hexameter poetry too): hence it is with dithyramb, epic and other poetry in mind that he makes some of his references to 'poetic' style in the *Rhetoric*, contrasting it with desirable standards for prose (1406a 5f., 11-14, 32, 1406b 1ff., 1407a 34ff.). But between *tragedy* and rhetorical prose the stylistic differential seems to be almost obliterated by Aristotle's principle, already quoted from *Poet.* 59a 12, that the poetic genre imitates ordinary speech (or

---

[5] See Appendix 1, § 1 (b) vi. For a discussion of the relation between the two passages see Morpurgo-Tagliabue 201ff., with due stress on some differences.

[6] On the style of contemporary tragedy see *Rhet.* 1404a 29ff. (comparing *Poet.* 49a 21ff.). Cf. Bywater viii-ix, Xanthakis-Karamanos 61.

vocabulary) as far as possible. If the *Rhetoric* does little to justify this idea, except by apparently supporting it with reference to *contemporary* poets at 1404a 29ff., it does at least make clear that for Aristotle to commend a relatively plain tragic *lexis* is for him to show respect for its serious significance. This is because Aristotle's fundamental view of language holds *clarity* to be the indispensable virtue, and this is taken to be best attainable by close adherence to ordinary vocabulary (*Poet.* 58a 18f.). Beyond this, all is a matter of additional decoration or garnishing, and such garnishing is by definition never essential.[7]

Hence Aristotle opens up a strong division between style and meaning, so that in some spheres (geometry is his wry example, at *Rhet.* 1404a 12) *lexis* – the stylistically conscious choice of words – can be reduced to a minimum, while, on the other side of the same coin, Aristotle can advocate in *Poetics* 24 that the poet should particularly apply himself to style in those parts of his poem which are lacking in 'thought' or characterisation: brilliant *lexis* would elsewhere detract from the effect of the more essential elements mentioned (60b 2-5). Style is separable from sense, and secondary to it. Clarity is the first aim for the writer or speaker with something to say. An admixture of language above the ordinary level is desirable for dignity of tone, but in prose this must not be allowed to excess. Stylistic excess is precisely a feature of some poetry, but in the genre which Aristotle values most highly, tragedy, the natural process of cultural evolution has brought about a shedding of distracting ornament.

But it would be wrong and misleading to complete these brief observations on Aristotle's conception of language and style without an acknowledgement of his most famous pronouncement on the subject. The 'greatest attribute of all' in poetic style is the use of metaphor – it is unteachable and a sign of natural ability; and it consists in the capacity to perceive likenesses. Moreover, it

---

[7] On Ar.'s use of the categories 'ornament' and 'garnishing' see ch. VIII n. 3 and Appendix 3 n.9. 60b 11-13 refers to stylistic heightenings as a concession to poets.

It helps to understand Ar.'s emphasis on clarity if we note the association between ambiguity and sophistry, disreputable rhetoric and the like: see e.g. *Top.* 130a 1ff., *SE* 165b 26ff., *Rhet.* 1375b 11-13, with W. B. Stanford, *Ambiguity in Greek Literature* (Oxford 1939) 13-16. Ambiguity is a means of disguising vacuity in both rhetoric and poetry (Empedocles!) at *Rhet.* 1407a 32ff. The wider use of style to dress up emptiness of thought is diagnosed in poetry at *Rhet.* 1404a 24f. (referring especially to *early* poetry: cf. *Poet.* 50a 35-8).

particularly suits the style of the two most important genres, epic and tragedy (*Poet.* 59a 5-13, 59b 35f.). Although metaphor can be analytically examined and classified, as it is in both the *Poetics* and the *Rhetoric*, it clearly remains resistant, in Aristotle's eyes, to a 'technical' understanding. It is only in the case of metaphor that we sense a complete harmony of meaning and style in Aristotle's view of language. The reason for this is that metaphor, although it *can* be regarded as a stylistic ornament alongside other types, is valued by the philosopher as a unique means of expressing certain perceptions. As *Rhet.* 1410b 10ff. explains, it is metaphor above all which communicates understanding and insight (whether serious or humorous) by *indissoluble* linguistic means.

Appendix 5
Interpretations of *katharsis*

This appendix is designed to supplement my arguments in ch. VI with a conspectus and critical appraisal of the main interpretations of the *katharsis* clause which have been put forward in the past or are current today. I cannot claim to be even remotely comprehensive, nor have I space to deal with all the nuances of individual treatments of the issue: Renaissance writers in particular tend to mix elements of different interpretations. I ignore some tediously idiosyncratic contributions, and attempt to identify the main schools of thought.

Various surveys of material on *katharsis* can be found in the following (see the Bibliography for further details where appropriate):

A. Döring, *Die Kunstlehre des Aristoteles* 263-306
Bywater's edn. of the *Poetics*, 361-5 (but cf. ch. VI n. 42)
J. Gillet, 'The Catharsis-clause in German Criticism before Lessing', *JP* 35 (1920) 95-112
M. Kommerell, *Lessing und Aristoteles* 268-72
G. Else, *CW* 48 (1954) 75-7
H. Flashar, *Hermes* 84 (1956) 12-18
V. Kostić, 'Aristotle's Catharsis in Renaissance Poetics'
B. Hathaway, *The Age of Criticism* 205-300
K Gründer, 'Jacob Bernays und der Streit um die Katharsis'
D. Keesey, 'On some Recent Interpretations of Catharsis'
C. Wagner, ' "Katharsis" in der aristotelischen Tragödiendefinition'
(For concepts of *katharsis* which do not purport to be interpretations of Aristotle see e.g. Henn 14-16 and Keesey 194-7.)

(1) The period of neo-classicism was dominated by the MORALISTIC or DIDACTIC view of *katharsis*, according to which tragedy teaches the audience by example – or counter-example – to

350

curb its own emotions and the faults which they may cause: we learn through *katharsis* to avoid those passions which can lead to suffering and tragedy. On this interpretation, whose roots lie deep in neo-classicism, *katharsis* becomes synonymous with direct ethical teaching or protreptic: see Hathaway 221 ff. It appears first in the Italians Segni and Maggi, and later in Corneille, Rapin and Dacier in France, Dryden and Johnson in England, to mention only the most prominent.

Four features of this interpretation should be noted: first, that it altogether ignores the homoeopathic element indicated in the *katharsis* clause (and confirmed by *Politics* 8); secondly, that it tends to put more weight on fear than on pity, since the former fits better with a didactic emphasis; thirdly, that this fear is wholly self-regarding: see e.g. Corneille's second *Discours*; fourthly, that the passions removed by *katharsis* are usually thought to be other than pity and fear – such things as anger, hate, envy, ambition.

It should also be mentioned that the moralistic interpretation sometimes incorporates the medical analogy drawn by Aristotle in *Politics* 8: this occurs first in Minturno, whose view of *katharsis* was composite (see Kostić 66f.); and Dacier (among others) calls tragedy 'une véritable médecine'. But the important point is that the medical analogy is *dispensable* to these and other similar writers; it is not central to the interpretation, as it is later to become for Bernays and others (see (4) below). Readings of the *katharsis* clause should therefore not be categorised on the basis of their recognition or lack of recognition of the medical analogy. Cf. (3) below on Milton.

The didactic view was decisively criticised by Lessing in *Hamburgische Dramaturgie* nos. 77–8: his own interpretation should not be confused with it, as it still sometimes is (see (3) below).

(2) In principle separable from the moralistic interpretation, though in practice often overlapping with it, is the notion of *katharsis* as the acquisition of EMOTIONAL FORTITUDE: through exposure to others' greater sufferings, our susceptibility to pity and fear in our own lives is lessened. Tragedy helps us to become inured to misfortune and so better able to tolerate it: thus the poetic experience is 'une sorte d'apprentissage du malheur', preparing us for life (C. Batteux, *Les Quatre Poëtiques d'Aristote* etc. (Paris 1771) vol. 1, 283).

Such an idea is interestingly first found in a later contemporary of Aristotle's, the comic poet Timocles (fr. 6 Kock, regarded as a direct

echo of Aristotle by Stark 57, 83 ff.). A similar idea occurs in Marcus
Aurelius, *Med.* 11.6 (referred to by e.g. Dacier, who rejects a 'Stoic'
view of *katharsis*, but whose own composite theory certainly contains
an element of acquiring fortitude). It would not in fact be inapt to
call this view loosely stoical; it has also been dubbed the Mithridatic
principle (by reference to M.'s use of prophylactics against poisoning):
Hathaway 214 ff. In the Renaissance the fortitude theory was
subscribed to, in varying degrees, by e.g. Robortello, Minturno and
Castelvetro: see Kostić 62f., 66-8.

This reading is often found in conjunction with (1), and the
distinction between them can be, and was, blurred by the common
didactic principle that tragedy teaches us to learn fortitude by
showing the fickleness of fortune. But, unlike the pure didactic
reading, the fortitude theory can be regarded as coping with the
homoeopathic aspect indicated by the *katharsis* clause in the *Poetics*:
we grow emotionally stronger through an experience which involves
the very emotions that are consequently toughened. There is
therefore some affinity with (3) below, but the significant difference
subsists between an interpretation, the present one, which makes the
reduction of emotional susceptibility a goal in itself, and the following
one, the kernel of which is moderation. Taken to an extreme (as in
strict Stoicism) the fortitude theory would presumably aim at total
immunity to emotion in our own lives – hardly an Aristotelian ideal.

(3) Groupable under the broad heading of MODERATION are
those readings of *katharsis* which relate it in some way to Aristotle's
notion of the mean. I have argued for one form of this view myself in
ch. VI. As indicated above, this approach differs from the preceding
by virtue of positing a process (or effect) of psychological attunement
or balance, not one of simple or invariable reduction: it is even
conceivable that *katharsis* is meant to entail a *heightened* capacity for
emotion on the part of those who are deficient in the appropriate
feelings (cf. *Rhet.* 1382b 34 ff., 1385b 19 ff.). The crucial factor, then,
in this school of interpretation is the Aristotelian concept of
habituation: the principle that our actions and experiences help to
shape our future capacities for the same actions and experiences. The
arousal of pity and fear, by the best tragic means, accustoms us to
feeling these emotions in the right way and to the right extent (cf. ch.
VI n. 39). It should be stressed that the neo-platonist texts which
refer to *katharsis*, and which probably derive in part from Aristotle's

early work, *On Poets*, explicitly and clearly refer to the principle of balance and the mean (cf. ch. I n. 2).

Vettori and Piccolomini are the two leading Cinquecento proponents of such a view: see Kostić 65f., 68. It was given a lucid statement by Daniel Heinsius, in ch. II of *De tragoediae constitutione* (1611), where, despite the use of a corrupt text of the definition of tragedy (and one which was conventional until the nineteenth century), the key points of Aristotle's response to Plato, and the essential standard of the mean, are both set out. Contrary to what is sometimes claimed, Milton's preface to *Samson Agonistes* (1671) should also be classed in this category, his paraphrase of *katharsis* being 'to temper and reduce' the passions 'to just measure'. (On Milton see Kostić 72, House 105, 110, Rees (1972b) 7-11). Milton's use of a medical analogy is *not* the essential point (see on Minturno in (1) above) and does not make him a precursor of the Bernaysian school, *pace* Bernays himself, 94f., Bywater *JP* 27 (1901) 267-75, Lucas (1968) 278. Twining 231-42, who professes agreement with Milton, can be cited as a further supporter of the moderation theory of *katharsis*, as can Lessing in the *Hamburgische Dramaturgie* nos. 77-8 (cf. ch. X pp. 312 ff. and nn. 40-3). Even after Bernays, some nineteenth-century Germans persisted with attempts to relate *katharsis* to Aristotle's ethical mean: cf. Gründer 509f. For modern adherents of such a position see ch. VI n. 40.

(4) The dominant modern trend has been to take *katharsis* as a process of emotional release or OUTLET – a harmlessly pleasurable means of expending pent-up or excessive emotions. The patron-saint (though not quite the founder) of this view is Bernays, who interprets the process as a *pathological* phenomenon: Aristotle's position in the *Politics* 8 passage is 'ein pathologischer Gesichtspunkt' (10). It is important, however, as I have already stressed in (3) above, not to identify the Bernaysian school of interpretation purely by reference to a medical analogy. The critical point is that Bernays and others have emphasised this analogy in order to give to *katharsis* the exclusive sense of therapeutic or quasi-therapeutic *relief*, and to rule out any question of an ethical dimension to the experience; whereas earlier writers such as Minturno, Milton and Dacier employed the medical analogy in combination with various types of moral reading of the doctrine. For discussions of *katharsis* within the Bernaysian consensus see e.g. Bywater 152-61, Dirlmeier *Hermes* 75 (1940)

81-92, Flashar (with a full-blown medical interpretation, but cf. ch. VI n.35), Schadewaldt, Lucas (1968) App II, Söffing 57-65.

I have already expressed some doubts about the outlet theory of *katharsis*, particularly when given a strong pathological colouring: cf. ch. VI pp. 190ff. and nn. 33, 35, 37. Here I pick out two related points:

i.   the theory does not satisfactorily account for the special phrasing of the *katharsis* clause, since it makes it say that the relief or outlet of the emotions is effected through their arousal: but how else? Why should Aristotle not have written simply 'effecting the *katharsis* of pity and fear'? And it is especially difficult to see why *katharsis* should be mentioned in the definition at all, if it is merely the 'Endeffekt', the return to normality after the turbulence of the tragic emotions, which Schadewaldt calls it.

ii.   Greek medicine cannot furnish a proper basis for the homoeopathic aspect of the phenomenon, and close scrutiny of *Politics* 8 shows that Aristotle does not appeal to medicine for one: his primary illustration is a ritual process (reinterpreted psychologically), and medicine is brought in as a secondary comparison (cf. ch. VI n. 37).

(5) Apart from (1), all the above interpretations at least agree in regarding *katharsis* as essentially a matter of emotional experience. But there have been some recent attempts to deduce from the *Poetics* a doctrine of INTELLECTUAL *katharsis*. Such positions must not be simply equated with the general and independently important proposition (for which see pp. 173ff.) that the tragic emotions depend on cognitive judgements about the dramatic action.

(a) Golden (1962) offers the first of many statements of the view that *katharsis* means intellectual 'clarification': it is 'a synonym for the process of inference ... described in chapter 4' (58). For later statements see Golden & Hardison 114ff. (conceding 'alleviation' as a byproduct, 119), and Golden's articles in *CP* 64 (1969) 145-53, *CQ* 23 (1973) 45f., *JAAC* 31 (1973) 473-9, *CP* 71 (1976) 77-85, *CJ* 72 (1976) 27-33, *Hermes* 104 (1976) 437-52 (*ad infinitum?*).

This theory rightly emphasises the cognitive status of mimetic art which Aristotle affirms in *Poetics* 4 (cf. pp. 71ff.), and it claims the merit of connecting *katharsis* with the earlier chapters of the treatise (but 49b 23f. need not mean that everything in the definition has been previously mentioned: on any argument, pity and fear have not been). The following objections, however, show decisively that it is unwarranted to make *katharsis* synonymous with the cognitive experience of mimesis (see also Wagner 71 ff. for a critique):

i.   the theory depends on the unjustified translation of 'pity and fear' in the definition as '[events arousing] pity and fear', and also takes the second part of the clause (*pathêmatôn*) dubiously to mean the events of the play.

ii. the theory wilfully ignores the evidence of *Politics* 8 (to refer, as Golden's 1972 article does (475) to '*the mere appearance* of the term catharsis in the *Politics*' (my ital.) is deliberately to suppress the cross-reference to a discussion of poetry (cf. p. 190 and n. 32).

iii. even disregarding point i above, the interpretation makes the first part of the *katharsis* clause redundant by virtual tautology.

iv. to claim that the *Poetics* is concerned 'with the nature of tragedy, not the response of the audience' (Golden & Hardison 116) is a *petitio principii*, as well as self-contradictory, since intellectual clarification must equally be experienced by audience or reader (Keesey 202 f. finds this a 'fruitful ambiguity' in the interpretation).

v.   the interpretation leaves Aristotle without a response to Plato's charges against the emotional irresponsibility of poetry: cf. Hubbard 88 n.2.

(b) Ničev (1970) esp. 33-90 and (1982) 10-15 suggests that *katharsis* means the removal of the spectator's false opinion about (and consequently his pity and fear for) the tragic agent, at the point at which the latter's culpability (N.'s view of *hamartia*) is perceived. The following objections will here suffice:

i.   the implications of the *katharsis* clause's phrasing are again ignored.

ii. according to *Poet.* 13-14 pity and fear are *aroused* by the change of fortune (the point at which N. would have them disappear).

iii. *Poet.* 52a 3f., N.'s key passage, similarly refers to the production of pity and fear in connection with the paradoxical turn of events (on which cf. ch. VII n. 15), not their removal.

(6) There are various theories which can be given the loose description of DRAMATIC or STRUCTURAL *katharsis* – theories, that is, which locate *katharsis* as an internal and objective feature of the poetic work itself. Twining 235 refers to an apparent instance in the eighteenth century; for Goethe's famous view see e.g. Bernays 4f. The main modern exponent of such an interpretation is Else (1957) 224-32, 423-50, who describes *katharsis* as 'the purification of the tragic act by the demonstration that its motive was not *miaron* [morally repellent]' (439). We come to realise, according to Else, that the agent is innocent and therefore not polluted, and so our emotions towards him are released (the theory having, after all, clear affective implications). The following is a selection of objections:

  i.   the link with *Politics* 8 has to be ignored (Else 231 n. 36, with some unease).
  ii. the objection made in 5 a i above applies also to Else's translation.
  iii. on Else's interpretation, *katharsis* belongs only to complex plots (444f.), yet it is part of the definition of the genre.
  iv. innocence does *not* generally guarantee freedom from pollution (Else 427-33 relies on Platonic evidence): thus in Soph. *OT* Oedipus is still polluted at the end, 1227f., 1424-9 (cited by E. himself, 431 n. 76, and cf. 426 n. 52). The phrase 'exculpation … from polluted intent' (447) illustrates the confusion.

For further criticisms of Else see e.g. Vickers App. I, and Wimsatt. Else is followed by Düring (1966) 173-5, and, with qualifications, by N. van der Ben, in Bremer (1976) 1-15. Partially akin to Else's are also the readings of Goldstein 573-7 (*katharsis* is 'some sort of ordering of pitiable and terrible material', 574), and H. D. F. Kitto, 'Catharsis', in *The Classical Tradition*, ed. L. Wallach (New York 1966) 133-47 ('a "cleaning-up" or "purifying" of painful incidents', leaving something 'orderly and significant', 146f.). These are both vulnerable to point (i) made above against Else. Kitto also leaves obscure the force of the first part of the clause, 'through pity and fear' (where K. 138 differs from Else): what would Aristotle mean by saying that the material of the play is ordered *through* the audience's pity and fear? But the simplest objection to both Kitto and Goldstein is to wonder why, when Aristotle's whole theory of poetry prescribes order, the special term *katharsis* should in one place be applied to this pervasive requirement (cf. Keesey 199).

Bibliography

This bibliography contains only those books and articles which are cited in the notes and appendices by author's name alone (with date of publication where necessary). It should be noted in particular that many works relating to the influence of the *Poetics* are mentioned only in the notes to ch. X.

Abrams, M.H., *The Mirror and the Lamp* (Oxford 1953)

Adkins, A.W.H., 'Aristotle and the Best Kind of Tragedy', *CQ* 16 (1966) 78-102

id., *From the Many to the One* (London 1970)

Allan, D.J., *The Philosophy of Aristotle*, 2nd edn. (Oxford 1970)

id., 'Some Passages in Aristotle's *Poetics*', *CQ* 21 (1971) 81-92

id., '*Eidê Tragôdias* in Aristotle's *Poetics*', *CQ* 22 (1972) 81-8

Anderson, W.D., *Ethos and Education in Greek Music* (Cambridge Mass. 1966)

Annas, J., 'Plato on the Triviality of Literature', in Moravcsik and Temko 1-28

Armstrong, D., and Peterson, C., 'Rhetorical Balance in Aristotle's Definition of the Tragic Agent: *Poetics* 13', *CQ* 30 (1980) 62-71

Atkins, J.W.H., *Literary Criticism in Antiquity*, 2nd edn. (London 1952)

Barnes, J., et al. (edd.) *Articles on Aristotle: 4.Psychology & Aesthetics* (London 1979)

id., *The Presocratic Philosophers*, 2nd edn. (London 1982)

Belfiore, E., 'Aristotle's Concept of *Praxis* in the *Poetics*', *CJ* 79 (1984) 110-24

Bernays, J., *Zwei Abhandlungen über die aristotelische Theorie des Drama* (Berlin 1880)

Bonitz, H., *Index Aristotelicus* (Berlin 1870, rpr. Graz 1955)

Boyancé, P., *Le Culte des Muses chez les Philosophes Grecs* (Paris 1937)

357

Bremer, J.M., *Hamartia* (Amsterdam 1969)

id., et al. (edd.) *Miscellanea Tragica in honorem J.C. Kamerbeek* (Amsterdam 1976)

Brink, C.O., *Horace on Poetry: Prolegomena to the Literary Epistles* (Cambridge 1963)

id., *Horace on Poetry: the Ars Poetica* (Cambridge 1971)

Brown, A.L., 'Three and Scene-Painting Sophocles', *PCPS* 30 (1984) 1-17

Browning, R., 'A Byzantine Treatise on Tragedy', in L. Varcl & R.F. Willetts (edd.) *GERAS: Studies Presented to George Thomson* (Prague 1963) 67-81

Burkert, W., 'Aristoteles im Theater', *MH* 32 (1975) 67-72

Burnett, A.P., *Catastrophe Survived* (Oxford 1971)

Butcher, S.H., *Aristotle's Theory of Poetry and Fine Art*, 4th edn. (London 1907)

Bywater, I., *Aristotle on the Art of Poetry* (Oxford 1909)

Collard, C., 'On the Tragedian Chairemon', *JHS* 90 (1970) 22-34

Collingwood, R.G., *The Principles of Art* (Oxford 1938)

Cooper, L., *An Aristotelian Theory of Comedy* (New York 1922, rpr. 1969)

id., *The Poetics of Aristotle: Its Meaning and Influence* (London 1923)

Cooper, L., & Gudeman, A., *A Bibliography of the Poetics of Aristotle* (New Haven 1928)

Crane, R.S. (ed.) *Critics and Criticism: Ancient and Modern* (Chicago 1952)

Croissant, J., *Aristote et les Mystères* (Paris 1932)

Dale, A.M., *Collected Papers* (Cambridge 1969)

Dalfen, J., *Polis und Poiesis* (Munich 1974)

Dawe, R.D., 'Some Reflections on Ate and Hamartia', *HSCP* 72 (1967) 89-123

Devereux, G., 'The Structure of Tragedy and the Structure of the Psyche in Aristotle's *Poetics*', in C. Hanly & M. Lazerowitz (edd.) *Psychoanalysis and Philosophy* (New York 1970) 46-75

Döring, A., *Die Kunstlehre des Aristoteles* (Jena 1876)

Dover, K.J., *Greek Popular Morality* (Oxford 1974)

Düring, I., *Aristotle's Protrepticus* (Göteborg 1961)

id., *Aristoteles* (Heidelberg 1966)

Eden, K., 'Poetry and Equity: Aristotle's Defense of Fiction', *Traditio* 38 (1982) 17-43

Else, G.F., 'Aristotle on the Beauty of Tragedy', *HSCP* 49 (1938) 179-204 id., *Aristotle's Poetics: The Argument* (Harvard 1957)

id., ' "Imitation" in the Fifth Century', *CP* 53 (1958) 73-90

id., *The Structure & Date of Book X of Plato's Republic* (Heidelberg 1972)

Finsler, G., *Platon und die aristotelische Poetik* (Leipzig 1900)

Flashar, H., 'Die medizinischen Grundlagen der Lehre von der Wirkung der Dichtung in der griechischen Poetik', *Hermes* 84 (1956) 12-48

Fortenbaugh, W.W., *Aristotle on Emotion* (London 1975)

Friedrich, R., '*Epeisodion* in Drama and Epic', *Hermes* 111 (1983) 34-52

Friedrich, W.H., 'Sophokles, Aristoteles und Lessing', *Vorbild und Neugestaltung* (Göttingen 1967) 188-209

Fritz, K. von, *Antike und Moderne Tragödie* (Berlin 1962)

Fuhrmann, M., *Einführung in die antike Dichtungstheorie* (Darmstadt 1973)

id., *Aristoteles: Poetik*, 2nd edn. (Stuttgart 1982)

Glanville, I.M., 'Note on Peripeteia', *CQ* 41 (1947) 73-8

id., 'Tragic Error', *CQ* 43 (1949) 47-56

Golden, L., 'Catharsis', *TAPA* 93 (1962) 51-60

id., '*Hamartia, Ate*, and Oedipus', *CW* 72 (1978) 3-12

Golden, L., & Hardison, O.B., *Aristotle's Poetics: A Translation and Commentary for Students of Literature* (New Jersey 1968)

Goldschmidt, V., *Questions Platoniciennes* (Paris 1970)

id., *Temps Physique et Temps Tragique chez Aristote* (Paris 1982)

Goldstein, H.D., 'Mimesis and Catharsis Reexamined', *JAAC* 24 (1966) 567-77

Gomme, A.W., *The Greek Attitude to Poetry and History* (Berkeley 1954)

Gould, J., 'Dramatic Character and 'Human Intelligibility' in Greek Tragedy', *PCPS* 24 (1978) 43-67

Gould, T., 'Plato's Hostility to Art', *Arion* 3 (1964) 70-91 (rpr. in N. Rudd (ed.) *Essays on Classical Literature* (Cambridge 1972) 80-101)

Grube, G.M.A., *Aristotle on Poetry and Style* (New York 1958)

id., *The Greek and Roman Critics* (London 1965)

Gründer, K., 'Jacob Bernays und der Streit um die Katharsis', in H. Barion et al. (edd.) *Epirrhosis: Festgabe für Carl Schmitt* vol. 2 (Berlin 1968) 495-528

Gudeman, A., *Aristoteles: Poetik* (Berlin 1934)

Gulley, N., 'Aristotle on the Purposes of Literature', in Barnes

(1979) 166-76

Halliwell, S., 'Plato and Aristotle on the Denial of Tragedy', *PCPS* 30 (1984) 49-71

Hardison, O.B., 'The Place of Averroes' Commentary on the *Poetics* in the History of Medieval Criticism', in J.L. Lievsay (ed.) *Medieval and Renaissance Studies 4* (Durham N.C. 1970) 57-81

Harriott, R., *Poetry and Criticism Before Plato* (London 1969)

Hathaway, B., *The Age of Criticism* (New York 1962)

Held, G. F., 'SPOUDAIOS and Teleology in the *Poetics*', *TAPA* 114 (1984) 159-76

Henn, T.R., *The Harvest of Tragedy*, 2nd edn. (London 1966)

Herrick, M.T., *The Poetics of Aristotle in England* (New Haven 1930)

Hogan, J.C., 'Aristotle's Criticism of Homer in the *Poetics*', *CP* 68 (1973) 95-108

House, H., *Aristotle's Poetics* (London 1956)

Hubbard, M.E., translation of the *Poetics* in D.A. Russell & M. Winterbottom (edd.) *Ancient Literary Criticism* (Oxford 1972)

Hutton, J., *Aristotle's Poetics* (New York 1982)

Janko, R., *Aristotle on Comedy* (London 1984)

Jones, J., *On Aristotle and Greek Tragedy* (London 1962)

Kassel, R. (ed.) *Aristotelis de arte poetica liber* (Oxford 1965)

Kaufmann, W., *Tragedy and Philosophy*, Anchor Books edn. (New York 1969)

Keesey, D., 'On Some Recent Interpretations of Catharsis', *CW* 72 (1979) 193-205

Keuls, E.C., *Plato and Greek Painting* (Leiden 1978)

Kitto, H.D.F., 'Aristotle and Fourth Century Tragedy', in M. Kelly (ed.) *For Service to Classical Studies* (Melbourne 1966) 113-29

Knox, B., *Word and Action* (Baltimore 1979)

Kock, T. (ed.) *Comicorum Atticorum Fragmenta*, 3 vols. (Leipzig 1880-88)

Koller, H., *Die Mimesis in der Antike* (Bern 1954)

Kommerell, M., *Lessing und Aristoteles* (Frankfurt 1940)

Koster, S., *Antike Epostheorien* (Wiesbaden 1970)

Kostić, V., 'Aristotle's Catharsis in Renaissance Poetics', *Živa Antika* 10 (1960) 61-74

Kristeller, P.O., 'The Modern System of the Arts', *Renaissance Thought and the Arts* (New Jersey 1980) 163-227

Lamberton, R.D., '*Philanthropia* and the Evolution of Dramatic Taste', *Phoenix* 37 (1983) 95-103

Lanata, G. (ed.) *Poetica Pre-Platonica* (Florence 1963)

Lesky, A., 'Zum Problem des tragischen', *Gesammelte Schriften* (Bern 1966) 213-19

Lieberg, G., *Poeta Creator* (Amsterdam 1982)

Lienhard, M.K., *Zur Entstehung und Geschichte von Aristoteles' Poetik* (Diss., Zurich 1950)

Lord, Carnes, 'Aristotle's History of Poetry', *TAPA* 104 (1974) 195-229

id., *Education and Culture in the Political Thought of Aristotle* (New York 1982)

Lord, Catherine, 'Tragedy without Character', *JAAC* 28 (1969) 55-62

Lucas, D.W., 'Pity, Terror, and *Peripeteia*', *CQ* 12 (1962) 52-60

id., *Aristotle: Poetics* (Oxford 1968)

Lucas, F.L., *Tragedy: Serious Drama in relation to Aristotle's Poetics*, 2nd edn. (London 1957)

McKeon, R., 'Literary Criticism and the Concept of Imitation in Antiquity', in Crane 147-75

Macleod, C., *Collected Essays* (Oxford 1983)

McMahon, A.P., 'Seven Questions on Aristotelian Definitions of Tragedy and Comedy', *HSCP* 40 (1929) 97-198

Marzullo, B., 'Die visuelle Dimension des Theaters bei Aristoteles', *Philol.* 124 (1980) 189-200

Meineke, A., *Fragmenta Comicorum Graecorum* vol. 1 (Berlin 1939)

Moles, J.L., 'Notes on Aristotle's *Poetics* 13 and 14', *CQ* 29 (1979) 77-92

id., 'Aristotle and Dido's *Hamartia*', *G & R* 31 (1984a) 48-54

id., '*Philanthropia* in the *Poetics*', *Phoenix* 38 (1984b) 325-35

Montmollin, D. de, *La Poétique d'Aristote* (Neuchatel 1951)

Moravcsik, J., & Temko, P. (edd.) *Plato on Beauty, Wisdom and the Arts* (New Jersey 1982)

Morpurgo-Tagliabue, G., *Linguistica e Stilistica di Aristotele* (Rome 1967)

Moulinier, L., *Le pur et l'impur dans la pensée des Grecs* (Paris 1952)

Murray, P., 'Poetic Inspiration in Early Greece', *JHS* 101 (1981) 87-100

Nehamas, A., 'Plato on Imitation and Poetry in *Republic* 10', in Moravcsik & Temko 47-78

Ničev, A., *L'Énigme de la catharsis tragique dans Aristote* (Sofia 1970)

id., *La catharsis tragique d'Aristote: Nouvelles Contributions* (Sofia 1982)

Olson, E. (ed.) *Aristotle's Poetics and English Literature* (Chicago 1965)
  id., *The Theory of Comedy* (Bloomington 1968)
Østerud, S., 'Hamartia in Aristotle and Greek Tragedy', *Symbolae Osloenses* 51 (1976) 65-80
Packer, M., 'The Conditions of Aesthetic Feeling in Aristotle's *Poetics*', *British Journal of Aesthetics* 24 (1984) 138-48
Parker, R., *Miasma* (Oxford 1983)
Pauw, D.A., 'The Rigorism of Aristotle in his *Poetics*: Fact or Fiction?', *Acta Classica* 21 (1978) 71-81
Pfeiffer, R., *History of Classical Scholarship: from the Beginnings to the end of the Hellenistic Age* (Oxford 1968)
Pickard-Cambridge, A.W., *Dithyramb Tragedy and Comedy* (Oxford 1927)
Pohlenz, M., *Kleine Schriften* vol. 2 (Hildesheim 1965)
Pollitt, J.J., *The Ancient View of Greek Art*, Student edn. (Yale 1974)
Post, L.A., *From Homer to Menander* (Berkeley 1951)
Potts, L.J., *Aristotle on the Art of Fiction*, 2nd edn. (Cambridge 1959)
Quinton, A., *Thoughts and Thinkers* (London 1982)
Radt, S.L., 'Aristoteles und die Tragödie', *Mnem.* 24 (1971) 189-205
  id., 'Zum 13 Kapitel von Aristoteles' *Poetik*', in Bremer (1976) 271-84
Redfield, J.M., *Nature and Culture in the Iliad* (Chicago 1975)
Rees, B.R., '*Pathos* in the *Poetics* of Aristotle', *G & R* 19 (1972a) 1-11
  id., 'Aristotle's Theory and Milton's Practice: *Samson Agonistes*', Inaugural Lecture (Birmingham 1972b)
  id., 'Plot, Character & Thought', in J. Bingen et al. (edd.) *Le Monde Grec: Hommages à Claire Préaux* (Brussels 1975) 188-96
  id., 'Aristotle's Approach to Poetry', *G & R* 28 (1981) 23-39
Robertson, J.G., *Lessing's Dramatic Theory* (Cambridge 1939)
Robins, R.H., *A Short History of Linguistics*, 5th edn. (London 1967)
Rose, V. (ed.) *Aristotelis ... Fragmenta*, 3rd edn. (Leipzig 1886)
Rosenmeyer, T.G., 'Design and Execution in Aristotle, *Poetics* ch. XXV', *California Studies in Classical Antiquity* 6 (1973) 231-52
Rösler, W., 'Die Entdeckung der Fiktionalität in der Antike', *Poetica* 12 (1980) 283-319
Ross, W.D., *Aristotle*, 5th edn. (London 1949)
Rostagni, A., *Aristotele Poetica*, 2nd edn. (Turin 1945)
  id., *Scritti Minori I: Aesthetica* (Turin 1955)
Russell, D.A., *Criticism in Antiquity* (London 1981)
Rutherford, R.B., 'Tragic Form and Feeling in the *Iliad*', *JHS* 102

(1982) 145-60

Schadewaldt, W., 'Furcht und Mitleid? Zur Deutung des Aristotelischen Tragödiensatzes', in *Hellas und Hesperien* vol. 1, 2nd edn. (Zurich 1970) 194-236

Schrier, O.J., 'A Simple View of Peripeteia', *Mnem.* 33 (1980) 96-118

Schütrumpf, E., *Die Bedeutung des Wortes êthos in der Poetik des Aristoteles* (Munich 1970)

Shankman, S., 'Led by the Light of the Maeonian Star: Aristotle on Tragedy and *Od.* 17.415-44', *Classical Antiquity* 2 (1983) 108-16

Silk, M.S., & Stern, J.P., *Nietzsche on Tragedy* (Cambridge 1981)

Smithson, I., 'The Moral View of Aristotle's *Poetics*', *JHI* 44 (1983) 3-17

Snell, B. (ed.) *Tragicorum Graecorum Fragmenta* vol. 1 (Göttingen 1971)

Söffing, W., *Deskriptive und Normative Bestimmungen in der Poetik des Aristoteles* (Amsterdam 1981)

Solmsen, F., 'The Origins and Methods of Aristotle's *Poetics*', *CQ* 29 (1935) 192-201

Sorabji, R., *Necessity Cause and Blame* (London 1980)

Sörbom, G., *Mimesis and Art* (Stockholm 1966)

Spingarn, J.E., *A History of Literary Criticism in the Renaissance*, 2nd edn. (New York 1908)

Stark, R., *Aristotelesstudien*, 2nd edn. (Munich 1972)

Ste Croix, G.E.M. de, 'Aristotle on History and Poetry', in B. Levick (ed.) *The Ancient Historian and his Materials* (Farnborough 1975) 45-58

Stinton, T.C.W., '*Hamartia* in Aristotle and Greek Tragedy', *CQ* 25 (1975) 221-54

Susemihl, F., & Hicks, R., *The Politics of Aristotle: Books 1-5* (London 1894)

Süss, W., *Ethos* (Leipzig 1910)

Svoboda, K., *L'Esthétique d'Aristote* (Brno 1927)

Taplin, O., *The Stagecraft of Aeschylus* (Oxford 1977)

Teichmüller, G., *Aristotelische Forschungen* 2 vols. (Halle 1867-9)

Thielscher, P., 'Die relative Chronologie der erhaltenen Schriften des Aristoteles nach den bestimmten Selbstzitaten', *Philol.* 97 (1948) 229-265

Tracy, H.L., 'Aristotle on Aesthetic Pleasure', *CP* 41 (1946) 43-6

Tumarkin, A., 'Die Kunsttheorie von Aristoteles im Rahmen seiner Philosophie', *MH* 2 (1945) 108-22

Twining, T., *Aristotle's Treatise on Poetry* (London 1789, rpr.

Farnborough 1972)

Vahlen, J. (ed.) *Aristotelis de arte poetica liber*, 3rd edn. (Leipzig 1885)

id., *Gesammelte philologische Schriften* vol. 1 (Leipzig 1911, rpr. Hildesheim 1970)

id., *Beiträge zu Aristoteles' Poetik* (Leipzig 1914, rpr. 1965)

Verdenius, W.J., *Mimesis: Plato's doctrine of artistic Imitation and its Meaning to us* (Leiden 1949, rpr. 1972)

id., 'Gorgias's Doctrine of Deception', in G. B. Kerferd (ed.) *The Sophists and their Legacy*, *Hermes* Einzelschriften 44 (Wiesbaden 1981) 116-29

Vernant, J.-P., & Vidal-Naquet, P., *Tragedy and Myth in Ancient Greece*, Engl. transl. (Brighton 1981)

Vicaire, P., *Platon: Critique Littéraire* (Paris 1960)

Vickers, B., *Towards Greek Tragedy* (London 1973)

Wagner, C., ' "Katharsis" in der aristotelischen Tragödiendefinition', *Grazer Beiträge* 11 (1984) 67-87

Webster, T.B.L., 'Fourth Century Tragedy and the *Poetics*', *Hermes* 82 (1954) 294-308

Wehrli, F., *Die Schule des Aristoteles* vol II (Basel 1945)

id., 'Die antike Kunsttheorie und das Schöpferische', *MH* 14 (1957) 39-49

Weinberg, B., *A History of Literary Criticism in the Italian Renaissance*, 2 vols. (Chicago 1961)

Will, F., 'Aristotle and the source of the Art-Work', *Phronesis* 5 (1960) 152-68

Wimsatt, W. K., 'Aristotle and Oedipus or Else', *Hateful Contraries* (Lexington 1966)

Winnington-Ingram, R.P., *Sophocles: an Interpretation* (Cambridge 1980)

Xanthakis-Karamanos, G., *Studies in Fourth-Century Tragedy* (Athens 1980)

Zeller, E., *Die Philosophie der Griechen*, vol. 2.2., 3rd edn. (Leipzig 1879)

Index

N.B. Collective page-references do not necessarily indicate a continuous treatment of a topic.

acting, theatrical, 46, 89, 114f., 126, 131, 140, 181, App. 3 *passim*
action, dramatic, ch. V *passim*, 203, 249f., 297f.
  see also s.v. *praxis*
Aeschylus, 40, 66, 95, 115, 147, 206f., 241, 244-7, 316, 346
aesthetic philosophy, Aristotle's, 3-6, 24f., chs. II-III *passim*
Agathon, 88, 114, 241f.
anagnôrisis, tragic recognition, see s.v. recognition & reversal
apangelia, poetic narrative, q.v.
Archilochus, 270, 277
Aristophanes, 10, 15, 17-19, 38, 45, 64, 83, 86, 88, 95, 113-15, 166, 239, 249, 273, 278
Aristoxenus, 187, 189
art, Aristotle's concept of, 42-62
  see also s.v. craft, and *technê*
Astydamas, 328f.
atuchia, misfortune, see s.v. *dustuchia*
audiences, of poetry, 103, 168-70, 194, 236f., 296, 334
Aurelius, Marcus, 64, 352
Averroes, 291

Batteux, Charles, 351
beauty, Aristotle's concept of, 92f., 97-9, 283f.
Bernays, Jacob, 191, 197f., 323, 351, 353

Brecht, Bertolt, 316f.
Butcher, S.H., 43, 320-2
Bywater, Ingram, 43, 321

Carcinus, 328f.
Castelvetro, Lodovico, 293, 298, 301, 313, 315, 352
Chairemon, 277, 328
chance, in tragedy, see s.v. *tuchê*
character(isation), in poetry, 54, 125, 138f., 143f., 149-67, 203f., 207f., 257, 267f., 326
Chicago school, 292, 317
chorus, of tragedy, 95, ch. VIII *passim*
  see also s.v. *melopoeia*
comedy, 65, 266-76, 333
Corneille, Pierre, 299, 301, 303-5, 307, 311, 313, 351
correctness (*orthotês*), in poetry, 3, 24f., 132, 335
craft, and poetry, 9f., 82-92
  see also s.v. *technê*
Crates, 269f.
Cratinus, 10, 259

Dacier, André, 301, 303, 307-9, 314, 321, 351-3
dance, 42, 45, 121f., 126, 128, 131, 240, 332, 339
Democritus, 6, 9f., 38, 83, 86, 113
desis (= *plokê*), dramatic 'compli-

Made in the USA
Lexington, KY
16 July 2012